Explaining local government

Manchester University Press

Explaining local government

Local government in Britain since 1800

J. A. Chandler

Manchester University Press

Manchester and New York

distributed exclusively in the USA by Palgrave

Published by Manchester University Press
Oxford Road, Manchester M13 9NR, UK
and Room 400, 175 Fifth Avenue, New York, NY 10010, USA
www.manchesteruniversitypress.co.uk

Distributed in the United States exclusively by
Palgrave Macmillan, 175 Fifth Avenue,
New York, NY 10010, USA

Distributed in Canada exclusively by
UBC Press, University of British Columbia, 2029 West Mall,
Vancouver, BC, Canada V6T 1Z2

British Library Cataloguing-in-Publication Data is available

Library of Congress Cataloging-in-Publication Data is available

ISBN 978 0 7190 6707 5 paperback

First published by Manchester University Press in hardback 2007

This paperback edition first published 2013

The publisher has no responsibility for the persistence or accuracy of URLs for any external or third-party internet websites referred to in this book, and does not guarantee that any content on such websites is, or will remain, accurate or appropriate.

Printed by Lightning Source

Contents

Acknowledgements

Sam Nolutshungu, when we were students, observed that he would one day write a book dedicated to 'myself without whom this work would never have been written'. However, I owe much to Sam for developing my interest in politics. In the context of this book I also wish to thank former Department of Political Studies colleagues at Sheffield Hallam University who have helped and encouraged this work, and especially Roger Ottewill and John Kingdom who have read and commented on most of the chapters. Other academics who have provided comments or support for the project include Christine Bellamy, Howard Elcock, Peter Hennessy, Chris Game, Steve Leach and David Pell. I have also received much help from librarians and archivists, in particular Alasdair Allen, University of Sheffield Library, and George Wade, Sheffield Hallam University Library. Thanks also to Jane Watt and Sue Blower who helped with proof reading. Thanks are also due to the many archives that permit access and quotations from their collections, and to the interviewees. Finally, many thanks to Krys Chandler whose encouragement and forbearance allowed this book to be written.

The study could not have been as thorough and detailed without the aid of a grant from the British Academy that enabled more extensive archival research than would otherwise have been possible.

Abbreviations

ACC	Association of County Councils
AMC	Association of Municipal Corporations
BMA	British Medical Association
BV	best value
CCA	County Councils' Association
CCGLF	Consultative Council on Local Government Finance
CCT	Compulsory Competitive Tendering
CIPFA	Chartered Institute of Public Finance and Accountancy
CPA	Conservative Party Archive
DoE	Department of the Environment
DETR	Department of the Environment, Transport and the Regions
DLO	Direct Labour Organisation
FAS	Funding Agency for Schools
GDP	gross domestic product
GLA	Greater London Authority
GLC	Greater London Council
ILEA	Inner London Education Authority
ILP	Independent Labour Party
JP	justice of the peace
LAA	Local Authority Associations
LCC	London County Council
LGA	Local Government Association
LGB	Local Government Board
LSP	Local Strategic Partnership
MBW	Metropolitan Board of Works
MCC	Metropolitan County Council
MHLG	Ministry of Housing and Local Government
NA	National Archive
NALGO	National Association for Local Government Officers
NHS	National Health Service
NPM	new public management
ODPM	Office of the Deputy Prime Minister
OFSTED	Office for Standards in Education
PWLB	Public Works Loans Board

RDA   Regional Development Agency
SRB   Single Regeneration Budget
UDC   Urban Development Corporation

Preface

During the House of Commons debates on the 1834 Poor Law Reform Act Colonel Torrens observed:

> A good system of local government he looked upon to be the perfection of all government ... As he was desirous, therefore, to interfere as little as possible with the influence which the local authorities of the country ought to possess he should propose as an amendment 'That no rules or regulations framed by the Commons should be binding on any parish without the concurrence of the majority of rate payers'.[1]

In 2004 the unelected agency the Audit Commission in its report on libraries in Cumbria awarded the elected Council two stars for this service and among numerous recommendations reported: 'Internal signage could be improved ... at the one in Carlisle it was difficult to identify where the lift was situated'.[2]

This volume explains how Britain has evolved from a relationship between central and local government based on the premiss of dual polity, expressed at its most extreme by Colonel Torrens, in which central and local government had separate spheres of interest into a framework in which central government or its agents may comment on the most minute detail of local government service delivery.

Local government in Britain in 1830 resembled in its structure the pattern of larger European nations or the United States with a bedrock of numerous community governments subject to a measure of control by a larger sub-regional authority representative of state interest. In post-revolutionary France and the United States there has been an ethos within elite and popular cultures that local governments should have considerable autonomy from the centre and are an important safeguard to ensure the dispersal of power as one of the foundations of a pluralist society. The patterns of local government in these liberal democracies over the last 200 years have modernised in terms of powers and functions in line with technological and social change but have retained not dissimilar structures. In contrast Britain during this period has radically restructured local government to create far fewer authorities with executive powers covering much larger populations than those of almost all comparable liberal democra-

cies. Underlying the restructuring is the evolving relationship between
central and local government. Attitudes to the role of local government
within the Constitution have evolved in Britain from placing a high value
on the separation of central and local authority to one in which the
Deputy Prime Minister can assert that 'Britain has become one of the most
centralised systems of government in the Western world'.[3]

In the late nineteenth and early twentieth centuries the study of local
government, outside the framework of legal guides for local government
personnel, orientated around historical explanations alongside philosophical analysis of its constitutional role and status. Utilitarian critiques of
the local government system in journals such as the *Westminster Review*
had a substantial historical base that drew opposition from proponents of
localism like Joshua Toulmin Smith in studies that provided a colourful if
not too thoroughly researched historical vision of Anglo Saxon community values.[4] By the second half of the nineteenth century books were
being published to chronicle the political development of the growing
municipal corporations.[5] Studies of the evolution of the local government
system did not, however, take on a systematic and rigorously researched
analysis of the system as a whole until the appearance of continental
European interest in British Government with works such as Gneist's
History of the English Constitution.[6] Gneist had suggested that the post-
1832 reforms of local government had replaced the duty to participate in
local community governance with an elected principle that under an
increasingly mass party system would lead to centralisation and loss of
communal duty. His analysis sparked the liberal Austrian historian and
lawyer Joseph Redlich to provide a substantive work on the local government system in Britain that revolved around the socio-economic battle
ground between liberal and conservative forces.[7] The work, translated
and aided by Francis Hirst, is remarkably modern in its capacity to relate
the development of the local government system in the nineteenth century
to the wider ideological conflicts between capital and landed interests,
and urban and rural values. This book similarly aims to explain the evolution of the structures of local government in Britain from the perspective
of the socio-economic and ideological forces that shaped the system.

Despite the many histories of specific local governments or of specific
periods of history there have been few studies that chart, let alone seek to
explain, the development of the local government system in Britain as a
whole. Shortly after the publication of Redlich and Hirst's work came the
first of the eleven-volume study of local government history by the Webbs.
They too were reacting against the ideas of Gneist and were concerned
initially to understand the system of British local governance in order to
pave the way for their ideas on the practical reshaping of the system. From
a political perspective the Webbs influenced a generation of Fabian-
inclined theorists such as G. D. H. Cole and W. A. Robson who adopted
a policy studies approach that discussed, with the aid of a measure of

historical background, the efficiency and effectiveness of the system and its representative character, but were much concerned to suggest new ways of organising the system. This approach was shaded in the 1960s by community studies that focused on power and decision-making in local government in order to evaluate pluralist theory. By the mid-1960s these works had a Marxist tinge and in the following decades a number of studies considered local government largely as an institution undertaking specific tasks of resource allocation and distribution that helped facilitate the maintenance of a capitalist state. This genre ceased to be particularly fashionable with the domination of Thatcherite New Right values in the 1980s, and it may be argued that mainstream analysis has returned more to the policy studies approach of Cole and Robson.

Historians, post-1945, inspired initially by Asa Briggs's *Victorian Cities*,[8] have emphasised the economic and social growth of urban communities and in particular the cultural impact of the nineteenth-century industrialised city.[9] Relatively few of these local studies however have concentrated on the political dimension of urban growth during the Victorian period. Important and valuable exceptions are Hennock's *Fit and Proper Persons*[10] or studies by Derek Fraser of politics in Leeds and other cities.[11] A number of works, for example Smellie's *History of Local Government*[12] and later the work of Keith-Lucas and Richards, became established as teaching texts.[13] More recently Young and Rao[14] have extended the history of local government from 1945 to the Blair administrations using a more extensive trawl of government records than characterised preceding studies. There have also been some important works in this field by writers on local politics that concentrate on more specific aspects of the local government system.[15] However, while charting events and explaining the motives of central politicians, these works rarely extend their analysis to a consideration of the socio-economic factors that drive the attitudes of particular governments and ministers. Exceptions to this trend are Bulpitt's[16] study of territorial politics and the rather neglected comparative study of Britain and France by D. E. Ashford.[17]

British studies of local governance have a tendency towards insularity with an implicit view that somehow the British structure and processes are the norm and it would be expected that any rational policy-maker devising a system from *tabula rasa* would arrive at a rather similar system. Reflection on the French or US systems of local government had a place in nineteenth-century studies. De Tocqueville's comments on local government in the USA were well read in Britain and subject to considerable comment from J. S. Mill, while Gneist and Redlich, well versed in the German local government tradition, brought comparison of these values into their writing on the British system. Much less attention, however, was paid to non-British structures by the Fabians, and the consequent policy studies-based genre of analysis in the first half of the twentieth century. Cole and Robson's major studies tend to be insular in their analysis and make relatively few references to European or French practice. Reference to parliamentary debate also suggests that while in the nineteenth century comparisons were made between British practice and that of other regimes, this seems less frequent in the early twentieth century. The contrast between the present system of British local government and those of the US and the larger countries of Western Europe is in need of serious explanation, but such an exercise would require more resources than could be given to this study. The final chapter of this book does, however, attempt to summarise the influences that have shaped the British system in the context of comparison between the development of local governance in France and the US.

The book focuses on local government as a political institution and in particular the changing structure of local government both in terms of the number and kinds of local authorities, the allocation of functions to each kind of authority and their patterns of internal decision-making. The study is not extended to cover all aspects of British local governance and hence uses the institutions of the local authority as an exemplar of forces shaping a wider range of institutions that include the health services or law enforcement. Britain is defined here as encompassing England, Scotland and Wales, but due to the very different social pressures in Northern Ireland consideration of that Province has been excluded. Since the central aim of this book is to explain the evolution of the structures, functions and management of local government in Britain, the book does not provide extensive details on the evolution of local authority services such as education, policing or housing given that there are studies which analyse the development of such tasks in considerable detail.

In order to explain the development of local government the evolving relationship between central and local government is a key concern of this study. Elements in the analysis of inter-governmental relations include the legal and constitutional status and powers of local authorities and their financial resources but underlying these issues are the changing political values of policy-makers at central and local levels of government and the political philosophies and socio-economic interests that drive political change.

The methodological perspective for this analysis is based on the view that the evolution of elements within a political system are shaped by the interaction of a network of agencies with an elite of central policy-makers who will themselves conflict as to their policy preferences and values. The factors that motivate demands for change are, in part, responses to technological and economic change and a concern to alleviate social hardship when this is affordable. However, reaction to economic and technological change is also shaped by the effect of those pressures on the social and financial standing of political actors and by the ideological values that are used to justify self-interest or to motivate individuals to take altruistic values to heart.

Notes

1 Hansard, Second Reading Poor Law Debate, vol. 23, col. 1340, 17 April 1834.
2 Audit Commission, *Comprehensive Performance Assessment: Libraries and Archive Services in Cumbria* (London: HMSO, 2004), online at: www. audit-commission.gov.uk/reports.
3 Office of the Deputy Prime Minister, *Your Region, Your Choice* (London: HMSO, 2003).
4 Joshua Toulmin Smith's works include *Local Self-Government and Centralization*, (London: John Chapman, 1851); *The Parish* (London: J. Sweet, 1854).
5 The two-volume study by J. T. Bunce, *History of the Birmingham Corporation* (Birmingham: Cornish Brothers, 1878, 1885), is a particular exemplar of this genre.
6 R. von Gneist, *History of the English Constitution*, trans. P. A. Ashworth (London: William Clowes, 1891).
7 J. Reddlich and F. W. Hirst, *Local Government in England* (London: Macmillan, 1903).
8 A. Briggs, *Victorian Cities* (London: Odhams, 1963).
9 P. J. Waller, *Town City and Nation* (Oxford: Oxford University Press, 1983); or, most recently, G. Tristam-Hunt, *Building Jerusalem: The Rise and Fall of the Victorian City* (London: Weidenfeld & Nicolson, 2004).
10 E. P. Hennock, *Fit and Proper Persons* (London: Edward Arnold, 1973).
11 D. Fraser, *Urban Politics in Victorian England* (London: Macmillan, 1976); D. Fraser (ed.), *Municipal Reform and the Industrial City* (Leicester: Leicester University Press, 1982).
12 K. B. Smellie, *A History of Local Government* (London: George Allen & Unwin, 1946).
13 B. Keith-Lucas and P. G. Richards, *A History of Local Government in the Twentieth Century* (London: George Allen & Unwin, 1978).
14 K. Young and N. Rao, *Local Government Since 1945* (Oxford: Blackwell, 1997).
15 In particular, B. Keith-Lucas, *The English Local Government Franchise* (Oxford: Blackwell, 1952) and *The Unreformed Local Government System* (London: Croom Helm, 1980); K. Young, *Local Politics and the Rise of Party* (Leicester: Leicester University Press, 1975); S. Goss, *Local Labour and Local Government*, (Edinburgh: Edinburgh University Press, 1988); J. Sheldrake, *Modern Local Government* (Aldershot: Dartmouth, 1992).
16 J. G. Bulpitt, *Territory and Power in the United Kingdom* (Manchester: Manchester University Press, 1983).
17 D. E. Ashford, *British Dogmatism and French Pragmatism* (London: George Allen & Unwin, 1981).

1

Local government before 1832

There is little left of the Roman administrative legacy for the provinces of Britain. Towns were established under Roman practice as *coloniae* and *municipium* for retired soldiers who were granted citizenship of the Empire.[1] Other townships, *civitates*, established by Britons were recognised as following local tribal laws:[2] 'A large measure of local government was conducted by the British themselves with official supervision and encouragement.'[3] All that remains of the Roman legacy are some of the towns themselves, including London as the capital city. The break up of the *pax romana* by the fourth century AD, and invasions by Anglo Saxons and, later, Vikings ensured that for most purposes towns and villages in Britain were self-governing. For many communities this involved domination by whoever had ownership of the land and control of armed men to keep farmers and labourers in check. As they grew in power the Anglo-Saxon kings established sufficient authority over the landowners to divide their territories into areas in which they established a lieutenant to protect the royal interest. Wessex was divided into shires before King Alfred's birth in 849[4] and Edgar I ordained in the tenth century that these should be divided into hundreds and smaller tithings,[5] and then sub-divided again into wapentakes, wards, lathes and rapes.[6] The growth in power of Wessex spread this territorial arrangement into the remainder of England, although it was not until perhaps the eleventh century that the Mercian kingdom was structured in this way.[7] During this period a legal distinction began to emerge between what was to be regarded as a 'town' as distinct from a large village: a town was regarded as a corporate body by the King or the nobility, and could act in law as if it were a single individual; thus, the town as a whole could own property, sue and be sued, and provide collective services. The term 'borough', derived from an earlier term meaning 'fortified place', emerged in the late Anglo-Saxon period to identify this form of community. Many smaller communities were also developing in later Anglo-Saxon England parishes as both ecclesiastical and temporal units of administration.[8]

By the time of the Norman Conquest practices for controlling local areas had emerged in a form that was in some respects still recognisable in the eighteenth century. The pattern was based on principles that had taken root in many areas of Europe. Landowners interfered in communal government according to local economic dominance and inclination. The Lord was not so inclined to be *primus inter pares* within the community but was rather its absolute ruler governing through his local court leet and appointing a bailiff to implement his authority.[9] Castles might be established within potentially rebellious towns to ensure their good behaviour.[10]

Parishes were based around the manor houses of landowners who had established churches on their lands to cater for the spiritual needs of themselves and their dependent communities.[11] They emerged as the administrative as well as ecclesiastic lower tier of administration after the ravages of the Black Death had emancipated the remaining peasants from dependence on their feudal serfdom. In areas where the manor and the court leet had declined, the parish took over as the unit of communal representation.[12] However, in some areas, even into the nineteenth century, as in Manchester, the court leet survived as a legally recognised unit of local governance.[13] By the fourteenth century larger towns that were centres of trade or manufacturing, with economic importance to rival the influence of landed interests, were able to exert a measure of self-government as boroughs, or burghs in Scotland, even though they were still relatively small communities partly restricted in size by the logistics of maintaining good water supplies, sanitation and fire precautions. London at the end of the fourteenth century had a population of around 35,000, and only York and Bristol had populations approaching 10,000.[14]

Above the community level the county and its divisions were the administrative units representing central government, and hence the monarch. In practice, the power of the monarch over a county or, in a few cases, larger towns acting effectively as counties in their own right, could be delegated to one or a number of powerful landlords. These communities as boroughs often received from the Crown a charter of incorporation establishing their rights and form of government. During the Middle Ages, as aficionados of the legend of Robin Hood will be aware, the King's senior representative in a county was normally the Sheriff;[15] but by the sixteenth century their frequent failure to rally the local gentry to support the Crown in times of need[16] led to a decline in the Sheriffs' political importance. Their influence was superseded by that of the Lord Lieutenant, the monarch's direct representative in the county and below them the justices of the peace (JPs), appointed usually at the Lord Lieutenant's nomination. The Lord Lieutenants were expected to report on the custody of county government to the King's representatives at the assize courts.[17]

The Civil War and its consequences

During the Tudor dynasty the Crown had become a powerful unifying political force and within this framework the county and the parish were expected to do the bidding of central government. The capacity of Elizabeth's Governments to establish the Poor Law shows that 'both parishes and property owners were agents of the central government; and that government could communicate a consistent policy to them, and commit them to it'.[18] The Civil War did much to unravel this trend. The political settlement that emerged from the strife of the 1640s and the 'Glorious Revolution' of 1688 ensured that the King must govern with the consent of a Parliament selected largely from major landowners. The unwise attempt by James II to revive his father's quest for absolutism prompted the revolt of the vast majority of landed and commercial interests, and the transfer of the monarchy to the firmly protestant William III who understood the need to protect his executive power by working with, rather than against, Parliament. These events put an end to the possibility that Britain would be governed by a powerful centralising monarchy, as in Louis XIV's France. The Crown's power was limited by the conventions that taxes were determined by Parliament and that those in government would respect landowners' interests in local matters in the parts of the country in which they held their estates. The quarter sessions, which were the courts under the immediate control of JPs in a county and, in some cases, a borough, dealt with both criminal cases and, for each county, local governance. Only the most serious felonies were sent for trial at the assizes, the courts established under direct control of central government, and by the eighteenth century a system of grand juries ensured that agents of landed interests could determine whether a case went to trial at an assize.[19] Power rested increasingly with landowners. The monarch could influence foreign policy, the army and the navy, but had little impact on local issues such as the development of local roads or the distribution of poor relief.

Parliament was dominated by aristocrats holding large estates. The grandest landowners acquired peerages and seats in the House of Lords, but wealth could also buy land or favours that ensured representation in the House of Commons. Not all landed gentry represented 'old money': successful merchants and adventurers could use wealth from trade and commerce to buy estates in order to gain political power and social status.[20] Although tensions between old and new money were socially significant, they were never so great as to generate conditions that would lead, as in France, to a revolution to overthrow the monarchy and aristocracy. Large landowners with an incentive to increase their fortune sought extra capital by borrowing or promoting joint-ventures with the commercial classes and consequently came to have an interest in the growth of the trade and commerce of the socially inferior merchant class. Both benefited greatly from political stability at home in securing the development of land and the commercialisation of agriculture, and in creating the means to wage war globally and secure fortunes through overseas trade and colonisation.

Central–local relations

Liberal and Fabian commentaries of the late nineteenth and early twentieth centuries suggest that the eighteenth-century system of local government resulted in growth of bizarre local customs and practices that
generated serious inequities throughout the nation.[21] This view has a
measure of truth but the situation was not, as such authors suggest, due
to an absence of central control. At one level the relationship between
central and local government might be characterised as that of a dual
polity in which central government dealt with issues of high politics, such
as the defence of the realm, the protection of the colonies and the encouragement of trade, leaving counties, parishes and boroughs responsible for
low politics, such as the relief of the poor.[22] However, such a view is
misleading from the perspective of the poor and the powerless, since
Parliament was carefully constructed to ensure that those who controlled
the local political systems acted in the interests of the landed elites. As
Prest observes, 'the relations between central and local government were
worked out in Parliament'.[23] Any substantive change to traditional land-
holding patterns, especially the enclosure of land, required Parliamentary
sanction. Extensions to the powers of a borough or measures to by-pass
its moribund corporation through the formation of some improvement
commission similarly required private Acts. The building of canals, turnpikes and railways which affected the established rights of communities
and individuals were also processed by such an arrangement. The eighteenth-century Parliament was far from reluctant to deal with local
matters but it was opposed to making blanket statutory public Acts that
imposed nationwide uniformity on the diverse legal and traditional
arrangement that had evolved over time. This attitude flowed into the
nineteenth century when, between 1800 and 1854, almost twice as many
private as public acts were passed by Parliament.[24]

The acquisition of a private act involved a complex procedure that
required evidence of local support and could, for a corporation, necessitate a local referendum. The proposal had to be drafted in accord with
legal conventions and was closely scrutinised by a parliamentary committee. The bill was best defended by supportive MPs. The process was often
facilitated by a paid parliamentary agent, usually a lawyer specialising in
this task.[25] Costs often deterred organisations from pursuing improvements in this way.[26] Private legislation was, therefore, feasible primarily
for the wealthy landowner, businessman or corporation. An impecunious
parish had little chance of raising the funds needed to oppose a private Act
or to foster their own schemes for improvement. By the early nineteenth
century this cumbersome and expensive procedure was beginning to be
undermined. Legislation had been possible in the previous century to
forward statutes granting corporations permissive powers. The Gilbert
Acts, permitting the consolidation of parishes into 'unions', was an

important step in developing such a strategy. By the 1830s permissive Acts had been passed for lighting and watch committees in Ireland and England, and for police services in Scotland which could be put into operation by petitions to Parliament from substantial rate-payers of a town or parish. The 1801 General Enclosure Act facilitated change by establishing a uniform set of rules that could be inserted in any land enclosure Act, thus simplifying the development of such legislation.[27]

Underlying the stability of this system was a deep-seated suspicion of a centralising government widely thought to be an agent more likely to enslave the population of Britain than be a force for the general improvement of society. Parliament was regarded as an essential bulwark against potential tyranny of the monarch and the government. From the writings of Locke wealthy landlords garnered the belief that they had a right to their property and that the State had no right to tax or regulate the use of their possessions without their consent. It was accepted that where someone owned land he should have power over the use to be made of that property. Landowners ought, therefore, to determine the decisions to be made in the area that affected their local estates and many factory-owners and urban commercial interests could similarly argue they had every right to govern the growing towns which had, in part, been created by their capital and enterprise. There was, therefore, both among Tories and Whigs a strongly ingrained hostility to centralisation coupled with a view that local economic interests should be the governing voice in, to use the terminology of the seventeenth century, 'the country', by which they meant the county in which they held their capital.[28]

Translated into popular culture this value generated the myth of the freeborn Englishman whose home was his castle and who was not to be subjected to oppression by either foreign or domestic despots. Thus, even before the emergence of a popular and identifiable liberal individualism fostering capitalist enterprise there was a groundswell of opinion among the wealthy favouring limited central government. The conclusion of a committee of enquiry on policing in London established by Peel in 1822 states:

> It is difficult to reconcile an effective system of police with that perfect freedom of action and exemptions from interference, which are the great privileges and blessings of society in this country and your Committee think that the forfeiture or curtailment of such advantages would be too great a sacrifice for improvements in police, facilities in detection of crime, however desirable in themselves if abstractedly considered.[29]

J.S. Mill in his autobiography observes that

> centralization was, and is, the subject not only of rational disapprobation, but of unreasoning prejudice; where jealousy of government interference was a blind feeling preventing or resisting even the most beneficial exertion of legislative authority to correct the abuses of what pretends to be local self

government, but is, too often, selfish mismanagement of local interests, by a jobbing and *borne* local oligarchy.[30]

In practice dual polity meant that landowners could control the localities in which they owned their estates and resolve differences between themselves through their membership of their national conclave, the British Parliament.

Local government and the franchise

The complexity of systems of representation from the boroughs ensured that electoral reform and local government reform had to be inextricably linked. The county franchise in England, which was the only electoral arrangement that had some uniformity, consisted of all men who owned freehold land or property to the value of £2.[31] Each county regardless of size returned two members of Parliament and this arrangement returned to the eighteenth-century House of Commons 112 of the total of 558 MPs.[32] Many, although not all, boroughs had been created so as to secure their representation in Parliament[33] The 1835 Commission of Enquiry into the Municipal Corporations in England and Wales observed that 'a great number of Corporations have been preserved solely as political engines and the towns to which they belong derive no benefit, but often much injury, from their existence'.[34] The franchise in boroughs varied widely. A substantial number of seats in the House of Commons were 'rotten boroughs' which returned two members of Parliament through a highly restricted and subornable electorate. According to Namier only twenty-two towns had an electorate of more than 1,000 and a further 22 one of between 500 and 100 voters; only 12 boroughs had a near universal male franchise.[35] Towns with over 1,000 electors tended to show deference to the great families rather than local business interests. The exception was the city of Westminster which by the nineteenth century had become a stronghold of radicalism. The majority of what may be termed rotten boroughs based their franchise on either the members of the corporation or a small coterie of freemen usually selected by the corporation but which could also comprise a few wealthy rate-payers owning property with sufficient rateable value to qualify for the vote. The right of a borough to elect an MP could be of great benefit to its leading citizens. As in all patron–client relationships the exchange of favours was a two-way process. Boroughs might solicit a number of candidates to stand, as there was much graft to be gained by competition for their vote. However, it was not infrequent for corporations, with the backing of local citizens, to give their preference to candidates who would provide the funds for major improvements within the town. In Tewksbury two candidates ousted the sitting members as they were willing to pay for the renovation of worn-out local roads. The successful candidates, a brewer and a merchant from London,

made their public entrance into the town with pickaxes and shovels carried
before them, and flags, with inscriptions thereon, of 'Calvert and Martin' on
one side and 'good roads' on the other.[36]

Enfranchised towns often supported politicians in the expectation of
receiving protection and favour. The Government could exert influence in
towns such as Harwich which were dependent on State spending on the
navy.

The influence of borough corporations on central government should
not be exaggerated although there was substantial ideological dispute
over the meaning and importance of representation. A considerable body
of opinion believed that an MP ought to be the representative of the
community that elected them and be subject to local instructions. Burke's
celebrated address to his Bristol constituents illustrated the view that the
MP should be free to use his own judgement as regards the interests of his
constituents.[37] While it was possible in a number of boroughs and counties for the representative in the Commons to be beholden to the demands
of the constituency to secure election, there were a much larger number of
constituencies in which local interests might seek an MPs support, but
they were in no position to make demands on him.[38] Some of the elite
were from aristocratic families with centuries' old connections to a
community, but others, such as Lord Sidmouth[39] or Robert Peel,[40] were
sons of successful merchants or professionals who had bought land and a
constituency for themselves and their heirs. These grandees did not see
themselves as owning their positions of power on the basis of popular
acclaim for the advantages they secured for their local areas. A consequence of these arrangements was that by the eighteenth century the
majority of MPs and members of the House of Lords were not dependent
for their position on securing the interests and demands of their
constituencies and hence, for many, their links with local government
were marginal. By the time of the 1832 Reform Act there was, therefore,
little affection or interest among the elites in the Whig and Tory parties
for local politics other than as a means of trading-in parliamentary seats
and securing a system through the JPs that could guarantee law and order
throughout the nation. Such a development paves the way for the characteristic and significant domination of local government by central government in the modern British political system and the absence of a role for
the national parliamentary representative, as in France or the USA, to
serve as a patron to his or her constituency by ensuring central largesse
flows to the locality.

The county

Improvements in agricultural technology and the growth in Tudor times
of sheep farming for wool had led to the enclosure of common land and
strip farms to create estates that were parcelled out into a patchwork of

medium-sized farms often tenanted by wealthier farmers who paid rents to the landowner. The wealthiest families might own several estates and often left their management to stewards while they enjoyed a life of luxury or political intrigue based in London or a spa town such as Bath. In the summer they entertained grandees of similar status in their country houses. Although some of these grandees were Lord Lieutenants and interested themselves in local matters, as indicated above, many were by 1800 indifferent to local concerns, seeing themselves as national leaders. The day to day running of local government in most rural areas rested more on the respectable but lower strata of country gentry, the squirearchy who farmed smaller but, nevertheless, still substantial estates. Traditionally, these worthies remained in their country houses and dominated, often as JPs, the life and values of their communities. Many lacked the economic capital to develop their estates to gain commercial advantage and tended, consequently, to form the Tory traditionalist backbone of the British polity. The less prosperous squires may have farmed the land themselves, alongside their farm workers, while the more successful will have become *rentiers* securing profits from a number of tenant farmers.

Within the village the parson was often next in status to the landowner and was appointable as an owner of property by virtue of the endowments that sustained his post in the Church. Since landowners frequently held the right to nominate who should occupy these 'livings' local vicars were often related to landowning families, perhaps, like the Reverend Bute Crawley as satirised by Thackery[41] in V*anity Fair*, a hunting, shooting and fishing relative of the squire of the parish. Many a bench of magistrates were peopled by Church of England clergymen while the routine work of running the parish was given to educated but impecunious curates. Other personnel of consequence were the stewards who managed the estates and lawyers who handled the landowners' legal affairs. Below the level of gentlemen, the farmers renting the larger parcels of the estate formed a relatively prosperous stratum. Rural Britain was, however, far from being a country wholly settled under a pattern of large or small estates. In regions characterised by smaller, independently owned farms, yeomen farmers could own sufficient land to give them a secure and relatively comfortable livelihood. Communities could be grouped around villages composed of small farmers and also tradesmen such as blacksmiths, tailors and weavers, who comprised a small, semi-industrial community and might be independent of the economic pressures that could be exerted by a powerful landowner. In open villages the social structure was far less hierarchical and villages not subject to the influence of a squire could be regarded by the elite as ill-organised and potentially lawless.[42]

By the eighteenth century, the government of the county was conducted primarily by the JPs who met in conclave at the quarter sessions. Although appointed by the Lord Lieutenant, in most counties the majority of landowners of substance could expect to be appointed as a JP and might regard themselves as seriously insulted if their claims were passed over. There were more JPs by the eighteenth century than were required to conduct judicial and administrative business of the county and many did not attend the quarter sessions which, on occasion, could even be cancelled for lack of attendant magistrates. Clergymen were often the more assiduous attendees and in some cases the work of the county was largely in the hands of Anglican parsons. Not all JPs were, however, from the traditional landed classes, and it was in urban areas sometimes necessary to appoint them from the lower professional strata of merchants, bankers and businessmen. In Middlesex, which was being consumed by 1800 in the expansion of London, the senior JPs included bankers who used the office for personal profit and the notorious Merceron family who controlled the parish of Bethnal Green, manipulating their powers to grant licences for public houses.[43] The power of magistrates derived from their capacity to regulate the activities of parish government coupled with their local economic influence. They had the statutory power to approve annually the accounts of parishes and to require them to undertake duties such as road and bridge maintenance. They could also adjudicate on appeals from residents of a parish against decisions on eligibility for paying rates or payments of poor relief,[44] or decide whether a particular country fair might be a nuisance and instruct constables to ban the festivity or prevent particular peddlers from operating in their county. Even farm labourers' wages could be influenced through Poor Law payments. The Speenhamland system linking poor relief to the price of bread derives from the deliberations of a group of Berkshire magistrates.

Magistrates formed a secretive local legislature allowing landowners to determine not only how regulations delegated to them by statute should be ordered but also to develop legal precedent.[45] While the judicial proceedings of the quarter sessions were usually open to the public, much of the business of county administration was conducted in private by small groups of JPs. Where matters affected a particular parish or group of parishes it was common practice, for much of the eighteenth century, for justice and administration to be undertaken through application to the local landowner or parson in their capacity as magistrates. This might involve dealing with complaints about the criminal activity of neighbours to determine whether to commit the accused for trial at the quarter sessions or, in lesser cases, to impose a summary fine. The remit of magistrates encompassed also administrative issues relating to parish supervision such as enforcing licensing rules for taverns, commanding local constables to collect appropriate tax arrears or resolving complaints of villagers against low entitlements from the Poor Law overseers. The Webbs report an entry in the diary of a Lancashire JP: 'He issues a precept to the constables of Failsworth and Gorton to appear at the next quarter session 'to answer the default ... in not paying in the bridge money'''.[46]

By 1800 almost all counties had petty sessions, usually held in the most distinguished inns of county-towns, attended by two or more JPs who oversaw justice and administration for specific areas. These semi-professional administrators tended, like twentieth-century civil servants, to believe that parish government was run by incompetent, lower class citizens who needed to be informed how to behave.[47]

The power of JPs was further strengthened by the role of the county as a military division to help muster soldiers for either national defence or for dealing with major outbreaks of civil disorder. By the time of Henry VIII the Lord Lieutenant and his deputies were the senior officers of a county militia; they appointed junior officers, for the most part landed gentlemen, who in their turn would recruit loyal dependants, such as their tenant farmers, to the force. After the Restoration of Charles II the militia gained further standing as a military force to balance the dangers inherent in a standing army.[48] Each parish was obliged to supply a quota of able-bodied men for the militia on pain of a fine imposed by the quarter sessions. In some areas enthusiastic landowners recruited their own volunteer levies, the yeomanry, usually from among their tenant farmers.[49] The militia and the yeomanry by the eighteenth century were, apart from times of national crisis as in the Napoleonic Wars when they would have been expected to repel invading forces, a means of supplementing local constabularies when faced with civil unrest. Through the militia, local landed interests had powers that could extend even into the boroughs, to suppress political and social unrest.[50] Magistrates could also request support from the professional army but usually found it more convenient to call out their own volunteer forces, using the professionals only in the most serious emergencies. Yeomanry was the force that turned the radicals' meeting in Manchester into the 'Peterloo Massacre'.[51]

The county itself undertook relatively few executive functions and was more an organisation for the control of local agencies and, broadly, the maintenance of law and order. The few county-level executive officers were either voluntary or poorly paid subordinates. Perhaps the most arduous office was that of High or Chief Constable. Several were appointed in most counties, for a year in office, usually from the smaller yeoman class of landowners or more prosperous tenant farmers. They were obliged to inform the parish constables of the decisions of the quarter sessions, organise the constables if there were threats of violence that could not be handled by a single parish and also to collect the county rates from parish officials. Until the late eighteenth century the role was usually unpaid, the holders of the office serving at some expense to themselves.[52] In the county town a clerk of justice handled the administrative work and record-keeping of the quarter sessions. As the county system of government developed, subsequent appointments included a treasurer, a county surveyor who took over the from the High Constables the maintenance of large bridges, the county hall and the prison, frequently contracting those tasks to local builders or farmers.[53]

The parish

According to the 1834 Poor Law Commissioners there were some 15,600 parishes in England[54] which, like French communes, true to their organic nature, varied greatly in area and population. A few had no inhabitants at all while the largest had over 50,000. Although the parish, or vestry,[55] is regarded as a rural institution, any urban area that had not been granted borough status was usually subject to parish government. Outside its ancient city, London was governed largely by vestries, as were the communities of the emerging industrial towns. Parishes had a range of rather ill-defined tasks. There were a number of duties enforced on the parish by statute, including administration of the Poor Law. The parish was also expected to secure law and order in its community, maintain local roads and bridges and provide for the up-keep of the local church. Parishes were also able to undertake many other tasks at their own discretion and, since the concept of *ultra vires* had not been developed until the mid-nineteenth century, could have a wide range of activities. In practice cost and custom limited what they did largely to their statutory tasks. However, in the greyer areas of legality, a parish might assume a central role in organising cakes and ale for the community by raiding the coffers to celebrate feast days, serving as a means of reconciling local quarrels or enforcing local custom.[56]

The government of parishes was traditionally supposed to be conducted through regular open meetings of all rate-payers in the community, including women.[57] Parishioners assembled in the vestry of the church or at a local hostelry to approve policies or make appointments by majority vote. The extent to which participative democracy characterised the open vestries varied widely. In some parishes decisions were made only by the wealthier farmers, who excluded paupers and those who had recently been in receipt of poor relief, and in others only the appointed officers of the parish determined its decisions.[58] Although most parishes were theoretically open and democratic, the influence of different strata of rural society will have ensured that certain members of the vestry could exert greater pressure than others. A dominant landowner may not regularly attend vestry meetings but could ensure through agents, especially the local rector, who often chaired the meetings, that his views were seriously considered. Many parishes had over time restricted participation and become select vestries in which only a small number of usually co-opted parishioners could determine their decisions. The system had emerged through private acts or by custom and was particularly entrenched in the London conurbation.[59] The select vestries were widely opposed by radicals, who saw them as generally corrupt, self-seeking organisations.

Efforts were made to democratise them, including an Act of 1831, steered through Parliament by the radical John Cam Hobhouse with the urging of Francis Place, to allow rate-payers in parishes with over 800 inhabitants to establish elected parish councils.[60]

The parish implemented most of its business through the appointment, usually, of unpaid officers selected by the parish meeting. In many cases these posts were assigned to the less affluent members of the community and shunned by those of higher status. Greatest responsibility rested on the overseers of the poor, who in many cases also collected local taxes, the parish constable who ensured law and order and the churchwarden. Additionally, the sometimes salaried surveyor ensured the maintenance of local roads. The post-holders were chosen by a variety of methods: villagers might be persuaded to take on posts, but in some parishes roles were allocated in a prearranged order, while in other parishes they might by custom be allocated to a particular family. Nominees selected by the parish were usually confirmed by the JPs who could therefore weed out politically or morally undesirable appointments.[61] Some people, usually the affluent, were exempt from that process, and it was even possible with a 'Tyburn ticket' to buy exemption through a transferable by sale privilege given originally to citizens who successfully brought to justice a criminal.[62] In larger parishes there were a number of lowly paid and lowly regarded employees of the parish, such as the attendants in the workhouse or the beadle, much derided by Dickens in *David Copperfield*, who acted partly as town-crier and assistant to the constable.[63]

Municipal government

The Webbs arrived at the view that the principal distinction between a municipality and other forms of urban government was the capacity to appoint JPs outside the framework laid down by the county.[64] The grant of a royal charter was not necessary to claim borough status. Many municipalities could not trace such a charter and had obtained certain privileges by practice and custom or had their charter revoked by James II, never to be restored by William and Mary.[65] The right to choose MPs was not held by all boroughs. As a charter or set of customary rights was unique to each borough, their organisation was highly individual. The principal function of many boroughs related to their capacity to appoint magistrates and a number also acted as if they were a county and held quarter sessions. Authority over law and order could be substantive, extending even, as in Banbury, to enforcing the death penalty.[66] In addition to local justice many boroughs provided a wide range of services for their communities, for example controlling their local markets or paving and cleansing the local streets. Coastal boroughs such as Penzance, Liverpool or Berwick operated harbours.[67]

Many boroughs – in Scotland, burghs – were governed by small councils of some twenty members, led by the mayor or, in some communities, a port-reeve, bailiff or provost; the mayor, or his equivalent, was usually elected by the councillors. Although many councils had originally been subject to election by their rate-payers, democracy was frequently subverted so that most councils were renewed through co-option by vote of the existing councillors. Thus, the corporation had in many boroughs become a self-perpetuating clique of leading families who were increasingly distant from its citizens. The Webbs give detailed accounts of the divisions that opened up between the closed corporation of Bristol and its leading commercial citizens.[68] In some communities, such as Liverpool and Leicester, the election of councillors was more open, the vote extending to all freemen of the city, a several-thousand-strong body of craftsmen and traders who had acquired their status through servicing apprenticeships, through birthright or by purchase of the right to trade in the community.[69] Occasionally, this group might form themselves into a corporation, which, as in Sandwich in Kent, ensured that town meetings were attended by at least 100 freemen.[70] As the foremost citizen, the mayor was also chief magistrate for the town and usually chaired judicial petty sessions and even the quarter sessions. He called and presided over council meetings and often had substantial executive powers to determine policies and ensure their implementation. A town clerk, usually an established local lawyer paid for his services by the corporation, was often second in importance to the mayor, as he could determine and argue for the legal rights of the community.

The boroughs of the unreformed local government system were frequently depicted as corrupt, self-perpetuating organisations concerned with gathering local taxes solely for the purpose of wining and dining the self-selecting corporation members. Such an impression was firmly embedded in the liberal consciousness by the Royal Commission on Municipal Government whose conclusion was quoted by Lord John Russell in the debate on the First Reading of the Municipal Corporations Act:

> There prevails among the inhabitants of a great majority of the incorporated towns a general, and in our opinion, just dissatisfaction with their Municipal Institutions, a distrust of the self-elected Municipal Councils, whose powers are subject to no popular control, and whose acts and proceedings being secret, are unchecked by the influence of popular opinion; a distrust of the municipal magistracy, tainting with suspicion local administration of justice, and often accompanied by contempt of the persons by whom the law is administered; a discontent under the burthens of local taxation, while revenues that ought to be applied for the public advantage are diverted from their legitimate use and are sometimes wastefully bestowed for the benefit of individuals, sometimes squandered for purposes injurious to the character and morals of the people.[71]

The reality was, however, far more complex. Some boroughs, although far from democratic, were entrepreneurial and did much to build the expansion and wealth of the community. Liverpool in the eighteenth century had a particularly forward-looking council which built the docks and warehousing that ensured the town became one of the most important ports in the country.[72] The Webbs also show how the smaller town of Penzance had an active corporation led by industrious mayors who were often prevented from developing public and commercial infrastructure by the reluctance of citizens to support the plans put forward by their council.[73] In many cases lack of activity among the borough councillors was a reflection not so much of incompetence but of the lack of any powers within their charters, especially that of raising a rate, to facilitate the development of relatively poor communities. Many boroughs with the capabilities to improve the streets, maintain harbours or provide more effective sanitation secured those powers through private acts of Parliament which were necessary to supplement the limited jurisdiction that they may have acquired through their original charters. The cost of acquiring such an act was often too great a burden for the citizens of a small borough.

The limited powers and capacities of most town governments or parishes in urban areas led in the late seventeenth century to the emergence of new structures for resolving the squalor and dangers of unplanned town development. In 1662 a Private Act of Parliament created commissioners for the City of London and the adjoining Westminster in order to clean the streets and rebuild sewers. The organisation that came to be known as the Commissioners of Scotland Yard consisted of twenty-one local worthies holding the post largely through their incumbency of other posts in London governments and was funded from contributions from wealthier householders.[74] In the first years of the eighteenth century a few town councils, Bristol and Beverley for instance, gained similar powers to ensure the cleansing of streets, and in 1748 a body of 'improvement commissioners', separate from the Town Council, was established by a Private Act in Liverpool for cleansing the streets.[75] From this point, there was a steady stream of local acts creating similar bodies in towns throughout Britain, so that by 1835 some 300 such organisations were in existence.[76]

Each commission tended to be distinctive in its structure and in the exact functions that it was legally entitled to perform, and many were restricted in their capacity to fulfil their duties by restraints on their fundraising. Many commissions tended to be, like the borough corporations, co-opted bodies and included a large proportion of the town councillors; others, however, had a substantial elected element, although most relied on a small number of more dedicated members for conducting their routine activities.[77] The functions of improvement commissions normally centred on clearing the refuse and filth from streets, and also in paving and lighting streets. Many had prototype building regulation powers that allowed them to prevent new buildings which would encroach on highways or to end practices such as leaving open cellar hatches in walkways, which was a continual hazard for the unwary, late-night, tipsy reveller. The commissions sometimes had powers to establish night-watch patrols and on occasion this was probably the central function of the organisation. The most successful commissions gradually became effective local authorities, as in Manchester where a highly energetic body, created in 1765 as a Police Commission, had by 1835 acquired additional powers to improve sanitation, remove obstructions from the streets and pioneered municipalisation by taking over the supply of gas to the town.[78]

London

Since the Middle Ages London was much the largest urban area of Britain and had long spilled over the boundaries of the City of London to form in 1801 a conurbation of 958,863 inhabitants, which was 11 times larger than the second most populous borough, Liverpool.[79] By the fourteenth century the City of London had gained considerable privileges from the Crown, partly in recognition of the role of its wealthier citizens in funding the wars and extravagances of monarchs. The City of London was governed by 4 interlocking 'courts' representing, at the lowest level, 26 ward councils, a Court of Common Hall consisting largely of liverymen associated with the trade guilds, a Court of Common Council consisting of freemen of the City and a Court of Alderman of 26 members elected for life. Presiding over this structure was the Lord Mayor, assisted by 2 Sheriffs who were elected annually by the Court of Common Hall from the 26 aldermen.[80]

The system of government in the City of London reflected a delicate balance of democracy and plutocracy. At the lowest level, local citizens through their ward organisations could, as in many parishes, exert considerable influence over the minor regulations important to their areas. However, substantive matters concerning trade and the interconnected relationship of the city with monarchy rested on an elite of merchants, bankers and masters of city guilds who guarded the economic privileges of the city against the interests of the King and the nobility. The structure survived the numerous changes related in this chronicle and is little changed in its formal structure today, if not in its practices and functions.

Surrounding the few square miles of the city, the conurbation of London comprised small towns, parishes and parts of the county administrations of Surrey, Middlesex and Kent. Greater London was, therefore, governed by an array of generally small authorities which often jealously guarded their independence from one another. The most widespread governing body was the parish vestry which, in many districts, retained an open form of government. Numerous local residents crammed into meetings in the parish churches when important matters required debate and some of the largest parishes, St Pancras for one, were changed to a select vestry through a Private Act in order to ensure more manageable meetings. Some larger and generally wealthier parishes, such as St Marylebone and St George's in Hannover Square, catering for well-heeled residents, were also select vestries. In poorer areas some theoretically open vestries had fallen under the control of powerful local families not unwilling to use the threat of violence to secure a corrupt, self-interested, city-boss system of government.[81] The parishes frequently governed alongside commissions established for specific purposes. Drainage of water by an Act of 1532 had been entrusted to eight commissions for sewers that were appointed bodies with a theoretically numerous membership that in some cases came effectively to be controlled by the contractors who undertook the work of the organisation.[82] With the laying out of new estates for wealthy Londoners many developers applied for acts of Parliament to secure separate paving commissions for the maintenance of streets and paths in these areas of opulence.[83]

Scotland

Scotland had evolved into a relatively united country under a monarchy by the time of the Norman conquest of England.[84] Shires were recognised before the eleventh century and by the twelfth century were established in the kingdom as legal divisions in which the major local power, the Sheriff, usually a landed aristocrat, held his courts that resolved both criminal and civil issues.[85] After succeeding to the throne of England James VI tried to translate English institutions to his native land in order to strengthen his influence against the power of the Sheriffs by establishing JPs within the Scottish county system. The Scottish nobility ignored the new arrangement and continued to govern primarily through the office of Sheriff as the principal law-enforcement officer in each county, working alongside the more ancient courts of the nobility.[86]

Following the Act of Union in 1707 and the putting down of the Jacobite rebellions there was increasing concern over the administration of justice in Scotland, particularly on account of the largely hereditary basis of the Sheriff's powers. In 1747 legislation restructured the office by appointing a 'Sheriff Depute' to counties, who had to be a lawyer with at least three years' experience, to conduct judicial proceedings. The Sheriff became a ceremonial figure while the 'Sheriff Depute' and a subordinate team of 'sheriff substitutes' became the central administrators of Scottish local judicial government by the eighteenth century.[87] Scotland, therefore, secured the division of judicial and administrative control of rural government much earlier than happened in England and Wales.

In 1667 the Scottish Government's administration of rural areas was transformed through the creation of the office of 'commissioner for supply' to raise taxes, appointing the holders of the office from representatives of the landed aristocracy and gentry.[88] The commissioners' principal power was in respect of the collection of a land tax to be sent to a receiver in Edinburgh for disbursement for Scottish and British Government expenditure. Their second most important role was repair of roads and bridges. The commissioner of supply continued to control much of the administration of the counties after the Act of Union, but was required to be in possession of land and hence pay taxes. However, this stipulation, if generously interpreted, enabled a large number of landowners to qualify as commissioners, although in practice relatively few regularly attended to their duties. Their meetings were called by a convenor elected from the commissioners who, by 1800, had come to be regarded as one of the significant leaders of the county, although he had few executive powers. By the nineteenth century some of the commissioners' powers were being distributed to other agencies.[89] Road Trustees, for example, were established in 1831,[90] and, following their creation in 1845, greater freedom was consequently delegated to parish governments to administer a Poor Law system for Scotland.[91]

As in England, by the twelfth century towns that had sufficient importance were being recognised with a charter.[92] Those receiving their charter direct from the King were referred to as 'royal burghs'. There were by the eighteenth century seventy such towns[93] of which a few, such as Glasgow, Edinburgh, Aberdeen and Dundee, had become substantial cities, although most were in reality merely large villages. In addition to the royal burghs a number of communities claimed to be burghs of barony by attaining either a charter from an aristocrat with rights under the Crown over a region of Scotland or a regality from a bishop. There were around 150 such creations,[94] although most were small communities.[95] The royal burghs like those of England were self governing and harboured a wide variety of councils, some elected but many acting as self-perpetuating oligarchies. Similarly their powers varied in accord with their charter or custom and practice and on occasion these powers were supplemented by private acts.

The service functions of local authorities

In the towns many services necessary for maintaining a reasonably comfortable environment were expected to be acquired privately by direct payment to contractors and workmen or through the employment of servants. Good sanitation and clean roads could be obtained in rich neighbourhoods through employing private road-sweepers or refuse-collectors. Many estates in eighteenth-century London or Bath were private enclaves employing their own service personnel which could include night-watchmen. In the late eighteenth and early nineteenth centuries development of turnpike trusts was motivated similarly by a view that services should be provided not on a communal basis but as profitable enterprises to be sold

to those willing to pay for the service or facility. In contrast to private
provision for the wealthy, there was also a pervasive ethos of voluntary
service for the community that formed the bedrock of any effective governance for the parish and county. The many tasks that were undertaken by
boroughs or parishes were usually based on custom, including care of
corporate property, or by private acts and were not, therefore, subject to
universal provision. It was expected that able-bodied residents of a village
would be prepared from time to time to take on offices in parish government or the county, without pay, and also be prepared to lend a hand in
road repairs or other tasks requiring maintenance of public property:

> It was, indeed, this principle of obligation to render public service ... that
> was, and remained far into the eighteenth century, the axle round which
> revolved all old established local institutions, whether manorial or parochial,
> of the Borough or of the County.[96]

Only a few communal functions, such as the care for the poor in a
community, were a national requirement. The task was formally assigned
to the parish in the Elizabethan Poor Law Act,[97] developed between 1597
and 1601. Anyone who was destitute was able to seek poor relief from
their home parish which was required to appoint overseers to raise funds,
determine eligibility for poor relief and distribute payment or support in
kind. Although many boroughs had systems for the relief of the poor, the
legislation required that the separate parishes within each borough were
responsible under the Act for raising a rate to relieve poverty. The
Elizabethan legislation established few guidelines as to how poor relief
was to be distributed. Traditionally, help was provided as out-relief in the
home of the paupers with money or food allocated to the aged and infirm.
The able-bodied poor were often expected to undertake tasks such as road
maintenance in return for support. Arrangements evolved in some
parishes for the poor to work on local farms with the parish subsidising
the wages paid by the farmer. This included the Speenhamland system,
devised in 1795, to supplement low wages with relief payment tied to the
cost of bread. The system created serious divisions in many parishes as it
allowed farmers to pay low wages at the rate-payers' expense and also tied
labourers to the land.[98]

By the seventeenth century it was recognised that by joining together
the Poor Law activities of separate parishes to establish a workhouse the
able-bodied poor could be more cheaply assigned to some useful tasks.
Parliament sanctioned the arrangement in Bristol through a Private Act in
1697 and this initiative was followed by other larger cities.[99] By the eighteenth century workhouses had become widespread in towns, and even in
some rural parishes, and in 1782 an enabling Act sponsored by Thomas
Gilbert allowed parishes the power to group together into Poor Law
Unions in order to establish larger houses for the poor.[100] The proposal
was in part motivated by a widespread view in Parliament that Poor Law

overseers were incompetent and the issues of poverty could better be dealt with by professionally run institutions.[101] In many cases, however, the workhouse was degraded into an establishment of last resort where there was little or no effort to keep its unfortunate inmates in humane conditions.[102] Scottish local government tended to provide poor relief through different principles and structures from those of England and Wales. Interpretation of Poor Law Acts as applied to Scotland had by the late eighteenth century generally decreed that the able-bodied poor had no right of help or support. Liberal economists of the time argued that this was a considerable asset to the Scottish economy and upheld Scotland as representing better practice than England. Greater support than in England and Wales was provided by voluntary charity collected by the Church, but this system fell under the control of the large landowners who, by 1800, came to dominate much of northern Scotland. The charitable lairds who were creating poverty by enforcing enclosures and clearances could afford to be so generous.[103]

It was the duty of the parish to secure law and order in its community. The task was entrusted to a constable who was usually an annual unpaid appointment by the parish council, although the same individual or family could monopolise the position for several years. The post was also often avoided by those who could buy themselves out of such potentially unpopular service. The constable in a small community could hope to exert some order as he would know the majority of local families and be sufficiently informed through local gossip of the behaviour of its less scrupulous citizens. The constable was authorised to whip unwanted vagrants before sending them on their way, although he could also provide money from parish accounts for travellers who had honourably fallen on hard times and needed funds to assist their journey.[104] The position of the constable was fortified by laws which provided substantial rewards to those who aided in the successful arrest and prosecution of felons, and a diligent constable could receive considerable compensation from his unpaid office through such means. However, the practice also led to the temptation to prosecute the innocent scapegoat for the sake of reward. The duties of the constable might also involve collecting local taxes and fines on behalf of the county, and could extend to tasks ranging from keeping a communal bull to service the cattle of the village to ensuring that beacons to alert the countryside about potential invasion were kept in readiness at times of crisis.[105] In the case of major social unrest the office of constable was wholly unsuited to the task of maintaining order. Serious disturbances that were endemic in rural areas undergoing transformation through enclosure and the mechanisation of agriculture had to be dealt with by the power given to JPs to read the Riot Act, which ordered hostile crowds to disperse on pain of calling out the county militia to quell the disturbance.

The transformation of the police into a modern bureaucratic force is attributed to Peel's 1829 Metropolitan Police Act. The idea of a single professional police force for a town was not new. The term 'police' was used in the eighteenth century by Whig reformers campaigning for a system of bringing criminals to justice by the amelioration of harsh sentences through a framework separate from that of the judiciary.[106] Oldham had established such a structure by a Private Act in 1826 and Bristol in the 1820s had some 170 policemen.[107] What was unusual about Peel's 1829 Act was that the force constructed for London had no local control and was an organisation dealing with local issues directly subject to the Government. The development of the Metropolitan Police is a significant indication of a changing political climate as regards central control of locally delivered services. Peel, perhaps alerted to the value of a large, co-ordinated police force by his service as the Government Minister for Ireland, had set up a Select Committee in 1822 to inquire into policing in the Metropolis. The Committee did not endorse developments that would lead to centralisation, but a few years later, following further scandal concerning parish governance in London and more liberal pressure for law and order, Peel managed, by excluding the City of London from the arrangement, to push through the Metropolitan Police force as a local administration directed wholly by central government.[108] The force was under the command of three Commissioners who reported directly to the Home Secretary. The arrangement created a model police force and was a possible blueprint for the evolution of services under central control, although it was to become one of the evolutionary dead-ends in the emergence of the nineteenth-century structure for local government.

In the eighteenth century, prisons, like the police, were a local responsibility and in rural areas subject to haphazard control by the JPs and the quarter sessions. Many boroughs also had their local prisons, which were subject to corporations and mayors in their capacity as magistrates. Prisons were an unwanted expense for local landowners, although until 1815 many were funded by fees extracted from the prisoners or their families. Abuse and the injustice of this arrangement led to an Act in 1815 abolishing payment of fees by prisoners, placing further costs on the rates. A growing clamour from humanitarian reformers such as John Howard and Elizabeth Fry, or radicals like Bentham, created increasing pressure for further reform. As Home Secretary in 1823 Peel passed the Goal Act to regulate many aspects of prison administration, but the measure did little to enforce better standards and it was not until 1835 that further legislation established a system of central government inspection of prisons and began to loosen the control of landowners over the penal system.[109]

Until Tudor times it was expected that the landowner, and hence in many cases the Lord of the Manor, was responsible for the roads that ran through his land, but a landmark Act of 1555 transferred this responsibility to the parish and in so doing initiated a view of local government as an agency to undertake common obligations for a locality.[110] The Act required a landowner to supply a cart and labourers to maintain the roads for up to six days a year and all un-propertied able-bodied labourers to provide the same amount of time without pay to maintain the roads. By the eighteenth century much of this voluntary help had been substituted through the use of unemployed paupers. Where some engineering expertise was needed, such as building a substantial bridge, professional masons were employed, who had to be paid for by borrowing capital and recouping the interest through tolls.

The growth of industry and commerce required the development of inexpensive and reasonably rapid systems for transport. The early eighteenth-century system of road maintenance undertaken by the parishes, supervised haphazardly by county surveyors acting on behalf of the JPs of the quarter sessions, was never capable of establishing a structured national transport system. Communities tended to concentrate most effort on the roads serving local farms rather than on any major highways crossing parishes which would interest the wealthy traveller and the vagrant but not the more sedentary local landowner.[111] As road traffic grew in volume and weight the network of roads was inadequate to serve the demands laid on them and in winter many major highways became boggy quagmires, often broadening into adjacent farmland as travellers tried to circumvent the more impassable stretches of the highway. The problem of maintaining major routes between towns was, by the seventeenth century, seen to require new strategies and led, in 1663, to a petition from the JPs of the counties of Hertford, Cambridge and Huntington for help to maintain the Great North Road. Parliament responded by granting a special statute to the quarter sessions to erect gates across sections of the road so that tolls could be collected to secure its maintenance. The idea was applied to only one section, at Wadesmill in Hertfordshire, and this became the first turnpike road in Britain.[112] Although a number of further Acts allowed quarter sessions to charge tolls for road maintenance, any trend towards giving the counties authority for maintaining major highways was brought to an end in the early eighteenth century. In 1706 an Act established a new ad-hoc authority, a 'trust', to collect tolls in order to maintain a section of the Great North Road in Bedfordshire. In 1711 Parliament responded to all further requests to set up tolls by permitting the creation of turnpike trusts through private Acts, which followed a standard format as to their composition and powers.[113] By 1832 the number of trusts that had been created was sufficient to make them, after the parish, the next most numerous type of local authority[114]

The turnpike trusts tended to consist of local landowners and usually included a number of JPs. Membership was renewed by co-option and hence the organisations became self-perpetuating oligarchies. Landowners and industrialists developed new roads largely as a means for ensuring that their estates or factories could be effectively linked to national trade routes, and there could be bitter arguments between communities and landowners over the direction of a turnpike. A common complaint was that wealth often diverted roads away from the direct flight of the crow to satisfy someone's commercial interest. Many toll roads failed to raise funds sufficient to secure their adequate repair, partly because of competition from other means of transport, and their status was to be reviewed every twenty-one years.[115] Turnpike trusts secured loans by mortgaging future income; when faced with increasing debt they ceased to effectively maintain their route, which could become almost as ruinous as the parish-maintained roads that had preceded them. Although the trusts could not gain direct funding through rates, many made use of the old requirement on parish councils to provide labour to maintain the roads. By the 1830s there was a strong body of opinion that argued for an end to toll roads.

Financing local governments

The principal source for financing local government activities within parishes, counties and by most improvement commissions was the rate as a tax primarily on property. The rate as a central source of revenue was established by statute in the Elizabethan Poor Law but certainly pre-dated that legislation.[116] Until the nineteenth century there were no fixed arrangements as to how rates were to be levied, and parishes had a variety of methods for their assessment and collection. In most communities an assessment was made of the value of a property and a rate in the pound was levied in accord with that value. In some areas a rate could be levied on fixed property, such as boats or machinery. In some communities land was rated while in others it was shops or houses. Rates frequently were not charged on the cottages of the poor who may well be in receipt of support from Poor Law funds or they might be levied not on the occupant but on the owner of a property, who 'compounded' the rate by passing on the charge to the occupant in the rent.[117] The most onerous element of the rates concerned contributions to the Poor Law funds but rates were additionally levied for functions such as maintenance of the parish church, highways and sewers, and payment of constables. Normally the parish vestry fixed the rate in the pound and determined when this was to be collected, giving the task of its collection to the overseer of the poor or the constable.[118] In addition to a parish levy the rate-payers had to meet the demands of the county which charged a rate on the parish as a whole that was then either paid from funds already collected by the parish rate or levied as an additional charge on the local rate-payers. It was also possible for JPs to require wealthier parishes to subsidise the Poor Law fund in less affluent parishes from their funds;[119] the High Constable had the unenviable task of persuading parishes to forward their contribution to the county.[120]

In urban areas raising funds was more problematical as the charters of incorporation of many towns did not allow for the imposition of rates, unless they were among the few which, like the counties, held quarter sessions. In some towns the corporation raised funds through its ownership of property, which, in a few cases, could bring in a substantive income. A number of towns were also fortunate to have received substantial bequests in trust funds from wealthy former citizens. In some towns their charter of incorporation allowed them to raise taxes on goods brought into the community. Bristol and Liverpool, for example, enjoyed considerable income from property and also levies on ships using their harbours.[121] In many cases, however, corporations had little responsibility for services in their towns given the paucity of resources with which to provide them.[122] The formation of an improvement commission was often a means to establish by private act both a body that could provide services and an organisation with the power to raise revenue sufficient to pay for them. Many commissions established a rating system to pay for their activities and some also charged for the use of their services: for example, Manchester Street Lighting Commission charged a rate to anyone living within 100 yards of one of its street lamps.[123] A further financial problem besetting all forms of local government was the issue of raising money for capital expenditure. This was frequently secured by borrowing money from wealthy landowners or professionals and paying back the sum, with interest, through the rate fund or by raising a further levy on the rate-payers.[124] Ideally, but not always successfully, the parish or county sought the generosity of local worthies who might be inclined to provide the funds needed for maintaining a bridge or to shore up a crumbling town hall.

The raising of revenue for local expenditure was no less of a controversial issue in the eighteenth century than it is throughout this history. In the absence of grants from the central exchequer to subsidise local services, and with the onus of supplying social services and infrastructure resting on local government, the burden of taxation was skewed towards the rates, and in an agrarian society these fell heavily on the owners of land. There was, however, little interest until the eighteenth century in looking to the State for financial aid to resolve the problem since it was for many landowners better to be subject to locally collected taxes, which could be more easily controlled by them, than national tariffs. Such an attitude led to a widespread view that underlay the relationship between central and local administration, according to which local government paid through rates on property for local spending on poor relief, roads and police, while central government raised revenue, principally through excise duty, for national defence and the machinery of justice and government. The interface between national and local duties was not, however, always clear, and since the Middle Ages there had been payments that crossed the boundaries, such as exchequer payments to county sheriffs for administering decisions taken by central government's courts of assize.[125] Some municipalities also received subsidies from the national exchequer or the civil list expenses of the Crown. The border town of Berwick, for example, received an annual payment from the civil list for maintaining the important crossing of the Tweed.[126]

Social pressures and technological developments, however, began to erode the formula. During the eighteenth century the contribution due to the Poor Law for overall taxation had nearly doubled.[127] The sum paid by each individual varied widely but could amount to a substantial proportion of the income of a moderately affluent citizen. The demands of the Napoleonic Wars greatly increased national taxation to pay for defence. Following the Wars the subsequent economic slump of the 1820s exacerbated the demands on Poor Law funds and the capability of householders to pay for them. Behind the demands for reform of the franchise, the Poor Law and the boroughs were major concerns about the rising proportion of income that was being diverted into local taxation.

Notes

1 A. Birley, *Life in Roman Britain* (London: Batsford, 2nd edn, 1981), p. 22.

2 A. L. F. Rivet, *Town and Country in Roman Britain* (London: Hutchinson, 1958), p. 64.

3 Birley, *Life in Roman Britain*, p. 22.

4 J. Blair, *Anglo Saxon Oxfordshire* (Oxford: Sutton Publishing, 1994), p. 102.

5 A. Williams, *Kingship and Government in Pre-Conquest England* (Basingstoke: Macmillan, 1999), p. 88.

6 S. Webb and B. Webb, *English Local Government*, 10 vols, vol. 1: *The Parish and the County* (London: Longmans, 1906), p. 284.

7 Williams, *Kingship and Government in Pre-Conquest England*, p. 88.

8 J. Clarke, *A History of Local Government of the United Kingdom* (London: Herbert Jenkins, 1955), p. 9.

9 S. Webb and B. Webb, *English Local Government*, vol. 3: *The Manor and the Borough* (London: Cass, 1963), pp. 11–32.

10 H. Swanson, *Medieval British Towns* (Basingstoke: Macmillan, 1999), p. 13.

11 W. E. Tate, *The Parish Chest: A Study of the Records of Parochial Administration in England* (Cambridge: Cambridge University Press, 1960), pp. 9–10.

12 B. Keith-Lucas, *The Unreformed Local Government System* (London: Croom Helm, 1980), p. 75.

13 Webb and Webb, *The Manor and the Borough*, pp. 99–113.

14 L. F. Salzman, *English Life in the Middle Ages* (Oxford: Oxford University Press, 1926), p. 78.

15 I. Gladwin, *The Sheriff: The Man and His Office* (London: Gollancz, 1974), p. 16. 'Sheriff' probably derives from the Anglo-Saxon 'shire-reeve' who as a prosperous local figure originally served as the go-between for a community and its protective Lord.

16 *Ibid.*, p. 271.

17 Webb and Webb, *The Parish and the County*, pp. 283–91.
18 P. Slack, *Poverty and Policy in Tudor and Stuart England* (London: Longman, 1988), p. 114.
19 R. J. Olney, *Rural Society and County Government in Nineteenth Century Lincolnshire*, vol. 10 of the 'History of Lincolnshire' series (Lincoln: History of Lincolnshire Committee, 1979), p. 12.
20 F. M. L. Thompson, *English Landed Society in the Nineteenth Century* (London: Routledge & Kegan Paul, 1963), pp. 36–42.
21 Webb and Webb, *The Manor and the Borough*, p. 726.
22 J. Bulpitt, 1983, *Territory and Power in the United Kingdom* (Manchester: Manchester University Press, 1983), refers to the later period of 1926 to the early 1960s as a dual polity in relation to England, Scotland and Wales in which high politics, such as foreign policy, trade relations and defence, were matters for Parliament, while the provinces dealt with low politics, such as social welfare and education. However, although he recognises for the eighteenth century that 'local politics was to be located in parliament, not local government' (p. 82), he suggests that the dual polity in England was an arrangement affecting local government as a consequence of the eighteenth-century settlement between Crown and Parliament.
23 J. Prest, *Liberty and Locality: Parliament, Permissive Legislation and Ratepayers' Democracies in the Nineteenth Century* (Clarendon Press: Oxford, 1990), p. 1.
24 *Ibid.*, p. 2; F. Clifford, *A History of Private Bill Legislation*, 2 vols, vol. 1 (London: Butterworths, 1885), p. vii.
25 J. Redlich and F. W. Hirst, *Local Government in England*, 2 vols, vol. 2 (London: Macmillan, 1903), pp. 346–7; Prest, *Liberty and Locality*, pp. 4–6.
26 S. E. Finer, *The Life and Times of Edwin Chadwick* (London: Methuen, 1952), p. 433, estimates that this could be over £1,500 for an uncontested Bill in the 1850s and much higher if there was opposition to the measure.
27 Prest, *Liberty and Locality*, pp. 7–8.
28 I. Roots, 'The central government and the local community', in E. W. Ives (ed.), *The English Revolution 1600–1660* (London: Edward Arnold, 1968), p. 40.
29 N. Gash, *Mr Secretary Peel* (London: Longmans, 1961), p. 313.
30 J. S. Mill, *Autobiography*, ed. H. J. Laski (Oxford: Oxford University Press, 1924 [1873]), p. 163.
31 E. J. Evans, *The Great Reform Act of 1832* (London: Routledge, 2nd edn, 1994), p. 4.
32 L. Namier, *The Structure of Politics at the Accession of George III* (London: Macmillan, 2nd edn, 1957), p. 62. In 1801, following the Anglo-Irish Act of Union, sixty-four MPs were additionally returned for Irish counties.
33 Keith-Lucas, *Unreformed Local Government System*, p. 16.
34 *Inquiry into the Municipal Corporations of England and Wales* (1835), p. 34, para. 73, *British Parliamentary Papers*, vol. 23: *Government: Municipal Corporations* (Shannon: Irish University Press, 1956).
35 Namier, *The Structure of Politics at the Accession of George III*, pp. 83.
36 *Ibid.*, p. 131.
37 J. Morley, *Burke* (London, Macmillan, 1879), p. 75.
38 J. Brooke, *The House of Commons 1754–1790* (Oxford: Oxford University Press, 1964), p. 45.

39 Viscount Sidmouth, Home Secretary and briefly Prime Minister, was the son of a successful lawyer who bought a Devon estate which was 'seldom visited by its owner the first Viscount' and was never modernised by him: F. M. L. Thompson, *English Landed Society in the Nineteenth Century* (London: Routledge & Kegan Paul, 1963), p. 180.

40 Gash, *Mr Secretary Peel*, pp. 14–40. Peel's father, who had made money in calico manufacture in Bury, Lancashire, moved to an estate near Tamworth, Drayton Manor, which enabled him to gain a seat in Parliament.

41 W. M. Thackery, *Vanity Fair* (Harmondsworth: Penguin Books, 1985), pp. 131–2.

42 Onley, *Rural Society*, p. 77.

43 Webb and Webb, *The Parish and the County*, pp. 559–80.

44 D. Eastwood, *Governing Rural England: Tradition and Transformation in Local Government 1780–1840* (Oxford: Clarendon Press, 1994), p. 32.

45 Webb and Webb, *The Parish and the County*, pp. 533–50.

46 *Ibid.*, p. 388.

47 Eastwood, *Governing Rural England*, pp. 105–6.

48 J. R. Western, *The English Militia in the Eighteenth Century* (London: Routledge & Kegan Paul, 1965), pp. 1–6.

49 Keith-Lucas, *Unreformed Local Government System*, pp. 67–8.

50 Western, *English Militia in the Eighteenth Century*, pp. 431–5, provides some examples of their use in suppressing disturbances in the late eighteenth century.

51 E. P. Thompson, *The Making of the English Working Class* (Harmondsworth: Penguin, 1968), p. 752.

52 Keith-Lucas, *Unreformed Local Government System*, pp. 47–9.

53 *Ibid.*, pp. 62–3.

54 *Ibid.*, p. 76.

55 Parishes were often referred to as 'vestries' because meetings were frequently held in a church's vestry. Church matters were an important issue for the parish meetings but it is probable that in their earliest form parishes had civil as well as ecclesiastic responsibilities.

56 Webb and Webb, *The Parish and the County*, pp. 51–60.

57 *Ibid.*, p. 15, footnote; in some parishes women might not be allowed to vote (p. 106); that this was a 'tradition' was particularly upheld by Joshua Toulmin Smith.

58 Keith-Lucas, *Unreformed Local Government System*, p. 77.

59 Webb and Webb, *The Parish and the County*, pp. 173–246.

60 D. Miles, *Francis Place 1771–1854* (Brighton: Harvester Press, 1988), p. 137; Keith-Lucas, *Unreformed Local Government System*, pp. 92–5.

61 Webb and Webb, *The Parish and the County*, pp. 15–32.

62 Keith-Lucas, *Unreformed Local Government System*, pp. 83–90.

63 Webb and Webb, *The Parish and the County*, pp. 32–5.

64 Webb and Webb, *The Manor and the Borough*, pp. 261–6.

65 Charters were first granted by Richard II, and Kingston on Hull's, in 1439, is regarded as the earliest: H. A. Street, *A Treatise on the Doctrine of Ultra Vires* (London: Sweet & Maxwell, 1930), p. 12. In his efforts to retain power and re-establish Catholicism James II removed the royal charter from many boroughs that opposed his views.

66 Webb and Webb, *The Manor and the Borough*, p. 281n.
67 *Ibid.*, pp. 409, 483, 520.
68 *Ibid.*, pp. 443–75.
69 Keith-Lucas, *Unreformed Local Government System*, p. 26.
70 *Ibid.*, p. 53.
71 *Report of the Inquiry into the Municipal Corporations of England and Wales*, p. 49; the passage was quoted by Lord John Russell in the First Reading Debate of the Municipal Corporations Bill, Hansard, vol. 138, col. 542, 5 June 1835.
72 Webb and Webb, *The Parish and the County*, pp. 135–43.
73 Webb and Webb, *The Manor and the Borough*, pp. 406–14.
74 S. Webb and B. Webb, *English Local Government*, vol. 4: *Statutory Authorities for Special Purposes* (London: Longmans, 1922), pp. 240–1.
75 *Ibid.*, p. 241.
76 *Ibid.*, p. 244.
77 *Ibid.*, p. 245.
78 *Ibid.*, pp. 258–73.
79 F. Sheppard, *The Infernal Wen: London 1808–1870* (London: Secker & Warburg, 1971), p. xvii.
80 *Ibid.*, p. 20.
81 Webb and Webb, *The Parish and the County*, pp. 80–6.
82 Sheppard, *The Infernal Wen: London 1808–1870*, p. 27.
83 One of first of these was created by a Private Act in 1826 by Cubbitt, a builder, for the development of estates in Belgravia on behalf of the Marquess of Westminster: Webb and Webb, *Statutory Authorities*, p. 247.
84 J. D. Mackie, *A History of Scotland* (Harmondsworth: Penguin, 2nd edn, 1978), pp. 23–34.
85 G. W. S. Barrow, *The Kingdom of the Scots: Government Church and Society from the Eleventh to the Fourteenth Century* (London: Edward Arnold, 1973), pp. 7–18.
86 A. Whetstone, *Scottish County Government in the Eighteenth and Nineteenth Centuries* (Edinburgh: John Donald, 1981), p. 27.
87 *Ibid.*, pp. 5–17.
88 W. C. Dundas, *The Development of Local Government in Counties in Scotland* (London: William Hodge, 1942), p. 17.
89 Whetstone, *Scottish County Government*, pp. 62–89.
90 Dundas, *Development of Local Government*, p. 13.
91 *Ibid.*, p. 17.
92 I. Maver, *Glasgow* (Edinburgh: Edinburgh University Press, 2000), p. 6.
93 W. E. Whyte, *Local Government in Scotland* (Edinburgh: William Hodge, 1925), p. 18.
94 J. G. Kellas, *Modern Scotland* (London: Pall Mall Press, 1968), p. 158.
95 Whyte, *Local Government in Scotland*, pp. 18–19.
96 Webb and Webb, *Statutory Authorities*, p. 355.
97 Particularly, 43 Eliz. I, c. 2
98 M. Bruce, *The Coming of the Welfare State* (London: Batsford, 1968), p. 55.
99 S. Webb, and B. Webb, *English Local Government*, vol. 7: *English Poor Law History, Part 1: The Old Poor Law* (London: Longmans, 1927), pp. 116–25.
100 22 Geo. III, c. 83.

101 Webb and Webb, *The Old Poor Law*, pp. 273–4.
102 R. Porter, *English Society in the Eighteenth Century* (Harmondsworth: Penguin, 1982), pp. 131–2, observes that 'out of 2,399 children received into London workhouses in the five years after 1750 only 165 were alive in 1755'.
103 M. J. Daunton, *Progress and Poverty: An Economic and Social History of Britain, 1700–1850* (Oxford: Oxford University Press, 1995), pp. 463–7.
104 W. E. Tate, *The Parish Chest: A Study of the Records of Parochial Administration in England* (Cambridge: Cambridge University Press, 1946), p. 184.
105 *Ibid.*, p. 185.
106 Gash, *Mr Secretary Peel*, pp. 308–10.
107 J. Field, 1981, 'Police, power and community in a provincial English town: Portsmouth 1815–1875', in V. Bailey (ed.), *Policing and Punishment in Nineteenth Century Britain* (London: Croom Helm, 1981), p. 46.
108 P. Rawlings, *Policing: A Short History* (Cullompton: Willan Publishing, 2000), pp. 113–17.
109 C. Harding, B. Hines, R. Ireland and P. Rawlings, *Imprisonment in England and Wales* (London: Croom Helm, 1985), pp. 143–5.
110 S. Webb and B. Webb, *English Local Government*, vol. 5: *The Story of the King's Highway* (London: Longman, 1913), p. 14; Phillip and Mary 2 & 3, c. 8.
111 W. E. Tate, *The Parish Chest*, p. 245.
112 Webb and Webb, *The Story of the King's Highway*, p. 115.
113 Webb and Webb, *Statutory Authorities*, pp. 156–9.
114 *Ibid.*, pp. 152–3.
115 Daunton, *Progress and Poverty*, p. 49.
116 E. Cannnan, *The History of Local Rates in England* (London: P. S. King, 2nd edn, 1912), provides a useful account of the growth and consolidation of the rating systems.
117 This system of compounding the rate was made legally permissible in the Stourges–Bourne Acts and was later to cause serious problems for assessing the right to vote after 1832 when the franchise was based on the rates paid by the householder.
118 Keith-Lucas, *Unreformed Local Government System*, pp. 137–9.
119 J. D. Marshall, *The English Poor in the Eighteenth Century* (London: Routledge & Kegan Paul, 1969), pp. 80–6.
120 Keith-Lucas, *Unreformed Local Government System*, pp. 140–1.
121 Webb and Webb, *The Manor and the Borough*, pp. 448, 482.
122 Webb and Webb, *ibid.*, p. 535, observe that Norwich had some substantial endowments for a few specific charities, e.g. a hospital, but little property to fund more general expenditure.
123 Keith-Lucas, *Unreformed Local Government System*, p. 142.
124 *Ibid.*, p. 143.
125 Webb and Webb, *The Parish and the County*, p. 305.
126 Redlich and Hirst, *Local Government in England*, vol. 2, p. 157.
127 P. Slack, *The English Poor Law* (Basingstoke: Macmillan, 1990), pp. 30, 34.

2

The impact of industrialisation

The political crisis that led up to the 1832 Electoral Reform Act is seen as a near-bloodless revolution that levered the landed elites from power in favour of urban merchants and industrialists, and, in the context of local government, led to the 1834 Poor Law Reform and the 1835 Municipal Corporations Acts that began the modernisation of the system.[1] While the 1832 crisis precipitated these major reforms, they were not a radical break with the past. Poor Law unions, improvement commissions and Peel's ideas on police and prisons were anticipating modernisation and central control, but there was no consistency evident in the direction in which these reforms were taking local government. While the Poor Law Amendment Act is depicted as the beginning of centralisation, the Municipal Corporations Act, along with the enfranchisement after 1832 of the urban conurbations, suggested the possibility of a more decentralised patron–client system, as obtained in France. In as much as there was a real break with the past following 1832, it was in the application of statute to establish nationally uniform legislation for specific types of local authority.

The capacity to compromise

Industrialisation was at the root of the social forces that restructured the British political system and, as part of the process, the system of local governance in the nineteenth century. Underpinning this evolution was the merging of differences between land and capital. By the eighteenth century trade and manufacturing was practised on sufficiently large a scale to produce wealth rivalling the economies of the great estates. The political conflicts over the Reform Acts or the Corn Laws may be seen as a consequence of the struggle of middle-class capitalists to remove the old feudal landowning aristocracy from power. However, this is a crude depiction of nineteenth-century conflict and compromise, as landowners and capitalists were not without common interests. Landowners with sufficient capital realised that money was to be made through manufacturing and commerce, and began where possible to develop such industries as coal-mining on their estates or, more often, invested in infrastructure such as

canals or in trading ventures in the developing colonial empire. The
Marquess of Bute was the major developer of the City of Cardiff, as were
the Earls of Dartmouth and Dudley for the West Midlands,[2] and Lord
Lowther constructed the port of Whitehaven. Landowners were gradually
becoming involved in an economy increasingly dependent on manufacturing and commerce. The involvement of Whig grandees in commerce
helped ensure the compromise that, after 1832, allowed landed interests
to share power with capital and hence prevent the cataclysm that had
engulfed France after 1789. The commercial interests of landowners facilitated the emergence of Robert Peel as a Tory Prime Minister willing to
lead landowners into an era in which they developed a common political
interest with industrial capitalists. Peel was only partially successful, and
was politically in eclipse at the time of his death, but his successors, for
example Disraeli, continued his work in building a Conservative Party
that by the end of the century attracted both landed and commercial
wealth and the deferent working class. Among the Whigs, Lords Grey and
John Russell were more firmly committed to an economy embracing land-
holding, manufacture and commerce. Later, William Gladstone, as a
statesman with both landed and manufacturing interests, had the vision to
establish a Liberal Party that could respect those concerns.[3]

The merging of landowning and manufacturing interests was, nevertheless, a gradual and contested process, as groups who financially or ideologically could not compete with the new order sought to retain the
eighteenth-century settlement. Owners of smaller enclosures without the
necessary capital and those lacking the inclination to develop the commercial potential of their estates or invest in trade had formed the bed-rock of
Tory values since the seventeenth century. By the nineteenth century the
farmers of medium-sized and smaller holdings also faced the worry that
commercialisation of agriculture and the importation of cheap food from
Europe and the United States would undermine their profitability and
make their estates vulnerable to purchase by the new as well as the established old wealth. These landowners found solace in the ranks of the Tory
Party which by the 1830s clustered round Wellington for hope and
support. Below the squirearchy the tenant and yeomen farmers felt the
threat of commercialism equally, but those who were not inclined to
deference towards the squire were more likely to support radicals such as
Cobbett and look back to a mythical age of bucolic peace and prosperity.

Radical and liberal opinion on local government

Local government had, as shown in the previous chapter, an integral role
in maintaining the eighteenth-century formula that political power was
secured through ownership of land. Industrial initiatives and many
supportive merchants and bankers were aware that landed interest was
holding back the progress of capital. Landowners should not, therefore,

levy taxes on and interfere with the governance of urban areas in order to stave off the conjoining of the interests of landownership and capital growth. Adam Smith argued that while towns were sustained by produce from the country, the landed estates were in turn dependent on the industry of the towns that created a market for their produce. Estates were also renewed by commerce as businessmen bought land in the country.[4] Where landowners have access to 'neither … foreign competition nor any of the finer manufactures … a great proprietor consumes the whole in rustic hospitality at home'[5] by the retention of large retinues of unproductive labour. In the long term landowners destroyed their own as well as the urban interest if they monopolised power by indulging in unproductive display or fighting unnecessary wars.

The capacity of landed interests to control the urban franchise was an anathema to capitalists, who objected both to the lack of parliamentary representation in the growing industrial towns and to the political control exerted in many of those communities by landowners who had done little or nothing to develop the cities into strongholds of the new economy. Only a few of the industrialising towns, like the ports of Bristol and Liverpool, had the right to be represented in Parliament; and among the growing inland cities of the north lacking representation in Parliament were Manchester, Leeds, Sheffield and Birmingham. London was probably the worst represented urban area with but 10 MPs when under a more even representation it would have been entitled to 60.[6] The pre-1832 franchise did not wholly exclude wealthy businessmen from Parliament: for those with wealth it was not impossible to gain a seat in the House of Commons through the purchase of a rotten borough. In the industrialising towns which had parliamentary representation, business representatives were more in evidence after the 1780s, but were still few in number.[7] The repeal in 1828 of the Test and Corporation Acts, which barred nonconformists from public office, enabled dissenting businessmen to stand for election to Parliament[8] and gave some promise that the business class would eventually match any Conservative landowning vote in the counties. Wealthy urban businessmen with the support of a more radical lower-middle and working class were, however, impatient with the unnecessarily complex and indirect processes through which they could obtain a seat in Parliament. A banker such as Thomas Attwood, who founded the influential Birmingham Union to campaign for electoral reform, was never likely to see the immediate changes he sought in the currency system without greatly increasing the chances of securing representation in Parliament for business interests.[9]

If businessmen were to be returned to Parliament from the newly enfranchised cities, they required the capacity to control the internal politics of the urban areas, in part to influence the selection of candidates, but also to parallel the established arrangements of patron–clientelism in rural areas. In as much as Parliament left landowners in control of the political and economic development of the areas local to their estates, so in Parliament post-1832 businessmen would, under dual-polity principles, be free to oversee the governance of their cities. Businessmen were also fully aware that if they or their close allies represented their cities in Parliament they would have far more power, under the conventions of the day, to sponsor private Bills to develop the infrastructure of their communities. Richard Cobden, who had cut his political teeth campaigning for the 1835 Municipal Corporations Act in Manchester, urged fellow citizens to support incorporation, railing in a pamphlet:

> The Lords of Clumber, Belvoir and Woburn, although they can no longer storm your town, and ransack your stores and shops, at the head of their mailed vassals, are as effectively plundering your manufacturers and their artizans; for by the aid of their parchment votes and tenant-at-will serfs, they are still enabled to levy their infamous bread tax upon your industry. And must you tamely submit to this pillage ...? ... [T]hen imitate your forefathers by union and co-operation; amalgamate all ranks in your town, by securing to all classes a share in its government and protection; give unity, force and efficiency to the intelligent and wealthy community of Manchester, and qualify it by organization, as it is already entitled by numbers, to be the leader in the battle against monopoly and privilege. In a word, INCOPORATE YOUR BOROUGH.[10]

Pressure from the labouring poor was a further potent element for reform. Following the French Revolution, the greatest fear of the landed classes was that the working classes and agrarian poor would join forces with the bourgeoisie and, inspired by intellectual radicals, seek the violent overthrow of the established order.[11] The self-educated artisan and the emerging working classes found support and ideas among radical intellectuals freed from the needs of patronage by the emergence of mass literacy and communication. Despite the stamp duties placed on newspapers to discourage mass readership, semi-clandestine societies to enable the labouring classes to gain information and discuss political change mushroomed in the early nineteenth century. Radicals could distribute their pamphlets to a wide audience and travel the country to speak to huge crowds of poor but intelligent followers.[12] Demands for the right to vote and the removal of barriers to holding government office on grounds of religious affiliation were central as the first step to achieving further emancipation. Die-hard Tories such as Lord Sidmouth recognised this threat. He implored Peel to preserve the unreformed boroughs, noting that 'without their influence ... hardly a single Conservative would have been returned', and that 'a seal will be put to republican uniformity of the reform Act – the new Common Council men will be the men of most revolutionary violence and least character in the Boroughs ... the radical members will be confirmed in their now tottering seats – Sound and quiet men will not be elected'.[13]

Although liberal opinion was in agreement on the need to widen the franchise and as a consequence reform the local government system, there were wide ideological differences among those supporting electoral reform. The business interests favouring *laissez faire* capitalism, as proposed by economists such as Adam Smith and Ricardo, looked towards free trade and less interference by government with the money supply and interest rates. They were, however, cautious about extending the franchise to those who owned no property, let alone to the poor, and many were enthusiasts for diminishing the cost of the Poor Law. In contrast more populist radical voices, such as Tom Paine's, argued for higher taxation of landed interest for the relief of poverty, education for the young and security for the old.[14] Paine argued that town charters which supposedly conferred rights were in effect a means of removing the right of citizens to choose their local government. Common sense, argued Paine, would invest power in the community, among all its citizens, rather than in a small, self-perpetuating oligarchy of councillors.[15] Paine also saw the workings of the settlement regulations of the Poor Law as a serious constraint on liberty:

> A native of England, under the operation of these charters and corporations, cannot be said to be an Englishmen in the full sense of the word ... His rights are circumscribed to the town, and, in some cases, to the parish of his birth; and all other parts, though in his native land, are to him a foreign country. To acquire residence in these he must undergo a local naturalization by purchase, or he his forbidden or expelled from the place.[16]

On one important issue concerning local government the liberal economists and the radicals were in agreement. Paine and Adam Smith were concerned that the growth of industrial cities was strangled by the restrictions on the free movement of labour inherent in the Poor Law.[17] However, a further facet of radicalism expressed a desire to return to an imagined age of agrarian freedom. The popular journalist William Cobbett disliked the Reformed Poor Law, seeing it as a policy to save money for the landed interest at the expense of the rural poor.[18] In his widely read writings he fulminated against the borough mongers who bought seats through a corrupted system of community politics but looked back to a mythical golden age of agrarian farming communities in which the grasping aristocrat or capitalist borough monger was prevented from abusing, through Parliament, the rights and property of the diligent small farmer and agrarian labourer. These values tapped into the deeper popular ethos concerning Whig suspicions of the power of the State that could be traced back to the ousting of James II in the 'Glorious Revolution' of 1688. Cobbett looked towards the emancipation of the rural farmer and labourer within an agrarian rather than an industrial society, in which local people rather than the aristocracy governed their rural townships through the open vestry. What was an even worse evil was domination by the wealthy merchants whom he termed 'borough

mongers'. Such differences among radicals and liberals concerning the
role of local government in an evolving British Constitution seriously
weakened their capacity to drive through significant changes to town or
county government.

The philosophical radicals and the centralised State

Only one major strand of English radical opinion, that of the 'philosophical
radicals',[19] developed anything approaching a coherent view of the role of
local government in the evolving British Constitution. Although their ideas
were not widely supported in the early nineteenth century, they were to
develop into the dominant values underlying attitudes to the role of local
government during the twentieth century. Bentham exerted a huge influence
over radical reformers and many of his disciples, such as Edwin Chadwick
and Joseph Parkes, were instrumental in promoting the reshaping of local
government after 1832. Laws, argued Bentham, should be based on the only
acceptable guide to ethical conduct, the greatest utility to the greatest
number of people, widely, but misleadingly, translated as the greatest happiness of the greatest number. The only effective judge of what constitutes
utility for an individual is that individual himself or herself; so to determine
the greatest possible utility for the greatest number could be done only
through democratic debate and compromise. In practice, within a large
polity where direct democracy was impossible this could be achieved only by
a representative assembly. The logic of Bentham's views dictated that an
elected Parliament should be the sovereign body of a society and that its
powers, therefore, could not be limited. Any organisation that proposed
policies not acceptable to Parliament would be seeking to increase utility to
its own members at the expense of the greater loss of utility to the majority
in the nation as a whole. Thus, a council representing a specific community
would be able only to undertake policies that differed from other communities' with the consent of the national Parliament. Bentham did not suggest
that all policies of the State should be determined centrally and be uniformly
administered throughout the country. Diversity was possible to suit local
circumstances, and to evaluate innovatory and experimental schemes for
administration, provided that such differences were acceptable to the
Parliament. The capacity of states in America to innovate and experiment
with new service-delivery mechanisms, Bentham considered, was of advantage provided the actions of one set of individuals did not damage the interests of others.[20]

Bentham finalised his ideas on political institutions in his practical
constitutional code, written towards the end of his life. Government
should be based on an annually elected Parliament that determined the
laws of the country and selected a Prime Minister who appointed ministers with whom he administered the policies of the nation. Below the
national level, Bentham proposed the formation of sub-legislatures in

districts. These appear to be relatively large-scale organisations that would 'under the authority of the [national] legislature' be responsible for the issues pursued by the Government, with the exception of foreign policy.[21] The administrative departments of the sub-legislatures would also mirror those of the national administration and hence could deal with some issues that would hardly be seen today as in the domain of local government. These included an army and naval sub-minister, on the grounds that militia should be raised locally and that localities would also sponsor and provide funds for ship-building. Health care and education were more conventional tasks that could be delegated under centrally determined principles to the sub-legislature. Bentham proposed that there should be at least one lower tier of devolved government below the district level which would be as close to the people as possible and subject to the administration of a single elected office. In the prosaic style of a philosopher who thought 'poetry was no more preferable than pushpin' Bentham titled the office the 'local headman'. The headman would chair local meetings and be subject to its wishes, although he would also exert a prefectoral role by implementing the decisions of the national or the district government. The headman would not only determine issues on the Poor Law or local roads, but also be an arbiter in the case of family disputes or problems relating to travellers in his area.[22]

The logic of Bentham's view created a problem for philosophical radicals deeply influenced by the idea that each individual should have the maximum liberty that was possible.[23] Many radicals torn between the centralising logic of Bentham and the appeal of *laissez faire* opposition to an over-powerful Government developed convenient if intellectually uneasy compromises between these strands of thought. The anonymous author of an 1836 article in the *Westminster Review* criticising piecemeal proposals to reform the City of London presents what would now be seen as an obvious case for uniformity and simplicity in the local government system: 'By and by – but let us be patient – the bright idea will occur to their minds that in every part of the country the people ought to have the same power.'[24] A uniform system of local administration was necessary, as 'all systems cannot be equally good, and it is everywhere desirable to have the best', and 'the task of legislation is greatly simplified and a vast amount of useless expenditure saved, by creating at once the machinery necessary for all local business that may arise'.[25] The author could, however, only partially accept Bentham's view that local government should be subordinate to the interests of central government: 'Municipal institutions are required, first, as part of the machinery for giving effect to the will of the national government', but local government should serve as 'the means of making local regulations which do not interfere with the rights or interests of the inhabitants of other districts and which do not violate the principles of general legislation and government recognised by the state'.[26]

The conservative radicals and decentralisation

As industrialisation and urban life increasingly became the accepted social norm throughout Britain, Cobbett's views came to be seen as increasingly picturesque but impracticable, although rural poverty remained an active concern even in the late nineteenth century. Opposition to centralisation passed to writers more attuned to the industrial and commercial realities of the mid-nineteenth century who could place the goal of local self-government in a more urban context and in the framework of a more consistent view of the role of local government within the State. The most prominent campaigner of this genre was the Birmingham-born lawyer Joshua Toulmin Smith who, once settled in London, became the leading light in the Anti-Centralization Union which was vocal in its opposition to the Health Acts of the 1850s.[27] Smith is too often dismissed as a romanticising Tory, and many of his ideas form a sound and logical, if not always historically accurate, system that owes more to radical liberalism than to old Tory values. Smith was a liberal in the sense that he believed individuals were free born and entitled to develop and express their own ideas and values.

For Smith, the best means of guaranteeing those rights was a democratic institution that regularly brought together a group of residents to determine the issues that affect their community. This organisation would be the open vestry or borough moot that Smith believed allowed the male residents of any community in Anglo Saxon times to freely resolve their common concerns. Smith maintained that the organisation of parish and town governments had since the Middle Ages been moving away from the basic principles of individual liberty.[28] Where issues had to be decided at a county or a national level, then the local communities should be represented in the larger organisation. Thus, Parliament was a body to be composed not of independent representatives but of delegates regularly made accountable to their electorate. The destruction of liberty came from the openness of organisations, including Parliament, to domination by individuals or small groups acting in their own interests rather than those of the community. Common law, which he regarded as being the outcome of agreements between free individuals, was to be preferred over parliamentary statute law.[29] Smith argued that self-interested organisations centralised policy making in their own hands to deprive individuals of their capacity to determine with their neighbours decisions for their common good and their capacity to think for themselves or become politically astute through self-education. Smith characterised the institutional expression of freedom in terms of two contrasting styles:

> Local Self-Government is that system of Government under which the greatest number of minds, knowing the most, and having the fullest opportunities of knowing it, about the special matter in hand, and having the greatest interest in its well-working, have the management of it, or control over it.

Centralization is that system of Government under which the smallest number of minds, and those knowing the least, and having the fewest opportunities of knowing it, about the special matter in hand, and having the smallest interest in its well-working, have the management of it, or the control of it.[30]

Local government and the Reform Act

The first major restructuring by the Whig–Liberal–radical coalition in 1832 was the Electoral Reform Act itself which promised parliamentary representation to the growing industrial towns and the removal of the *raison d'être* of many rotten boroughs.[31] The Act was a compromise between reformers and their Tory opponents rather than a crushing defeat for the landed interest. It removed representation in Parliament from 56 boroughs, ensuring that many of these communities lost their sole *raison d'être* and halved the representation in another 30 boroughs to a single MP. In exchange the larger industrialising towns were given representation, with 22 boroughs, including Birmingham, Manchester and Sheffield, acquiring 2 MPs each and 19 boroughs gaining one. Towns in Scotland gained a further 8 MPs, with Edinburgh and Glasgow returning 2 MPs while the smaller burghs were grouped into single constituencies. In the boroughs the vote was given to all males owning property to the value of £10.[32] The changes increased the number of electors by an estimated 49 per cent[33] but fell far short of securing fully democratic government, and gave little advantage to the upper-working-class artisans whose mass campaigning had done much to bring about change. The powerful landowners could still control seats in Parliament and place their lieutenants in the House of Commons. In forty-five boroughs in 1865 parliamentary representation was influenced by a single family.[34] The county representation was substantially increased with addition of sixty-seven MPs for English and Welsh counties. What the Act secured was recognition that ownership of land or the patronage of a landowner was not the necessary route for wealthy commercial interests to secure a place in the House of Commons, but as Finlayson observes: 'If then the electoral system after 1832 recognised new elements in the country and society, these had to exist within a framework which still gave great scope to many of the older elements.'[35]

The creation of new parliamentary boroughs in the expanding industrial cities formed the basis for a significant new relationship between a borough, its MPs and its electorate by facilitating the potential development of a patron–client relationship between central and local government. The electorates of the new parliamentary boroughs were generally too well-populated to be easily bought and many new voters were too idealistic to be susceptible to bribery. Thus, it was possible for such cities to secure in Parliament representatives who would use their position to favour the interests of their constituencies. In the 1833 House of Commons 39 of the 57 MPs elected for newly created urban constituencies in England and Wales had local connections and at least 23 were local manufacturers, bankers or were involved in commerce.[36] The possibility of a French style of political system in which economic leaders of urban and rural areas would be sent to Parliament by their electorates to defend local interest was, however, never to become a significant factor within Britain. A third of the newly enfranchised urban seats, even in 1833, were represented by landowners or merchants with few prior connections with the town. Almost all of the MPs elected for those cities maintained a substantial house in London and, while this may be a necessity for a hard-working Westminster MP, the pull of London society would have diverted at least some attention away from their more provincial responsibilities.

Once the court and later the offices of government ministers had been centred in London, the capital became a magnet for anyone aspiring to a position of national power and authority. The ambitious landowner, by the eighteenth century, was engrossed in a relatively closed and small world of high politics concerned with foreign wars, diplomacy, trade relations and public finance, largely for the navy and the army. The correspondence of the major figures in government in the 1830s, such as Wellington, Peel or Lord Liverpool, suggest that they had only passing interest in local affairs, leaving the management of their estates, not to mention the routine tasks of a JP in securing order, stability and poor relief in rural areas, to lesser figures.[37] Since many Peers and MPs had no need to follow the dictates of local worthies for the seats they represented, it cannot be expected that the up-and-coming class of liberal and radical MPs who had the ambition to become influential in the high politics of trade and currency reform or foreign policy was any more inclined than their landowning adversaries to fix their attention on the detailed management of industrialising cities.

Democratic local government was for many leading radicals a necessary stepping-stone to national goals rather than an entity they valued because it would promote local power and wealth. Attwood, for instance, was greatly interested in reform of the currency system. Joseph Parkes was concerned to advance the reform of the boroughs not through an interest in local politics *per se* but out of a concern to fatally damage the Tory cause.[38] Following his local successes in Manchester, Cobden advanced to national prominence through the development, together with John Bright, of the Anti-Corn Law League as an instrument for challenging the power of the landed classes. By the 1840s he had ceased to have any substantive interest in local politics, and although an alderman in Manchester he attended only ten of the City Council meetings between 1840 and his resignation from the authority in 1844.[39] Cobden's subsequent correspondence with Bright and with Joseph Parkes makes little mention of local government issues such as the development of the Poor Law or of Health

Boards, and neither he nor Bright spoke in Parliament on these matters. When they did refer to local concerns it was often to belittle local politicians. Bright, for example, wrote to Cobden in relation to the Crimean War that 'there has been a great rejoicing ... mayors and men of that class, the "small great officials", have been very busy. Liverpool's mayor for one – Doncaster's for another';[40] and he observed that on the occasion of a visit by the Queen to Manchester the Mayor will not 'present an address as full of slip slop and flattery as the Queen is often condemned to listen to'.[41]

The Poor Law

Apart from the Reform Act itself Grey's ministry directed its initial reforming zeal on local matters to the restructuring of Poor Law provision rather than of the municipal boroughs. Radicals and *laissez faire* liberals who had supported the 1832 electoral reform expected nothing less. The Government also recognised that there was sufficient depth of concern over the rising cost of poor relief in rural areas that even the most die-hard Tory accepted that they may be financially advantaged by reform. J. D. Marshall observes that, even allowing for the inaccuracy of early statistical data, expenditure on the poor 'rose from about two million pounds in 1784 ... to just short of six million in 1815. It fluctuated widely around the latter figure for most of the succeeding years to 1833.'[42] It was widely accepted by liberal economists that generous poor relief would provide no incentives for the poor to seek better-paid work. Thomas Malthus argued that giving aid to the poor would allow earlier marriages among those unable yet to support themselves, let alone a family, and a consequent rise in the population that could not be sustained by economic growth.[43] During a time of rising costs both landowners and commercial–industrial liberals found this an attractive argument. A further serious problem was the inability of a localised system of poor relief to adapt to a society transforming from a predominantly agrarian economy based on high levels of self-sufficiency to an urban industrial economy based on mobility of labour and cycles of high and low demand for workers.

There was a wide range of solutions proposed to mitigate the problem of poverty and its spiralling costs, but none of the attempts at reform had made significant progress, partly because of the difficulties of arriving at a workable solution that could gain widespread consensus, but also 'because there was a long tradition that the Cabinet did not intervene in parochial or municipal affairs'.[44] In 1832 serious rioting in some agricultural areas, fuelled by resentment that promises to supplement low wages with poor relief were falling far short of what farm labourers had anticipated, created a further pressure for reform. The riots were quelled by county militia but their occurrence suggested to many landowners that the Poor Law was failing to maintain law and order.

The Whig Government entertained reform by appointing a Royal Commission of 7 members, under the chairmanship of the Bishop of London, aided by 3 dignified Tories as well as four younger Whigs including the economist Nassau Senior and William Coulson who had worked as an amanuensis to Bentham. [45] There was no secretary and much of the administrative work was undertaken by the more energetic Whig members. The Commission met usually on a weekly basis and, in the absence of any central understanding of the differing systems of poor relief in the parishes, conducted a substantive survey by Assistant Commissioners of Poor Law administration. The following year two further Assistant Commissioners were added, one of whom was the indefatigably industrious Edwin Chadwick who had lived in Bentham's household. The final report of 1834, written by Nassau Senior and Chadwick,[46] has become a classic of pioneering work in social studies and surveys. The Webbs observed that in the supervisory arrangements 'we note the hand of Edwin Chadwick, but we listen to the voice of Jeremy Bentham'.[47]

The conclusion of the Commissioners concerning the means of delivering poor relief steered a compromise between the view that assistance was a humanitarian necessity and the economist argument popularised by Malthus. Chadwick established an eligibility principle that to some extent satisfied the economist critique by insisting that those who received poor relief should not be better off than anyone employed in basic labour. Poor relief to the able-bodied was, therefore, only to be given within workhouses at a level of subsistence lower than would be received by a labourer in employment.[48] The Commissioners argued, with the backing of voluminous evidence from the surveys annexed to the report, that small parishes generally lacked the means in money and personnel to operate an effective system of poor relief and were unable to establish the substantial segregated workhouse dividing the idle from the deserving poor and men from women.[49] In addition it was shown by the Assistant Commissioners that in England the rates were generally lower in the more populous rather than the smaller parishes. [50] Poor relief was placed under the control of larger units of administration which would be formed by amalgamating parishes for that purpose into Poor Law unions[51] under the control of the elected representatives of rate-payers who would be more likely to seek and impose economies in the delivery of poor relief than the open parish vestry. Economies were subsequently widely practised and applied by Union officials, including local doctors contracted to give medical support for the poor. The tendency of the reformed Poor Law unions to impose on local doctors their penny-pinching orders and diminish a source of income for many poorer general practitioners was a grievance that helped to create the British Medical Association, instilling in its membership a disdain for both the Poor Law and, more generally, local government that would contribute a century later to the antipathy among doctors to local government's close link with a 'national health service'.[52]

The second element of the structural change was that the poor law unions would be subject to national supervision rather than the haphazard jurisdiction exerted by the quarter sessions and local magistrates. Such an arrangement was essential if there was to be a standardised national system of poor relief, as 'the good example of one parish is rarely followed in the surrounding parishes, bad examples are contagious and possess the elements of indefinite extension'.[53] Such a view echoes the much later thinking of the 'New Liberals' at the beginning of the twentieth century – and even the 'best value' attitudes of the early twenty-first. The Commission had seriously considered taking the operations of the Poor Law wholly out of the parishes by placing it under central control, including raising taxes nationally and, therefore, removing the issue altogether from local government. The reasons for not advancing along this path anticipated modern New-Right critiques of central government, arguing that over time a centralralised administration would become inefficient if it were not close to local private interest and also would be far too costly a burden on national taxation.[54] It is also probable that such a suggestion would have been far too radical to pass through the House of Lords.

Chadwick and Nassau Senior rejected the idea that Parliament should regulate the overview of Poor Law regulation on the grounds that they themselves could not deal with the minutiae of local differences to be taken into account in a provision that was uniform in principle. They therefore advocated a three-person Commission, small so as to be inexpensive, which would, by employing Assistant Commissioners, oversee the uniform implementation of the Poor Law. The system recommended was, they argued, to be based on arrangements that had been instituted to regulate savings banks and friendly societies.[55]

The Poor Law Reform had an untroubled passage through Parliament and, despite several amendments by the House of Lords, its central principles became law by August 1834.[56] Few legislators opposed reforms that might lower the cost of the Poor Law and only a few radicals like Cobbett saw the Bill as an infringement of the right of the poor to receive an appropriate level of social security. There was, however, an underlying concern among MPs and the Peers over the method being used to bring about a new system of central inspection. The Government did not enthuse over the proposed Commission, but assured opponents of the idea of a board that the Commissioners would favour good practice and would force smaller parishes or badly run systems of poor relief into the framework of the Act only on an incremental basis. However, as Chancellor of the Exchequer Lord Althorpe observed,

> the local authorities or the local magistracy, however well intentioned they
> might be, deprived as they were of their sources of general information and
> comparison open to a Board of Commissioners, and however excellent their
> motives, biased as they must be by local prejudices and local feeling, it was

plain that such a quarter would not be the fittest one to vest with a discretionary power for carrying the measure into effect.[57]

Many MPs who otherwise supported the Bill raised doubts about the
capability of a small number of centralised Commissioners to appreciate,
let alone correct, the different practices for operating the Poor Law system
throughout the country. As one MP observed, he did not envy the
Commissioners who would have to tell southern labourers to 'live the
same way as the labourers of the northern counties, and that their
wheaten loaf was to be changed to a barley one'.[58] Sir Henry Willoughby
summarised the essence of dual-polity values, saying that he

> did not object to a Central Board acting as a Board of Control; he did object
> to one which appeared intended to interfere and meddle in matters which the
> ratepayers could settle and adjust much better for themselves.[59]

The Government may have accepted the idea of the Poor Law
Commission without fully recognising its potential implications for local
discretion. The lack of substantial Tory opposition to the House of Lords
on the reformed Poor Law reflected the interest of the landed oligarchy to
divest themselves of much of the burden of taxation that they contributed
to the maintenance of the poor.

The 1835 Municipal Corporations Act

A paradox of the Whig Government was that the Municipal Corporations
Act retained the principle that, in contrast to the reformed Poor Law,
central government should not interfere in essentially local matters. The
demand for restructuring the boroughs was, like the reform of the Poor
Law, an aim of radicals that could not be dismissed by their more tenta-
tive Whig allies. It was not, however, a policy that offered any clear
advantages to rural interests and hence was more likely to be subject to
obstruction from the House of Lords. Once the Whigs attained power
they immediately moved towards democratisation of urban local government in the one area, Scotland, where their influence was not strongly
challenged by Tory landowners. In 1833 an Act was passed without
substantive dissent to require that all Scotland's royal burghs adopt a rate-
payer franchise and establish common regulations for the conduct of elections and the constitution of local authorities.[60]

Similar legislation for England and Wales was much more contentious.
In July 1833 the Grey's Government appointed a Royal Commission to
inquire 'into the state of municipal government in England and Wales',[61]
composed of twenty largely young and up-and-coming Whig lawyers and
chaired by Whig MP John Blackstone. Its secretary, Joseph Parkes, was a
solicitor, a radical dissenter and friend of Frances Place. The Committee
undertook a thorough investigation of the state of municipalities, paralleling the meticulous study of the Poor Law Commission. Ten teams of

two Commissioners looked in detail at the boroughs within specific areas of England and Wales. London was an eleventh area for study but its problems were considered to be so unique and difficult that it was excluded from the review in the expectation of a later separate enquiry.[62] Although the investigation provided four volumes of generally objective evidence, the relatively short final report[63] was hurriedly written by the Commission's chairman and secretary, without much reference to the weight of collected evidence, and was designed to be strongly condemnatory of the municipalities. Two members of the Commission refused to sign the report, which anyway was never thoroughly discussed by all the members.[64] While the report found little fault with a few corporations, such as Liverpool, it highlighted the petty corruption and ineffectiveness of the many run down closed small town corporations. The report conveyed the impression that scandals in a particular authority were translatable to the majority of boroughs and presented a picture that, if taken without a measure of scepticism, could only prompt a government and the public to demand radical reform.

On the day the report was published a new Whig administration under Lord Melbourne took office. To the surprise of many of the Commission's members, Melbourne was favourable to the need for reform[65] and proceeded to prepare legislation, although he was much concerned about the threat to the Church of England that would result from enfranchising middle-class dissenters in the towns.[66] The initial proposals passed through the House of Commons with little opposition from either Whigs or Tories, but met fierce resistance from an Upper House galvanised by Lord Chancellor Lyndhurst, who was probably motivated by political ambition and the hope of undermining Peel and his supporters in the modernising Tory Party as much as by his dislike of the Bill.[67] Among the wrecking amendments proposed by the Lords was that at least a third of councillors should be aldermen appointed for life. The Lords also employed delaying tactics by questioning in their House representatives of boroughs that claimed to be unjustly vilified in the report. Against the background of much popular agitation the Lords were eventually obliged to compromise with the Commons on the Bill. In September Peel had informed his Tamworth constituency that he supported reform on the evidence presented by the Commission[68] and held his ground against the Lords. Wellington sided with Peel at a party meeting at Aspley House and 'to the great relief to my mind', wrote Peel,[69] paved the way for a compromise with the Whigs and Peelites in the Commons.[70]

The Commissioners had considered the claims of 285 communities and found 246 of them were legally entitled to borough status; but of these only 178 were regarded as of sufficient size to be scheduled in the Act as reformed boroughs.[71] The Act effectively ended the pretensions of over 100 communities to remain as boroughs. Equally importantly, the boroughs retained by the Act had to adopt standard procedures for election and governance and thus the varied powers that typified the old char-tered boroughs were swept aside. The corporations of the reformed boroughs had also to govern as trustees and representatives of their towns and not as if they themselves owned the corporation. The legislation did not immediately create new boroughs even in the large un-incorporated industrial towns. Communities that considered themselves to be worthy of borough status had to petition the Privy Council for a charter of incor-poration which would then institute an inquiry, collecting arguments from those for and against the communities' claims. An unopposed request could be granted by an order in council, but if opposed the request could be sanctioned only by an act of Parliament.[72]

The councils of the new municipal boroughs were to be elected for a three-year term in office, with a third retiring each year. As a concession to the House of Lords, candidates in all but the smallest boroughs would be selected from wards rather than the community at large and the coun-cillors would select a third of their members as alderman who would enjoy office for six years before the need for re-election by the council. The vote was entrusted to all rate-paying male occupants of premises who and had paid their rates to the town council for at least the three preced-ing years. Those paying rates on property in the town but living up to seven miles outside its borders could also qualify for the vote. Women and any non-rate paying males, including lodgers and tenants who did not pay rates directly, did not therefore have the vote. Anyone in receipt of Poor Law assistance was also excluded.[73]

The boroughs under the terms of the Act took over the property and the resultant responsibilities of the former corporations. This presented the new authorities with rather different fortunes as some of the former boroughs, Liverpool for one, had extensive assets, whereas many others had little property and had made little impact on the town's infrastruc-ture. However, the Act gave the boroughs powers to raise a rate in order to fund any deficits they may incur, although this had to be charged on a common formula to all property holders and removed many individual fund-raising practices that some boroughs had accrued through common-law consents.[74] The new boroughs were given but few additional respon-sibilities, of which the most important was to establish 'watch committees' to deal with issues of law and order and so form local police forces. They also had responsibility for ensuring the lighting of streets. It was never the intention of the Act, given the divisions on the issue in Parliament, to substantially increase the powers of boroughs, but rather to establish them in a uniform structure in urban areas that could make use of their potential powers. A significant element of the Act that contrasted with the provisions of the reformed Poor Law was that the municipalities were regarded as independent of substantive central super-vision apart from the requirement of permission from the Treasury to sell or lease property.[75] There was no thought in 1835 that Parliament or the

Government should supervise borough corporations. The principles of eighteenth-century control through a restricted franchise and the need for a local act to extend the powers of a corporation remained firmly in place in the minds of both Tories and Whigs.

One of the most significant consequences of the Act was the separation of the judicial role of the former boroughs from the administrative functions of the new councils. Radicals had campaigned for a system of elected magistrates to dispense justice on relatively minor issues within the boroughs and the Bill put forward by the Whigs had gone someway to satisfying that requirement by allowing councils to choose magistrates who would be chaired by a centrally appointed recorder.[76] Under pressure from the Lords this proposal was dropped in favour of an arrangement that the Government appointed the magistrates, with the mayor of the borough acting in theory as a JP during his time in office. This decision effectively began a process leading to an almost complete separation between local government and the local judiciary. Licensing of inns, which was a particularly politically sensitive issue, had been given to the boroughs in the original Act but was also omitted in order to avoid conflict with the House of Lords.[77] Licensing remained with the magistrates.[78] A further omission from the Act was any mechanism to incorporate into the new municipal authorities the many agencies such as improvement commissions that had been created by separate Acts. Thus, the Act did not diminish the trend, given impetus in the Poor Law Reform Act, to by-pass the executive functions of local authorities through the creation of ad hoc agencies for special purposes. Pressure to get the legislation through the Commons and Parliament, and the amendments forced on the radicals by the House of Lords, ensured that the 1835 Act for all its innovation was ill-drafted and a legal mess. Following its approval, there was a succession of minor Acts to clarify uncertainties created by the legislation,[79] and in 1882 it was fully overhauled by a more consolidated Act to regulate municipal authorities.[80] Despite its shortcomings the Municipal Corporations Act rather than the reformed Poor Law was to prove the foundation of the principles for the structure of local government by the twentieth century into relatively large and populous multifunctional local authorities.

Notes

1 K. B. Smellie, *A History of Local Government* (London: George Allen & Unwin, 1946), pp. 21f., for example, tends to perpetuate the myth that the origins of the current local government system began in 1832.

2 J. Davies, 'Aristocratic town-makers and the coal metropolis', and R. Trainor, 'Peers on an industrial frontier: the Earls of Dartmouth and Dudley', in D. Cannadine (ed.), *Patricians, Power and Politics in Nineteenth Century Towns* (Leicester: Leicester University Press, 1982).

3 G. R. Searle, *Entrepreneurial Politics in Mid-Nineteenth Century Britain*

(Oxford: Oxford University Press, 1993), p. 296.

4 A. Smith, *The Wealth of Nations*, vol. 1, ed. E. Seligman (London: Dent, 1964), pp. 362–4.

5 *Ibid.*, p. 363.

6 L. Namier, *The Structure of Politics at the Accession of George III* (London: Macmillan, 2nd edn, 1957), p. 63.

7 *Ibid.*, pp. 84–5.

8 E. J. Evans, *The Great Reform Act of 1832* (London: Routledge, 2nd edn, 1994), p. 40.

9 C. Flick, *The Birmingham Political Union* (Folkestone: Archon & Dawson, 1978), pp. 18–19.

10 R. Cobden, *Incorporate Your Borough* (1835), in W. Axon, *Cobden as a Citizen: A Chapter in Manchester's History* (London: Fisher & Unwin, 1917), p. 2; the capital letters are Cobden's.

11 See, for example, E. P. Thompson, *The Making of the English Working Class* (Harmondsworth: Penguin, 1969).

12 *Ibid.*

13 Peel Papers, Add. 40420, fo. 26, 9 June 1835. Locations of the archival material cited in this book are given at the start of the Bibliography.

14 T. Paine, *The Rights of Man*, ed. H. Collins (Harmondsworth: Penguin, 1969), pp. 262–83.

15 *Ibid.*, p. 242.

16 *Ibid.*, pp. 243–4.

17 *Ibid.*, p. 245.

18 W. Cobbett, *Cobbett's Legacy to the Labourers* (London: Cobbett, 1834), p. 8.

19 John Stuart Mill devised the term 'philosophical radicals' to refer to a group of utilitarian thinkers that he had assembled in the 1830s to discuss the ideas of his father, James Mill, and Jeremy Bentham.

20 T. P. Peardon, 'Bentham's ideal republic', in B. Parekh (ed.), *Jeremy Bentham: Ten Critical Essays* (London: Frank Cass, 1974), p. 132.

21 B. Parekh (ed.), *Bentham's Political Thought* (London: Croom Helm, 1973), p. 224.

22 *Ibid.*, pp. 224–7.

23 These issues are raised in J. A. Chandler, 'The Liberal justification for local government: values and administrative expediency', *Political Studies*, 37:4 (1989), pp. 604–11.

24 Anon., 'Municipal reform, as required for the metropolis', *Westminster Review*, 25, Jan.–July (1836), p. 71.

25 *Ibid.*, p. 72.

26 *Ibid.*, p. 74.

27 For a succinct review of his ideas, see W. H. Greenleaf, 'Toulmin Smith and the British political tradition', *Public Administration*, 53:1 (1975), pp. 25–44.

28 J. T. Smith, *The Parish* (London: J. Sweet, 1854), p. 203.

29 *Ibid.*, he did, however, like many Victorian democrats, exclude those on poor relief from the franchise: J. T. Smith, *Local Self-Government and Centralization* (London: John Chapman, 1851), p. 244.

30 Smith, *Local Self-Government and Centralization*, p. 12.

31 2 & 3 Will. IV, c. 45 and c. 44, which determined constituency boundaries.

32 Disenfranchisement in more open boroughs was avoided by allowing electors who did not have this qualification but voted under the old system and were still able to retain their vote.

33 Evans, *The Great Reform Act of 1832*, p. 76.

34 F. B. Smith, *The Making of the Second Reform Bill* (Cambridge: Cambridge University Press, 1966), p. 17.

35 B. A. M. Finlayson, *Decade of Reform: England in the Eighteen Thirties* (London: Edward Arnold, 1969), p. 17.

36 Data from *Dod's Parliamentary Companion* (London: Dod's Parliamentary Communications, 1833); sixteen of the MPs did not specify their occupation.

37 Papers of these political figures are archived in the British Library; on Sidmouth see also F. M. L. Thompson, *English Landed Society in the Nineteenth Century* (London: Routledge & Kegan Paul, 1963), p. 180.

38 W. Thomas, *The Philosophic Radicals: Nine Studies in Theory and Practice, 1817–1841* (Oxford: Clarendon Press, 1979), pp. 244–304.

39 Axon, *Cobden as a Citizen*, p. 122.

40 Bright Papers, Add. 43384, 21 Sept. 1855, fo. 16.

41 *Ibid.*, Add. 43383, 25 Aug. 1851, fo. 209.

42 J. D. Marshall, *The English Poor in the Eighteenth Century* (London: Routledge & Kegan Paul, 1969), p. 23.

43 Daunton, *Progress and Poverty*, pp. 4–5.

44 S. Webb and B. Webb, *English Local Government*, vol. 8: *English Poor Law History, Part II: The Last Hundred Years*, vol. 1 (London: Longmans, Green & Co., 1929), p. 33.

45 *Ibid.*, pp. 45–6; D. Fraser, *The Evolution of the British Welfare State* (Basingstoke: Macmillan, 2nd edn, 1984), p. 41.

46 *Report of the Royal Commissioners for Inquiry into the Administration and Practical Operation of the Laws for the Relief of the Poor*, Session 4, Feb.–15 Aug., 1834, vol. 26; S. G. Checkland and E. O. A. Checkland (eds), *The Poor Law Report of 1834* (Harmondsworth: Penguin, 1974).

47 Webb and Webb, *The Last Hundred Years*, vol. 1, p. 79.

48 Finer, *The Life and Times of Sir Edwin Chadwick*, pp. 82–95.

49 Webb and Webb, *The Last Hundred Years*, vol. 1, pp. 45–6; Fraser, *Evolution of the British Welfare State*, p. 41.

50 Checkland and Checkland, *Poor Law Report of 1834*, pp. 439–44.

51 The Act (22 Geo. III, c. 83) promoted by Thomas Gilbert MP in 1782 that facilitated the creation of Poor Law Unions among parishes wishing to provide a workhouse common to then all. He had promoted another Act (22 George III, c. 64) that year concerning Houses of Correction which had been established to ensure vagrants were put to work. Both Acts jointly are referred to as the Gilbert Acts.

52 F. B. Smith, *The People's Health* (London: Croom Helm, 1979), pp. 346–62.

53 Checkland and Checkland, *Poor Law Report*, p. 398.

54 *Ibid.*, p. 417; Webb and Webb, *The Last Hundred Years*, vol. 1, pp. 74–5.

55 Checkland and Checkland, *Poor Law Report*, pp. 417–18.

56 An Act for the Amendment and Better Administration of the Laws Relating to the Poor in England and Wales: 4 & 5 William IV, c. 76.

57 Hansard, vol. 23, col. 881, 17 April 1834.

58 *Ibid.*, vol. 24, col. 1031.
59 *Ibid.*, col. 1037.
60 E. W. Whyte, *Local Government in Scotland* (Edinburgh: William Hodge, 1925), p. 18; 3 & 4 Will. IV, c. 77.
61 *Report of the Inquiry into the Municipal Corporations of England and Wales* (1835), *British Parliamentary Papers*, vol. 23: *Government: Municipal Corporations* (Shannon: Irish University Press, 1956), p. 3.
62 This was conducted ineffectively and did not lead to legislation.
63 *Report of the Inquiry into the Municipal Corporations of England and Wales* (1835).
64 Webb and Webb, *The Manor and the Borough*, pp. 712–22.
65 P. Zeigler, *Melbourne* (London: Collins, 1976), p. 213.
66 Webb and Webb, *The Manor and the Borough*, p. 750.
67 B. Keith-Lucas, *The English Local Government Franchise: A Short History* (Oxford: Blackwell, 1952), p. 54.
68 Peel Papers, Add. 40421, fo. 16, Speech at the Town Hall, Tamworth, 4 September 1835.
69 *Ibid.*
70 The Municipal Corporations Act 1835: 5 & 6 Will. IV, c. 75.
71 Redlich and Hirst, *Local Government in England*, vol. 2, p. 125.
72 W. B. Odgers, and E. W. Naldrett, *Local Government* (London: Macmillan, 2nd edn, 1909), pp. 80–1.
73 Keith-Lucas, *English Government Franchise*, pp. 60–3, calculated that immediately after 1835 the Parliamentary vote in towns was probably greater than the municipal vote, since the Reform Act allowed those in towns who had previously voted for an MP, but no longer qualified under the new arrangements, the right to continue to vote. Excluding such individuals who would gradually leave the band of earthly voters, the municipal franchise was still only slightly higher than the parliamentary franchise.
74 Redlich and Hirst, *Local Government in England*, vol. 1, p. 396.
75 Webb and Webb, *The Manor and the Borough*, p. 753; writing in a different age, the authors complain that the absence of controls was a serious omission in the legislation.
76 *Ibid.*, p. 740.
77 Redlich and Hirst, *Local Government in England*, vol. 1, p. 127.
78 In the 1790s magistrates started being far more restrictive in granting licences to the extent that in 1830 Parliament allowed the sale of beer on payment of a fee: Keith-Lucas, *Unreformed Local Government System*, p. 64.
79 Webb and Webb, *The Manor and the Borough*, p. 751, cite 16 such Acts in the 8 years following 1835.
80 The Municipal Corporations Act 1882: 45 & 46 Vict., c. 50.

3

Compromise and confusion: the ad hoc local governments of mid-Victorian Britain

Pressures to restructure local government, it may be argued, derive from the concern of practically minded national and local politicians and administrators to adapt its many institutions to deal with the problems thrown up by the growth of cities, the need for a more mobile workforce, the social consequences of enclosures or the demand for improved systems of transport. Smellie argues that

> Behind the reform bills themselves were revolutions in industry and transport, in medical and engineering science and in the technique of taxation, which made it impossible for the government to disclaim responsibility for the essential elements of social security. Between 1832 and 1888 the growth, and the movement of population, shattered the way of life that was common before the railway and the urban life of the machine age.[1]

Similarly, David Roberts states that it would be unwise to attribute to the utilitarians the reforms that ushered in central funding and inspection of local services.[2] There was a widespread realisation that in urban areas government was breaking down.[3] Rapidly growing industrial centres could not be managed effectively by parish government that ran alongside, in some areas, the vestigial role of the court leet. Supervision by magistrates of locally provided services formed an inefficient county-wide as distinct from a national inspectorate. The parishes were, as the Poor Law Commission of 1834 argued, too small to administer for local needs in an industrialising society and had to be replaced by larger and more economically viable units of local governance capable of taking advantage of economies of scale designed for a more mobile society.

These arguments do not, however, take account of the retention of parish-sized units of local government in other industrialising countries, such as France or the USA, where many local services were provided by smaller communities either acting in partnership with larger authorities or employing external private sector contractors.[4] It was not impossible after 1832 to forge a system of local government based firmly on the parish with the more strategic services being managed by the county, and there were those who envisaged just such a framework. There was, however, neither the political will nor the means to secure such change. The development of local government in the mid-nineteenth century to accommodate social change within the framework of ad hoc agencies, beginning with the Poor Law unions, reflected an unsatisfactory compromise between Whigs and Tories who could both see the need for some measure of modernisation and were, with the exception of the philosophical radicals, opposed to centralisation, but were not willing to give powers to the opposing faction. Llewelyn Woodward observes that following the death of Peel in 1850 parliamentary politics 'reflect the hesitancy and quick changes of opinion inevitable at a time when the issues were so much confused and in many cases so new that old party distinctions did not apply to them'.[5] The uncertain development of local government reflects this period of the breaking of old parties and the forming of new coalitions. Liberals and radicals wished to establish elected county councils that would undermine the influence of the JPs, but the Tories had sufficient influence in Parliament to block any attempts to reform the parish or the county. An impasse developed that was expediently resolved by ad hoc solutions satisfying neither Conservatives nor reformers. Modernising Liberals successfully pressed for legislation to regulate the growing technical and social demands, but would not allow the State's new powers to be given to the unelected Tory-controlled quarter sessions. Governments, therefore, by-passed the county and the parish by either creating the ad hoc arrangements for each service, gradually extending local auditing and inspection as in the case of schools, or as in the case of the prisons taking over the service.

Among radicals and Liberals there was agreement on the need to remove unelected Tory gentlemen from rural government but little consensus as to the pattern of government that should replace the old system. Within many communities rate-payers' motives in resisting change were also bound up with personal concerns over the expense of reforms. Successive Liberal and Conservative Governments had no desire to reap the electoral unpopularity of increasing national taxes in order to gain greater control over local government by subsidising improvement through central grants. The rural rate-payers who demanded more government subsidies were unwilling to accept that this would inevitably be accompanied by greater central controls. Developments to by-pass any need to create larger authorities or raise local taxes through the growth of private-sector services to community government also faltered, with the Turnpike Authorities as a central example, and, as the following chapters show, an ethos of municipal inclusivity in the towns. A final problem was that prior to the creation of the Local Government Board (LGB) there was no department of State to cut the Gordion knots by co-ordinating a vision of and a strategy for local government as a system.

The failure of central control of the Poor Law

The Poor Law Board, created in 1834, consisted of three members who, according to the Webbs, 'were not badly chosen'.[6] The chair, Frankland-Lewis, had held ministerial posts and had helped draft the Sturges–Bourne Reports promoting plural voting.[7] Chadwick had to be content with becoming the Secretary to the Board. Chancellor of the Exchequer Lord Althorp informed him: 'your station in society was not such as would have made it fit that you should be appointed one of the Commissioners'.[8]

However, class was not an insuperable barrier to preferment for the most able, and realistically Chadwick was too combative and unbending to be a suitable choice for a politically sensitive post. Lord Althorp admonished Chadwick not long after his appointment: 'I will frankly tell you that if the appointment rested with me I should think that any want of cordiality between you and any one of the Commissioners an insuperable objection to you.'[9] Chadwick did not accept his role as Secretary with good grace and was quickly at odds with the Commissioners, who were inclined to be more cautious and pragmatic in their implementation of the principle that all relief should be provided within workhouses run by unions of parishes.[10]

During its first two years the Commission successfully established Poor Law unions throughout the south of England and, later, the rural Midlands. The early successes reflected the paternalistic power of the landed elite in many rural areas as the new system did little to erode the power of the magistrates. Assistant Commissioners who were charged with forming the new Unions were generally younger sons of established land-owning families who could discuss reorganisation with local men of consequence, usually the magistrates, on an equal footing. Arrangements within many Unions had more to do with the interests of the squires and parsons than those of the lowly rate-payers, let alone the poor themselves.[11] Much greater difficulty was faced by the Commissioners from 1837 onwards, when they sought to impose the local parish unions and the workhouse system in industrialising cities and towns in the north of England. The Act was ill-designed to deal with unemployment caused by business slumps that left many without work through no fault of their own. Labourers took to the streets in protest at what they saw as possible incarceration for the failures of their employers and the economy as a whole.[12] The Government urged the Poor Law Commissioners to proceed with caution in the face of likely civil disturbance.[13] Gradually most of these areas were forced to create unions, partly as an Act of 1836[14] had given them a new responsibility for registering births, marriages and deaths and allowed them to be formed initially for such a purpose before they took on their responsibilities under the 1834 Act. The protests against the Poor Law unions also declined as the indignation of urban working-class leaders transferred to a more general demand for political emancipation. As Fraser observes, 'the anti-poor law movement ... was the mid-wife of Chartism'.[15]

The violence of opposition to the new system declined as it became impossible to implement the workhouse test as fully as Chadwick and Nassau Senior had intended. The Poor Law Commissioners found that they lacked many of the powers necessary if the agency was to enforce their views on local administration. The Commission could interfere with procedures of the Poor Law guardians, but if local boards of guardians refused to follow the precepts of the 1834 Act they could be compelled to conform only by use of the cumbersome legal procedure of *mandamus*:[16]

> The Commissioners could prevent rates being spent on guardians' feasts, or on outdoor relief to the able bodied, but they could not compel guardians to spend. Guardians could be made to close an insanitary institution but could not be forced to spend more than 50 pounds, or one tenth of the average annual rate, on improving it.[17]

The unions formed through Gilbert's Acts could resist change as the Commission had no power to overturn the legislation that established them. By 1840 over 2 million citizens in 799 parishes still remained outside the Board's control because of such Acts and they were not brought into line until 1868.[18] It was also impossible to establish the practice that poor relief could be obtained only within the workhouse, and in most areas systems of outdoor relief continued to provide much of the support for the poor. As the Poor Law Commission began to face increasing difficulties, political support withered away. In 1837 the Government acceded to requests for an investigation into the operation of the Act which disappointed the critics by generally praising the Commission. When the original five year term of the agency required renewal in 1839, Parliament prolonged its life for only a year at a time. In 1841 the ailing Whig Government attempted to continue the Act for a further ten years but met with such backbench hostility, led from the Tory side by the young Disraeli, that the proposal was withdrawn. The succeeding Tory Government of Robert Peel, despite considerable opposition, was able to renew the Commission for a year and then later for a further five years.[19]

The mood of hostility against the centralising Commission did not, however, disappear and was brought into focus in 1845 by a widely reported scandal concerning the Andover Poor Law Union, that paupers crushing bones from animal carcasses were so hungry they were eating rotten meat from the debris.[20] The Whig Government under Lord John Russell which took power in 1847 restructured the Poor Law Commission the following year, in the wake of a report on the Andover case, by ensuring that the Board became a department under the control of a government minister. The new Poor Law Board was composed of a number of ministers but, like the Board of Trade, it was never intended to meet.

Effectively the Board's President was the Minister for the Poor Law. Placing the Board under direct ministerial control gave the Government greater authority over this aspect of local administration. At the time, however, it was seen as a means of ensuring less interference since it could be assumed that the governments would be less inclined to intervene in local matters than would an independent agency under the influence of utilitarians like Chadwick.

The Public Health Acts

As understanding of the causes of disease grew during the 1840s and 1850s, the poor-relief system became increasingly involved in health care as they began providing hospitals and medical services for the poor.[21] Chadwick had published ideas on the connection between disease and poverty and, thwarted in his ambitions to steer the Poor Law, turned increasingly to campaigning on the issue of sanitation.[22] After unsuccessfully pressing the Poor Law Commissioners for an enquiry, he by-passed their obduracy by turning to his parliamentary supporters. The Bishop of London, who was one of his major supporters, was able to announce in 1839 that Lord John Russell[23] was requesting the Poor Law Commission to inquire into the causes of ill-health in the country. Chadwick was given leave by the Commissioners to write the report, partly to divert his critical focus from their administration. Published in 1842, his findings excited popular interest by clarifying the link between disease and crowded, insanitary, urban slums. Light dawned that diseases could be prevented by extensive public works to dispose of sewage more efficiently, by supplying fresh water and by constructing better ventilated homes. The concern for improvements in public health led to an expansion in the numbers of private acts seeking to establish local improvement commissions and in 1841 and 1842 backbench essays in statutory legislation concerning public health included measures by Lord Nomanby to establish effective drainage systems and get rid of back-to-back houses.[24] In 1843 the Government demonstrated serious interest when Sir Robert Peel, spurred on by the threat of a cholera outbreak, appointed the Royal Commission on the Health of Large Towns and passed in 1846 a Nuisance Removal Act.[25] The Act allowed local governments facing a deadly epidemic to seek Privy Council approval to allow magistrates to remove nuisances and provide better drainage and water supply, and to charge property-owners for the work. The agencies given this task were municipal boroughs or improvement commissions and, in their absence, the Poor Law guardians. The Act pointed the way to adding public health and the related elements of public works, planning and housing to the responsibilities of the boards of Poor Law guardians in rural areas. Attachment of supervision to the Privy Council further suggested that Government was in no mood to make the local administration of health care a matter for direct interference.

Fears of a cholera epidemic in the mid-1840s promoted politicians to accept demands for more substantial legislation on health and sanitation. A Bill began its Parliamentary life under the supervision of Lord Lincoln, the Minister for Woods and Forests in Peel's last ministry. Lincoln wanted to establish ad hoc sanitary authorities throughout the country to be responsible for developing clean water and sewage systems. He decreed that, as with the boards of guardians, even in the post-1835 boroughs the proposed local Health Boards would be separately elected authorities subject to direct government supervision by the Home Office.[26] Lincoln's successor in Russell's 1846 Whig administration, Lord Morpeth, succeeded in steering the 1848 Health of Towns Act through Parliament.[27]

Morpeth's Act established a three-person General Board of Health to supervise the creation of local Health Boards and to inspect their operations. One member of the General Board was to be a government minister.[28] The General Board had powers to compel a community to establish a local board of health if it had a higher mortality rate than the average for the country while other communities, including parishes acting on their own, could request permission to establish a local board of health by sending a petition signed by a tenth of its rate-payers to the General Board. This provision effectively enabled a minority within any area to initiate the creation of a local board against the wishes of an elected borough, improvement commission or parish council. The Whigs reversed Lincoln's Tory doubts concerning the 1835 Act and decreed that municipal authorities could be local Health Boards.

Local Health Boards could also consist of combinations of boroughs and parishes. Improvement commissions could also request to be restructured into local Health Boards. Once established the local boards had the power to undertake the supply of water, drainage and sewage disposal, and the paving of streets, and could implement these tasks themselves rather than use private contractors. It was also possible for a local board to buy land outside its own area to, for example, build a reservoir.[29] Apart from the specific power to impose the Act on a community, the General Board was able to ratify the appointment of local medical officers and surveyors, sanction borrowing by local boards and had some powers over burials. It was an organisation that could encourage, warn and keep records, but which did not itself execute public works and lacked even the limited authority of the Poor Law Board.[30]

The Act met relatively little resistance in its passage through Parliament. The success of the Bill may have been a consequence of fears of further cholera epidemics which were spreading throughout the Continent. Moreover, as both Tory and Whig frontbenches had supported the principle of the Bill, backbench criticism was muted. Radicals, Whigs and Tories were, in any case, concentrating their efforts at this time on the easier task of dismantling the Poor Law Commission. Given his pre-eminent role in researching and popularising the need for sanitary reform, Chadwick was appointed as one of the three members of the General Board.[31]

Outside of Parliament the General Board of Health was an immediate target of suspicion from supporters of decentralised local governments and was the particular *bête-noir* of the influential Anti-Centralization Union created in 1854 under the leadership of Joshua Toulmin Smith. It is difficult to place a recognisable political label on the Anti-Centralization Union, which claimed it was of 'no "Party"'[32] and as such could have appeal across a range of disparate interests. These included Tory country MPs who formed a constant if declining band of opponents to central controls as well as a vociferous band of largely London interests who had a variety of objections to the General Board. A number disliked Chadwick's authoritarian style, and some disagreed with his technical proposals for resolving the problems of sewage disposal.[33] Other opposing interests favoured the existing arrangements of sewerage authorities and commissions in London and a few had business interests in water supply that they wished to protect.[34] When in 1854 it became necessary to renew the General Board's term of office that had been limited to 5 years, Home Secretary Palmerston attempted to place it under his department's supervision, but the proposal was defeated by 9 votes. Chadwick, who with the other Commissioners had placed his office at the minister's disposal, was thus bereft of an office. The Government subsequently reconstructed a new General Board of Health on an annual basis until 1858, when the unloved institution was finally laid to rest, but Chadwick was never again asked to take a role in public life.

The major responsibility for health advice was subsequently located in the Privy Council[35] whose Chief Medical Officer, John Simon, previously Medical Officer of Health for the City of London, became the most influential voice on public health policy until the creation of the LGB in 1871. Chadwick was well acquainted with Simon and both men worked passionately for improvements on public health but differed significantly in their approach. Simon had trained as a surgeon and strongly supported control by professionals while Chadwick was disposed more to the line that came to be adopted by the mature Civil Service, that the generalist had to be on top and the professional on tap.[36] As a former employee of a local authority, Simon was, in contrast to Chadwick, initially more amenable to allowing local governments freedom to develop and implement innovations. The role of central government was to spread good practice rather than impose uniformity. Continued outbreaks of preventable contagions such as cholera and smallpox later compelled Simon to take a more centralist view. While a few progressive authorities adopted good practices and discretionary legislation on health, it was difficult for medical inspectors and radical politicians to stand by and watch poorly run, narrow-minded, parsimonious local corporations and boards preside over conditions that harboured the breeding-grounds of preventable contagious diseases. During the 1860s Simon insidiously toughened inspection and made it increasingly difficult for a responsible local authority to evade its duty to ensure public health.[37] The Sanitary Act of 1866 significantly increased local authority powers to compel citizens to clean up their towns.[38] Local vestries which had in the previous year been designated as sewer authorities were given the same powers as boroughs to deal with insanitary conditions.[39] Any complaint to the Government from an individual citizen that poor water or sewage facilities were damaging public health could trigger an enquiry. Depending on the findings the Government could appoint a contractor to undertake necessary work and claim the costs from a local authority.[40] Central government was beginning to accrue powers to take over local services that were being neglected by local governments.

An issue concerning both public health and religious values created a further group of ad hoc agencies, the Burial Boards. As the cities, and in particular London, grew in population church cemeteries became so overcrowded they were becoming not only macabre but dangerous to sanitation.[41] The 1852 Burial Act,[42] applying only to London, permitted a vestry to establish a new burial ground for themselves or with other vestries and to govern them with a separate Burial Board. The legislation was extended to other areas of the country under Burial Acts from 1852 to 1885 that regulated where and how cemeteries should be regulated and effectively established an adoptive power of local government to lay the dead to rest.[43]

Roads and highways

The lack of any clear consensus on the form and structure of local administration also dogged efforts to establish structures to improve the highways and by-ways to meet the steadily increasing traffic that flowed from industrialisation and prosperity. The advance of the railways in the mid-nineteenth century created a terminal crisis for most Turnpike Trusts since they could not compete for lucrative heavy goods traffic or long-distance travel, and with declining revenue most became uneconomic and bankrupt. Outside the turnpike network was a further problem of adequately surfacing the numerous country roads under the protection of local parishes. Engineers such as Thomas Telford had pioneered a new science of road-building that, he for one, saw as needing far better organisation, expertise and capital than could be provided by a parish vestry.[44]

The reforming Whigs were reluctant to hand over the task of road maintenance to the predominantly Tory county quarter sessions and were aware of widespread popular resentment at the tendency of JPs to stop rights of way across their own lands.[45] The General Highways Act of 1835 established a more professional structure for dealing with non-turnpike roads by consolidating earlier legislation in a single act that confirmed the parish as the unit for maintaining the roads but dropped the obligation of local rate-payers to voluntarily maintain them and, therefore, required their upkeep to be secured by hired labour, hopefully under the supervision of a professional surveyor.[46] The Whig Government also encouraged parishes to amalgamate into highway districts and allowed larger parishes to form specific highway committees but almost none took up the offer. Action to create larger highway authorities was promoted in 1842 as a consequence of the Rebecca riots in south Wales in which smallholders, some of whom dressed up as women to avoid detection, attacked and destroyed toll gates and houses.[47] The protest was driven by rate increases to cover losses made by turnpike trusts which had to be met by the parish as the body responsible for road maintenance, if no other agency was capable of undertaking repairs. The riots led to the creation of highway districts in south Wales under the super-vision of a County Highways Board. Although successful, this system did not become the blueprint for dealing with road maintenance in the rest of Wales or in Britain as a whole.[48]

It was not until 1862 that a Highways Act empowered the Home Office to force parishes into highway districts to be governed by Highways Boards that would include both locally elected members and a number of JPs.[49] The Home Office did little to promote the Act and not all county quarter sessions bothered to enforce the measure. Those that did could choose different groupings of parishes to form the Highways Board, such as the area covered by a Poor Law Board. Many small parishes found a loophole to subvert the merging of their powers with their parochial neighbours. The Health Acts of 1848 and 1858 enabled health authorities to have responsibility for road maintenance and hence many parishes peti-tioned to become Health Boards after 1862 so that they could resume control over their roads without interference from the quarter sessions. An Act was necessary the following year to restrict the formation of Health Boards to areas of at least 3,000 inhabitants.[50] In 1878 the future assignment of road maintenance was given a clear steer when an Act required any restructuring of Highways Boards to make the sanitary district the unit responsible.[51] The problem of the insolvent turnpike trusts also remained as a burden on the many authorities responsible for road maintenance and it was not until the 1870s that Parliament began as a matter of policy not to renew Turnpike Trust Acts and hence forced the roads to become a responsibility of at least one of the often several possi-ble local governments covering the area.[52] It was not until the 1894 Local Government Act that Highways Boards and the power of the parishes to maintain highways were abolished by transferring this responsibility to the urban and rural districts. Problems in determining boundaries between the new authorities and their inclusion in a single county ensured that it was not until 1900 that the last parishes gave up responsibility for highways' maintenance.[53]

Education boards

By 1800 the development of manufacturing and its concomitant liberal values stimulated demands for better schools. The growth of nonconformist churches, which were popular with liberal industrialists, also introduced a substantial political opposition to the dominant role of the Anglican Church in the provision of education. In 1816 Henry Brougham succeeded in establishing a parliamentary inquiry into the state of education in London and the depressing findings stimulated the creation of a wider and more permanent survey of education in Britain. Brougham unsuccessfully sponsored a Bill to require each parish to provide elementary schooling.[54] Despite this failure the survey of education provision nationally gave ample evidence to supporters of State involvement that public funding was necessary to improve the intellectual capacity of the country.[55] In the wake of electoral reform, a measure for modest State intervention was introduced by Lord Althorpe to allocate £20,000 of Treasury money for the building of schools to be distributed by two national charitable societies largely to the industrialising urban areas.[56] Suggestions for a board of commissioners to look into the development of teacher training were, however, defeated.

The religious conflict stirred up by the renewal of Anglican vigour through the Oxford Movement, the growing influence of nonconformism and the reassertion of Catholic rights, especially in Ireland, ensured that education was to become a highly contested issue. Anglicans fought to maintain what they saw as their right to influence national education. The Government of Lord John Russell, by then much embroiled in religious controversy connected with Ireland, side-stepped the issue by placing the control of Exchequer funding for schools in the hands of a Privy Council sub-committee which would consequently ensure that the issue was not a matter which must be defended in Parliament by a government minister. The sub-committee consisted of five government ministers, but day to day operations were handled by its secretary, Dr Kay Shuttleworth, aided by an Education Department of the Privy Council.[57] Among its first activities was to establish in 1840 a Schools' Inspectorate to ensure some national supervision of State-funded local education provision.[58]

Despite attempts in the 1850s to legislate for a system that would ensure more uniform and efficient provision of elementary education, this was not resolved until the 1870 Act sponsored by W. E. Forster in Gladstone's first administration. All boroughs and parishes were given the opportunity to establish elementary schools but where this was not secured the Privy Council's Education Department was given powers to enforce such provision by creating elected school boards able to charge rates to secure some of the funding necessary to build and maintain schools. Many boroughs and parishes took no action and hence facilitated the creation of yet another layer of ad hoc government, the school boards.

School boards were to have between 5 and 15 members, including women, who were also able to vote for them.[59] London had its own large school board. The Act also established a still operable division between elementary schools funded by the public sector and those that received some of their income from a charitable endowment, usually under the control of the Church. In 1876 a system of school-attendance officers was created and the 1880 Mundella Act[60] made it compulsory for all children up to the age of 12 to attend school. Moves were also made in the 1870s and 1880s to reduce the need to pay school fees although the principle of free education for all at elementary level was not finally secured until the Fisher Act of 1911.[61]

Police and prisons

Following Peel's creation of the Metropolitan Police in 1829 and the 1835 Municipal Corporations Act, most major conurbations had some element of professional policing. In 1836 Chadwick, who early in his career had developed ideas for a centralised police force,[62] persuaded Lord John Russell to establish a royal commission on the prevention of crime partly with the aim of securing better policing of the Poor Law Act.[63] The Commission's report proposed Home Office co-ordination of police forces throughout the country and the creation of county forces under the control of magistrates. The ideas were far too centralist to gain widespread support and, as the proposed county forces would take over the police in the newly created municipal boroughs, they unleashed a torrent of criticism even from Chadwick's liberal allies.[64]

Russell's Government confined legislation to the permissive Rural Police Acts of 1839–40 which allowed quarter sessions to establish professional police forces. Later Acts of 1842 and 1850 gave further substance to county police by allowing payments to be made to parish constables and the appointment of more senior police superintendents. By the 1850s all of the English counties had adopted some elements of these Acts but only eighteen had formed a county-wide paid police force.[65] The patchwork development of local police forces was due, in part, to the reluctance of many magistrates and rate-payers to bear the extra costs involved and, in part, to satisfaction in some areas with the older methods of policing. Demands for a more organised system of policing were fuelled in the 1850s by fears of increased crime on the part of soldiers demobbed from the Crimean War and discharged criminals who, before an Act of 1853, would have been transported and abandoned in the colonies.[66] In 1856 following a few failed attempts, Palmerston succeeded in passing an Act[67] which required counties and boroughs to establish police forces. The police services would be required to be professional and adequately equipped and housed, and were subject to inspection through the Home Office. In order to help mitigate the costs of such a change, funds were granted from central government to support police services.

There was an insidious decline in local authority powers over the prison service that had begun with the institution of a national Prisons' Inspectorate in 1835 and then enhanced in 1865 by an Act that allowed the Home Office to minutely regulate the management of prisons.[68] Following the 1865 Act counties and boroughs were contributing to a service they at best administered but could not control. Under pressure to reduce the costs of local administration on landowners, Disraeli's Government passed the 1877 Prisons Act which transferred responsibility for prisons entirely to central government.[69] This was the first transfer of a major service traditionally under local control to central government. As late as 1922 the Webbs observed:

> A great administrative service, extending throughout the whole country, which had been for centuries within the sphere of Local Government was transferred *en bloc* to a department of National Government. In no other branch of public administration has such a change been made in England ... English preference for local over central administration has hitherto always proved too strong to overcome.[70]

In the second half of the twentieth century many local services were, however, to follow this early precedent, but not solely, as in this case, to satisfy the economic concerns of rural squires.

Finance

The development of new tasks for local government, to be carried out in a more uniform and efficient manner, placed immediate strains on the financial relationship between central and local government. It became increasingly difficult to retain the balance in which local vestries, municipalities and the quarter sessions raised their funds for local services while national taxation was levied primarily for the costs of national defence. The restructuring of the Poor Law was in part an initiative to retain this framework despite increasing tax demands to cater for the greater costs of poor relief. Despite strong presumption towards separate national and local responsibility in paying for their services, reforming ministers even before 1832 raided central government coffers to pay for locally administered reforms. Without such a mechanism ministers could have little expectation that vestries or quarter sessions would take advantage of permissive legislation. Among the first examples of central funding for locally administered initiatives were Peel's support for the Metropolitan Police in 1829[71] and Althorp's distribution of funds to local charities for building schools in 1834,[72] although neither grant subsidised local government directly. In order to mitigate growing rural concern over increases in rates a select committee appointed to inquire into the problem in 1834 reported in favour of subsidising the county rate from the national exchequer for tasks that could be seen as local subsidies for national expenditure.[73] The proposal led to central government paying the county administrations for half the expenditure for successful prosecutions at assizes, although they did not accept that this should apply to all possible subventions, such as funding for police.[74]

The first major shift in the pattern of funding took place in 1846, largely as a means of securing agreement for the abolition of the Corn Laws. Peel's proposals on tariffs were countered by some landowners with the demand that a greater proportion of what were nationally required activities, such as the full cost of the assizes and partial payment for maintaining prisons, should be met by the Exchequer. With reluctance Peel conceded by providing the full cost of the assizes and giving grants towards the salaries of medical officers of health and some teachers.[75] In 1856 the Police Act further increased the growing portfolio of national grants by providing funds for police pay and uniforms. In 1867 medical officers of health were subsidised for expenses incurred in programmes of vaccination.[76]

The principle that central government payments to local authorities were made for expenditure incurred in meeting national needs began to crack in the late 1860s under the strain of predominantly country Tories' protests at increases in rates. A highly efficient interest group, the Chambers of Agriculture, established initially to campaign on policies concerning cattle disease, formed a separate Local Taxation Committee, led by land-owning Conservative MP Sir Massey Lopes. The organisation quickly established a permanent office with professional workers and had the support of eighty-three Tory MPs.[77] The movement won the support of many a squire and, as a Conservative force, had sufficient strength – either via the House of Lords or splits among Whigs in the Commons – to undermine any initiative of Gladstone's Liberals to resolve the interlinked issues of democratisation of county government and the restructuring of local taxation. Compromise on the issue was impossible largely because Gladstone's strict financial orthodoxy involved, as a matter of principle, the view that central government should not subsidise local expenditure. In a letter to Goschen, the President of the Poor Law Board, Gladstone asserted: 'My judgement is very hostile to taxing the Exchequer for local purposes. Even Sir R. Peel went too far in that direction.'[78]

Massey Lopes pressed his case by demanding the formation of a royal commission on local taxation, and the ambitious Goschen decided to use the pressure to his own advantage by turning down the request with the promise of a major restructuring of the system of rural government.[79] He succeeded in creating a select committee, which included Lopes, to inquire into the division of rates between owners and occupiers and the constitution of local bodies. This successfully pushed a wedge between rural and urban interests by showing that while rates had doubled in thirty years the increase fell more heavily on the boroughs than on rural areas.[80] He

followed the initiative with Bills to restructure parish and county government and reform local taxation. The proposals were not a priority for
Gladstone and were dropped, apart from one element, the creation of a
Local Government Board.[81] Massey Lopes continued with his demands
for relieving the burden on the rate-payer and succeeded in 1872 in
gaining Commons support for a motion on that issue, but this was steadfastly ignored by Gladstone. The strength of the organisation was sufficient to prompt Goschen to make economies in the Poor Law system and
for Gladstone to promise that the pressure group would always be
consulted on local tax issues. Gladstone did not, however, concede the
Local Taxation Committee's principal demand that more items subject to
county expenditure should be subsidised by central grants.

Disraeli's Government, formed in 1874, was more inclined to bow to the
pressure from the Tory Sir Massey Lopes and transferred half of the expenditure on police and a proportion of spending on the care of the mentally ill
under the Poor Law to central grant aid.[82] A further and far more significant
concession to county demands for lower taxes was the transfer of the prisons
to central government.[83] After 1877, with a decline in national finances, the
Conservative administration was more reluctant to make further concessions to the interest group. However, the agitation had importantly ensured
that the Conservatives and the rural interest could accept the principle of
central provision of local finances and hence opened up the route to the
concomitant principle of central control. Liberal proponents of local independence, such as Redlich and Hirst, commented:

> The budget of 1874 brings the history of grants in aid to a point at which
> logic and chronology permit us to pause. Their later history ... is a record of
> degeneration. The earlier grants in aid were for national purposes and were
> intended to secure efficiency. The later grants assume more and more the
> character of mere doles to relieve some favoured class out of the purse of the
> general tax payer.[84]

Neither the two major parties nor interests seeking to restructure
county government or to defray the rate burden through central government aid were, therefore, satisfied with the structure of county government and finance following the 1874 budget. The Local Taxation
Committee continued to campaign for rate support and added the need
for subsidies to defray extra costs on local authorities to maintain roads
following the demise of many turnpikes. Elements of the Tory rate-relief
lobby also began to support the idea of elected county councils as a means
of ensuring lower rate demands.[85]

In the longer term Sir Massey Lopes and his predominantly Tory landowning supporters were, probably unwittingly, sowing the seeds for
greater centralisation. The extent to which they appreciated that central
government was unlikely to subsidise local expenditure and yet not be
tempted then to control local government through that means is not clear.

The Poor Law Reform Act began to loosen the hold of local landowners through the appointment of independent auditors to check the accounts of boards of Poor Law guardians. The arrangement was strengthened in 1844 to allow the Poor Law Commissioners to combine boards of guardians and parishes for auditing purposes and require the appointment of a district auditor who was to take over the role of inspecting accounts and reporting publicly unlawful expenditure by the JPs. The procedure was subsequently applied to the health boards in 1875 and to the county and district councils on their creation. By 1879 the LGB had taken over the appointing of auditors from the rural authorities.[86] Local customs such as payments for mole-catchers or subsidies for a sparrow-shooting club were brought to an end.[87]

Not only was the growth of centrally directed auditing diminishing the power of JPs to control local expenditure, there was also the slow and insidious beginnings of central inspection for nationally funded services, as is illustrated in the emergence of the Schools' and Police Inspectorates. A further restraint on local government during the mid-Victorian years was the formal assertion by the courts of the principle of *ultra vires*. In its earliest form the grant of a charter allowed a corporation to act as if it were a person and therefore with constraints but by the eighteenth century there had emerged a legal understanding that a municipal corporation could not exceed the duties specified in its charter. The 1835 Municipal Corporations Act had maintained that boroughs had to safeguard rate-payers' contributions and as early as 1837 a legal ruling prevented a local corporation from subsidising a church.[88] The *ultra-vires* rule was formally established by the courts in respect of the activities of railway companies that wished to diversify their activities to undertake functions not permissible in the private legislation that had set up their business,[89] but this principle also began to be applied to local authorities,[90] perhaps spurred on by the largely Tory sentiments of much of the judiciary.

The formation of the LGB

The creation of the Poor Law Board under the control of a government minister in 1847 had created a department which for the first time supervised an important local government function and as a consequence the Board had a significant influence over the rating system and some aspects of local expenditure. The Board was not, however, represented in the Cabinet until 1859, until which time it had passed through the hands of six junior ministers.[91] In the late 1840s there was a possibility that the increasingly redundant post of Commissioner for Her Majesty's Woods and Forests would take on this role as the lead spokesperson for the health board, but the office ceased to be in the Cabinet from 1852. Following the winding-up of the General Board of Health, responsibility in Whitehall for the growing activities of local government was widely dispersed. The

majority of health-care powers were given to the Privy Council, although
responsibility for the prevention of contagious diseases rested with the
War Office. A Local Government Act Office, within the Home Office,
dealt with appeals maintaining that a local authority was not undertaking
its duties under sanitary legislation and also in sanctioning loans for
development of sewage schemes.[92] A separate Home Office department
also supervised Burial Boards.[93] Relief of the poor remained with the Poor
Law Board, which also was extending its remit into the fields of education
and health care. Palmerston in 1859 promoted its president to Cabinet
status where the office remained a fixture until the department's transformation in 1872. As an office represented in the Cabinet, a president of the
Board, for example Goschen, emerged as the lead figure in developing
policy towards local government.

The creation of a department to bring together ministerial direction of
central services relating to local government derives, in part, from
Goschen's failed initiatives to resolve the problems of local taxation and
also from a distinct initiative on the part of public health reformers to
reassert a more central role in government. With the growth in understanding of the causes of infectious disease and the importance of vaccination, governments found it increasingly inadvisable to stand aloof from
the issue. Following mounting professional pressures, the British Medical
Association and the Social Science Association jointly submitted evidence
to the Privy Council, arguing the need to develop larger sanitation authorities employing a full-time medical officer with the power to enforce
public health legislation.[94] In response, the Government established in
1868 the Royal Sanitary Commission to resolve the problem of the
divided administration of health services. Its report concluded that the
scattered units of local government should be consolidated into multi-
purpose agencies subject to election by rate-payers on the basis of a two-
tier county and district structure.[95] In addition there should be a new
statute on public health that would apply compulsorily to all local authorities rather than being a permissive power. The Commissioners further
concluded:

> The administration of the Laws concerning the Public Health and the Relief
> of the Poor should be presided over by one Minister as the Central Authority
> ... the Central Authority should have full powers of general supervision and
> inspection and defined powers of central control and direction over all Local
> Health Authorities.[96]

The Royal Sanitary Commission's conclusions were of sufficient weight
to induce Gladstone to rescue the idea of a Local Government Board from
the wreck of Goschen's financial proposals. Although the Commission
had in mind a Ministry of Health, the Government, aware of the earlier
hostility to the Board of Health, established a Local Government Board
which combined the Privy Council's health responsibilities, the Local

Government Act Office and the Poor Law Board. The new organisation was, like the Poor Law Board which it replaced, a government department presided over by a minister. The Act to establish the LGB was steered through Parliament in 1872 with little opposition by Sir James Stansfield, who had succeeded Goschen to become the final President of the Poor Law Board[97]. Prior to the Act there had been some debate between medical professionals, such as Sir John Simon, and ministers on whether the new department could be a federation divided into separate Health and Poor Law sections. To the chagrin of health reformers the LGB quickly evolved into an organisation under the domination of Poor Law bureaucrats. Although the LGB was assigned three permanent secretaries representing its different elements, within a year it came to be dominated by the former Permanent Secretary of the Poor Law Board, Sir John Lambert, who had been a member of the 1868 Sanitary Commission and had argued strongly for a unified ministry. Lambert was supported by Stansfield, who continued in office as the first President of the LGB, and by Gladstone, both of whom were concerned to avoid giving the Conservatives the impression that they were creating a spendthrift department.[98]

Under Lambert's guidance the values and practices of the Poor Law Board permeated the new department and its primary interest was with the efficient administration of the Poor Law rather than with public health[99]. Sir John Simon, although continuing as Chief Medical Officer but now located in the new Board, found himself, rather like Chadwick before him, in a subordinate role, with his ideas being given much less attention that he had hoped. Lambert ensured that Simon was given little access to the minister and constantly amended and interfered with his medical advice.[100] Simon appears to have been a victim of the emerging Civil Service ethos that power should lie with the generalist administrator and not the professional advisor. He struggled on with the situation until 1876, when he resigned over threatened economies in vaccination services and efforts to secure, outside of his control, the inspection of medical officers. Simon at least had the satisfaction that his resignation was accompanied by widespread public concern, in contrast to the enthusiasm that greeted the earlier fall of Chadwick.[101] By the 1890s Gladstonian Liberals, Salisbury's Conservatives and conservative civil servants such as Lambert had created an LGB wedded to Poor Law parsimony and class discrimination, which made it relatively efficient as an administrative agency but far from a base from which to create a welfare state. This short-term victory for conservative values was to be the undoing of the LGB in the early twentieth century and along with its demise the one other forgotten concern which Gladstone and Salisbury had cherished, the relative independence of local units of administration.

Notes

1 Smellie, *History of Local Government*, p. 23.
2 D. Roberts, 'Jeremy Bentham and the Victorian administrative state', in Parekh (ed.), *Jeremy Bentham: Ten Critical Essays*.
3 This is recognised by Disraeli in his depiction of Manchester, as fictionalised in his novel *Sybil*.
4 A defence of small local government in the USA is, for example, provided by V. Ostrom, R. Bish and E. Ostrom, *Local Government in the United States* (San Francisco, CA: Institute of Contemporary Studies Press, 1988).
5 L. Woodward, *The Age of Reform 1815–1870* (Oxford: Clarendon Press, 1962), p. 161.
6 Webb and Webb, *The Last Hundred Years*, vol. 1, p. 105.
7 The other two were George Nicholls who had developed the pioneering Southwell workhouse and John Shaw Leverve, an able young politician and an under-secretary in the colonial office who had been a member of the 1834 Commission: ibid., pp. 105–7.
8 Chadwick Papers, Box 1864, fos 175–80, Lord Althorp to Chadwick, 8 May 1841.
9 *Ibid.*, fo. 15, Lord Althorp to Chadwick, 15 April 1835.
10 Finer, *Life and Times of Sir Edwin Chadwick*, pp. 113–14.
11 M. A. Crowther, *The Workhouse System 1834–1929* (London: Methuen, 1981), p. 36.
12 J. Prest, *Liberty and Locality: Parliament, Permissive Legislation and Ratepayer's Democracies in the Nineteenth Century* (Oxford: Clarendon Press, 1990), pp. 11–12.
13 M. E. Rose, *The English Poor Law 1780–1930* (Newton Abbott: David & Charles, 1971), pp. 109–11; N. C. Edsall, *The Anti-Poor Law Movement* (Manchester: Manchester University Press, 1971), pp. 187–211.
14 An Act for Registering Births, Deaths and Marriages in England: 6 & 7 Will. IV, c. 86.
15 D. Fraser, *The Evolution of the British Welfare State* (Basingstoke: Macmillan, 2nd edn, 1984), pp. 50–1.
16 The legal requirement that an organisation undertake those duties stipulated by statute or common law.
17 Crowther, *Workhouse System 1834–1929*, p. 35.
18 Webb and Webb, *The Last Hundred Years*, vol. 1, p. 119.
19 Webb and Webb, *The Old Poor Law*, pp. 172–9.
20 Webb and Webb, *The Last Hundred Years*, vol. 1, pp. 179–88.
21 R. G. Hodgkinson, *The Origins of the National Health Service* (London: Welcome Trust, 1967), p. 621.
22 Finer, *Life and Times of Sir Edwin Chadwick*, pp. 154–63.
23 At the time Home Secretary in Melbourne's second Cabinet.
24 Hodgkinson, *Origins of the National Health Service*, p. 634.
25 The Nuisance Removal Act: 9 & 10 Vict., c. 96; 'nuisances' in Victorian upper-class speech means sewage and filth.
26 W. C. Lubnow, *The Politics of Government Growth* (Newton Abbott: David & Charles, 1971), pp. 79–80.
27 11 & 12 Vict., c. 63.

28 Initially this was the Commissioner of Woods and Forests.
29 For detailed accounts see Lubnow, *Politics of Government Growth*, pp. 81–4; Prest, *Liberty and Locality*, pp. 30–6.
30 Lubnow, *Politics of Government Growth*, pp. 80–1.
31 Finer, *Life and Times of Sir Edwin Chadwick*, p. 338.
32 Anti-Centralization Union, *Government and its Measures in 1857* (London: Edward Stanford, 1857), p. 3.
33 C. Hamlin, *Public Health and Social Justice in the Age of Chadwick: Britain 1800–1854* (Cambridge: Cambridge University Press, 1998), pp. 302–34.
34 R. Lambert, *Sir John Simon 1816–1904* (London: MacGibbon & Kee, 1965), pp. 147, 158–9.
35 The Privy Council, historically the advisory body to the monarch, was by the nineteenth century nominally subject to the Lord President of the Council, a Cabinet member, but became a repository for functions that were not of sufficient substance or were too politically sensitive to warrant their own minsiterial department, or Board: H. J. Hanham, *The Nineteenth Century Constitution: Documents and Commentary* (Cambridge: Cambridge University Press, 1969), pp. 340–1.
36 Lambert, *Sir John Simon 1816–1904*, pp. 266–9.
37 *Ibid.*, pp. 424–60.
38 29 & 30 Vict., c. 90.
39 Lambert, *Sir John Simon 1816–1904*, pp. 383–91.
40 Prest, *Liberty and Locality*, p. 209.
41 Finer, *Life and Times of Sir Edwin Chadwick*, p. 230.
42 The Burial Act: 15 & 16 Vict., c. 85.
43 W. C. Ryde, *The Local Government Act 1894* (London: Reeves & Turner, 1894), pp. 36–9.
44 Hamlin, *Public Health and Social Justice in the Age of Chadwick*, pp. 264–6.
45 Webb and Webb, *Story of the King's Highway*, pp. 203–5.
46 5 & 6 Will. IV, c. 50.
47 Webb and Webb, *Story of the King's Highway*, p. 218.
48 *Ibid.*, pp. 217–20.
49 25 & 26 Vict., c. 61.
50 Webb and Webb, *Story of the King's Highway*, pp. 206–10.
51 *Ibid.*, pp. 213; 41 & 42 Vict., c. 77.
52 Webb and Webb, *Story of the King's Highway*, p. 222.
53 *Ibid.*, p. 214.
54 S. J. Curtis, and M. Boultwood, *An Introductory History of English Education since 1800* (London: University Tutorial Press, 4th edn, 1966), pp. 54–5.
55 J. Stuart Maclure (ed.), *Educational Documents* (London: Methuen, 5th edn, 1965), pp. 18–28, provides extracts from the Parliamentary surveys.
56 Curtis and Boultwood, *Introductory History of English Education*, p. 54.
57 *Ibid.*, pp. 56–8.
58 *Ibid.*, p. 54.
59 *Ibid.*, p. 75.
60 The Elementary Education Act: 43 & 44 Vict., c. 23.
61 The Education (Administrative Provisions) Act: 1 & 2 Geo. V, c. 32.
62 Finer, *Life and Times of Edwin Chadwick*, pp. 29–31.

63 *Ibid.*, p. 127.
64 *Ibid.*, pp. 164–89.
65 C. Steedman, *Policing the Victorian Community* (London: Routledge & Kegan Paul, 1984), p. 14.
66 *Ibid.*, pp. 24–5.
67 The County and Borough Police Act: 19 & 20 Vict., c. 69.
68 S. Webb and B. Webb, *English Local Government*, vol. 6: *English Prisons under Local Government* (London, Frank Cass, 1963 [1922]), pp. 186–200; the Prisons Act: 28 & 29 Vict., c. 126.
69 The Prisons Act, 1877: 40 & 41 Vict., c. 21.
70 Webb and Webb, *English Prisons under Local Government*, p. 201.
71 Smellie, *History of Local Government*, p. 54.
72 Curtis and Boultwood, *Introductory History of Education*, p. 54.
73 Webb and Webb, *The Parish and the County*, p. 607.
74 Redlich and Hirst, *Local Government in England*, vol. 2, p. 157
75 *Ibid.*, pp. 159–60; C. Bellamy, *Administering Central–Local Relations 1871–1919* (Manchester: Manchester University Press, 1988).
76 Bellamy, *Administering Central–Local Relations*, p. 25.
77 *Ibid.*, pp. 28–9.
78 Gladstone Papers, Add. 44536, fo. 198, Gladstone to Goschen, 19 Jan. 1869.
79 *Ibid.*, Add. 44161, fos 150–3, Goschen to Gladstone, 15 Jan. 1869.
80 G. J. Goschen, *Local Taxation* (London: Macmillan, 1871), details the report with annexed correspondence.
81 H. G. C. Mathew, *Gladstone 1808–1889* (Oxford: Oxford University Press, 1997), p. 219.
82 Bellamy, *Administering Central–Local Relations*, pp. 28–9; Redlich and Hirst, *Local Government in England*, vol. 2, pp. 160–1.
83 The Prisons Act, 1877: 40 & 41 Vict., c. 21.
84 Redlich and Hirst, *Local Government in England*, vol. 2, p. 161.
85 Bellamy, *Administering Central–Local Relations*, p. 36.
86 W. A. Robson, *The Development of Local Government* (London: George Allen & Unwin, 3rd edn, 1954), pp. 374–5.
87 W. B. Odgers and E. J. Naldrett, *Local Government* (London: Macmillan, 2nd edn, 1909), p. 264.
88 Robson, *Development of Local Government*, p. 262n; *Attorney General* v. *Aspinall*, 1837.
89 *Colman* v. *Eastern Railway Co.*, 1846, prevented a rail company ending at Harwich from operating steam ships to meet their trains: J. Street, *A Treatise on the Doctrine of Ultra Vires* (London: Sweet & Maxwell, 1930), p. 2.
90 Street, *Treatise on the Doctrine of Ultra Vires*, p. 15; *R.* v. *Wood*, 1855.
91 Webb and Webb, *The Last Hundred Years*, vol. 1, p. 193.
92 Evidence of Tom Taylor, Head of the Local Government Act Office, to the Royal Sanitary Commission: Minutes of Evidence, 26 April 1869, *British Parliamentary Papers: Health General*, vol. 9 (Dublin: Irish University Press, 1970), pp. 9–25. Tom Taylor was a man of many parts and apart from his work for the Civil Service was editor of the satirical weekly *Punch*.
93 *Ibid.*
94 Bellamy, *Administering Central–Local Relations*, p. 112.

95 *Report of the Royal Sanitary Commission*, Cmnd 281 (London: HMSO, 1871), pp. 74–5.

96 *Ibid.*, p. 75, para. 13.

97 The Local Government Board Act, 1871: 34 & 35 Vict., c. 70; Lambert, *Sir John Simon*, p. 115; Hansard, vol. 208, 21 July 1871, cols 79–82, Second Reading Debate of Local Government Board Bill.

98 Bellamy, *Administering Central–Local Relations*, p. 119.

99 Webb and Webb, *The Last Hundred Years*, vol. 1, pp. 198–9; Bellamy, *Administering Central–Local Relations*, pp. 120–56.

100 Lambert, *Sir John Simon*, pp. 526–46.

101 *Ibid.*, p. 571.

4

Municipal government to its zenith

The 1835 Act enabled but did not compel industrial towns to establish municipal corporations let alone develop the publicly owned infrastructure that by 1900 made the governments of the larger cities such as Birmingham, Glasgow or Manchester into complex bureaucracies closely intertwined with the commercial and social life of their communities. The status and influence of the great industrial towns were signalled by the magnificence of the town halls built as clubs for the industrial and commercial elites who comprised the majority of councillors and aldermen. It is suggested that the building of these 'New Jerusalems' was motivated by a spirit of civic pride encapsulated by a strong religious conviction that good Christians should be involved in the life of their community to spread God's largesse to society. However, it may also be claimed that less altruistic motives informed the interest of business elites. The development of complex bureaucratic municipal government began at a faltering pace, motivated in some cities by locally sponsored political initiatives, but in others by a belated response to central government demands. The pace of change, however, accelerated from the 1870s with substantial municipal purchase of infra-structure and energy companies, stimulated in part by the backward city of Birmingham catching up with developments elsewhere.

Incorporation and improvement

Many local authorities prior to the 1835 Act were divided along party lines,[1] although in many closed vestries a single party, usually the Tories, had come to dominate the council to the exclusion of rivals within the community. The formation of elected municipal councils and the repeal of the Test and Corporations Acts ensured in many municipalities bitter party competition between long-established Tory families and the newly empowered industrialists who generally saw themselves as Liberals. The skills of forming ward organisations and canvassing were developed in towns where there were open elections in the eighteenth century and were immediately in operation in boroughs after the 1835 Act.[2]

The 1835 Act applied to existing boroughs. Towns such as Leeds and

Liverpool were required to disband their previously closed corporations and set up a new council based on rate-payer elections. Large towns that did not have a corporation could only gain corporate status by petitioning the Privy Council to be allowed to apply the 1835 Act. Some like Manchester, which gained borough status by 1838, were quick off the mark but in others rate-payers hesitated to embark on what many feared would be an expensive business that would but replace one oligarchy with another. Sheffield, for example, initially rejected the idea, only 1,970 rate-payers petitioning the Privy Council in support as against 4,589 opposed. Among the objections were Tory fears that 'mob orators would lead the ignorant to elect persons for municipal office', and also that Sheffield had grown larger than the neighbouring boroughs of Doncaster and Chesterfield and so clearly could flourish without such status.[3] Many opponents were lower rated citizens who feared increases in costs, and there was also a general radical disquiet that incorporation would put the industrial masters of the town in judgement over their employees.[4] The issue re-emerged in 1839 with the threat that the Police Act would replace local police commissioners with a county force. A further attempt at incorporation resulted in a majority of all residents still opposed, but by 6,949 votes to 5,607 rate-payers favoured the idea. The legal process of securing incorporation was therefore put in motion, resulting in Sheffield gaining borough status in 1843.[5] Sheffield was not the slowest of the eligible towns to seek incorporation. Bradford did not secure borough status until 1847.[6]

The Municipal Reform Act itself had never been intended by the Whigs to launch new services at tax-payers expense rather than remove closed Tory corporations. Improvements came but gradually even after the 1848 and 1858 Health Acts gave the cities further permissive powers. Many improvement initiatives coalesced around a Whig–Liberal alliance supporting an innovative municipal corporation as opposed to an older oligarchy of predominantly Tory interests seeking to maintain the *status quo*. However, there were many exceptions to such a pattern. The city of York, that had previously been controlled by a Whig corporation, within two years of the 1835 Act voted the Tories into power, led by the rail magnate George Hudson, who retained his pre-eminence as Mayor on three occasions until his fall from grace in 1846.[7] The city of Liverpool accelerated its growth in services only after the Toies gained a majority on the Municipal Council in 1842.[8]

Among the majority of towns that had Whig, Liberal and radical majorities the breakdown of old party allegiances and the substantive differences between non-Tory factions often ensured stalemate concerning improvements. *Laissez faire* liberals could be unwilling to launch into costly, publicly funded developments, while radicals and, later, Chartists were on occasion prepared to support the Tory cause against improvements on the grounds that they should not pay for resolving the environmental problems created by the manufacturers.[9] Politics in Leeds after incorporation typically centred on the most expensive improvement needs for the city, in this case the supply of clean water. Although the Council had a strong Liberal majority, powers to supply clean water required a private bill that was vigorously opposed by the Tories. Liberals campaigned for public control of the inefficient private company in charge of water supplies, while Tories argued that municipal ownership would be inefficient and that it would be unfair to those with a private supply. The matter was resolved by the intervention of the Earl of Harewood who refused to sponsor the necessary legislation until both parties sorted out their differences. They agreed in 1837 that the private company would sell half its shares to the municipality and in 1852 the joint-venture became a wholly municipal one.[10] The issue of proper sewer facilities was opposed by the minority Tories and also, on the grounds of cost, by Chartists who in 1842 won a majority on the old Leeds vestry that sent sufficient members to the Leeds Improvement Commission to control its deliberations. The Liberal Borough Council and the magistrates who supported improvements pressed ahead and received the necessary government support with the 1842 Leeds Improvement Act which made the Improvement Commission redundant and willing to hand over its last remaining powers to the borough.[11] Despite the borough gaining powers over health improvements, Leeds Corporation was nevertheless slower than many other cities in forwarding major improvements.[12]

Following incorporation Sheffield politics evolved around a similar divide. A bitter division emerged over sanitary improvements with the local Chartist leader, Issac Ironside, adopting Toulmin Smith's views on local independence against centralising sanitary authorities and the Borough Council. The Chartists captured control of Sheffield Poor Law Vestry which ensured their control of the local Highways Board created by a Private Act in 1818. Ironside argued that the Vestry was more democratic than the borough with its rate payer franchise and sought to secure any improvements to drainage through the Highways Board but then overreached himself by seeking support to supply gas as well as sewage services to Sheffield.[13] The protracted struggle delayed improvements but Ironside was in the longer term unable to legally press his case and his overbearing tactics lost him many supporters. In 1864 the Town Council adopted the 1858 Health Act and following the necessary enquiries the Highways Board was wound up as it did not cover all areas of the growing city and had lost its principal role.[14]

In Birmingham underlying divisions between radicals supporting the more democratic open vestry as opposed to a municipal authority based on a restricted franchise crystalised around the continuing presence of improvement commissions.[15] Birmingham had petitioned to become a municipal corporation in 1838 but power to develop infrastructure was also held by Street Commissioners operating within the boundaries of the municipality who fought strenuously against the emergence of a rival organisation. The two groups tended to polarise around Conservative and radical positions.

Faced with the *fait accompli* by the Corporation, the Street Commissioners campaigned for their own local act to allow them rather than the corporation to improve sanitation. The battle was eventually resolved in 1851 in favour of the corporation taking improvement powers through a Private Act which involved the winding-up of the Street Commissioners,[16] who were forced to concede on the grounds that the 1848 Health of Towns Act would have led to central government eventually placing all sanitation powers in the hands of the Corporation. Following the consolidation of a single authority in Birmingham, few improvements were forthcoming. The Council during the 1850s was dominated by an economist party led by the Tory editor Thomas Allday, described by the Birmingham historian John Bunce as 'violent in speech, prone to make personal charges and engage in personal attack', whose ideas on local government were embodied by the one desire to keep down the rates.[17] Attempts to improve the water supply through municipal ownership by private act in the 1850s were ruined by the Tory economists who were able, despite being in a minority on the corporation, to organise popular dissent against the Bill in the referenda necessary to pursue the issue.[18] Following Allday the more respected but, nevertheless, economically cautious Thomas Avery became the dominant force on the local authority and secured rather modest improvements in sanitation and water supply.[19]

Consolidating the boroughs

By the late 1840s, developments in municipal government were often due as much to central governments taking the side of local forces demanding change as to a widespread demand for improvement among rate-payers. Liberal governments were inclined to grant petitions for incorporations, as in Bradford when in 1847 Lord John Russell's Government accepted such a petition even though it was opposed by a larger dissenting list.[20] The process of absorbing into a single authority the ad hoc Improvement and Highways Commissions was a one-way process that by the 1840s was being favoured by both Peelites and Whigs. Unless faced by extensive local pressure, Parliament was pleased to sanction the private acts that incorporated the older agencies into the municipal councils and, with very few exceptions, such as the Liverpool Docks and Harbour Board,[21] decisions on these matters were not likely to be reversed. In 1857 changes to the municipal code made it permissible for boroughs to seek the incorporation of improvement commissioners and by 1879 only fourteen still remained in boroughs.[22] Even though the political climate in central government was becoming more favourable to unified municipal corporations the rate-payers did not all leap at opportunities for the development of new facilities. As table 4.1 indicates, many boroughs delayed taking advantage of the 1848 or 1858 Health Acts, partly out of suspicion of potential centralised inspection of services, but also as a consequence of fears of higher expenditure. In 1850 the Public

Table 4.1 Growth of city functions

City	Incorporation	Health Acts	Commissioners	Libraries	Gas	Electricity	Tramways	Water
			Take-over					
Birmingham	1838	1857	1851	1860	1875	1899	1904–11[a]	1876
Glasgow	1833	1862[b]	1846	1899	1869	1890	1871[c]	1852
Leeds	1835	1866	1842	1868	1870	1898	1894	1837–52[d]
Liverpool	1835	1846[e]	1846	1852	X	1896	1897	1847
Manchester	1838	1868	1843	1851	1843[f]	1890	1870	1844
Sheffield	1843	1864	1864	1856	X	1899	1896	1888

Notes: [a] Briggs, *History of Birmingham*, vol. 2, p. 97; the city had leased lines to private companies since 1884.
[b] Police Board extension to appoint MOH prior to the 1867 Public Health (Scotland) Act: Mayer, Glasgow, p. 172.
[c] Glasgow leased tramway lines.
[d] Leeds partially owned the water company by 1837 but took up an option to fully take over water supply in 1852: Fraser, *Urban Politics in Victorian England*, pp. 154–60.
[e] Liverpool had anticipated the 1848 Health Act.
[f] Acquired from Police Commission: N. J. Frangupulo (ed.), *Rich Inheritance: A Guide to the History of Manchester* (Manchester: Manchester Education Commiteee, 1962), p. 58.
X: Service remained in private hands.

Libraries and Museums Act gave permissive powers to establish these services but there was scarcely a rush to adopt the legislation. Manchester, which up to the 1870s was in the vanguard of municipal development, led the way on this proposal but many larger towns such as Birmingham or Leeds did not establish libraries for a further ten years. As late as the 1870s there were laggard, penny-pinching authorities such as Birmingham that did not appoint a medical officer until obliged to do so through the 1872 Public Health Act.[23]

Concern for public health, more than any other factor, was a spur to regeneration and led more forward-looking towns by the 1860s to the conclusion that poor housing in the absence of town-planning required by-laws to regulate building.[24] The expanding cities also began to realise they needed to deal with problems of narrow streets and poor-quality buildings by engaging in the wholesale reconstruction of an area of the city rather than simply piecemeal orders to pave a street or remove buildings causing an obstruction. In theory local authorities had powers to build houses from the mid-nineteenth century after Lord Shaftsbury in 1851 piloted through Parliament Acts that allowed local authorities to build lodging houses for the poor, take out loans to raise the necessary capital and also subsidise the rents through payments from rates.[25] In practice few local authorities responded to the measure, with only Huddersfield making serious use of the Acts.[26]

In 1868 the Artisans' and Labourers' Dwellings Act gave medical officers of health the power to condemn property as unfit for habitation, but placed the onus and costs of remedies on the property-owners rather than on public bodies.[27] A more significant step was achieved through the efforts of Home Secretary Sir Richard Cross, who sponsored the 1875 Artisans' Dwellings Act which gave towns with a minimum population of 25,000 power of compulsory purchase of property and land in areas considered hazardous to health, provided approval following an inquiry was obtained from the LGB and a Bill presented to Parliament. Joseph Chamberlain as Mayor of Birmingham had advised the sponsors of a Bill and immediately initiated a major redevelopment of the city centre, which gained legislative approval in 1876 and was completed in 1881, to create the present commercial nucleus of Birmingham around Corporation and New Streets.[28] The Metropolitan Board of Works and its successor, the London County Council (LCC), also began to seriously clear slums and build housing for rent,[29] although few other towns were able to match the grand designs of Birmingham, partly due to the extensive capital that was needed for such a project.

While many cities satisfied little more than the minimum requirements of the Health Acts, local authorities embarked rather earlier on their own grandiose building plans to develop their town halls as iconic symbols of the importance of the corporations to their communities. Birmingham's Street Commissioners had created a Grecian-style Town Hall in 1828 which transferred to the Borough in 1851, although it was not until 1879 that the city completed its Council House.[30] Liverpool was among the earliest boroughs to construct a great building in the form of St George's Hall, completed in 1847 by private subscription. [31] The Mayor of Bradford, Samuel Smith, in 1851 led a successful campaign to build St George's Concert Hall as a private venture through the sale of shares in the enterprise.[32] Leeds responded with an attempt to parallel this approach but, failing to raise the required private investment, councillors agreed a proposal to build a rival great civic building in the form of a new Town Hall for the borough, raising the funds by loans secured and paid for by the municipality. The building was completed in 1858 and was the first of many town halls that did much to lift the grandeur and authority of city centres.[33] Manchester followed the Leeds example, commissioning Alfred Waterhouse to design a splendid gothic edifice with Ford Maddox Brown murals,[34] at a cost of £1 million, and completed in 1877.[35] Even relatively small northern cities such as Dewsbury and Bolton acquired their own grand municipal buildings. While the magnificent town halls are lasting monuments to Victorian design and civic pride, their construction at great cost should not be praised unduly. Leeds rate-payers may have sacrificed a considerable expenditure on an iconic status symbol which effectively served as a club for industrialists and professionals involved in local politics but had yet to employ a medical officer of health. In this context there are shades of the reviled pre-1835 property-owning corporations that feasted well but provided few services.

Taking off

The first forty years of the reformed boroughs suggest a pattern of sporadic and contested growth, whereas the next forty years ushered in what many commentators see as the golden age of municipal government that culminated by the end of the century in the established municipality subsidising the rates through profitable trading services and spearheading major infrastructure developments. The engine of growth in city expansion was at root industrial development and the concomitant increase in urban populations and subsequently areas. In 1851 54 per cent of the population of England and Wales lived in urban areas and 25 per cent of that figure were in towns of over 100,000 inhabitants; by 1901, however, 79 per cent of the population were in urban areas and 44 per cent were in the largest towns.[36] The population of Birmingham, for example, grew to 600,000 by 1887 due to increases in population and boundaries,[37] and Glasgow's increased from 77,385 in 1801 to 395,503 by 1861.[38] Expansion filled in many of the spaces between communities and better transport allowed residents in outlying areas to regularly visit city and town centres.

Until the 1880s the boroughs in England and Wales were kept largely to the arrangements established for them by the Boundary Commission following the 1835 Act even though many boroughs were pushing against their bounded cages. In 1885 several Health Boards in Manchester opted to join the city in order to ensure cleaner water supplies at lower cost and they were followed by a further influx of authorities in 1890.[39] The expansion of city boundaries was, however, often contested. Birmingham, for example, in 1876 successfully opposed a petition from neighbouring Aston to become a borough which would have made the expansion of Birmingham more difficult. The Government was not disposed towards a greater Birmingham and only a few of the neighbouring Health Boards showed any desire to be incorporated in the generally higher rated town, although several were merged into the authority in 1891. It was not until 1909 that the Aston Manor, which had by then become a borough, and a further five district councils were added to Birmingham under a Liberal Government that was more prepared to see the extension of large local authorities.[40]

Smaller towns sensed that the climate favouring expansion was to their benefit also. Alexander details the successful expansion of Reading, with the support of the LGB, through Private Acts in 1886 and 1911 against the wishes of the major property-owners in the incorporated areas. [41] A steady stream of smaller towns also sought borough status after the 1850s as their populations expanded with industrialisation. Middlesbrough, for example, was a village with a population of 154 according to the 1831 Census but by 1861, with its rapid development as a coal-exporting port, it had a population of nearly 20,000 and had applied and obtained borough status in 1853.[42] Incorporation was, however, an expensive process until 1877, when an Act permitted existing sanitary districts to sponsor such petitions and charge the cost to the rates.[43] Between 1835 and 1860 only 20 towns had been added to the list of the original 178 sanctioned through the Municipal Reform Act. The 1877 Act led to a renewed impetus to turn health authorities and later urban districts into boroughs. By 1888 there were 280 boroughs and a further 30 were created by 1901.[44]

Since 1835 there had been numerous changes to the powers and operation of municipal authorities and there also remained some confusion as to the status of pre-1835 chartered boroughs that had not been subsumed under the Act. A Royal Commission which reported in 1880 retraced the footsteps of the 1834 Commission but without unravelling the shocking data that gave grist to the mill of radical opinion. The prosaic findings of the Commission led in 1882 to an Act[45] that codified many of the changes post-1835 in the status of the boroughs and became the central legal document guiding the constitutions of borough councils until 1933. The Act established clear guidelines for the formation of new boroughs through a petition, signed by householders, to the Privy Council that could then rule on incorporation. A companion Act in the following year also removed the last vestiges of the pre-1835 system by establishing that only boroughs coming under the terms of the Act qualified for such status, and hence all towns not subject to the 1835 Act lost any claim to be a borough.[46]

In Scotland expansion was less problematic as a succession of acts increased the number of burghs. The General Police (Scotland) Act of 1850 allowed unincorporated urban areas to form ad hoc police burghs which also took on the powers of a Health Board. The police burghs were given a more uniform status by Acts of 1892 which allowed a community with 700 or more inhabitants to be classified as a town and establish its own police force. The Act effectively incorporated many of the small burghs of barony or regality.[47] In 1900 a further Act ensured that these smaller urban authorities were governed under regulations that were uniformly applied, dependent on population size, with other burghs.[48] Compared to English boroughs, Scottish burghs could be very small communities and those in the vicinity of large cities tended to be absorbed by the principal government of the growing conurbation. In 1888 a Boundary Commission for Glasgow allowed the City to incorporate a number of adjoining police burghs into a Greater Glasgow.[49]

Municipalisation

The growth of urban government is characterised by the municipalisation of utilities. Municipal ownership of services was, of course, not a new phenomenon and many of the pre-1835 corporations owned profitable services such as markets or harbours. Many ad hoc street commissions also assumed control of utilities. Manchester Police Commissioners, for example, pioneered public ownership of gas supplies, beginning modestly with a venture to light the lamp above the police station door in 1817. This seemed such a successful venture that they secured a Private Act in 1824 to supply gas to the city. The municipality took over this commitment when it assumed the powers of the Police Commissioners in 1843.[50] Public ownership was, then as now, accompanied by tensions between private and public interests over the efficiency of public-owned companies and it was not until the 1870s that any conscious ideology of public ownership entered the thinking of city fathers. Municipalisation of gas production and delivery prior to the 1860s followed a pattern rather similar to municipal ownership of water supplies in that it was pioneered by a few authorities where problems of supply created a specific local difficulty. For the most part local authorities left the supply of gas in private hands until the municipal 'take off' of the 1870s, but by 1882 there were 148 local authorities with municipal gas undertakings.[51]

The development of complex city government which owned and delivered essential services is most extensively attributed to the work of Joseph Chamberlain when Mayor of Birmingham. Chamberlain was not a native of Birmingham but arrived in the city at the age of 18 with the mission of reviving an ailing family business. He was introduced to local politics by the Unitarian minister Robert Dale who was seeking support from manufacturers to secure free elementary education for the city and nationally.

Chamberlain swept to national prominence through this campaign as a leader of the National Education League, and only when it was thought that education would become a municipal task did he stand as a councillor. His abilities quickly ensured that he was elected as Mayor and forsaking his industrial interests turned full time to local and then national politics.[52] He held office as Mayor for three years and during that period ensured that a previously rather lethargic authority caught up and even surpassed the civic growth of Manchester through acquisition of sanitary powers, water supply and gas services, as well as slum clearance in the centre of the city, to create a new commercial centre.[53] However, enthusiasm for developing the city did not last long into his parliamentary career and he resigned the post of mayor in 1876 with some self-doubts[54] when elected an MP, although he retained the position of alderman until 1880.[55]

Chamberlain's success in transforming Birmingham's finances and its importance as a model urban government was in part due to his ability to push at an open door given that most of its voters realised how far the city lagged behind its rivals' developments. As Briggs points out, Birmingham was not a pioneer in any major aspect of municipal growth. [56] The importance of Chamberlain was as a publicist, and his later fame focuses attention on his role as an advocate of the virtues of civic splendour and zeal, even though, while he never wholly lost interest in the values of local government, his political interests had moved to national and international affairs. In this context Chamberlain's career is similar to those of politicians such as Herbert Morrison or David Blunkett who reached prominence early in their political life as successful local leaders but once in Parliament and then the Cabinet were never wholly dedicated to the local political system.

Chamberlain's initiative did however ensure that many cities began after 1870 to take new technologies into public ownership. Cities began to be involved in electricity supplies almost as soon as the technology was available to make large-scale generation a viable proposition. A parliamentary Inquiry in 1879 favoured private acts to establish large-scale electricity supplies through streets. The Health Board of the small town of Cockermouth experimented with electric street-lighting as early as 1881.[57] Local governments were initially thought ideal for electricity supply as early generators could distribute power to a source only a few miles distant.[58] In 1882 Chamberlain as President of the Board of Trade passed the Electric Lighting Act that permitted streets to be dug up for the installation of electricity cables through private acts sponsored by municipalities or private companies and gave local authorities the remit to purchase private electricity companies at relatively low cost following twenty-one years of their operation. A subsequent Act of 1888 extended the period for which companies could avoid possible municipalisation to forty-two years.[59] Bradford pioneered municipal electricity generation in 1899, followed in 1891 by the London borough of St Pancras and, in 1894, by Portsmouth, Hampstead and Ealing.[60] By 1900 most large cities controlled their electricity supply, although some were slow to begin establishing municipal supplies, fearing competition with their munici-palised gas services.

The pressures opposing or favouring public provision of profitable serv-ices similarly created a confused balance of power relating to the construction of tramways. In the 1860s G. F Train, an American, began developing tramways in cities and in 1868 Liverpool secured a Private Act to allow the municipality at a future date to buy tramways established in the city. Parliament intervened in 1870 with legislation allowing private companies to operate tramways, subject to local authority regulations, and local authorities to apply to the Board of Trade to construct tramways, but not to run trams. However, local authorities could purchase a tram system in their area after twenty-one years of private sector operation of the service. This confused balance restricted the municipal growth of such ventures until in 1882 Huddersfield built tram tracks but could find no private company to run the service and gained modification of legislation to ensure that in the absence of private sector interest it could operate the trams itself. By the 1890s, with tramways becoming less profitable, it became much easier to secure government consent for full municipalisation of these services and by 1905 there were 161 municipal tramway services.[61]

London

The largest city in Britain did not follow the path of civic development taken by Birmingham, Glasgow and Manchester. The absence of London from the more general sanitation legislation, in particular, and any form of modernisation, in general, had concerned many Liberal and radical parliamentarians obliged to experience the squalor of the metropolis ever since the 1835 Inquiry shelved the task of including the City of London in its remit. Benthamite radicals suggested that the metropolis be governed through a uniform system of local authorities established for the country as a whole.[62] Less radical reformers campaigned for open vestries, an end to the exclusiveness of the City and the need for sanitation authorities. Toulmin Smith railed against the many vestries of greater London that had decayed into corrupt, closed systems, but opposed the creation of an elected greater London authority.[63] In addition to the divided voices for reform were interests with contracts tied to specific vestries, rivalries between local communities swallowed up in the growing conurbation[64] and, finally, the financial self-interest and wealth of the City of London.

In 1847 under the threat of a further cholera epidemic, Lord Morpeth engineered a Royal Commission headed by Chadwick to consider sanita-tion in London.[65] The metropolis was defined as a twelve-mile radius with Charing Cross at its centre. The Commission reported within two months and its findings led to the abolition of the seven Crown Commissions for

Sewers to create a single Metropolitan Sewers Commission for the whole of London apart from the City.[66] The old sewer authorities were constantly attacked by Chadwick and his allies for inefficiency but had, nevertheless, a creditable record of new construction since 1800, given the legal restrictions that hampered their work.[67] The Sewers Commission had twenty-three members, who were mostly ardent supporters of Chadwick's views.[68] Their powers were, however, limited to drainage, although Chadwick attempted to secure legislation the following year to include widened responsibility for paving and water supply. He also expected the Commission to be subservient to the General Board of Health then being created. None of these plans came to fruition, as the powerful vestries in metropolitan London exerted sufficient pressure on the Government to undermine the threat of a potential all-London authority.[69] Pressure for the reform of sanitation and the archaic system of government led to the creation of a Royal Commission to inquire into the condition of the City of London, which effectively considered the conurbation as a whole. The report published in 1854 rejected a widely held view that a reformed city should be enlarged to take control of metropolitan London as this would 'defeat the main purpose of municipal institutions'[70] by creating too large an authority[71] and recommended that the 1835 Municipal Corporations Act be applied to the city, except for its police who should be merged with the Metropolitan Police. For the conurbation outside the city the report recommended the creation of seven municipal councils to cover each of the parliamentary constituency areas of London and the formation of a conurbation-wide Metropolitan Board of Works that would be responsible for sanitation and drainage.[72]

Under the guidance of Sir Benjamin Hall Parliament passed the Metropolitan Local Management Act in 1855 which established the ad hoc agency of the Metropolitan Board of Works (MBW) to construct a drainage system that would prevent sewage being deposited into the Thames in the heart of London.[73] The Act was a compromise between groups wishing to retain the *status quo* and the enthusiasts grouped around Chadwick seeking radical reform.[74] The new body was also given powers to widen streets, and in a further Act of 1855 acquired the duties of a body created in 1844 to regulate building standards for London. The formation of the MBW to cover an area of some 74,000 acres shaped the future boundaries of the London conurbation until the creation of the Greater London Council. In the absence of any other body to represent the larger London area, the MBW accrued further powers such as the inspection of gas supplies in 1860 and of the fire brigades in 1866, and later the right to construct tramways and parks, and to undertake slum clearance.[75]

The 1855 Act also restructured the system of parish government within the metropolis, although it rejected the seven large authorities proposed by the Royal Commission and instead more modestly established 23 of the largest parishes as parish vestries to be governed by councils elected by rate-payers in households rated for the Poor Law at £40 or, in poorer parishes, £25. Smaller parishes were grouped together into fifteen districts boards whose members were elected by their constituent parish vestries. The 6 largest vestries elected 2 members to serve on the MBW while the others had a single representative. The City of London contributed a further 3 members to the MBW.[76] The newly constituted authorities had responsibility, guided by the MBW, for drainage into the main sewers, street-cleansing, paving and lighting, and numerous tasks of regulation such as inspection of cellars.[77] They were also required to appoint a medical officer of health and an inspector of nuisances.[78]

Although never seen as a complete solution to London's administrative problems, the MBW could claim considerable achievements in the forty-four years of its existence. During the twenty years preceding its creation there had been several attempts to create an effective sewage system for London all of which had been defeated on grounds of expense, technicality and the lack of a centrally co-ordinated authority. Ambitious plans had been drawn up but left on the table unfunded. The MBW might not have had any greater success in pushing forward an effective scheme had not the unusually hot summer of 1858 made it impossible to hold parliamentary sessions at Westminster due to 'the great stink' from the open sewer that was the Thames. Disraeli informed himself of the proposals on the table[79] and ensured that Parliament sanctioned the MBW's chief engineer Sir Joseph Bazalgette to construct probably the single most ambitious, yet unseen, public work of the Victorian age, the main London sewerage system. The work was completed at huge expense by 1864, but proved to be a remarkably robust and effective system.[80]

The City of London had escaped any change following the 1835 Municipal Corporations Act and further reform measures in 1837. It avoided pressure for sanitary reform in 1847 by agreeing to draft its own legislation, with the proviso that it would accept the intrusion of the Metropolitan Sewers Commission to secure main drainage in the Square Mile. The City evaded major reform initiatives for the next forty years, although an Act of 1858 marginally compromised its powers. Subsequent failed attempts at reform by private members in 1859, 1863, 1867, 1868, 1869, 1870 and 1875[81] attest both to the hostility of radicals towards the city and to the capacity of the financiers to avoid parliamentary interference. The Bills of 1867 and 1868, introduced by John Stuart Mill himself, marked a tendency noticeable in later proposals towards decentralisation by giving more powers to London's local districts.[82] Gathorne-Hardy, Poor Law President in Derby's Conservative Government, informed Disraeli that he found 'the London question a very puzzling one', in the sense that MPs were being pressured to act but that there was no clear line within Parliament on an approach that could lead to a successful reform.[83]

In 1880, following the defeat of yet another reform bill at the hands of city vested interests, a group of radical Liberals led by J. F. B. Firth prompted its sponsors to establish a London Municipal Reform League to secure government support for change. The League succeeded in its initial aim of getting Liberal governments interested in pushing through the restructuring of the Metropolis.[84] The greatest challenge to the City of London came with a Government Bill proposed by Home Secretary Lord Harcourt in 1884 that would have extended the power of a restructured and elected City of London government over the MBW's area.[85] Gladstone supported the proposal, though with reservations on Harcourt's refusal to give police powers to the restructured authority. Opposition to the Bill was orchestrated by Conservative leaders in the City of London who that year had chosen Robert Fowler MP, a private banker and 'acknowledged leader of the City Conservatives',[86] as Lord Mayor in view of the threat of democratisation. Their tactic was to spend lavishly to keep potential supporters away from the debate. The city 'hired bullies to disturb and break up' meetings of groups such as Firth's Municipal Reform League and paid for its own well-publicised meetings to act in its defence.[87] The Bill was received by an almost empty House of Commons. Delays ensued in scheduling further debate which, when they took place, resulted in adjournment, and the measure effectively ran out of time and was abandoned.[88]

The capacity of the City of London to resist change rested on both its wealth and the influence of its senior policy-makers. 'Bankers tended to go into Parliament strictly to benefit the business . . . and in the 18th century the influence of the banker, merchant and tradesman put the City into a state of quasi-permanent opposition to the Government of the day'.[89] These interests were resistant to the break-up of a city government that was as much concerned with facilitating gentlemanly connections between businessmen and financiers – through sponsoring dining circuits and convivial ceremonials such as the Lord Mayor's Banquet – as it was with resolving the sanitary problems that festered in the slums of Whitechapel. Following the defeat of the Harcourt Bill, a Parliamentary Committee investigated the city's campaign and, while reluctant to openly accuse the authority of outright corruption, suggested that it would have a case to answer if taken to court.[90] In reality, the city probably secured its aims as much by the manipulation behind closed doors of influential fellow-legislators. Although the city remained inviolate, the activities of Firth's interest group were instrumental in reshaping London in the 1888 Local Government Act.

Professionalism and bureaucracy

The elected status and growing complexity of the large municipalities led them to pioneer the structures and procedures for decision-making and administration that characterised local authorities until the Local Government Act of 2000. Committees established to deal with specific local government functions were present in some of the larger pre-1835 corporations such as Liverpool and the 1835 Act itself reinforced such an arrangement by requiring that each of the reformed boroughs established a watch committee, which did not necessarily report to the full council but tended to remain semi-detached from other branches of a local authority. Larger local authorities by the 1870s had evolved the framework that lasted for most of the twentieth century, in which the full council debated major policy issues but in general ratified without discussion the many administrative decisions of the sub-committees. The division of larger local authorities into semi-autonomous committees defined the decision-making structure within many large authorities. The senior politicians of the majority party, often secure from the frequent need to face the electorate as aldermen, occupied the chairs of the major committees and in many cases ran them as their personal empires. Co-ordination of an authority's policy was usually a matter of wrangling and horse-trading between committee chairs, although a strategic finance or general purposes committee might perform a co-ordinating role. The formal position of the leader of a council as the *primus inter pares* of the majority group did not emerge in the nineteenth century. White observes that in Liverpool the chair of the finance committee could be regarded as the leader of the Council.[91] In many authorities the position of mayor was seen as the most senior policy-initiating and co-ordinating role, which could, as in the case of Joseph Chamberlain in Birmingham[92] or Samuel Smith in Bradford,[93] be held by an individual for a number of years, customarily three.

The growth in the functions and status of borough governments transformed larger corporations from amateur bodies relying on part-time senior officers and a few full-time employees into complex bureaucracies staffed by professionals. In the pre-1835 boroughs the mayor and the councillors were not only policy-makers but overseers who ensured that decisions were implemented. Although the 1835 Municipal Corporations Act stated that the town clerk could not be appointed for life, and so in effect own the office, the newly formed boroughs initially kept largely to the pre-1835 pattern, expecting the mayor to both decide and implement policy and to contract-out administrative services to professionals in private practice. Manchester, for example, employed a part-time town clerk until 1846 when the solicitor, Joseph Heron, undertaking the work came to be employed full-time by the borough.[94] Many of the medical officers of health appointed after 1848 were doctors who continued, part-time, in private practice, their number including, against his better judgement, John Simon, the Medical Officer of Health for the City of London.[95] Treasurers were usually the manager of the bank used by the authority rather than an employee of the borough. Gradually the newly formed boroughs began employing their senior officers on a full-time basis and expected them to be at the top of a Weberian hierarchy of bureaucrats or, as chief officers, of the council committee that appointed them. Liverpool's Sanitary Act of 1846, which incorporated the town's Improvement Commissioners into the Borough Council, was an important step towards professionalisation. The Act allowed the Borough to appoint a medical officer of health, who, after 1848, was a full-time employee,[96] a borough engineer and an inspector of nuisances,[97] and set a precedent that was urged on other local authorities through the 1848 and 1858 Health Acts. Some of the larger municipalities appointed full-time officers only much later. Birmingham's first permanent financial officer, a financial clerk, was appointed in 1858[98] and a full-time town clerk was not established until 1868.[99] At the same time the corporation ended a not uncommon arrangement whereby the staff of the town clerk were his own employees paid directly by himself rather than the local authority.[100]

The wages, salaries and status of senior officers carried weight within their communities. Since town clerks had always been lawyers of local consequence who worked part-time for their boroughs, they needed to have a salary and status similar to those of successful professionals working in the private sector. Similarly, the next significant layer of the nineteenth-century officer hierarchy, the chief medical officer, expected the status accorded to doctors by the wider community. With the growth of highways and water supplies, the professional engineer also became an important fixture. After 1870 municipalisation ensured further expansion in the numbers of professional senior officers. Among the highest paid were the managers of water undertakings, gas works and, later, transport and electricity services, who were generally taken into local government employment as the permanent chief officers of the previously private utilities. Town clerks reflected their *primus inter pares* status by commanding the highest incomes. In Liverpool in 1851 the town clerk was paid the then princely sum of £2,000 per annum, while the borough surveyor received £1,000 and the borough engineer and medical officer of health £750. Less qualified professional staff received more modest salaries.[101] Even a small, recently incorporated borough such as Workington was by the 1890s paying the town clerk a substantial £250 per year, with the surveyor and manager of the gas works receiving around £170, and smaller sums were provided for financial accountants, rates and gas payments collectors, the inspector of nuisances and the part-time medical officer.[102]

The framework developed in the nineteenth century in the large city authorities such as Liverpool and Manchester was replicated by smaller authorities without serious reflection. By the end of the century the senior officers of the county boroughs were managing staffs of a considerable size. Even in 1866, at the height of its economising period, Birmingham Public Works Department had 391 men in employment and 52 horses, and by 1884 those numbers had risen to 624 employees and 89 horses.[103] The status and working conditions of the growing numbers of local government employees, whether in the municipalities, health districts or, later, the counties and urban and rural districts, were subject from the outset to strong demarcation between salaried officers, waged clerical staff and the manual workers. Below the chief officers and their deputies were the clerks, normally men, until the demand for soldiers in the First World War brought women into those ranks.[104] The clerks copied the letters signed by the chief officer, collected the rents and rates and kept the account books for their department. Recruitment to the white-collar rank and file was from school leavers who had shown promise but whose parents had insufficient means to further their education. Selection also involved a high incidence of nepotism. Not infrequently recruits were related to either councillors or the chief officers and on occasion favouritism resulted in jobs for the incompetent and the illiterate.[105] Employment in local government service was, despite the mundane nature of some of the clerical work, a position that paid appreciably higher wages than could be obtained from manual work and was, subject to good behaviour, likely to be a permanent post. Local government service was, therefore, a prized position for sons of the working class.

Although professional groups had by 1900 gained widespread recognition and authority provided they functioned in symbiotic consensus with local and central government, there were a number of would-be professional bodies that lacked the status and prestige or exclusivity to gain full respectability with employers and government. The earliest of such groups is perhaps the National Union of Teachers, founded in 1870, representing the many rather badly paid teachers being recruited into the growing education system. The first specifically local government-orientated body, the National Association of Local Government Officers (NALGO), was formed in 1905 largely as a means of organising a wider grouping of senior professionals within local government. NALGO was led by its senior officers rather than the rank and file members in most authorities and, following the First World War, was active in seeking the development of a more uniformly professionalised and appropriately educated workforce.[106] NALGO maintained its professional status into the 1960s and did not up to that time seriously consider itself an organisation that should demean its status by threatening industrial action.[107] Blue-collar unions in local government, such as those of the gas and general workers founded in 1889, represented the labourers in trading organisations that were being taken over by local government. In 1899 the Municipal Employees' Association was founded which in 1924 amalgamated with the Gas Workers' Union to form the General and Municipal Workers' Union. In the same year a union to represent workers for the London vestries took shape and eventually evolved into the National Union of Public Employees.[108] The Workers' Union representing many local transport workers became a major element in the Transport and General Workers' Union, which included a large segment of local authority workers.[109]

The franchise, party politics and local elites

It was not until the late nineteenth century that permanent mass party organisations based on a subscribing membership began to emerge in the larger towns. The major stimulus to the growth of mass parties was the 1867 Electoral Reform Act. There had been no substantial changes to the restricted male-only owner–occupier franchise established for borough elections in 1835 until the Second Reform Act which, by prohibiting compounding of rates, effectively ensured that all householders paid rates directly and, therefore, qualified as borough electors. The 1869 Municipal Franchise Act further increased the number of voters in towns by cutting the length of residency for qualification to vote from 30 to 12 months.[110] Although intended as a minor reform, the Act was amended by Jacob Bright, brother of John Bright, to state that use of the masculine gender also applied in this case to women. The amendment quietly crept through the Commons and ensured that women could vote in borough elections, although the advance was substantially reversed by the courts in 1872 which ruled that as married women were wholly subservient in law to their husbands the ruling could apply only to unmarried women.[111] The 1882 Municipal Corporations Act later confirmed the right of women to vote, but specifically excluded them from standing for election.[112]

The Birmingham Liberal Association is widely regarded as the first mass party in Britain. Under other names the Association had served as an irregular cadre of political leaders meeting for the purpose of selecting candidates and securing their election for parliamentary elections. In 1867, when Birmingham was awarded three parliamentary seats but electors had but two votes, it was seen as important to organise the Liberal vote across their slate of three candidates to prevent the third seat falling to a Conservative. Such action required careful co-ordination of Liberal voting at ward level and led to the formation of permanent ward committees for the Liberal Association with subscribing members. The electoral success of this strategy, plus a concern to exclude from the Borough Council Liberals who did not subscribe to the radical principles of Chamberlain and his allies, ensured that Liberal associations at ward level became a permanent fixture.[113] The success of the Birmingham Liberal caucus was imitated extensively in the next ten years in other cities, with some using the framework devised in Birmingham and others adopting their own local variants.[114]

Even though the franchise was gradually widening during the nineteenth century this did not result in the formation of local councils that mirrored the status of their voters. A central feature of the later Victorian municipalities was the high social esteem within their community of local leaders as compared to their status a century later.[115] Councillors and aldermen in late Victorian towns were predominantly owners and managers of local businesses or professionals in local partnerships. Birmingham Town Council in the 1880s and 1890s was composed of, among others, 23 per cent substantive businessmen, 16 per cent small-business owners and 19 per cent professionals.[116] Manufacturers comprised 38 per cent, merchants 24 per cent and lawyers 14 per cent of

Sheffield city councillors in 1900.[117] The first LCC included 18 per cent describing themselves as gentlemen, 31per cent professionals, 16 per cent manufacturers and 24 per cent bankers, merchants and shop-owners.[118] In Glasgow the position of mayor was held exclusively from 1833 to 1902 by prosperous manufacturers or commercial leaders, such as the founder of publishing houses Sir William Collins and John Blackie, or business magnates such as Sir James King, a director of the Clydesdale Bank and the Caledonian Railways.[119]

Political domination by the industrial–commercial elite was also prevalent in smaller boroughs.[120] In Glossop in 1900 the 'real rulers of the town were the industrialists, who dominated its political and social organizations. They led the political parties, controlled the Borough Council, took turns to be mayor.'[121] In some towns, as in Swindon for example, the major employer could control the borough: 'Officials of the Great Western Railway had for long played a prominent part in local politics and indeed when Swindon achieved the full dignity of a municipality in 1900 the first mayor to be elected was Mr G. J. Churchward, the Locomotive Superintendent.'[122] The proportion of small and large business interests and professionals serving as councillors could, however, vary over time and also between local authorities. Birmingham in the 1850s was more a Council of small-business owners such as shopkeepers but greatly increased the numbers of larger manufacturers by the end of the century, in contrast Leeds progressively lost most of its professional and large manufacturer representation by the 1870s.[123]

The emergence of mass parties, despite their capacity to return the manufacturing and professional elite to the council chambers, created considerable unease and tensions within the national party leaderships. It was seen on the one hand to be essential to encourage the development of local parties in response to the extension of the electorate. In 1874 the Liberal Party had reorganised its system for promoting the registration of electors by forming the Liberal Central Association. However, mass democratic parties were seen to threaten central control. There were strong forces, especially in the Liberal Party, urging democratisation to ensure that ward branches could influence the policies and leadership of the national party. Such a view was promoted by Chamberlain with the backing of his Birmingham caucus and in 1877 many of the local Liberal Associations formed a National Liberal Federation to pursue further democratisation of the party. The Federation maintained an uneasy relationship with the party during Gladstone's leadership, especially when, under Chamberlain's radical influence, the Federation pressed its own version of Liberal Party policy. The crisis arrived over Irish Home Rule in 1885 when the Federation backed Gladstone's policy on Ireland against Chamberlain, who subsequently resigned from the party and later joined the Conservatives. The disappearance of Chamberlain's influence allowed Gladstone to merge the Federation with the centrally controlled Liberal

Association and secure a new constitution for the party machine that freed the leadership from being influenced by rank and file members of provincial urban party associations.[124]

The Conservatives after 1832 had organised elections through county bodies co-ordinated loosely by Carlton House. After the 1867 Electoral Reform Act Conservative clubs sprang up in many cities. National party leaders, as in the Liberal Party, had no wish to lose central control to these local creations. In 1870 Disraeli established, under the control of W. E. Gorst, a central office that became the basis of the mass Conservative Party, to serve as the 'hand maiden' of the movement but not its controlling element. In the early 1880s Gorst and Randolph Churchill sought to democratise the movement by allowing greater powers to the mass party, but this was resolutely blocked by Lord Salisbury.[125] Local Conservative parties, therefore, retained influence in local politics and, subject to central approval, could select parliamentary candidates but were never closely integrated with central decision-making.

There was clearly little chance that the developing mass party system within either the Conservatives or Liberals would provide a mechanism that had strong local influence over the national leaderships. The patron–client ties that characterise France's and the USA's central–local relations were not destined to appear in Britain. The Liberal and Conservative parties were developed, in Duverger's[126] parlance, as cadre parties based on politicians appealing to a national audience following co-option into a ruling group by those already in positions of power. In the late nineteenth century, despite electoral reform, many parliamentary candidates were parachuted into constituencies through the influence and patronage of powerful national leaders rather than through support from local party machines, and even those who emerged out of success within the local political arena were likely, once elected, to seek the favour of their leaders in pursuit of a national as opposed to a local reputation. Chamberlain, for example, although building a party machine in Birmingham, first sought election to Parliament for Sheffield in 1873.[127] The division between the mass party organisations and the leadership in both the Conservative and Liberal parties, and, as will be noted later, the Labour Party, removed a potentially powerful link between local government activists and central government. In both parties a relationship emerged that both mirrored and fortified the consensus between central and local government. Local parties could supervise the selection of councillors and, subject to central party surveillance, the selection of parliamentary candidates. They were also able to influence policy at the local level, but in practice this was normally left to the councillors who dominated the local party structures. National parties did not attempt to interfere with local political parties, but neither were local parties expected to influence central policy-making or the selection of the national parties' leaders.

Civic pride and commercial interest

Briggs, Hennock and Tristram Hunt emphasise the development from the 1870s of municipal pride and the civic gospel as central factors that attracted the commercial and social elites of the growing cities to municipal politics.[128] These ideas are rooted in developments in Birmingham, where Unitarian ministers George Dawson and, later, Robert Dale drew large numbers of influential liberal citizens by their sermons which were premissed on the view that salvation should be found in the positive application of virtuous acts rather than by faithful adherence to orthodox religious observance. Dawson was politically active in establishing a free library in Birmingham[129] which, he informed the audience at its opening, 'is the expression of a conviction on your part that a town like this exists for moral and intellectual purposes':

> A great town exists to discharge to the people of that town, the duties that a great nation exists to discharge towards the people of that nation … a great town is a solemn organisation through which should flow, and in which should be shaped, all the highest, loftiest and truest ends of man's intellectual and moral nature.[130]

For Dale the prosperous citizen should demonstrate Christian purpose for the good of the nation and the community in which they worked and lived. Building a thriving municipality so as to facilitate education, access to culture and sound environmental services was an undertaking of admirable Christian virtue.[131] Dawson and Dale are regarded as having a major influence on the most celebrated champion of civic grandeur, Joseph Chamberlain.

The example of Birmingham in the 1870s can too readily be seen as representative of all cities or towns in Victorian Britain. The Birmingham nonconformists reached a wide and influential audience, lecturing frequently in other northern cities, but intellectually there were other influences at work in the promotion of the civic gospel. The development of compulsory and accessible elementary education that prompted much of Dale's concern for municipal politics in Birmingham is paralleled by the high-church New Liberal Thomas Hill Green who himself served on Oxford City Council and education boards and had far more lasting intellectual influence. In a secular form these values were also developed, with reservations, by J. S. Mill who, unlike Dawson or Dale, is not infrequently referred to in parliamentary debates of the time as an authority on local government.[132]

That the civic pride in late Victorian Britain was inspired by altruistic ideologies concerned to secure sober self-improvement among urban cadres of industrial–commercial interests can be challenged by rival interpretations. Neo-Marxist theorists such as Castells,[133] Dunleavy[134] and Saunders[135] depict the city as a means for securing the reproduction of labour to benefit capital and capitalists who had great interest in guiding and steering their local communities. Manufacturers had much to gain by municipal control of utilities that were essential for the well-being of their businesses. They could benefit from the cheap supply of gas and electricity and also from excellent public transport within their communities that could improve their supply of labour. Many civic leaders were, like Chamberlain, aware of the value of schools and colleges in ensuring a supply of capable workers for their businesses:

> The sixth standard is a very elementary matter. It merely means that a child should be able to read and write with fluency, do a common sum in practice and make out an ordinary invoice such as shall be required in any shop or warehouse in the country. You will agree that a less education than that would be of no use at all to a child in his battle in later life.[136]

The oligarchies that controlled the cities also saw to it that the cities could benefit their cultural life. The large parks set out in most cities were located predominantly in the wealthier areas, and it was concert halls and art galleries rather than music halls that were constructed with public largesse. The palatial city halls built at this time, much the grandest public buildings in late Victorian Britain, became gentlemen's clubs for businessmen wherein to develop profitable networks and reach consensus on mutually improving the competitive advantage of their cities against rival conurbations. Social status could also be acquired through municipal service. In Glasgow, Birmingham, Manchester and Liverpool mayors were often recompensed nationally for their labours with the award of a knighthood.

It is impossible to guage the extent to which the civic gospel of the late nineteenth century was a product of religious inspiration and altruism or, following neo- Marxist theory, a consequence of the economic self-interest of the leading manufacturers and commercial interests in the expanding cities. The two values can become inextricably linked. Economic self-interest may be justified through moral and spiritual sentiments while economic interest may be tempered by moral and altruistic considerations. In the growth of urban government in Britain there are examples of both altruism and self-interest. A substantive element of the recreational and cultural capital of Victorian cities was philanthropic action. In Sheffield, for example, almost half the park land had been bequeathed by wealthy citizens serving on the city's council.[137] Chamberlain contributed substantially to Birmingham's art collections. Many far-sighted civic leaders could firmly believe, with some justification, that better infrastructure for their towns benefited both their own business interests and the health and well-being of the labouring class. However, municipal leaders also ensured that their economic interests were safeguarded. Sir Fredrick Mappin, a Sheffield alderman and leading member of the local Liberal party who had a municipal art gallery named in his honour following his donation of pictures to the town, was also a major shareholder in the local gas company and was described by a contemporary editor as 'unshaken in his opinion that gas making ... ought never to pass into the unholy hands of an elected body'.[138]

Notes

1 J. Bulpitt, *Party Politics in English Local Government* (London: Longmans, 1967), p. 57.
2 B. Barber, 'Sheffield Borough Council 1843–1893', in C. Binfield, R. Childs, R. Harper, D. Hey, D. Martin and G. Tweedale (eds), *The History of the City of Sheffield, 1843–1993*, vol. 1: *Politics* (Sheffield: Sheffield Academic Press, 1993), p. 31.
3 National Archives, Kew (hereafter NA), PC/1 1491.
4 Barber, 'Sheffield Borough Council 1943–1893', p. 27.
5 *Ibid.*, pp. 27–9.
6 A. Elliott, 'Municipal government in Bradford in the mid-nineteenth century', in D. Fraser (ed.), *Municipal Reform and the Industrial City* (Leicester: Leicester University Press, 1982), p. 116.
7 A. Peacock, 'George Leeman and York politics', in C. H. Feinstein (ed.), *York 1831–1981* (York: William Sessions, 1981), pp. 234–8.
8 B. D. White, *A History of the Corporation of Liverpool 1835–1914* (Liverpool: Liverpool University Press, 1951), p. 29.
9 This occurred, for example, in Sheffield where the Chartist radical Isaac Ironside opposed municipal control and reform, as cited below.
10 D. Fraser, *Urban Politics in Victorian England* (Basingstoke: Macmillan, 1976), pp. 154–60.
11 E. P. Hennock, *Fit and Proper Persons* (London: Edward Arnold, 1973), pp. 190–1.
12 *Ibid.*, p. 109.
13 Fraser, *Urban Politics in Victorian England*, pp. 108–11.
14 Barber, 'Sheffield Borough Council 1843–1893', p. 37; NA, MH 13, p. 165.
15 Fraser, *Urban Politics in Victorian England*, p. 172.
16 *Ibid.*, pp. 170–3.
17 J. Bunce, *History of the Birmingham Corporation*, vol. 2 (Birmingham: Birmingham Corporation, 1885), p. xxxii; see also A. Briggs, *Victorian Cities* (London: Odhams, 1963), pp. 212–13.
18 Briggs, *Victorian Cities*, p. 214.
19 Fraser, *Urban Politics in Victorian England*, p. 174.
20 Elliott, 'Municipal government in Bradford in the mid-nineteenth century', p. 116.
21 The Liverpool Docks had been established by the old pre-1835 corporation and was a major source of revenue from the city, but in the 1850s private interests such as rail companies and public interests including the city of Manchester obliged the local authority to loosen control on the harbours and hive them off into a jointly controlled Merseyside Docks and Harbour Board: White, *History of the Corporation of Liverpool 1835–1914*, pp. 67–78.
22 Redlich and Hirst, *Local Government in England*, vol. 1, pp. 132, 356.

23 Hennock, *Fit and Proper Persons*, p. 114.
24 *Ibid.*, p. 115; Liverpool and Sheffield were pioneering authorities in building regulations.
25 L. F. Orbach, *Homes for Heroes: A Study of the Evolution of British Public Housing 1915–1921* (London: Seeley Service, 1977), pp. 36; 14 & 15 Vict., c. 34.
26 J. B. Cullingworth,*Town and Country Planning in Britain* (London: George Allen & Unwin, 6th edn, 1976), p. 38.
27 J. English, R. Madigan and P. Norman, *Slum Clearance* (London: Croom Helm, 1976), p. 16.
28 Bunce, *History of Birmingham Corporation*, vol. 2, pp. 455–85.
29 English, Madigan and Norman, *Slum Clearance*, p. 19.
30 Bunce, *History of the Corporation of Birmingham*, vol. 2, pp. 545–9.
31 T. Hunt, *Building Jerusalem* (London: Weidenfeld and Nicolson, 2004), pp. 174–5.
32 Briggs, *Victorian Cities*, p. 153.
33 *Ibid.*, pp. 166–70.
34 Hunt, *Building Jerusalem*, pp. 183–4.
35 Briggs, *Victorian Cities*, p. 135.
36 P. J. Waller, *Town, City and Nation, England 1850–1914* (Oxford: Clarendon Press, 1983), p. 8.
37 A. Briggs, *History of Birmingham*, vol. 2 (Oxford: Oxford University Press, 1952), p. 141.
38 I. Maver, *Glasgow* (Edinburgh: Edinburgh University Press, 2000), p. 83.
39 N. J. Frangopulo, 'A story of municipal achievement', in N. J. Frangopulo (ed.), *Rich Inheritance* (Manchester: Manchester Education Committee, 1962), p. 62.
40 Briggs, *History of Birmingham*, vol. 2, pp. 144–5.
41 A. Alexander, *Borough Government and Politics: Reading 1835–1985* (London: George Allen & Unwin, 1985), pp. 90–130.
42 Briggs, *Victorian Cities*, pp. 248, 253.
43 40 & 41 Vict., c. 69.
44 Waller, *Town, City and Nation*, p. 243.
45 The Municipal Corporations (Consolidation) Act, 1882: 45 & 46 Vict., c. 50.
46 Waller, *Town, City and Nation*, p. 246; C. Oakes, *Wright and Hobhouse on Local Government and Local Taxation in England and Wales* (London: Sweet & Maxwell, 6th edn, 1928).
47 W. E. Whyte, *Local Government in Scotland* (Edinburgh: William Hodge, 1925), pp. 17, 19.
48 J. Kellas, *Modern Scotland* (London: Pall Mall Press, 1968), p. 158.
49 Maver, *Glasgow*, pp. 99, 156.
50 T. I. Williams, *A History of the British Gas Industry* (Oxford: Oxford University Press, 1981), p. 27.
51 *Ibid.*, p. 28.
52 P. T. Marsh, *Joseph Chamberlain: Entrepreneur in Politics* (New Haven, CT: Yale University Press, 1994), p. 75.
53 *Ibid.*; R. Jay, *Joseph Chamberlain: A Political Study* (Oxford: Oxford University Press, 1981), pp. 22–8, provides a succinct account of his municipal service.

54 Chamberlain Papers, JC5/16/55, Chamberlain to Collings, 30 June 1876.
55 Bunce, *History of the Corporation of Birmingham*, vol. 2, p. 568; he resigned as an alderman on being asked to join Gladstone's Cabinet: Chamberlain Papers, JC6/1/94, Chamberlain to Harris, 6 May 1880.
56 Briggs, *Victorian Cities*, p. 188.
57 B. J. Bradbury, *History of Cockermouth* (Workington: Richard Byers, 1995), p. 100.
58 B. J. O'Neill, 'The development of the electricity supply industry in north west Kent 1882–1914', *Local Historian*, 30:2 (2000), pp. 165–77.
59 L. Hannah, *Electricity Before Nationalisation: A Study of the Electricty Supply Industry in Britain to 1948* (London: Macmillan, 1979), pp. 5–6.
60 *Ibid.*, p. 8.
61 H. Finer, *Municipal Trading* (London: George Allen & Unwin, 1941), pp. 51–3.
62 Anon, 'Municipal reform, as required for the metropolis', *Westminster Review*, 25 (Jan.–July 1836), pp. 71–103.
63 J. T. Smith, *The Metropolis and its Municipal Administration* (London: Trelawny Saunders, 1852).
64 J. Davis, *Reforming London: The London Government Problem 1855–1900* (Oxford: Oxford University Press, 1998).
65 Finer, *Life and Times of Sir Edwin Chadwick*, pp. 314–18.
66 *Ibid.*, pp. 322–31.
67 D. Sunderland, 'A monument to defective administration? The London Commission of Sewers in the early nineteenth century', *Urban History*, 26:3 (1999), pp. 349–72.
68 F. Sheppard, *The Infernal Wen: London 1808–1870* (London: Secker & Warburg, 1971), p. 267.
69 Finer, *Life and Times of Sir Edwin Chadwick*, pp. 326–31.
70 W. A. Robson, *The Government and Misgovernment of London* (London: George Allen & Unwin, 1939), p. 56.
71 Sheppard, *Infernal Wen*, p. 278.
72 Robson, *The Government and Misgovernment of London*, pp. 57–61.
73 The Metropolis Local Management Act 1855: 18 & 19 Vict, c. 120; Davies, *Reforming London*, p. 12.
74 Finer, *Life and Times of Edwin Chadwick*, pp. 421–9.
75 Robson, *Government and Misgovernment of London*, p. 60.
76 Davis, *Reforming London*, pp. 12–13.
77 Often the dark and unsanitary habitation of the most poor in the cities.
78 Lambert, *Sir John Simon 1816–1904*, p. 225.
79 Disraeli Papers, Box 53, fos 5–90.
80 D. Owen, *The Government of Victorian London 1855–1889* (Cambridge, MA: Harvard University Press, 1982), pp. 47–73; the cost of the scheme eventually exceeded £4 million.
81 Robson, *Government and Misgovernment of London*, p. 76.
82 A. M. McBriar, *Fabian Socialism and English Politics 1884–1918* (Cambridge: Cambridge University Press, 1966), p. 189.
83 Disraeli Papers, Box 98/3, fo. 5, 16 Dec. 1866.
84 McBriar, *Fabian Socialism and English Politics 1884–1918*, p. 189.
85 Davis, *Reforming London*, pp. 74–95.

86 D. Kynaston, *The City of London*, vol. 1: *A World of its Own 1815–1890* (London: Chatto & Windus, 1994), pp. 370–1.
87 Robson, *Government and Misgovernment of London*, p. 77.
88 *Ibid.*, pp. 74–6.
89 Kynaston, *City of London*, vol. 1, p. 22.
90 Report of the Select Committee on London Corporation (Charges of Malversion) 1887; Owen, *Government of Victorian London*, pp. 204–5.
91 White, *History of Liverpool Corporation*, p. 91.
92 He was Mayor from November 1873 until June 1876, when he was elected an MP for Birmingham: Bunce, *History of the Birmingham Corporation*, vol. 2, pp. 567–8.
93 Mayor from 1851 to 1854; A. Elliott, 'Municipal government in Bradford in the mid-mineteenth century', in D. Fraser (ed.), *Municipal Reform and the Industrial City* (Leicester: Leicester University Press, 1982), p. 140.
94 Waller, *Town City and Nation*, p. 283.
95 Lambert, *Sir John Simon 1816–1904*, pp. 109–10.
96 *Ibid.*, p. 109.
97 White, *History of the Corporation of Liverpool 1835–1914*, p. 43.
98 Bunce, *History of the Corporation of Birmingham*, vol. 2, p. 520.
99 Briggs, *History of Birmingham*, vol. 2, p. 125.
100 Bunce, *History of the Corporation of Birmingham*, vol. 2, p. 520.
101 White, *History of the Corporation of Liverpool 1835–1914*, p. 96.
102 Minutes of Workington Borough Council, Dec. 1893, p. 166.
103 Bunce, *History of the Corporation of Birmingham*, vol. 2, p. 78.
104 A. Spoor, *White-Collar Union: 60 Years of NALGO* (London: Heinemann, 1967), pp. 4–8.
105 Spoor, *ibid.*, p. 8, reports that George Bernard Shaw when a member of the St Pancras Vestry discovered the appointment of an illiterate clerk and was opposed by staff when he insisted on introducing some form of examination to recruit staff.
106 Spoor, *White-Collar Union: 60 Years of NALGO*.
107 M. Laffin, *Managing Under Pressure: Industrial Relations in Local Government* (Basingstoke: Macmillan, 1989), pp. 48–9.
108 A. Marsh, *Directory of Trade Unions* (Aldershot: Gower, 5th edn, 1991), p. 336.
109 Laffin, *Managing Under Pressure*, p. 48.
110 The Municipal Franchise Act 1867: 32 & 33 Vict., c. 55.
111 P. Hollis, *Ladies Elect: Women in English Local Government 1865–1914* (Oxford: Oxford University Press, 1987), p. 31; Keith-Lucas, *The English Local Government Franchise*, p. 166.
112 Hollis, *Ladies Elect*, p. 306.
113 Hennock, *Fit and Proper Persons*, pp. 131–8.
114 H. J. Hanham, *Elections and Party Management* (London: Longmans, 1959), pp. 125–54.
115 This concern is a central issue in R. V. Clements, *Local Notables and the City Council* (London: Macmillan, 1969).
116 Hennock, *Fit and Proper Persons*, pp. 34, 44.
117 H. Mathers, 'Sheffield municipal politics 1893–1926: parties, personalities and the rise of Labour', Ph.D thesis, University of Sheffield, 1979.

118 Data from J. Lloyd, *London Municipal Government: History of a Great Reform 1880–1888* (London: P. S. King, 1910), p. 69; see also a rather different but complementary occupational classification in G. Clifton, 'Members and officers of the LCC, 1889–1965', in A. Saint (ed.), *Politics and the People of London* (London: Hambledon Press, 1989), p. 6.
119 Cowns & Gray Ltd, *The Lords Provosts of Glasgow 1833–1902* (Glasgow: Cowans & Gray, 1902).
120 See for example J. Garrard, *Leadership and Power in Victorian Industrial Towns* (Manchester: Manchester University Press, 1983), pp. 13–35, for data on the dominance of manufacturers and business interests on Rochdale, Salford and Bolton town councils.
121 A. H. Birch, *Small Town Politics* (Oxford: Oxford University Press, 1959) p. 34.
122 G. Blaxland, *J. H. Thomas: A Life for Unity* (London: Fredrick Muller, 1964), p. 37.
123 Hennock, *Fit and Proper Persons*, pp. 225–7.
124 L. Lowell, *The Government of England*, vol. 1 (London: Macmillan, 1910), pp. 501–34.
125 See for example *ibid.*, p. 552 for a near-contemporary account; or R. T. McKenzie, *British Political Parties: The Distribution of Power within the Conservative and Labour Parties* (London: Mercury, 2nd edn, 1963), p. 7; or A. Ball, *British Political Parties: The Emergence of a Modern Party System* (Basingstoke: Macmillan, 1987), p. 38.
126 M. Duverger, 1964, *Political Parties* (London: Methuen, 1964).
127 N. Murrell Martin, *Joseph Chamberlain: The Man and the Statesman* (London: Hutchinson, 1900), pp. 95–6.
128 Briggs, *Victorian Cities*; Hennock, *Fit and Proper Persons*; Hunt, *Building Jerusalem*.
129 W. Wright, *The Life of George Dawson* (Birmingham: Percival Jones, 1905), p. 122.
130 *Ibid.*, p. 151.
131 Hennock, *Fit and Proper Persons*, pp. 61–79, 154–69.
132 For example H. H. Fowler in the First Reading of the 'Parish Councils' Bill: Hansard, vol. 10, col. 702, 1893.
133 M. Castells, *The Urban Question* (London: Edward Arnold, 1977).
134 P. Dunleavy, *Urban Political Analysis* (Basingstoke: Macmillan, 1980).
135 P. Saunders, *Social Theory and the Urban Question* (London: Hutchinson, 1981).
136 Chamberlain Papers, JC4/1, fo. 41, Speech by Chamberlain in Stroud, 26 March 1872.
137 H. Keeble Hawson, *Sheffield: The Growth of a City 1893–1926* (Sheffield: J. W. Northend, 1968), pp. 186–93.
138 Barber, 'Sheffield Borough Council 1843–1893', p. 48.

5

Restructuring local government

Few across the British political spectrum were satisfied with the evolution of the local government system following the 1832 Reform Act. While municipal government could lead the way to reform, the system could not evolve in rural areas because of the lack of any workable consensus in Parliament that could establish multi-purpose local government structures. The legislative compromises and resultant ad hoc developments were creating as complex a pattern of local government in rural areas and small towns as existed in the eighteenth century. During the last third of the nineteenth century the political factors standing in the way of a consensus to remodel local government declined in their potency. The engine driving change was the growing consensus between Conservatives, Liberals and radicals. Disraeli and Derby's 'great leap in the dark'[1] that widened the franchise in 1867 demonstrated that working men would in large numbers continue to support the established parties and political order. It was, therefore, possible to widen the franchise for local government in rural areas, put county government on an elected basis and hence end the need for ad hoc governance without greatly damaging the Tory cause.

The creation of county councils

Prior to 1832 most radicals wanted to replace the administrative powers of the magistrates with elected councillors[2] and had chipped away at some of the powers of JPs. Acts in 1828 and 1830 had deprived magistrates of much of their powers over licensing public houses;[3] they ceased to inspect factories in 1830 and by 1835 the prisons were subject to Home Office guidance.[4] Select Committees to inquire into the finance of county government were established in 1834 in both the Lords and the Commons; but, while the Lords predictably sought alleviation only of the cost of assize and quarter-session judicial costs,[5] the Commons suggested a Royal Commission. This was established the following year and reported in 1836.[6] The Commission had none of the reformist zeal of the parallel study of municipalities but went beyond its initial brief on finance to recommend that councils be established to deal with county finance although much of the decision-making power of the county would remain in the hands of the magistrates.[7] This proposal was a watered-down version of an idea put to the Commission by the Scottish radical MP Joseph Hume, a man much driven to seek economies in public administration, to create county boards elected by ratepayers to deal with county finance that would elect a small board to undertake on a more frequent basis the administrative tasks of the JPs.[8] The proposals were not accepted, but Hume pressed ahead with his ideas, sponsoring Bills in 1836 and 1837. He gained some support from Lord John Russell, but the reforms were wholly unacceptable to landowners in the Lords and the Commons. The issue remained on the agenda for radical reformers but gained no sponsorship in Parliament until 1848 when a meeting of Lancashire Guardians, alarmed at the rising Poor Law rate, pressed for change in county finances which would allow them a share in county government with the JPs. The initiative gained widespread national support and the ageing Joseph Hume was recruited to present a Bill to support their ideas.[9] The attempt made no progress but the Guardians persisted with the campaign, with unsuccessful Bills in 1851 and 1852.[10] The issue was also pursued by Liberal backbenchers in 1868.[11]

By the 1860s Tory squires were increasingly finding themselves in a cleft stick on the issue of county finance and control of the county. Through the Local Taxation Committee led by Massey Lopes they demanded some alleviation of the cost of county administration that fell predominantly on landed property and, therefore, their estates, but they faced predominantly Liberal Parliaments that were unlikely to lessen the landowners' financial burden without also demanding a reciprocal diminution in their control over the county. Goschen, in his ambitious proposals for local government reform in Gladstone's 1868 Cabinet, attempted to create boards to govern the counties, composed of chairs of elected parish councils who would be selected from among themselves and would be balanced by an equal number of JPs. Goschen also proposed the creation of urban and rural sanitary districts. The ideas generated strong opposition in Parliament and had to be abandoned.[12] The Conservative Government of 1874–80 was too dependent on the support in Parliament of county landowners to risk changes to the power of the JPs. Disraeli showed little interest in the subject. Sclater-Booth, President of the Local Government Board,[13] informed Disraeli in 1876: 'I am proposing to do nothing in the way of improvement or simplification of local government so that we should show as much activity as possible in the direction of sanitary reform.'[14] Massey Lopes gave Disraeli fulsome support for his efforts of behalf of the rate-paying landowner.[15] It required a new government to stimulate change.

In the longer term it was becoming increasingly difficult for the Tory squires and the Lords to resist some reform of rural government. After 1867, with the national franchise extending to urban householders, the unelected counties were even more at variance with democratic trends. Gladstone announced his intention to restructure local government in the Queen's Speech of 1882 on the advice of the President of the LGB, J. G. Dodson, for a local measure to parallel more extensive national electoral reform. Dodson was concerned to placate the opposition and initially proposed that a third of county councillors be magistrates, but he later abandoned the idea and settled for an authority that was fully elected by those eligible to vote for Poor Law guardians.[16] The Bill was, however, shelved to make way for electoral reform, as it was thought important to change the franchise before embarking on restructuring local government. Following the 1884 Electoral Reform Act, which gave all male household-ers in rural areas a vote in parliamentary elections, it was clearly insup-portable to retain county administration in the hands of appointed local worthies. Sir Charles Dilke, who had replaced Dodson, with the support of a Cabinet Committee drafted a Bill which would have created county councils to take over the powers of the Poor Law unions, the rural police and the administrative duties of the quarter sessions. It also proposed a lower tier of district councils. Dilke laid much emphasis on devolving to the counties many of the powers of surveillance over parishes held by the LGB.[17] There was, however, considerable division in the committee on the exact powers of the county councils, and the pressing demands of the Irish problem led to the postponement of legislation on the issue. The ideas were put in abeyance by the fall of the Liberals in January 1885, but they were briefly revived when the party returned for a further twelve months in office the following year. Joseph Chamberlain as President of Poor Law Board was able to continue refining Dilke's radical proposals[18] until the Irish question sent Chamberlain's Unionist faction into coalition with Salisbury's Conservatives and brought to an end Gladstone's administra-tion.

Salisbury was not adverse to further steps towards democracy, realising that 'representative bodies are the fashion of the day'.[19] Charles Ritchie, the President of the Local Government Board, who sponsored the County Council's Bill observed at its first reading: 'The Government of the coun-ties by the Quarter Sessions is undoubtedly an anomaly.'[20] Salisbury had little sympathy for the objections of Conservative squires to the loss of their administrative powers and on several occasions privately disparaged the thick-skinned, parochial-minded rural magistrate.[21] As a Tory grandee Salisbury could view the lesser landowners with a measure of disdain and probably realised they did not represent a force that would secure the future of Conservatism. Salisbury's readiness to pursue a major and controversial reform of county government was also a response to the split in the Liberal ranks. Chamberlain had demanded in his 1885 'unau-thorised radical programme' the creation of wholly elected local authori-ties based on municipalities, townships and districts.[22] If Ireland was to be retained as an integral part of the United Kingdom with the help of former radicals, it was necessary to grant Chamberlain's Unionists concessions on their domestic policy agenda. Chamberlain was in Canada on Board of Trade business during much of the negotiations on the Bill but kept himself informed of progress and conveyed his views to the Prime Minister. Salisbury wrote in February 1888 to Chamberlain:

> We have acceded to your views on the County Government Bill to a great extent, putting aside for the present those subjects where they presented the greatest difficulties. That is to say we have adopted the Borough Constitution and mode of election for the County Council: but have left the control of the Police with the magistrates and have not meddled with the poor law or the function of transferring any part of local taxation directly to the occupier.[23]

Salisbury was prudently removing from the Liberal proposals the issues that would be most objectionable to Conservative landowners. Transfer of Poor Law functions to the elected counties, Salisbury argued, 'seems to me, look at it how you will, rather like leaving the cat in charge of the cream jug'.[24] The Bill, as first put to Parliament, would have created lower tier urban and rural districts in areas not covered by municipalities. These clauses were removed even before the committee stage. The restructured Bill successfully negotiated its Second Reading but in committee was subject to some pruning. The most controversial elements were proposals to give county councillors rather than magistrates the power to grant licences for the sale of alcohol and to require the county to financially compensate innkeepers who forfeited their licence. Popular demonstrations prompted by the highly vocal temperance movements led to amendments retaining these powers in the hands of magistrates. In general, the central compromises on the Bill were conceded in private rather than on the floor of the House through delicate negotiations between Conservatives and Unionists and concessions to local Tory opinion. The complex Bill dominated parliamentary sessions without attracting large numbers of MPs to the debates, and by 13 August it received the Royal Assent.[25]

The 1888 Act broadly established the legal basis and structure of the county councils on the pattern created for the municipal boroughs in 1835. They were legally corporations able to own property and be sued, as if a person. The county councils, like the boroughs, were composed of councillors, elected for 3 years, who themselves would elect a further quarter of the council as aldermen, who held office for 6 years. The election of county councillors was established in a separate County Electors Act[26] that made the qualifications for a county vote the same as for the boroughs, bringing the franchise for local elections more in line with the parliamentary franchise by extending the vote to tenants of rooms or of land valued at £10 or more per year.[27] The counties took over the administrative role of the JPs, which in practice amounted to relatively few functions in comparison with the powers they were to gain in the twentieth century. A list of county functions, as in 1888, in a standard contemporary text on local government makes curious reading. The county

> repairs all main roads and county bridges. It provides, maintains and visits pauper lunatic asylums. It prevents the pollution of rivers; it carries into execution the laws relating to destructive insects and contagious diseases in animals; it protects wild birds and conserves fish ... it registers Dissenting chapels and the rules of various societies ... It regulates all Local Government elections. It pays the salary of the clerks to the justices and the costs of the Assizes and Quarter sessions; it pays half the cost of the clothing and pay of the county police ... It grants licences for music and dancing and racecourses; it insists on the proper use of weights and measures; it protects the purchaser of coal and bread.[28]

The Act provided for the transfer of substantial powers from central government to the counties through statutory orders to appease some doubting Tories. In practice the Local Government Board (LGB) used its powers of delegation only to transfer to counties powers to supervise the actions on specific tasks of districts and parishes.[29] Following the 1835 Municipal Corporations Act, the new counties divided judicial powers from local administration and hence retained the JPs and the quarter-session courts outside the framework of the elected county councils. The police powers of the county were also limited as Conservatives feared their control by popularly elected councils. The composition of police committees was equally apportioned to elected county councillors and to nominees of the quarter sessions, hence JPs.

Proposals for the creation of county councils inevitably raised demands from larger boroughs concerning the retention of their powers and privileges within the framework of the new authorities. Many towns enjoyed the status of being quarter session authorities in their own right which in practice meant they did not contribute rates to the county in which they were situated. From a Unionist point of view there was strong pressure to ensure that most boroughs were not obliged to pay county rates, whereas this was a far more desirable outcome for the predominantly Tory counties. Ritchie thus proposed that only the 10 largest boroughs with populations over 150,000 should be made into county boroughs that would have the powers of both a county and a borough. The concession encountered strong opposition from Liberal MPs representing substantial cities that would be excluded from this arrangement. Opposition was led by the prominent Liberal representative of Wolverhampton, Henry Fowler who was later to sponsor the 1894 Local Government Act. Fowler argued that urban areas which had better standards of services and higher rates were likely to be exploited by the counties and forced to pay an unfair contribution to rural areas. Ritchie, mindful of the support for the boroughs from Chamberlain began making concessions and eventually drew a firm line at 50,000 as the necessary minimum population for county borough status, with the addition of even smaller historic county towns such as

Canterbury. The Act created seventy-two county boroughs[30] which were effectively single-tier unitary authorities and, by so doing, the basis for the twentieth-century conflict between county and borough interests.[31]

The diverse size and complexity of county boundaries created a problem. Several counties were traditionally divided into separate quarter sessions, such as Suffolk or Sussex, others had outlying areas surrounded by other counties, and many boroughs were in two or more counties. It was reported in 1878 that of the 650 Poor Law unions only 343 were wholly contained within a single county or borough.[32] Prior to 1888 a group of MPs had published a series of studies on the issue and unsuccessfully promoted several Bills to resolve the maze of overlapping boundaries between local authorities.[33] In preparation for local government reform, Ritchie established a Boundary Commission in 1887, although it had yet to get off the ground when the 1888 legislation came before Parliament.[34] A simple expedient was adopted to deal with Poor Law unions by placing each one in the county in which the largest element of its population resided and giving powers to the LGB to split unions or amalgamate remnants of a union on the wrong side of a county border with a neighbouring union in that county. The issue of counties with more than one quarter session was subject to resolution, in a piecemeal fashion, during the debates on the 1888 Bill, with some MPs arguing for larger counties on the basis of economy and others demanding recognition of the rights of the quarter session for a specific area. The latter cause won the day, and Suffolk, Yorkshire and Sussex, for example, were divided into separate counties for administrative purposes. When the Boundary Commission eventually reported after the passage of the 1888 Act it was left to the counties to decide how to interpret their recommendations, and in most cases no change occurred. The area of each new county remained, therefore, as varied in population and dimension as it had been constituted prior to the Act.[35]

Tory acquiescence to the 1888 Act was in a large measure due to a resolution of the much contested issue of the burden of the rates on landowners. In exchange for standing for election the squirearchy received from their Conservative Government some relief from paying for county government. Gladstone's Cabinet had in 1881 established an inter-departmental committee to inquire into local government finance which suggested transferring revenue from the carriage tax to local authorities and a proportion of income tax to defray the extra expenditure on roads, as well as a further exchequer grant without attachment to specific revenue sources. The proposal never reached the stage of legislation although the principle of assigning certain taxes to local government remained on the table.[36] A failed local government Bill of 1885 proposed to allocate to local authorities the proceeds from the duty on alcohol and house sales. In 1886 the defection of Chamberlain's Unionists brought into Salisbury's camp the, by now, acknowledged authority on local government finance, George Goschen, who in 1887 became Chancellor of the Exchequer. Goschen firmly supported the idea of assigned revenues by replacing the majority of grants in aid to local governments that had accrued in England, Wales and Scotland with the revenue from excise licences that previously had gone to the Exchequer, in addition to a new tax on horses-and-carts and half of all probate duties. The tax on transport was withdrawn, after much opposition, but the other two taxes were carried and became a principal source of local income.[37] Since the revenue from probate had little connection with the operation of local authorities themselves, the policy was criticised by Redlich and Hirst as just a step away from ensuring that local authorities would be obliged to manage their affairs efficiently by raising their income locally.[38]

The impact of the 1888 Act was in practice undramatic in terms of the control of rural government. The election of a Conservative Government following the 1884 Electoral Reform Act demonstrated to most leading Tories that they could secure popular support in rural local elections. In introducing the 1888 Bill, Ritchie observed, with regard to the status of the country gentleman 'under such a system', that, far from losing out, 'I firmly believe that ... he will preserve that great influence which happily he now possesses'.[39] Ritchie was justified in his assumption. The landowners who had governed through the quarter sessions used their influence in the county party machines to secure their uncontested election to the new county councils. The first elections to counties occasioned some strongly fought contests, but thereafter most seats were secured by the sitting candidate without a vote. In Surrey, for example, 53 per cent of the seats were not contested in 1889, but at the next election, in 1892, 72 per cent were uncontested, and this pattern continued until 1939, when 74 per cent of county seats in Surrey were won without an election being necessary.[40]

Local government in Scotland was restructured in the wake of the English reforms, although the differing structures of the system required separate and far from identical legislation. In 1885 pressure for a measure of independence led to the creation of a Scottish Office and a Minister for Scotland. The Office was allocated to a succession of Scottish aristocrats who developed the role predominantly as an office for co-ordinating elements of local and central administration in the province with the Westminster Government. Prior to the formation of the Scottish Office a number of ad hoc boards had co-ordinated local services, such as the Poor Law or education. These were largely managed by a small number of lawyers with political connections sound enough to ensure their selection through patronage.[41] The Scottish counties were made the central element of the system of rural government in the Local Government (Scotland) Act of 1889. The franchise for the counties created by the Act was similar to those for the English counties, which took over the powers of the commissioners of supply, the county road trustees and many public health powers of the parishes, in addition to the non-judicial functions of the JPs. In advance of English legislation, the Act gave to the Scottish counties the power to create district committees to which could be delegated responsibility for roads and public health.[42] The civil parishes that had been created in 1845 retained only their original Poor Law functions,[43] though under the 1894 Act they were to be governed by an elected parish council rather than part-elected and part-nominated boards which in rural areas were dominated by landowners.[44] Government supervision of the Poor Law was transferred from the Board of Supervision to the LGB for Scotland.[45]

The LCC and the London boroughs

There were, however, serious differences within Salisbury's Government concerning metropolitan reorganisation. Chamberlain's Unionists supported single-tier city governments and hence an inclusive government for London. Salisbury feared a concentration of power in urban centres that might open the way for radical policies and, like the Thatcher Government in 1985, preferred the conurbation to be governed by a number of smaller elected authorities.[46] In 1887 and 1888 two unsuccessful Conservative-sponsored backbench Bills had proposed such an arrangement, which was initially the favoured option of the Government. However, in deference to the Unionists, the Cabinet compromised by proposing a somewhat stronger County Council for London and left to one side the issue of second-tier authorities.[47] Against this background Ritchie took the opportunity of the 1888 Bill to create the LCC which covered the same area and functions of the consequently abolished MBW. Additional powers acquired by the LCC included the appointment of medical officers, responsibility for major roads and controls over disease in farm animals.[48] The Metropolitan Police was retained under Home Office control. The new body was given an ambivalent status in relation to the City of London since the LCC took over the role of the MBW in the 'Square Mile'. The City, nevertheless, continued as a 'non-administrative county' in that it retained the judicial powers of a quarter-sessions county along with its many lower tier local government functions.[49]

Despite its limitations the LCC quickly gained status among metropolitan politicians, attracting substantial politicians from the Right and Left to stand for election in 1889.[50] Liberals, joined by socialist groups, formed the Progressive party to campaign for a more powerful LCC, while Conservatives established themselves as the Moderate party. The Progressives were the more successful, winning 73 seats and a clear majority in the 118 seat LCC[51] and elected as chair Lord Rosebery, former Liberal Home Secretary and future Prime Minister, with Firth as his deputy. The political composition of the LCC confirmed Salisbury's and many Conservatives' suspicions of powerful urban authorities and did nothing to alleviate the Conservative Party's concerns over the independence from central control of democratically elected councils. Conservatives continued to campaign for relatively powerful London boroughs that would be a substantial counterweight to the LCC. The Liberals, therefore, left aside the issue of further reform in the capital when developing the 1894 Act, given that they had no wish to oblige the Conservatives by creating districts that might challenge the LCC. A Royal Commission was established in 1893 to investigate the merger of the LCC and the City of London[52] but the return to power of the Conservatives in 1895 paved the way for a Bill to reconstruct local government in the metropolis in accord with Salisbury's ideas.

In 1899 a London Government Act created twenty-eight metropolitan boroughs within the area of LCC. These boroughs, based on the areas of the larger vestries merged with smaller vestries, took over the responsibilities of those vestries and many ad hoc commissions.[53] The new creations as London boroughs were to have their own elected mayors. Westminster was declared a city and hence had a Lord Mayor, and Kensington was dignified as a Royal Borough. The powers of the London boroughs were substantial and involved public health responsibilities, including drainage into the LCC's main sewers, street maintenance and cleansing, refuse collection, parks, museums, libraries and galleries.[54] No effort was made to establish systems to co-ordinate the often duplicated responsibilities of the London boroughs with those of the LCC. Balfour, in proposing the Bill, made a virtue of this arrangement, stating that any connections would

> inevitably drag those councils into the political vortex in which London County Council appears to flourish ... I look forward to these municipal boroughs having a great and most legitimate influence with the London County Council.[55]

Reconstructing parishes and districts

In his failed 1871 Act Goschen had proposed that the parish should be the cornerstone of the local government system. The creation of parish governments based on the direct democracy of parish meetings had been widely publicised and supported by Toulmin Smith and the Anti-Centralization Union and also gained respect from Conservatives opposed to radically restructuring the Constitution.[56] A further advantage of parish government for some more advanced Liberals was as a means of allowing agricultural labourers to gain some independence and a means of self-development outside of the oppressive controls exerted by landowners. A powerful movement to provide allotments and smallholdings for village labourers took firm root among Liberal Party members. Jesse Collings, an associate of Chamberlain, had convinced Gladstone of the advantages of the compulsory purchase of land to provide smallholdings for agricultural labourers under the slogan of their right to 'two acres and a cow'.[57] The 1887 and 1890 Allotments Acts gave parishes the power to purchase land to provide smallholdings.[58]

Restructuring parish government as a cornerstone of the sub-county system of local government was not a policy favoured by modernists, who regarded the units as being too small to have significant powers. Added to this view was the Tory landowner's fear that a Liberal Government may pass power to a democratic parish in which landless labourers would spend lavishly on poor relief and local services at the expense of the propertied rate-payer. There was, therefore, a strong cross-party coalition opposed to the significant strengthening of parish government. An influential study of local government authored jointly by a Tory and a Liberal MP excluded the parish as the lower tier authority as parishes were too variable in size and unlikely to attract able officers.[59] Supporters of larger district councils still had to decide whether the unit should be based on Poor Law unions, health districts or even the highways authorities. As the Poor Law unions administered a generally unpopular function, the Health Boards carried more favour with modernisers and were the units favoured in the abandoned clauses to establish district authorities in the 1888 Local Government Act.[60]

After 1888 Salisbury's Government continued to develop legislation to reform sub-county government,[61] but it was Gladstone's Government of 1892 with Sir Henry Fowler as President of the LGB that picked up much of the work of its predecessor and by 1893 published a Local Government Bill that was not dissimilar to the proposals for district councils in the 1888 Act. There was substantial cross-party agreement among Conservative and Liberal leaders on the issue. Chamberlain, now a Conservative, secretly wrote to Fowler offering his good offices to promote the main elements of the Bill.[62] Although the Bill created elected district councils within each county, it was, nevertheless, widely presented as restructuring parishes and came to be popularly known at the time as the Parish Councils Bill. The Act democratised parishes by removing select vestries, but at the same time required all parishes with more than 300 inhabitants to elect a council to manage its tasks. Villagers could attend and speak only at an annual meeting. Only the smallest parishes were to be governed by the direct democracy of a meeting attended by all parishioners. The role of the parishes was also fortified by retaining legislation in the 1887 and 1890 Allotments Acts that allowed parishes to compulsorily purchase land for allotments and smallholdings, subject to final appeal to the LGB.[63]

Although some contemporary commentators considered that by reconstituting parish government local people in rural areas would use their powers to 'change the face of rural England',[64] the Act provided few executive powers. Parishes could own property, establish allotments, consent to the opening and closing of rights of way, repair footpaths and create and care for recreation grounds, but they had limited resources for achieving such ends and could raise no more than sixpence in the pound as a rate. At best the parish could act as a pressure group for the interests of its area, but any substantive powers that it was originally given to deal with insanitary or obstructive buildings and, later, to comment on building plans were subject to district or county approval. Many supporters of the Bill and possibly even Gladstone may not have thought that the Act would marginalise the parish, but few probably looked closely at the implications of their restricted powers as compared to those of the districts. Among backbenchers the possibility of ineffectual parishes was not a major issue in parliamentary debates, with the exception of concerns over the proper body to deal with church endowments and charities.[65]

The 1894 Act created effective multi-purpose local authorities below the level of the county by transferring the powers of the ad hoc health and highways boards to the districts. The new county districts, as the authorities were collectively called following the pattern established for the Health Boards in 1872, were divided into urban and rural districts. The urban districts were generally small towns of varying size, with the smallest having a population of only 219, while the largest, Wallasey, had 53,500 inhabitants.[66] The rural districts tended to have fewer powers, although many were more populous than the urban districts. Both absorbed the powers of the health districts but urban, rather than rural, districts had control over street lighting, public baths and recreation areas, which were reserved for parishes in rural areas.[67] Councillors were elected to district councils for three-year terms, with one third of a council standing each year in which an election was to be held. The 1894 Act still left the boards of Poor Law guardians and of Education as separate ad hoc authorities, although steps were being taken in the 1894 Act to incorporate the former by ensuring that the electorate and electoral divisions for parishes were the same as those for the Guardians.

Education

The creation of elected county and district authorities and the restructuring of London government removed any misgivings on the part of Liberals that had held back the allocation of new social services to multi-purpose local authorities as opposed to elected ad hoc agencies. The opportunity to use the newly formed county councils to administer education was grasped in Wales, in 1889, following the recommendations of Lord Aberdare's Committee's[68] review of secondary education in the Principality. The Act entrusted secondary education in Wales to joint authorities of the county councils and boroughs. This was not such a simple political proposition for England where the Anglican and Roman Catholic Churches were reluctant to relinquish their role through their domination of charitably aided grammar schools, even though they found it increasingly difficult to sustain such schools financially.

Liberal nonconformists were by no means happy with Anglican dominance over secondary education. Fiscal and sectarian stress led in 1894 to the creation of a Royal Commission under the chairmanship of Viscount Bryce that led in 1899 to the formation of the Board of Education as a department of State. The Commission also recommended the adoption by England of the Welsh system for post-compulsory school-age education[69] by giving the county councils responsibility for this sector although it was assumed that for elementary education the School Boards would remain.[70] An attempt in 1896 to introduce an Act that would give county councils the responsibility for both elementary and secondary education failed to pass, due to hostility among Liberals to the possibility that church schools would be funded by rate-payers.[71] A further crisis beset the Education Board in 1898 when an auditor's opinion, upheld by the courts, ruled that local education boards should not fund secondary education. The issue was resolved by the Conservative Government in 1902 with Balfour's Education Act that abolished the ad hoc education boards and transferred their function, plus the responsibility for secondary education, to local authorities.[72] Counties and county boroughs were given responsibility for secondary education, although boroughs with a population exceeding 10,000 and urban districts with over 20,000 inhabitants could seek responsibility for elementary schools. Local authorities were given responsibility for funding the running costs of church-aided voluntary schools although the premises of the schools would be maintained out of church funds. Policy-making and supervision of the schools' systems were vested in education committees of the local authority which could also co-opt a minority of non-councillors to their ranks.[73]

In England and Wales only the Poor Law unions remained as a significant single-purpose agency for local governance. The Balfour Act generated intense opposition especially from non-conformist churches in Wales. Dissenting churches resented the idea that rate-payers should fund Anglican and Catholic Church schools and a number of Welsh counties attempted to defy the legislation by refusing to fund church-sponsored schools. They found a resolute champion in the rising star of New Liberalist David Lloyd George. The Conservative Government in 1904 neutralised the threat of non-compliance through an Act which gave the Government powers to fund the aided schools directly, should the local authorities default on their payments, and then reduce the grant allocation for education to the local authorities by the necessary sum.[74] The Government's success in undermining efforts by the new local authorities to refuse central legislation was a precursor of further conflicts in the new century.[75]

Scotland was not included in the 1902 Act and retained a system of School Boards until 1918 when an Act restructured the boards into education authorities which covered the four major cities, legally referred to as the scheduled burghs of Glasgow, Edinburgh, Aberdeen and Dundee, and each of the counties. The authorities were not, however, incorporated, as in England and Wales, into the burghs and counties but remained separately elected organisations with their own members and officers.[76]

Central–local relations and the new structures

Despite pressures to fund the increasing powers given to local authorities, most leading politicians in the Conservative and Liberal Parties still did not believe that they should interfere closely with the activities of local government. Palmerston observed in the debate on the 1854 Police Act that he

> attached great importance to the principle of local self-government. He thought it quite impossible to overrate the great national importance of employing the persons connected with the different districts of the country in administering the officers of those districts so far as it was possible to do so. He should be sorry on that ground to place the police of the country under a separate government and control like that of London.[77]

Gladstone, following Palmerston's view, instructed Local Government Board President Dodson, as he grappled in 1882 with framing a County Councils Bill,

> that your measure, with which I hope your name will be honourably associated, should not only be a great Local Government Bill, but a great decentralisation Bill: that to the utmost possible extent administration by the local authority, subject to fixed rules and conditions, of money raised for it by the Imperial authority, and handed over to it subject to those rules and conditions, should be the principle of our local expenditure and should replace the principle of administration from the Centre which has of late been forcing itself into our system. Also that the rules and conditions should be carefully revised and not as such some absurd rules under which we now bribe the local authority to keep more police than it wants.[78]

John Morley, Gladstone's official biographer, argued in a series of articles in *The Times* in 1889 that decisions on social matters should be devolved to municipal government since local people would be best able to judge and take a discerning interest in the reforms necessary for their own communities.[79] Conservatives demonstrated even less enthusiasm for local government restructuring, especially during Disraeli's tenure as leader, as indicated by his Government's lack of response to pressures for county reform. In as much as politicians held the view that local issues were best left to local political elites, the civil servants who had secured positions for much of the nineeenth century, largely through their patronage, also held such a position. Within the LGB the compromises made by officials over the implementation of the Poor Law had set the dominant ethos within the department, despite the protestations of more centralising public health reformers such as Sir John Simon.[80]

Support among Conservatives and Gladstonian Liberals for a dual polity did not, however, entail, as discussed earlier, that local government was in a position to pursue wholly separate interests from those of the centre. The arrangement continued to be based on the assumption that political figures elected to the leadership of local authorities would be of the same classes of landowner or capitalist as was the membership of Parliament. Local leaders could, therefore, be trusted to pursue policies that would not be radically opposed to central values, as they were closely networked into the values of the ruling elites. The safeguards to secure this arrangement continued within the newly restructured system. The extension of local powers, like the municipalisation of essential services such as gas and electricity, was still refined through the procedures used to secure private acts. The Conservatives, once they were assured that the leaders of the elected county councils would still be predominantly country gentlemen, could in 1903 extend the power to seek private acts to the counties.[81] Underlying these values was the assurance, still very evident in electoral returns, that the franchise would continue to return to the leading positions in local authorities either substantial businessmen and professionals in the towns or the county gentry in rural Britain. Nevertheless, by the late nineeenth century a pattern was emerging of innovations by a few advanced local authorities in social developments such as health care or education that were adopted by the majority of more penny-pinching towns or districts only after central government had taken up the local initiative and encouraged others to engage with change. The emerging generation of Liberals, however, had a concern to compel rather than to encourage reform.

Resetting the consensus on central–local relations

Although in the final years of the nineeenth century the dual polity, like the landowner and the country house staffed by innumerable servants, retained ascendancy, socio-economic developments and resultant intellectual pressures were undermining this framework. Politically, democratisation had an important impact by removing the ties that bound elite political families to local government in order to secure power at national level through the purchase of safe seats in the Commons. The Reform Acts of 1867 and 1884, the secret ballot introduced in 1872 for both national and municipal elections, and the Municipal Elections (Corrupt and Illegal Practices) Act of 1884 laid to rest the system of rotten boroughs and any desire on the part of wealthy politicians to protect closed corporations to secure their position in Parliament. The rural conservatism of Cobbett, who had seen individual freedom largely in terms of a rural society tied to corrupt landowners, was becoming increasingly unintelligible in an industrialising society. Democratisation in national and local government also undermined a major plank of radical populists such as Toulmin Smith by removing their argument that the open vestry was the only truly democratic form of government. Smith died in 1869 and the pressure groups he had created to sustain the idea of the open vestry died with him.

The emergence of a professional Civil Service and powerful representative interest groups was also insidiously transforming the operation of government from an elitist structure in which decision-making involved bargaining among members of the landed elite to a pluralist structure in which the Government and civil servants resolved much of their business through consultation with the middle-class representatives of professional groups and associations. The rationalisation of local government began to create common interests among local authorities and the professional officers who were being consolidated in national representative bodies. In Scotland the royal burghs had established a representative body as early as the sixteenth century.[82] A rather gentlemanly representative group for JPs involved with county government had been established as early as 1810 to ensure that they were consulted on the development of new roles for the counties.[83] English local authorities began forming corporate bodies to determine their collective interests with the inauguration in 1873 of an Association of Municipal Corporations to represent the post-1835 borough councils. The need for collective action was stimulated the previous year by parliamentary amendments to a Private Bill sponsored by Sheffield Town Council which would have seriously undermined the capacity of local authorities to take over private companies.[84] Concern over the implications of the proposal was taken further by the town clerks of Nottingham and Manchester who convened a meeting of borough representatives to create the Association and also appeal, successfully, to Gladstone to ensure the defeat of the offending amended Bill.[85] Following the 1888 Act the County Councils' Association (CCA) was established on the foundations of the Society for the Clerks of the Peace.[86]

The development of associations for the urban and rural districts, which followed immediately afterwards, had been preceded for the urban areas by a Local Boards' Association, formed in 1890. Parish councils did not, however, form an association until 1947.[87] Local government professionals paralleled these developments with their own associations. The Institution of Municipal Engineers was founded in 1873 and a Sanitary Inspectors' Association in 1883. The predecessor of the Chartered Institute of Public Finance and Accountancy emerged in 1885.[88] In most cases the new professional organisations for local government officers were expected to work alongside a wider professional body for their particular craft and hence most professionals in local government were members of at least two professional bodies. Medical officers of health were, for example, likely to be members of the British Medical Association and the Sanitary Inspectors' Association.[89] These associations were able to command a measure of respect from the Civil Service and came to be seen as the representative voice of the practitioners in those technical fields.

As economic and political change diminished demands for a highly decentralised system of local government, liberal intellectual opinion, which influenced both radical politicians and ambitious young civil servants, was emerging as a powerful body of opinion, arguing that local government could not be left entirely to its own devices. At one level liberal and radical pressure for greater control was driven by common-sense practicalities. Scientific and technological developments ensured better public health, fuel supplies and transport but these advances could be achieved only by technically educated professionals who increasingly argued that these resources required economies of scale that were out of the reach of small, poorly staffed units of local administration. Both Chadwick and Sir John Simon were concerned to centralise service standards in relation to health care as much from an interest in effective application of new technologies as from any deep-seated ideological concern for personal freedom. The logic of their arguments could influence practically minded government ministers. Sir Benjamin Hall, for example, appointed President of the Board of Health in 1852, had previously been an outspoken critic of Chadwick and had opposed any move to lessen the independence of local vestries but, when faced with the problem of cholera epidemics and the recalcitrance of many boards of guardians, was soon obliged to use the coercive powers available to him within sanitary legislation rather than rely on the voluntary adoption of sanitary powers.[90]

Intellectually, concern to secure professionally led social and economic improvement within a democratic framework stimulated the publication in 1861 of Mill's *Essay on Representative Government* whose chapter on local government remains applicable in Britain in the early twenty-first century. A major difference between a champion of decentralisation like Toulmin Smith and Mill concerned the approach of each to human nature. Smith based his ideas on a romantic notion that individuals could work together in harmony to resolve their common problems and that each individual could add to the common stock of wisdom. Mill, in contrast, while fully aware that autocracy could never provide stable or benign government, believed that only a few well-educated individuals could develop strong principles on which to base a progressive and harmonious society. Mill was influenced by a fear that stalked the corridors of Whitehall and Westminster that, as the franchise was tentatively but progressively widened, Britain would fall under the tyranny of an uneducated and prejudiced majority.[91] Self-government was for Mill of importance as a means of securing civic education and the development of a society that could provide able leaders and understanding subjects. Local government also served as the means for ensuring practical political experience for local leaders who may reach the more advanced heights of national politics.

Executive government must, however, be controlled by a small elite since effective political decisions could no more be made by popular committees than could decisions be made on a battlefield without power having been allocated to an officer in command.[92] Accountability of government must also be confined to a Parliament of the most able and principled minds in society. Thus, Mill proposed that liberal democracy should be limited to ensuring that the less educated masses would periodically select their betters to a representative assembly that would in turn appoint an elite executive government to devise policy for their approval and secure its execution. For such a system to work, like Disraeli and Lord Derby he saw the working-class deferent voter who could ensure a principled Parliament of intellectuals 'as the sculptor saw an angel imprisoned in a block of marble'.[93] Applying this broader view to local government, Mill could not accept populist local government based on the idea of an open vestry. Although well aware, through his reading of De Tocqueville, of New England township open governments, he dismissed such structures as 'primitive governments' and as an emanation from 'special circumstances',[94] and advocated, largely for the reasons he developed in relation to the national Parliament, the creation of representative local governing bodies. Mill, however, considered a more restricted local franchise and the retention of plurality voting on the grounds that as

> the principal duty of local bodies consists of the imposition and expenditure of local taxation, the electoral franchise should vest in all who contribute to the local rates, to the exclusion of all who do not ... there is more justice as well as policy in allowing a greater proportional influence to those who have a larger money interest at stake.[95]

The parish, if based on a small village, was not an ideal unit for local government since it would likely be too small to include people of sufficient ability to form a competent executive:

> Such small places have rarely a sufficient public to furnish a tolerable municipal council; if they contain any talent or knowledge applicable to public business, it is apt to be concentrated in some one man, who thereby becomes the dominator of the place.[96]

Anticipating the later development of local government, Mill argued for multi-purpose local authorities based on towns or elected county councils.[97]

The role of local government within the national political system similarly followed the elitist view that only a few were sufficiently educated to be capable of effectively leading government. Following Bentham, Parliament should be sovereign in relation to local government as the institution would be more likely to include individuals with the education and ability to frame the basic principles that should govern society and these should be accepted by the lesser folk who may control a local authority. Local policy-makers could, however, be superior to central government in their knowledge of their local area and hence an important value of a local authority was to apply central principles to the peculiar circumstances of a specific community. Through such delegation of power the local authority would have an important role in removing minor issues of local concern from the extensive work load of the centre. Mill argued:

> The authority which is most conversant with principles should be supreme over principles, whilst that which is most competent in details should have details left to it. The principal business of the central authority should be to give instruction, of the local authority to apply it.[98]

Mill's views on local government, as laid down in the 1860s, may not have influenced all politicians of his day, but they are at least prophetic in that they came to describe many aspects of the current structure and attitudes to local government that persist into the twenty-first century. Local authorities are multi-purpose, governed by elected representative bodies to be led by small executives and are constitutionally subservient to central inspection and control. They are, moreover, to be viewed as organisations of capabilities inferior to those of central government and as such are more likely to be subject to indifference, if not condescension. These attitudes in the late nineeenth century paved the way for larger, more professional, local authorities and in the twentieth century they gradually gnawed away at the integrity and independence of the system.

Intellectually, as the nineeenth merged into the twentieth century, liberalism was such a broad church that it encompassed a wide range of views on the status of local government. At one extreme Spencer's Darwinian enthusiasm for the survival of the fittest gave no scope to either national or local social-welfare initiatives. More attuned to the practical and altruistic inclinations of reform minded politicians were the values that came to be known as 'New Liberalism' which derived from the writings of Thomas Hill Green and David Ritchie who were attempting to reconcile individualist utilitarian thought with the collectivism of Rousseau, Kant and Hegel. While individuals should be free, and indeed have a duty, to develop their potential through their own responsible actions, it was the duty of the State to provide services to enable each individual to maximise her or his potential in a competitive society. Green was most interested in promoting State education in practical terms as the means to secure State support to enable equality of opportunity, but even though he stood for election as an Oxford town councillor there is little guidance in his principal writings on the role of specific agencies of State in securing this aim.[99] He argued that elementary education should be available at no cost, but paid for by both the Exchequer and the rate-payer, while the availability of secondary education could be widened under the existing system of endowments, scholarships and fees without extensive public involvement.[100] On the drink trade, however, Green did argue that local rate-payers ought to have the power to license public houses.[101]

The more Hegelian followers of T. H. Green, such as Bernard Bosanquet, saw the State as the expression of the general will of its citizens, and to the extent that the town or district expressed such a purpose for the neighbourhood it was therefore one of the most politically important relationships affecting citizens.[102] These liberal idealists could find common cause with the earlier enthusiasm for civic virtue as expressed by the Birmingham preachers Dawson and Dale, even though the implications of Boasanquet's ideas, just as much as Bentham's suggested that where conflict occurred the locality must give way to the State.[103] Unlike the philosophical radicals, the liberal idealists found little place for individual freedom and as such did not recommend themselves to the politicians who sought to implement New Liberal values. Mill's concern for individual liberty and Green's belief that the State should facilitate equal opportunity were to provide, therefore, the mainstream of reformist values in the early twentieth century. New Liberal ideas were further developed by later theorists L. T. Hobhouse and J. A. Hobson whose writings demonstrate little interest in local government as an institution worth considering as a means of delivering a welfare state. While they strongly argued for much greater levels of State intervention to alleviate poverty than would have been acceptable even to Green, they did little to specify how those services should be delivered. The politicians who were to put their values into practice thus began a process that provided a measure of equality of opportunity through a centralising State rather than local authorities.

Notes

1 Lord Derby in the Third Reading of the 1867 Reform Bill: Hansard, vol. 952, col. 952, 6 Aug. 1867.
2 Webb and Webb, *The Parish and the County*, p. 557.
3 This move was in response to concern from radicals that JPs were interfering in free trade in relations to sales of beer: S. Webb and B. Webb, *The History of Liquor Licensing in England principally from 1700 to 1830* (London: Frank Cass, 1963).
4 S. Webb and B. Webb, *English Prisons Under Local Government*, pp. 111–12.
5 The Government accepted this recommendation in 1834 and transferred part of these costs to the Exchequer.
6 Keith-Lucas, *English Local Government Franchise*, p. 94.
7 There were four members of the Commission, one of whom was also on the Municipal Corporations Committee, while the others were respected but not particularly radical lawyers.
8 Keith-Lucas, *English Local Government Franchise*, p. 95.
9 J. Prest, *Liberty and Locality* (Oxford: Oxford University Press, 1990), p. 16.
10 Hansard, vol. 114, cols 1268ff., 12 March 1851.

11 *Ibid.*, vol. 190, cols. 1206 and 1542, 6 March 1868.
12 These ideas were published in Goschen, *Local Taxation*, pp. 189–218, providing his First Reading speech on the Bill and extracts from the proposed legislation.
13 Under Disraeli this post was not in the Cabinet.
14 Disraeli Papers, Box 119/2; fo. 208, 31 Jan. 1876.
15 *Ibid.*, Box 134/ 4, fo. 1.
16 Monk Bretton Papers, Box 55. (Dodson became Lord Monk Bretton).
17 *The Times*, 14 October 1885.
18 Keith-Lucas, *English Local Government Franchise*, p. 109.
19 A. Roberts, *Salisbury: A Victorian Titan* (London: Weidenfeld & Nicolson, 1999), p. 499.
20 Hansard, vol. 323, col. 1642, 19 March 1888.
21 Roberts, *Salisbury*, pp. 499–500.
22 N. M. Marris, *Joseph Chamberlain* (London: Hutchinson, 1900), p. 217.
23 Chamberlain Papers, JC3/1/88, Salisbury to Chamberlain, 1 February 1888.
24 Keith-Lucas, *English Local Government Franchise*, p. 110.
25 The Local Government Act, 1888: 51 & 52 Vict., c. 41.
26 The County Electors Act 1888: 51 & 52 Vict., c. 10.
27 Keith-Lucas, *English Local Government Franchise*, pp. 74, 114–15, 232.
28 W. B. Odgers and E. J. Naldrett, *Local Government* (London: Macmillan, 2nd edn, 1909), pp. 210–11; by 1909 education had been added to the list.
29 P. G. Richards, *Delegation in Local Government* (London: George Allen & Unwin, 1956), pp. 22–3.
30 Odgers and Naldrett, *Local Government*, p. 25.
31 Lipman, *Local Government Areas*, pp. 146–51.
32 *Ibid.*, p. 127.
33 Their writings included: W. Rathbone, A. Pell and F. C. Montague, *Local Administration* (London: Swan Sonnenschein, 1885); R. S. Wright and H. Hobhouse, *An Outline of Local Government and Local Taxation* (London: Sweet & Maxwell, 1884). The group spanned the party divide and Albert Pell succeeded Sir Massey Lopes as chair of the Local Taxation Committee; see also Lipman, *Local Government Areas*, p. 128.
34 Lipman, *Local Government Areas*, pp. 136–7.
35 *Ibid.*, pp. 153–8.
36 C. Bellamy, *Administering Central–Local Relations 1871–1919: The Local Government Board and its Fiscal and Cultural Context* (Manchester: Manchester University Press, 1988), pp. 38–9.
37 Redlich and Hirst, *Local Government in England*, vol. 1, pp. 198–200.
38 *Ibid.*, p. 201.
39 Hansard, vol. 323, col. 1655, 19 March 1888.
40 R. M. Ottewill, 'County elections in Surrey: the first sixty years, 1889 to 1949', unpublished paper (2005).
41 H. J. Hanham, 'The development of the Scottish Office', in J. N. Wolfe (ed.), *Government and Nationalism in Scotland* (Edinburgh: Edinburgh University Press, 1969), pp. 51–70.
42 W. E. Whyte, *Local Government in Scotland* (London: William Hodge, 1925).
43 W. C. Dundas, *The Development of Local Government in Scotland* (London: William Hodge, 1942), p. 15.

44 Whyte, *Local Government in Scotland*, pp. 239–40.

45 *Ibid.*, p. 240.

46 J. Davis, *Reforming London: The London Government Problem 1855–1900* (Oxford: Oxford University Press, 1998), pp. 104–5; Robson, *Government and Misgovernment of London*, p. 90.

47 K. Young, *Local Politics and the Rise of Party* (Leicester: Leicester University Press, 1975), pp. 37–8.

48 Livestock was still being herded through London to wholesale markets such as Smithfields.

49 Robson, *Government and Misgovernment of London*, p. 80.

50 Four MPs and a Peer were elected to the authority in 1889.

51 Young, *Local Politics and the Rise of Party*, p. 39.

52 Robson, *Government and Misgovernment of London*, pp. 88–9; the Royal Commission on the Amalgamation of the City and County of London reported in 1894.

53 The London Government Act, 1899: 62 & 63 Vict., c. 14.

54 Robson, *Government and Misgovernment of London*, p. 97.

55 *Ibid.*, p. 95.

56 Rathbone, Pell, and Montague, *Local Administration*.

57 J. Collings and J. Green, *Life of the Right Honourable Jesse Collings* (London: Longmans, 1920), p. 182; Collings in 1886 moved an amendment to the Queen's Speech on this issue which led to the defeat and resignation of the Salisbury Government. Although the issue was but the pretext for the defeat, it consequently gained much greater public attention.

58 50 & 51 Vict., c. 48; 53 & 54 Vict., c. 65.

59 Rathbone, Pell and Monatgue, *Local Administration*; William Rathbone was a Gladstonian Liberal while Albert Pell was a Tory supporter of Massey Lopes and one-time chair of his Committee; Montague was a barrister.

60 Rathbone, Pell and Montague, *Local Administration*, pp. 100–3.

61 Bellamy, *Administering Central– Local Relations*, pp. 243, 263.

62 Chamberlain Papers, JC5/31/13, Chamberlain to Fowler, 7 February 1894; E. H. Fowler, *The Life of Lord Wolverhampton* (London: Hutchinson, 1912), p. 271.

63 W. C. Ryde, *The Local Government Act 1894* (London: Reeves & Turner, 1894), p. 50.

64 Odgers and Naldrett, *Local Government*, p. 64.

65 See for example Hansard, vol. 18, cols 83–108, 2 Nov. 1883.

66 Odgers and Naldrett, *Local Government*, p. 122; figures for 1901.

67 *Ibid.*, p. 138.

68 Formed in 1881 and chaired by Lord Abedare, the Departmental Committee on Intermediate and Higher Education in Wales suggested an increase in the number of non-denominational schools in the strongly nonconformist Principality: J. Stuart-Maclure (ed.), *Educational Documents* (London: Methuen, 1965), pp. 112–20.

69 The Commission quickly realised that there was no clear delineation to be made in the existing structure of English education between primary and secondary levels.

70 H. C. Barnard, *A History of English Education* (London: London University Press, 2nd edn, 1961), pp. 204–13; S. J. Curtis and M. E. A. Boultwood, *An*

Introductory History of English Education Since 1800 (Cambridge: University Tutorial Press, 4th edn, 1966), pp. 94–103.

71 Curtis and Boultwood, *Introductory History of English Education Since 1800*, pp. 94–101.

72 *Ibid.*, pp. 162–70.

73 *Ibid.*

74 K. O. Morgan, *Wales in British Politics 1868–1902* (Cardiff: University of Wales Press, 1970), pp. 191–5; the Education (Local Authority Default) Act, 1902: 4 Edw. VII, c. 18.

75 Curtis and Boultwood, *Introductory History of English Education Since 1800*, p. 170

76 W. E. Whyte, *Local Government in Scotland* (Edinburgh: William Hodge, 1925), p. 334.

77 Hansard, vol. 133, col. 1267, 2 June 1854.

78 Gladstone Papers, Add. 44252, fo. 42, Gladstone to Dobson 10 Jan. 1882.

79 D. A. Hamer, *John Morley* (Oxford: Oxford University Press, 1968), pp. 308–9.

80 Refer to chapter 4 for further details on this attitude.

81 The Act of 1888 had not extended this power to the county councils, giving rise to an increasingly anomalous situation, granted that the 1894 Acts bestowed this power on urban and rural districts. This was rectified in the 1903 County Councils (Bills in Parliament) Act: 3 Edw. VII, c. 9.

82 Keith-Lucas and Richards, *History of Local Government in the Twentieth Century*, p. 180.

83 K. Isaac-Henry, 'The Association of Municipal Authorities and the County Councils Association: a study of the influences and pressures on the reorganisation of local government, 1945–1972', Ph.D thesis, University of London, 1980, p. 58.

84 *Ibid.*, p. 54.

85 *Ibid.*, p. 57.

86 *Ibid.*, p. 58.

87 Keith-Lucas and Richards, *History of Local Government in the Twentieth Century*, p. 180.

88 K. P. Poole, *The Local Government Service* (London: George Allen & Unwin, 1978), p. 18.

89 Robson, *Development of Local Government*, p. 322.

90 Lambert, *Sir John Simon 1816–1904*, pp. 222–5.

91 J. S. Mill, *Considerations on Representative Government*, in *John Stuart Mill: Three Essays*, ed. R. Wollheim (Oxford: Oxford University Press, 1975), pp. 179–98.

92 *Ibid.*, pp. 211–28.

93 The phrase was used in *The Times*, 18 April 1883, on the second anniversary of Disraeli's death.

94 Mill, *Representative Government*, p. 364.

95 *Ibid.*, p. 366.

96 *Ibid.*, p. 371.

97 *Ibid.*, pp. 368–9.

98 *Ibid.*, p. 377.

99 P. P. Nicholson, *The Political Philosophy of the British Idealists* (Cambridge:

Cambridge University Press, 1990), p. 197.
100 *Ibid.*, pp. 165–77.
101 *Ibid.*, p. 177.
102 B. Bosanquet, *The Philosophical Theory of the State* (London: Macmillan, 1965), p. 286.
103 *Ibid.*, p. 298.

6

The turning point: growth with decline

In 1900 local government appeared to have a clear purpose within the Constitution along with resources and prestige much greater than had been the case fifty years previously. The Acts of 1888, 1894 and 1899 for England and Wales and parallel legislation for Scotland provided a platform to vest responsibility for delivering a wide range of public services in multi-purpose local authorities. During the first decades of the twentieth century local governments gained many new services as both Liberals and Conservatives accepted the new structures for local governance. Much of this advance was the consequence of 'New Liberal' values and their application to improve the education and health of every stratum of the population. However, despite expansion in services, the proponents of social reform also began to roll back the powers and prestige of local government. The New Liberal values that influenced reform-minded politicians of all parties and the fears of Conservatives and Liberals over the growth of what they saw as a potentially socialist party in their midst ensured that central government could not trust local authorities to pursue the policies that were now expected of them.

Social reform, liberal values and the role of local government

The Liberals led by Asquith and Lloyd George did not incorporate local government in their emerging vision for their really big ideas concerning the growth of welfare in the form of payment of old-age pensions and health care. Irrespective of theory, the adherents to the new interventionist philosophy appear, like Chadwick and other practically minded followers of Bentham, inclined to believe that local government was more a hindrance than a help to the mission of the State to efficiently provide equality of opportunity for all. The introduction of old-age pensions undermined the principle that alleviating poverty in old age was a responsibility of the Poor Law as the State took charge of ensuring that everyone had the capacity to provide for the problems of old age during their working life. Pensions were therefore provided through funds from insurance schemes and the Exchequer rather than from the rates and were the responsibility nationally of the Customs and Excise Board, to be distributed through the post offices. Asquith believed that the scheme had to be national in scope and free from local variations that would arise if it were connected to agencies of local government.[1] Such a view came not only from New Liberal thinking but from that of the Fabians. Sydney Webb advised the Government:

> I am convinced that the individual pension must (with whatever local aid) be chargeable to the Treasury. This involves Treasury *award* and Treasury management – which I greatly respect. The reasons are
> A) Extreme differences between place and place ... some places have few pensioners others have many ...'no amount of aid ... up to 75% would prevent Local Pensions being a burden terribly crushing on the poorest authorities, in Ireland in particular
> B) The dangers of restoring all of the Laws of Settlement.[2]

Local government, although capable of administering the scheme was consequently largely excluded from funding or distributing pensions.[3]

The 1912 National Health Insurance Act which provided funding for medical care of employed workers through contributions from government, employer and employee similarly by-passed local government and the boards of Poor Law guardians. The scheme was supervised by National Health Insurance Committees, established for England, Wales, Scotland and Ireland, operating under the control of a junior government minister and the Civil Service, and at local level subject to administration by panels of doctors and the private insurance companies approved to pay out benefits. The Act was crafted by a careful balancing of the interests both of the British Medical Association and of the private insurance companies who profited from their widespread small-scale policies sold on a doorstep-collector basis to working-class households.[4] Neither group was likely to warm to its development as a service that would closely involve local government interest and participation. The doctors had been antagonised by the subordination of their role within the reformed Poor Law ever since its inception in 1835.[5] As such, the scheme had important negative implications for the role of local government and arguably medicine in general as it represented a triumph for those who emphasised the curing of illness rather than the nineteenth-century concerns of Chadwick and Simon for its prevention through public services, which had been the foundation of local government's contribution to improving the health of the nation.

The creation of a national system of labour exchanges by Winston Churchill as President of the Board of Trade undermined the preceding attempts by local authorities to alleviate unemployment. Chamberlain, when briefly President of the LGB in 1886, established a scheme to allow local authorities to help the unemployed through public works schemes. This arrangement had been reinforced by Walter Long as Conservative President of the LGB in 1904 by encouraging the formation of joint committees of guardians, councillors and charities to investigate possible schemes for providing work through local authority special projects. In 1905 these were given greater permanency in the Unemployed Workmen Act which allowed local authorities to raise a halfpenny rate to fund schemes for employing men who were temporarily out of work due to circumstances of the economy.[6] Some local authorities had established labour exchanges under this scheme[7] following, like many of the initiatives of the time, the pioneering work of Bismark's Germany. Many authorities attempted to find work in construction, manual work in hospitals or develop the fashion for farm colonies to put the unemployed back to work. Few local authorities were, however, satisfied with the Act and many complained that it was not possible to find serious work for any skilled unemployed workers other than in construction trades. At an Association of Municipal Corporations' (AMC) meeting on the operation of the Act, a Birmingham representative complained about the unavailability of suitable work for unemployed artisans such as jewellers and a Bristol delegate criticised farm colonies as it was impossible to make farmers out of urban workers in three months.[8] It was argued that the schemes of public works to create jobs were based on the 'tiding over' of work rather than the creation of permanent jobs, and that the situation could be improved by a comprehensive system of labour exchanges. Churchill's idea was much influenced by the Webbs and by the up-and-coming social activist William Beveridge,[9] who was recruited by Churchill into the Board of Trade to lead the development of labour exchanges. Beveridge in principle 'favoured a centrally controlled thoroughly nationalised system – as likely to secure greater efficiency and uniformity', but thought that workers and employers would prefer a local system.[10] Churchill went for the nationalised option, probably as it would be connected with the scheme for national insurance, and, as he later stated, labour availability was a national not local issue.[11] The scheme established in the Labour Exchanges Act of 1909[12] was partly facilitated by taking into central control a number of the exchanges that had been created by local authorities.

At the centre of the developing ethos of central disdain for local government was the LGB. Among adherents to New Liberalism there was a widely held consensus that the stigmatising LGB undermined the belief that each individual who, for no fault of their own, was poor, unemployed or incapacitated had a right to receive from the State support that would enable them to have a decent standard of living and the opportunity to develop themselves. These values were underlined in the minority report of the Poor Law Royal Commission that had been established in 1905 to review the 1834 Act.[13] Beatrice Webb and George Lansbury as Commission members argued that poverty was a function largely of social conditions and that the State should guarantee a minimum level of subsistence to all except the most confirmed wastrel. Both the minority and majority reports were agreed on the need to remove the boards of guardians and transfer their responsibility for alleviating poverty to local authorities. The majority report wished to incorporate the board of Poor Law guardians as a whole into local government while the minority report wanted to allocate different aspects of poverty to the appropriate committees of a local authority and, hence not to view destitution as a specific issue.[14]

The LGB, the department with greatest responsibility for social change, appeared to reformers like Lloyd George and Churchill to be sunk in the depths of nineteenth-century lethargy. Responsibility for the Board's apparent lack of activity is often placed on John Burns, its President from 1905 to 1914.[15] Radicals and socialists such as the Webbs[16] initially had high hopes of major reform from Burns, a self-taught engineer and in his early years a socialist activist from a working-class background in Battersea. He was a pioneer of mass trades union activism, effectively leader of the London Borough of Battersea and a founder member of the LCC.[17] Burns, however, had no enthusiasm for the proposals for reform advanced by the Royal Commission on the Poor Law. The LGB, he argued, had made sufficient changes to move with the times by giving more outdoor relief, especially to families, and there was no need for reform. The Webbs concluded that Burns had become besotted with his department and was controlled by the old Poor Law officials.[18] Nevertheless, Burns was capable of appointing outsiders to important roles within the department such as, in 1908, Arthur Newsholme to the post of Chief Medical Officer.[19] Burns had a not untypical attitude to poverty and poor relief, according to which it was always possible for the industrious to find work.[20] Like many self-made working men, Burns thought simply that those who could, but would not, work were to be stigmatised while for the others they should '[a]bolish the workhouse ... provide the able bodied poor with work. Send the sick to hospitals, the aged with their pensions to friends.'[21] Asquith saw in Burns a competent, safe pair of hands in terms of thriftful administration and additionally a minister who could represent respectable working-class opinion in the Government.[22] Asquith also believed that many of the problems of poverty could be resolved by developments such as pensions and national insurance outside the sphere of local government.[23] In a wider context Asquith and Lloyd George saw the LGB as an agency for local interests rather than the means to secure major social reform. Burns, for all his lack of radicalism concerning poverty, ought not to be dismissed entirely as an ineffectual champion of local government. In 1909, for example, he brought forward legislation to facilitate town planning and, unlike many of his successors, did nothing to undermine either the advance of municipalisation or the capacity of local authorities to expand their services without substantive monitoring and regulation from central government. He showed considerable enthusiasm for local government as a means of facilitating community development, maintaining: 'It was De Tocqueville who said that it was in the commune (meaning the municipality) that the free force of the people rested, and he was right.'[24] Arguably, Burns was the last minister with responsibility for local government to retain intact the dual-polity ideal.

From the LGB to the Ministry of Health

The apparent lethargy and *laissez-faire* values of the Poor Law-dominated LGB did little to endear the department to more radical opinion. A post-Gladstonian generation of New Liberal politicians establishing social security and health care were making the ethos of the Poor Law redundant and the LGB seemed a reactionary and anachronistic element within government. Churchill characteristically rejected a suggestion by Asquith that he might replace Burns at the LGB.

> There is no place in the Government more laborious, more anxious, more thankless, more choked with petty and even squalid detail, more full of hopeless and impossible difficulties: and I say deliberately that so far as the pace and comfort of my life are concerned, I would rather continue to serve under Lord Elgin at the Colonial Office without a seat in the Cabinet than go there. It is however only on public grounds that I submit the following considerations to you.
>
> I have had very little training in the detail of domestic politics such as would seem necessary at the L.G.B. I have never piloted a Bill of any importance through Parliament (that kind of work exhausts me). I cannot claim any acquaintance with a proper grounding in the Poor Law or the law of rating – two absolutely basic subjects. Five or six absolutely first class questions await immediate attention – Housing, Unemployment, Rating Reform, Electoral Reform, Old Age Pensions – I presume to say nothing of minor measures and exacting day to day administration. On all of these I shall be confronted by hundreds of earnest men who have thought of nothing else all their lives, who know these subjects – as I know military and colonial things – from experience learned in hard schools, or else men who have served for many years on local bodies.
>
> Dimly across gulfs of ignorance I see the outline of a policy which I call the Minimum Standards. It is national rather than departmental. I am doubtful of my power to give it concrete expression. If I did, I expect before long I should find myself in collision with some of my best friends – like for instance John Morely, who at the end of a life time of study and thought has come to the conclusion that nothing can be done.[25]

Charles Masterman, when offered a junior minister appointment in Burns's LGB, accepted the position on the understanding that Asquith intended that the department be radically reformed.[26] Pressure for change came from an increasingly influential cadre of 'earnest young men', among them Robert Morant, from 1911 the head of the English National Insurance Commission and previously permanent secretary to the Board of Education, and George Newman, Chief Medical Officer to the Board of Education, both of whom had become increasingly interested in developing a structure for health care in parallel to that of education.[27] The reform-minded civil servants were particularly fearful that the LGB would become the repository of such a wide range of social responsibilities as to become incapable of achieving anything. Morant observed in 1908 to Beatrice Webb:

> If they continue to throw every new job at the head of the LGB, to cast into its seething pot all housing difficulties, all town planning, all old age pensions difficulties, all unemployment difficulties (and Bills) as well as all Poor Law and Public Health and all auditing of local expenditure – the office will be a perfectly hopeless one for anyone to try and control into a state of even comparative efficiency.[28]

Morant and Newman were plotting the creation of a Ministry of Health, free of Poor Law values prior to the outbreak of the First World War and had succeeded in interesting Lloyd George in the idea.[29] The reforming civil servants found a powerful ministerial ally in Christopher Addison, an enthusiast for New Liberal ideas, who had distinguished himself as a successful surgeon. He entered Parliament in 1910 as a Liberal, was important as an advisor in the development of national medical insurance and by 1915 became Minister for Munitions and then, in 1917, Minister for Reconstruction.[30] As a doctor Addison was far more concerned to shape accessible health services for the nation as a whole than to concern himself with local government and community politics. He observed:

> From the time of the Insurance Act onwards some of us, particularly Morant, Newman and myself, had looked forward to the establishment of strong Central Health Agency. The application of medical knowledge, in so far as it could only be applied by public agency, was lagging grievously behind the advance of knowledge.[31]

Addison suggested the development of a Ministry of Health to Lord Rhondda, President of the LGB in the Lloyd George coalition Government, who appears to have warmly accepted the idea. The proposal was initially opposed by the major health insurance societies which were concerned that health issues should be kept separate from the activities of Poor Law administration, as indicated in following exchanges:

> J. H. Thomas: The Local Government Board is connected with pauperism, and speaking for insured persons and emphasizing the Trade Unions, we hate it, we are opposed to it, and we will not have it any price at all. (*Applause*)

> Lloyd George: That is sufficiently emphatic and it seems to evoke the common assent of all present.

> Addison: What is it you will not have? The association with pauperism or the association with the Local Government Board?

J. H. Thomas: Making the Local Government Board the Authority ... I am not concerned with a building, I am not concerned with a name, but I am concerned in having one Authority to deal with one subject. (*Hear, Hear*)

Lord Rhondda: I take it that your one and only objection to the Local Government Board is that, by association with the Department the new Ministry would give a taint of pauperism to the work.

J. H. Thomas: Mr Hayes Fisher (knows I am not being personal) when I say that I would attack the Local Government Board root and branch. It is moribund and out of date.[32]

The creation of the Ministry of Health was seen by its medical sponsors as a means of developing better hospitals through control of local authority and Poor Law medical facilities and integrating these tasks with preventive health-care systems that stemmed from the sanitation and housing responsibilities of the LGB. In a paper urging the creation of the new Ministry, the sponsors of the idea, including Addison, pleaded with the Government for a reorganisation of the Poor Law as part of the scheme since

the new Ministry of Health would be condemned from the outset in the eyes of practically all that part of the population that is most concerned, if all the great new health activities which its establishment is to inaugurate were to be associated, at its very centre, with all the prejudice, the odium and dislike at present inseparably connected in the public mind with the very name of the poor law.[33]

Similar ideas were urged by Lord Rhondda, who threatened resignation if Lloyd George could not persuade the Conservative leader in the coalition Government, Bonar Law, to accept the creation of a Ministry of Health.[34] Bonar Law acquiesced to the change and, following pledges to satisfy the insurance lobby, the local authority associations and the medical profession, a draft Bill was sent to the Cabinet in March 1918. In Cabinet the idea ran into strenuous opposition from Tory supporters of the LGB, where Lord Rhondda had been replaced by the Conservative Hayes Fisher who was already getting embroiled with Addison's ambition to increase spending on public housing. Lloyd George and Bonar Law eventually gave sufficient support to the idea to ensure that the LGB was replaced in 1919 by the Ministry of Health with Addison as its first minister.[35] The Ministry brought together the LGB and the Insurance Commissions. The Poor Law legacy that defeated the medical profession as represented by Sir John Simon was thus itself defeated by a doctor some fifty years later, although the compromises to secure the new department did not establish a Ministry of Health as free of the Poor Law as Addison might have hoped. The Cabinet had in 1918 accepted the proposals of the Maclean Committee[36] which reworked the differences in the 1909 Poor Law Commission reports and recommended that the Poor Law be scrapped and its activities distributed to larger local authorities. However, resolute defence by Hayes Fisher ensured that the coalition Government finally agreed to retain the disparate boards of guardians and divide the new Ministry into a section for health and a section on the Poor Law.[37] The latter section was restructured and staffed predominantly with senior officials from the National Health Insurance Commission rather than the more conservative dual-polity minded LGB. Honigsbaum observes: 'The new Ministry was thus practically the old NHI Commission under another name.'[38]

Housing and town planning

The battles to establish the Ministry of Health were intertwined with pressure from Addison and his allies to develop the department as a base for substantive government intervention in slum clearance and the construction of new housing for the poor. Lloyd George warmly supported the idea and gave the policy the imprimatur of a vote-winning slogan, 'Homes fit for heroes'. Better housing was considered by Addison, and many medical predecessors, as one of the keys to ensuring improved public health. The problem with the permissive housing legislation prior to 1918 was that it willed the possibility but not the means to clear slums or build affordable rented accommodation. The 1890 Act necessitated expensive compensation to owners of slum property and provided no help towards the cost of rebuilding in order to rehouse people who were unlikely to afford economically viable rents.[39] Councillors and aldermen who were generally from the manufacturer or shop-keeper classes in the cities and the landed gentry in the rural areas were not inclined to launch into welfare programmes without substantial financial support. Even potential schemes to re-plan the commercial areas of cities were fraught with difficulties. The Birmingham improvement scheme required additional borrowing to establish itself and did not make a surplus until 1938.[40] John Burns on taking office found that in 5 rural areas the preceding Acts had resulted in the construction of only 44 houses by the local authorities.[41] In 1909 the first legislative recognition was given to the idea of town planning[42] which gave local authorities powers to regulate the development of new housing schemes. The Act was the most positive legislation of Burns's tenure at the LGB following on from the pioneering private sector garden city schemes such as Port Sunlight and Ebeneezer Howard's prototype scheme in Letchworth.[43] However, without financial support, little action was taken in relation to this initiative,[44] with only Birmingham developing new estates under the Act before 1914.[45]

Lack of substantive local authority initiatives on housing was viewed by the social welfare enthusiasts as an indication of the conservatism of local authorities and their lack of interest in the social welfare of their communities: 'The lesson that local authorities were teaching – which was, that left to their own devices, they would do as little as possible – was not being learned.'[46] Lloyd George stated in a speech on housing shortages reported in *The Times*:

> There are two way of dealing with it. One is leaving it to the local authorities (much laughter). I see you have settled that, and I do not mind telling you that we agree with you. We agree that if there was plenty of time, and no particular hurry, the local authorities might do it better and more economically. But there is not plenty of time ... We have, therefore come to the conclusion that the central Government has got to do it ... (Loud cheers)[47]

Although prior to 1914 Lloyd George had enthusiastically championed government support to build houses for the poor, it was not until he became Prime Minister that he set up a Committee to inquire into making good the shortages due to economies and lack of labour during the war. The Committee found that 175,000 more homes were needed for working people. The LGB under Hayes Fisher promised to provide some help to local authorities towards the costs of building housing for rent, but as it promised no definite sum few local authorities felt it prudent to initiate the work.[48] Addison with Lloyd George's support continued to develop a housing policy from the Ministry of Reconstruction, adding to the ferocious inter-departmental battle between Addison and the beleaguered Hayes Fisher at the LGB. The latter's support for the *status quo* was a defence of private capital. He informed Addison: 'I am most anxious to go to considerable lengths in an endeavour to keep alive private enterprise which in the past has provided at least 95% of the housing in this country.'[49] However, the conflict was also a clash between new liberal values and the nineteenth-century consensus on the dual polity. Hayes-Fisher believed that Addison's scheme would be expensive and would compel local authorities to build houses that they and the public did not want, under the assumption that the State would later pay for the schemes. As a consequence local authorities would not be eager to collect rents, and 'if this becomes law it will almost be impossible to compel local authorities to take over these houses'.[50] Addison, on the other hand had no doubts about the need for central government to compel local authorities to implement national policies. He believed that local authorities were unadventurous, badly led and poorly staffed, and would be incapable of pushing ahead with social reform unless compelled to do so by central legislation and supervision. Addison reported to Lloyd George on the progress of housing policy:

> I cannot conclude this survey without calling your attention to what I believe is one matter most vitally affecting the practical application and working of our reform proposals, that is, the character of the personnel, procedure and quality of our Local Authorities. I have made it my business to see a great deal of a large number of them during the last five months and I am impressed more than anything else with the poor quality and unintelligent

working of a large number of them.[51]

In an earlier memorandum, written when Minister of Reconstruction, Addison observed that the failure to deal with housing

> is that in many cases the Councillors take little interest in the question or, at any rate, adopt a low standard with regard to housing. Frequently the Councillors themselves are interested parties.
> The only remedies for this state of affairs are:-
> i) Regular supervision on the part of Central Authority
> ii) Power on the part of Central Authority to enforce the adoption of a high standard of administration and this can only effectively be done by *grants in aid of local rates which Central Authority can withhold in the event of administration being unsatisfactory.*[52]

Addison, however, reluctantly concluded that local rather than central administration was necessary to implement housing policy, on the grounds that it

> must be remembered that housing erected during the year or two following the war will be scattered in comparatively small numbers all over the country, and their supervision by a central authority, even if delegated to local agents, would involve costly and complicated machinery. On the other hand local authorities employ expert officials who could with comparative ease supervise such property within their areas.[53]

Before joining the LGB prior to its restructuring as the Ministry of Health, Addison had prepared a Housing and Town Planning Bill to ensure that local authorities would receive subsidies for money spent above the product of a penny-rate for house construction and slum clearance. The Act[54] passed in 1919 gave local authorities the incentive to build substantial council estates, and the emergence of Labour councils in the cities with greater ideological enthusiasm for housing the poor added to the extent that this measure became the basis for a transformation of city landscapes and the social direction and policies of local authorities. However, the Act also demonstrated a further ratcheting of constraints on local authorities as it contained clauses that could compel them to provide housing at the Government's demand.

The emergence of the Labour Party

The opportunity for working men to gain a role, however minor, in local government had existed for centuries within the system of open vestries. In a few municipal authorities post-1835 it was possible for activists bordering on the 'lower classes' to become municipal councillors. In Sheffield in 1846, for example, two members were elected for the Chartist movement, one described as a farmer and the other the troublesome Isaac Ironmonger, an accountant who according to opponents was more a debt-collector and a socialist.[55] During the 1880s with the emergence of a substantial working-class vote trade unionists secured the election of working-class representatives at national and local levels through gaining Liberal support. Most of the larger towns had a small group of Lib–Lab councillors although many of these were enthusiasts for liberal values. The division of the Liberals led by Chamberlain's Unionists and increasing industrial unrest in the 1890s convinced many trade unionists and working-class radicals that alliance with the Liberals would achieve little for their class and they began founding political organisations to secure, if not socialism as in Hyndeman's Socialist Democratic Federation (SDF), at least working-class representation without compromise with the employers' political parties.[56] John Burns was one the first councillors elected on a purely labour ticket unencumbered by Liberal support, gaining election to the newly formed LCC in 1889 as an SDF member.

In addition to predominantly working-class groups were numerous other middle-class socialist organisations, of which the Fabians had by the turn of the century emerged to be easily the most influential under the impact of intellectuals such as the Webbs, George Bernard Shaw and Graham Wallas.[57] In the 1892 elections six Fabians including Sidney Webb secured election to the LCC.[58] From many diverse local socialist parties, a national Independent Labour Party emerged in 1893 and by 1899 the Trades Unions Congress had established the Labour Representative Committee as the forerunner of the Labour Party. By 1900 there were, for example, 26 Labour representatives on West Yorkshire municipal councils[59] and in 1913 the Labour Party was able to field 494 candidates in municipal elections, of whom 196 secured election.[60]

Attitudes towards local government within the Labour Party were, like the Party itself, a patchwork of ideas. On the extreme left were Marxist radicals but they were few in number and had relatively little influence within the Labour Party.[61] What influence they did have was, moreover, generally unfavourable to the power and status of local government which was seen as an instrument of the capitalist State that, unless captured by fellow travelling socialists, could not be a means of securing popular ownership of the means of production. Hyndman, arguing for a 'commune' for London in 1887, sought a Greater London Council and lower tier district councils to be elected by universal adult suffrage under the belief that this would ensure that wealthy vested interests in the City of London and the vestries would not corrupt municipalisation in the interests of the owners of production rather than the people.[62] Robert Tressell takes this line in the *Ragged Trousered Philanthropists* where the *petit-bourgeois* councillors of Mugsborough hatch a scheme to gain profit from the shares they own in a bankrupt electricity company by selling the business to the council and ensuring that the rate-payers subsidise their unwise investment.[63]

The central weight of, if not intellectual input to, the nascent Labour

Party lay with the trade unions. The party leaders who came from a background of conflict with industrial employers had little but passing thoughts on the nature of local government. Many of the earlier leaders of the party, such as Keir Hardie, focused on gaining better remuneration for working men and women and securing better working conditions, a shorter working day and control over the decisions of their employers. This, they believed, could be secured only by nationalisation or by effective national government regulation of working conditions. For many trade unionists local authorities were too small to be capable of securing such aims and did not touch the vast array of employees. Hardie, who had once stood unsuccessfully for a county council seat but never otherwise interested himself in local government, argued in opposition to John Burns in 1905 that national rather local taxation was the better source of aid to alleviate unemployment.[64] Hardie saw a role for local government in securing socialism through municipalisation or decreasing unemployment through work creation only in the context of a nationally directed alleviation of poverty.[65] As Morgan observes, Keir Hardie

> claimed to support devolution ... and to be opposed to centralization. Yet the kind of reforms he advocated ... would inevitably entail an immense expansion of collectivism, with resultant expansion of the civil service and government control.[66]

Many of the Labourinclined trade unionists followed the same route by accepting the enthusiasm of New Liberal politicians and civil servants for national rather than local initiatives to secure the social reforms that would realise the potential of poorer classes.

In the early years of the Labour Party the most influential systematic stream of thought directed towards local government emerged from the Fabians and in particular Sidney Webb. The first 100 Fabian tracts written between 1884 and 1900 included 43 that discussed issues relating to the activities of local government and the Poor Law, 11 of them written by Sidney Webb himself.[67] Webb's views were not far removed, and may have stemmed from, the radical liberalism of Firth's Municipal Reform League which advocated municipal ownership of productive monopolies such as gas and electricity, and water distribution.[68] Webb differed from Firth in considering that the local authority itself should supply these services direct, rather than handing their operation over to contractors, and that the development of collective services would, through their efficiency and support for welfare policies, expand to gradually overwhelm the private sector of capital. The municipalisation of services was important for Webb as a means to assuage fears that socialism through public ownership meant excessive centralisation of power:

> Many students, however, still have the idea that Socialism implies a rigidly centralized national administration of all the details of life. This is an entire misapprehension of the Socialist position ... in England, Socialist and

Individualist alike will probably desire to make the regulation of taxation of private industry matters of centralization, whilst actual public administration will probably be municipal. Factory Acts and the Land Tax will probably be national, but gasworks and tramways local.[69]

Sidney Webb's insistence on municipalisation and the importance of voluntary societies to lessen the dangers of centralisation are reiterated in his later works,[70] although Beatrice, who he met first in 1889, toned down his enthusiasm for municipal independence by her advanced liberal enthusiasm for the State to secure a 'national minimum' of service provision for every citizen. The view is staunchly upheld nearly a century later by the Blair Government. Central government should determine what the minimum standard of provision should be for a wide range of services, including not only health and education but the physical environment. Local authorities would have a significant role in imposing the national minimum, although it

> need hardly be added that that the enforcement of the National Minimum in all its ramifications will not be required only in the respect of the undertakings of capitalist profit makers. The national industries and services, the enterprises of Local Authorities and of voluntary associations of consumers ... will all have to adopt as, as the necessary basis of their activities, a corresponding fencing off of the 'downward way' ...[71]

The Webbs' mature ideas on the structure of local government involved a highly flexible system of that would be based on small community wards electing councillors who would represent them in a wide range of agencies established in relation to local circumstance and the size of area necessary for effective administration of any particular service. In cities the wards may make up an authority undertaking the majority of local services but in rural areas ward councillors may be represented in a number of differing agencies covering, as appropriate, different areas for particular services.[72] A serious problem with the Webbs' commitment to municipalisation is that they never provided further argument for local autonomy as a basis of individual freedom and democratic choice, and thus never gave substantive grounds to the Labour Party for securing local autonomy from national control, while their idea of the national minimum gave later politicians good reason to accept that local government should ultimately be subject to central regulation.

The next generation of Fabian-influenced academics, who included G. D. H. Cole and W. A. Robson, retained the Webbs' enthusiasm for developing local government in helping both to secure the ownership of the means of production, in part through municipalisation, and to ensure decentralisation of power. However, they did not develop some of the more radical aspects of the Webbs' later thinking on local government, such as their flexible ward-based structures.[73] A strong consensus emerged among this influential group that in order to secure relative independence it was essential that local government was restructured into units more capable of mobilising the political weight necessary to withstand the pressure for control by the centre. For Cole this should be achieved in England primarily by the formation of seven elected regional authorities which would be concerned with planning unitary boroughs for urban areas and, for rural areas, unitary county districts, larger than the existing rural and urban districts but smaller than the existing counties. The local authorities would undertake more detailed service delivery but should, thought Cole, transfer the more strategic functions, such as gas and electricity supply, to the regions.[74] Robson, with some modifications, similarly advocated a system of local government based on single-tier counties and county boroughs, and, within each county, district committees made up of county councillors augmented by some locally elected non-county-council members.[75]

The ideas of Fabian-inclined academics generated within the Labour Party, and in the thinking of some Liberals and Conservatives, the view that local authorities played an important role in the British Constitution, but included too many small authorities lacking the resources to be effective either in delivering services or in establishing a sound basis for decentralisation of power. Clement Attlee, a councillor, mayor and effectively leader of the London Borough of Limehouse in the 1920s, warmly recommended to a correspondent the Webbs' multi-volume *History of Local Government* as an explanation of eighteenth-century central–local relations.[76] In a letter to his brother Tom, written from India on a parliamentary committee visit, he observed that the District Officer system in India was far too centralised, resembling the French prefectoral system, and recommended a system of local government very similar to that envisaged by Cole and Robson. 'I have always been in favour of a system with (A) Parish Councils (B) County Districts larger than R.D.Cs but smaller than counties (C) Regional Authorities.'[77]

There emerged in the minds of many Labour leaders a view, not dissimilar to that of the New Liberals, according to which local government had limited powers over equality of opportunity issues and the redistribution of wealth. This message was emphatically communicated to Minister of Health Alfred Mond and, a week later, to Lloyd George, at the height of the Poplar crisis, by a delegation of London mayors on the issue of relief for the unemployed. The principal spokesman was Herbert Morrison, the Mayor of Hackney and future stalwart of the Attlee governments, who with the support of his fellow-representatives spelt out the limits of local and central authority on the matter:

> You are talking as if the problem of unemployment was a responsibility resting on the local authorities. I want to say with great respect the problem of unemployment as such ... is essentially a national problem ... You come to us and talk about helping the local authorities; it is a national problem and it is nonsense to talk about assisting the local authorities. The whole point is

that the local authorities are prepared, through their machinery, to help the Government in solving a national problem, and we decline to accept financial responsibility for what are essentially national problems.[78]

The following week the deputation met Lloyd George, whose response anticipated New Labour's enthusiasm for partnership:

> Countries who look entirely to the State generally find themselves let down in the end, because there is a sort of feeling that you need not worry, the State will do it for you. The State cannot; the State did not do it in the war except with the co-operation of all interests ... You must, somehow or other, find a scheme where the State will do its share, where the employer will do his share, where the banker will do his share, where the manufacture and where the Trade Unionist will do his share. You must get everybody in ....[79]

Poplarism

The growth of the Labour Party in local and national politics removed Liberals and Conservatives from control over urban local authorities and undermined the role of the town hall as a club for gentleman industrialists. The emergence of the party also promoted the decline of the Liberal Party and during the inter-war years shifted the balance of power in central government in the Conservatives' favour. In the 1890s the Conservatives had absorbed Chamberlain's Unionists whose radicalism, when accommodated within Disraelian paternalism, gave some potential for a sympathetic stance towards the municipalisation of essential infrastructure as a means to aid industrial and economic growth, and provide for a modest development of locally implemented social welfare schemes. With the emergence of Labour, much of this sympathy dissipated. Conservative governments in the inter-war years feared that Labour extremists would take control of local governments in order to conduct socialist experiments that would tax the rich to redistribute resources to the idle poor and also use the nineteenth-century liberal interest in municipalisation to the socialist ends of securing wholesale public ownership of the means of production. The future Prime Minister, Neville Chamberlain, who followed in his father Joseph Chamberlain's footsteps as a mayor of Birmingham, was predisposed to be sympathetic to local government[80], but in 1926 observed:

> I see in the Labour attack a deliberate intention to seize local power to commit local bribery in one form or other: it can be done with tram fares or house rates or even gas & electricity charges quite as effectively as with out relief. And secondly they admit frankly that a Labour majority in the councils will create a more favourable atmosphere for carrying out the acts of a Labour Government; an ominous suggestion in view of the way they behaved in some places during the General Strike. More than ever I am disposed to think that I shall have to get powers to 'West Ham' Local Authorities.[81]

In the minds of those most susceptible to fears of working-class revolution the Labour Party within local government appeared in the 1920s to be a significant force threatening liberal capitalism. The spectre of 'reds under the bed' found a focus in the confrontations between several Labour-held London boroughs and boards of guardians over the Poor Law and the provision of a reasonable wage to workers. The long-term implications of the battles waged in the first instance by Poplar Borough Council from 1919 to 1925 were to have major significance for the relationship between local and central government. Labour won control of Poplar Borough Council and its Poor Law guardians in 1919, taking over some of the poorest neighbourhoods in London. With George Lansbury, later to be leader of the national Labour Party, as its most prominent member, the Poplar Council increased spending on the authority's services.[82] Poplar encompassed some of the poorest of London's poor and yet had one of the lowest rateable values in the country from which to glean revenue to pay for their support. Limited schemes had been established during the war to redistribute rates collected for London as a whole to the poorer boroughs, but these were, according to Poplar's Labour leaders, inadequate to resolve their problems.

In 1921 the frustrations of the Council boiled over into direct action to force the issue of rate equalisation by refusing to collect or pay the rate precepts requested by the LCC, the Metropolitan Police or the London Asylums Board.[83] Lawyers for the LCC found that the only legal redress was either the ineffectual recourse to seizing property belonging to Poplar Borough Council or to apply to the High Court for a writ of *mandamus*. The Government was not unsympathetic to redistribution but was also resolutely opposed to the councillors' brinkmanship and accepted that if they wished to be martyrs this would be granted.[84] The Poplar councillors, when faced with the High Court's order, continued to refuse payment and in September 1921 they were imprisoned for contempt of court. They gained instant nationwide publicity and sympathy. It had been the hope of the councillors that their stand would be supported by other Labour-controlled London boroughs, but the response was mixed. Only the boroughs of Bethnal Green and Stepney, under the guidance Clement Attlee, refused to pay the LCC precept. Prominent among the Labour opponents of confrontation was Herbert Morrison, then secretary of London's Labour party and leader of the Labour group on Hackney Council. Morrison counselled legal pressure and led a delegation first to the Minister of Health, the Liberal Alfred Mond, and, failing to get a satisfactory response, then to Lloyd George who conceded that the Poplar councillors had a serious point and suggested that a meeting of London's mayors be convened to discuss with Poplar's representatives the rating inequalities. The imprisoned councillors were released on the grounds that they regretted having to confront the courts and hoped the conference would resolve their concerns.[85] Following the meeting with the mayors,

Mond brought the immediate crisis to an end by conceding that there was much substance to Poplar's protests by raising significantly the levies to be distributed to the poorer authorities from the wealthier London boroughs and boards of guardians.[86]

Having secured a victory, the Poplar councillors and Poor Law guardians continued to press forward their socialist objectives. The board of guardians began increasing levels of payment for the unemployed over and above limits were set by the Minister of Health,[87] but was soon in serious debt and sought government help to secure its viability. Following an inquiry into Poplar's situation, Mond rediscovered a deterrent in the 1834 Poor Law Amendment Act which allowed him to determine the extent of relief to be given by a Poor Law union. He informed the Poplar Guardians that if they kept to the limits of payment set he would resolve their debts. The guardians refused initially, but reached a compromise that allowed them to remit to the Minister any excess payments needed to be given in emergency cases. Soon after the Conservatives took office in 1922 Neville Chamberlain took over the Ministry of Health. He was not inclined to appease the Poplar socialists and began moves to transfer the responsibilities of the Poplar Poor Law Guardians to the LCC. Following the 1923 general election, the first – minority – Labour Government put paid to Chamberlain's idea. The Labour Minister of Health John Wheatley, probably the most left-wing member of MacDonald's Cabinet, immediately rescinded the restraining order under the 1834 Act, and also any surcharges that might have been incurred by their earlier spending, provided the Poplar Guardians did not further increase the cost of relief payments in the Borough.[88]

Following the fall of the Labour Government in 1924, Neville Chamberlain returned to the Ministry of Health to resume unfinished business, but soon found that, although the Poplar Guardians had kept to their side of the bargain with Wheatley, other Poor Law boards were following their precedent. The guardians of West Ham, who were outside the County of London and not, therefore, protected by redistribution of rates, were incurring considerable debt due to high levels of payment to the poor and were also rumoured to be undertaking their tasks corruptly. In September 1925 the ministry refused to bail out the West Ham Board of Guardians, which then had no money with which to pay its paupers. Chamberlain arranged an unprecedented system of paying tradesmen to supply food and fuel to the poor in West Ham from government funds until agreement was reached with the West Ham guardians[89] to moderate their payments in return for repayment of their debts. Increasing unemployment and the General Strike of 1926 ensured that West Ham's debts and the guardians' willingness to give way reached crisis point.[90] Chamberlain resolved the problem through an Act[91] that allowed the Minister for Health to replace a board that was unable legally to undertake its functions and immediately substituted the West Ham guardians with two officials. The Act was used subsequently to replace two other boards, Chester-le-Street and later Bedwellty, while the initial defaulter, Poplar, managed to avoid such a fate.[92]

The Poplar Guardians were becoming less of a problem to Chamberlain only because the attention of their radical Labour members had transferred to a battle over the borough council's policy to recompense their lowest paid manual workforce with higher wages than had been agreed between trade unions and the London boroughs. Poplar's policy was being followed also by the Borough of Bethnal Green. In 1923 the district auditor decided to surcharge the councillors on the grounds that through their action they had 'not paid due regard to the interests of their ratepayers'.[93] The councillors challenged the auditor's ruling and the case was finally resolved against them in the House of Lords, which established the principle that an auditor could recommend sanctions against elected councillors should they be considered to be acting unreasonably. The councillors appealed to the Minister for remission of the surcharges. Chamberlain, realising that to impose the surcharge would be to give prominent Labour politicians once again the popularity of martyrdom, remitted the surcharge after receiving an assurance from the councillors that they would lower the wages paid to their employees. Nevertheless disgruntled Conservatives in London sought a judicial review, and the courts ruled that the minister could not remit payment of the surcharge. Chamberlain decided finally that legislation was needed to enable him to remove from office councillors who incurred the auditor's wrath. In 1927 the Minister for Health acquired powers to remove from a local authority for five years any councillor surcharged in excess of £500.[94] The Act gave central government a powerful new weapon with which to ensure that its policies would be imposed on dissenting local authorities.[95] The Poplar councillors had won battles but only at the cost of their war by forcing the Government to change the rules of the game through the imposition of a much tougher regime of central controls.

Notes

1 M. Bruce, *The Coming of the Welfare State* (London: Batsford, 1968), p. 178.
2 Asquith Papers, Box 75, fo. 133, Sydney Webb to Haldane, Dec. 1908.
3 Local government did, however, initially have some involvement in local committees administering the scheme alongside the Customs and Excise officials to ensure that it was received only by those eligible for payment.
4 Bruce, *Coming of the Welfare State*, pp. 213–20.
5 F. B. Smith, *The People's Health 1830–1910* (London: Croom Helm, 1979), pp. 346–62.
6 Bruce, *Coming of the Welfare State*, pp. 184–8.
7 D. Fraser, *The Evolution of the British Welfare State* (Basingstoke: Macmillan, 2nd edn, 1984), p. 171.

8 Association of Metropolitan Corporations Minutes 1907: Meeting of a Special Committee of the Council and Representatives of Distress Committees, 12 Dec. 1907.
9 J. Harris, *William Beveridge: A Biography* (Oxford: Oxford University Press, 1977), p. 139; B. Webb, *Our Partnership* (London: Longman, 1948), p. 404.
10 Harris, *William Beveridge*, p. 149.
11 *Ibid.*, pp. 149–50, 152.
12 The Labour Exchanges Act 1909: 9 Edw. VII, c. 7.
13 Royal Commission, *The Poor Law and Relief of Distress*, Cd 4499 (London: HMSO, 1909).
14 Fraser, *Evolution of the British Welfare State*, pp. 159–62.
15 Keith-Lucas and Richards, *History of Local Government in the Twentieth Century*, p. 163; J. Brown, *John Burns* (London: Royal Historical Society, 1977).
16 Webb, *Our Partnership*, p. 330.
17 Brown, *John Burns*.
18 Webb, *Our Partnership*, pp. 393–4.
19 J. M. Eyler, *Sir Arthur Newsholme and State Medicine 1885–1935* (Cambridge: Cambridge University Press, 1997), p. 220; Newsholme was an innovatory Medical Officer of Health for Brighton and was the first external appointment to the post of Chief Medical Officer since Sir John Simon.
20 Brown, *John Burns*, pp. 113–15.
21 Burns Papers, Add. 46306, 30 Oct. 1892, Public lecture on the work of municipalities.
22 Brown, *John Burns*, p. 201; see also Hansard, vol. 16, cols 836–42, 8 April 1910.
23 Hansard, vol. 16, cols 836–42, 8 April 1910.
24 Burns Papers, Add. 46306, Speech, 7 Dec. 1903.
25 Asquith Papers, Box 11, fo. 10, Churchill to Asquith, 14 March 1908.
26 *Ibid.*, fo. 95, Masterman to Asquith, 13 April 1908.
27 F. Honigsbaum, *The Struggle for the Ministry of Health* (London: Social Administration Research Trust, 1970), pp. 9–19.
28 Passfield Papers, 2/4/D/1, fo. 22, Robert Morant to Beatrice Webb, 10 May 1908.
29 Eyler, *Sir Arthur Newsholme and State Medicine 1885–1935*, p. 334; NA, MH/139–2, Newman Diaries, 6 and 8 July, 1914.
30 K. Morgan and J. Morgan, *Portrait of a Progressive: The Political Career of Christopher, Viscount Addison* (Oxford: Clarendon Press, 1980).
31 C. Addison, *Politics from Within, 1911–1918*, 2 vols, vol. 2 (London: Herbert Jenkins, 1924), p. 221.
32 Lloyd George Papers, LG/F224, fo. 2, p. 22; Hayes-Fisher was then the Conservative President of the LGB.
33 Addison Papers, Box C/127, 30 August 1917.
34 Lloyd George Papers, F/43/5/23, 20 June 1917 and F/43/5/25, 25 June 1917, Lord Rhondda to Lloyd George.
35 Addison, *Politics from Within*, pp. 221–32.
36 LGB, *Transfer of Function of Poor Law Authorities: England and Wales*, Cd 8917 (London: HMSO, December 1917).
37 Morgan and Morgan, *Portrait of a Progressive*, pp. 76–8.

38 Honigsbaum, *Struggle for the Ministry of Health*, p. 56.
39 Addison Papers, C/150, fo. 141, Ministry of Reconstruction, Preliminary Paper on Slums, March 1918.
40 A. Briggs, *History of Birmingham*, vol. 2: *Manor and Borough, 1865–1938* (Oxford: Oxford University Press, 1952), p. 18.
41 Brown, *John Burns*, p. 139.
42 The Housing and Town Planning, etc., Act, 1909: 9 Edw. VII, c. 44.
43 J. B. Cullingworth, *Town and Country Planning in Britain* (London: George Allen & Unwin, 6th edn, 1976), p. 17.
44 L. F. Orbach, *Homes Fit for Heroes: A Study of the Evolution of British Public Housing 1915–1921* (London: Seeley Service, 1977), p. 39.
45 Brown, *John Burns*, p. 172.
46 Orbach, *Homes for Heroes*, p. 39.
47 *Ibid.*, p. 42.
48 *Ibid.*, pp. 50–67.
49 Addison Papers, C/120, fo. 167.
50 *Ibid.*
51 Addison Papers, C/127, 3 July 1919.
52 *Ibid.*, C/150, fo. 141; italics in original.
53 *Ibid.*, C/120, fo. 7.
54 The Housing (Additional Powers) Act, 1919: 9 & 10 Geo. V, c. 99.
55 Barber, 'Sheffield Borough Council 1843–1893', in C. Binfield *et al.* (eds), *History of the City of Sheffield*, vol. 1: *Politics*, pp. 29–30.
56 H. Pelling, *The Origins of the Labour Party 1880–1900* (Oxford: Clarendon Press, 1965).
57 N. Mackenzie and J. Mackenzie, *The First Fabians* (London: Weidenfeld & Nicolson, 1977).
58 A. M. McBriar, *Fabian Socialism and English Politics 1884–1918* (Cambridge: Cambridge University Press, 1966), p. 198.
59 K. Layburn, *The Rise of Labour* (London: Edward Arnold, 1988), p. 16.
60 R. McKibben, *The Evolution of the Labour Party 1910–1914* (Oxford: Oxford University Press, 1974), p. 85.
61 See, for example, Pelling, *Origins of the Labour Party 1880–1900*.
62 H. M. Hyndman, *A Commune for London* (London: Justice Printery, 1887).
63 R. Tressell, *The Ragged Trousered Philanthropists* (London: Granada, 1965), pp. 306–7.
64 K. Morgan, *Keir Hardie: Radical and Socialist* (London: Weidenfeld & Nicolson, 1975), p. 75.
65 *Ibid.*, p. 206.
66 *Ibid.*, p. 209.
67 McBriar, *Fabian Socialism and English Politics 1884–1918*, pp. 350–2.
68 *Ibid.*, pp. 196–7.
69 S. Webb, 1890, *Socialism in England* (London: Swan Sonnenschein, 1890), pp. 109–10.
70 The Webbs set out mature ideas for local government in S. Webb and B. Webb, *A Constitution for the Socialist Commonwealth of Great Britain* (Cambridge: Cambridge University Press, 3rd edn, 1975).
71 *Ibid.*, p. 323.
72 *Ibid.*, pp. 224–8.

73 G. D. H. Cole, *The Future of Local Government* (London: Waverley Book Company, 1921), pp. 155–62.

74 Cole, *Future of Local Government.*

75 Robson, *Development of Local Government*, pp. 146–73.

76 Attlee Papers, Box 142, fos 2–83, 30 Nov. 1937; Attlee was a councillor, the Mayor and effectively leader of the London Borough of Limehouse in the 1920s.

77 *Ibid.*, fos 2–27, 9 Nov. 1928.

78 Lloyd George Papers, F/196/7/7, pp. 9–10, 16 Sept. 1921.

79 *Ibid.*, F/196/7/6, p. 15, 22 September 1921.

80 He remained for some years an MP on Birmingham City Council and expressed great pride in helping establish its municipal bank, and in his letters can on occasion be very supportive of some Labour-controlled author-ities: N. Chamberlain, *The Neville Chamberlain Diary Letters 1921–7*, ed. R. Self, vol. 2: *The Reform Years, 1921–1927* (Aldershot: Ashgate, 2000), p. 425.

81 *Ibid.*, p. 374; as shown below 'West Ham' refers to the suspension of a local authority.

82 Lansbury had been a member of Hyndman's SDF and became editor of the Labour newspaper the *Daily Herald*; he was from 1932 to 1935 leader of the Labour Party.

83 N. Branson, *Poplarism 1919–1925* (London: Lawrence & Wishart, 1979), p. 28.

84 NA, CAB/23, vol. 27, Home Affairs Committee Minutes, 17 August 1921.

85 Branson, *Poplarism 1919–1925*, pp. 61–101.

86 NA, CAB/23, 80th Meeting, 17 October 1921.

87 Under the Local Authorities (Financial Provisions) Act, 1921: 11 & 12 Geo. V, c. 67.

88 Keith-Lucas and Richards, *History of Local Government in the Twentieth Century*, pp. 74–84.

89 *Ibid.*, p. 87.

90 Chamberlain, *Neville Chamberlain Diary Letters*, vol. 2, pp. 313, 353, 374.

91 The Boards of Guardians (Default) Act, 1926: 16 & 17 Geo. V, c. 20.

92 Keith-Lucas and Richards, *History of Local Government in the Twentieth Century*, p. 88.

93 *Ibid.*, p. 81.

94 The Audit (Local Authorities) Act, 1927: 17 & 18 Geo. V, c. 31.

95 Keith-Lucas and Richards, *History of Local Government in the Twentieth Century*, p. 84; Chamberlain, *Neville Chamberlain Diary Letters*, vol. 2, p. 413.

7

The slow road to 'modernisation'

The inter-war years were dominated by a resurgent Conservative Party. Many of its members' sympathies still lay, as regards local governance, on the Salisbury plain of a dual polity. However, fears that urban government might be captured by socialists and used to further ownership of the means of production compelled Conservatives to reluctantly interfere in local politics. Even Conservatives like Neville Chamberlain who sympathised with New Liberal values of equality of opportunity tempered their support for the larger enterprising local authorities once Poplarism suggested to them the dangers of the cat being in charge of the jug of cream. Thus, Conservatives seeking to curtail the advance of municipalisation by the 1920s could succeed in placing constraints on the expansion of independent urban governments while favouring the continued integrity of the more rural county council.

Growth and rivalry between authorities

Following the creation of county and district governments at the end of the nineteenth century county boroughs and boroughs continued to multiply at the expense of the counties and districts. The 1888 Act allowed boroughs with a population exceeding 50,000 to apply for county borough status through either a private act of Parliament or the less costly and more frequently used procedure of an application to the LGB, which would result in an inquiry by an inspector into the entitlement of the borough to 'county' status, and, if approval was forthcoming, the new classification would be made by statutory order. A similar inquiry was undertaken when boroughs or county boroughs sought to extend their territory within a county by annexing neighbouring districts.[1] Between 1889 and 1923 the procedure had led to the creation of 23 new county boroughs to add to the 61 created in 1888,[2] and 109 requests for re-classification as county boroughs, 55 per cent of which involved areas in excess of 1,000 acres.[3] There were also numerous requests for the creation of urban district authorities and boroughs. Under the Municipal Corporations Act of 1882 and the 1888 County Councils Act, a borough could be created through a petition to the Privy Council. An applicant town had to have a population of at least 10,000, the support of the majority of the rate-payers and proof of industrial viability and satisfactory local governance in the area.[4] Fifty-five new boroughs had been created by 1926, while only one lost its borough status.[5] Some 270 new urban districts also were formed by 1926, either at the request of counties under the 1888 Act or, more usually, through the Public Health Act of 1875 which allowed an area to claim such a status, subject to LGB agreement that it formed a unit for the effective deployment of public health services in terms of water supply and drainage.[6]

By 1913 the County Councils' Association (CCA) was sufficiently worried about loss of territory that they made a stand against applications for county borough status by Luton and Cambridge which would have removed the one substantial urban centre of each county. The CCA sent a delegation to Asquith demanding an Inquiry into changes in the status and boundaries of authorities but, receiving no support, mobilised sufficient county-based MPs to vote down the Cambridge and Luton plans in Parliament.[7] The First World War put paid to further boundary changes until the re-election of a Conservative Government ensured a more favourable response to county interests. In 1923 Bonar Law's Government appointed a Royal Commission on Local Government, chaired by the Earl of Onslow, to inquire into the creation of new authorities and the extension of local government boundaries. The Commission issued reports in 1925, 1928 and 1929, and, expanding its brief, became a body to make recommendations on a wide range of functional overlaps in local authority business.

The first report[8] argued that further growth of the boroughs should be slowed down, if not eliminated, and subsequent legislation ensured that county borough status could be conferred only via the expensive route of a 'local act' and only if the population of a borough exceeded 75,000, while territorial extensions of boroughs and county boroughs would be secured by an order rather than an act and only if no objections were made to the change. [9] Doncaster, which became a county borough in 1926, was the last ever to be created.[10] Following the Onslow report and the subsequent 1926 Act[11] the expansion of county boroughs by incorporating existing centres of population diminished, though they were still able to absorb adjacent rural areas in which to build over-spill estates to cope with the increases in their population.[12] Between 1929 and 1938 of the 256 boroughs 189 underwent boundary alteration.[13]

The second Onslow report[14] dealt with reorganisation of the boundaries of boroughs and of urban and rural districts, and again it favoured the county councils, advising that, given that they had played a lead role in reorganisation under the 1888 Act, they undertake regular co-ordinated reviews of boundaries within their territories. The proposal was accepted in the 1929 Local Government Act, and the Local Government Act of 1933 established that reviews should take place only at intervals of ten or more years. Most counties undertook reviews, with a consequent sharp reduction by 1939 of 328 district boundaries.[15] During the 1930s, 206 urban districts and 236 rural districts were abolished and only 49 urban and 67 rural districts were created,[16] although 33 urban districts were promoted to the status of boroughs.[17] As Ottewill shows for the review in Surrey, the larger authorities within a county, given their more substantial voting power in council, were usually able to absorb smaller authorities, despite local protests.[18] From 1939 there were no changes to the structure of the English local government until the recommendations of the second Boundary Commission and of the Herbert report came on stream.[19]

A major area of contention post-1918 was the boundaries of the LCC, which wished to extend its area of influence beyond its relatively narrow confines to encompass the metropolitan conurbation.[20] In 1921 the Government appointed a Royal Commission to investigate the problem under the chairmanship of former Speaker of the House of Commons Viscount Ullswater. The Commission was, according to Robson, 'an unmitigated fiasco'.[21] The evidence given by the Conservative-controlled LCC was limited to arguing that its powers should extend to the urban conurbation as a whole but, fearing the hostility of surrounding local authorities, it did not give any steer to the Commission as to how large or how powerful the extended LCC would be. The London Labour party led by Herbert Morrison argued more cogently for a greater London authority that would take over large sections of the surrounding counties, have strategic powers over transport, the fire service and education, absorb many conurbation-wide agencies, such as the Port of London Authority, the Metropolitan Water Board and the Joint Electricity Authority, and, in the light of Poplar, would equalise grants between the London boroughs. The surrounding local authorities defended their own interests, with county boroughs such as West Ham and some of the smaller boroughs proposing that the outer-London area should be divided into county boroughs. Predictably the CCA argued against proposals to absorb any of their members' territory into a Greater London. The Royal Commission was as equally divided as the local authorities. The majority report rejected any arguments suggesting an extension of the LCC, maintaining that as joint-working under existing boundaries was practicable in other parts of the country this should also be possible in London. A minority report took up the county borough case, while a more radical report supported by two commissioners advocated an arrangement similar to the plans of Herbert Morrison and the London Labour party for a Greater London Council.[22] These views were to have their day, but not for another thirty years. Given such a divided outcome, no serious action was taken by the Government.

The decline of municipalisation

There had always been a measure of concern among private contractors concerning the municipalisation of specific gas, water and electricity services. As socialists began pushing for public ownership of the means of production, Conservatives began to see the policy as an ideological trojan horse. The Liberty and Property Defence League in its annual report for 1892–93 was actively opposing municipal management as 'costly, inefficient and more or less corrupt'.[23] Publications of a strongly partisan flavour began denouncing the efficiency of municipalised ventures.[24] The courts began a strict imposition of the new-found principle of *ultra vires* to deter local enterprise. Manchester City Council in 1901 was prevented from undertaking a parcel service as an extension of its buses and tramway functions[25] and, later, the LCC was prevented from operating buses to support its tramway functions. A Joint Committee of the Houses of Commons and Lords was established in 1900 to consider the pressure from the volume of local legislation on the issue. Its report, under the promptings of Lord Avebury, expressed reservation concerning the debts that would be incurred by local authorities through injudicious acquisitions, the dangers of corruption, over-payment to workers at tax-payers' expense and the problems of work overload for councillors.[26]

Despite a heavyweight membership, including Lord Rosebery, the Joint Committee decided it had insufficient time for a full Inquiry and recommended its re-appointment in the following session of Parliament. The Inquiry was revived in 1903 but made no seriously adverse comment against the practice other than recommending improved systems of accounting to ascertain the extent to which municipal ventures made a loss or a surplus.[27] Although the *status quo* remained intact, attempts to widen municipal enterprise also failed to gain support. Sir Charles Dilke and Arthur Henderson failed to push a Bill through the Commons in 1906 that would have given powers to local authorities to trade without the need to secure consent through private acts.[28]

By this time the issue was the subject of considerable public debate, with several publications, some sponsored by the Conservative London Municipal Society, opposing municipalisation,[29] and many such as George Bernard Shaw's *The Common Sense of Municipal Trading*[30] and numerous Fabian Society tracts in support. John Burns as President of the LGB and an LCC councillor had actively supported municipalisation and was not inclined to reverse his position on the issue. Following his departure the war relegated the subject to the back-burner. After 1920 the Labour Party continued to carry the flag for municipalisation and on eight occasions between 1921 and 1939 unsuccessfully promoted Bills that sought to follow Dilke and Henderson's 1906 proposal to give local authorities, subject to safeguards on borrowing and viability, powers to establish business ventures without having to seek approval through private legislation.[31]

Conservative resurgence during the inter-war years ensured that the Government and Parliament swung sharply against the development of municipal trading. Conservatives in the House of Commons were increasingly reluctant to sanction private bills facilitating municipal enterprise. Problems were put in the way of municipalisation by the Select Committee evaluating private bills, which established the principle that trading organisations were not to use any surplus generated from their ventures to subsidise the general rates but should plough back any gains to consumers through lower prices or further investment in the business. All but the most anodyne schemes put forward by local authorities were refused,[32] and it became a matter of principle, even during the 1929 Labour minority Government, to exclude further municipalisation of electricity, water or tram services, as these were subject to existing statutes.[33] The 1925 Rating and Valuation Act ensured that local authorities had to make clear to their communities how much money they were paying to particular services so that any losses made by trading ventures were more transparent to the local electorate.[34]

The case of municipal savings banks was symptomatic of the reluctance growing in the Conservative Party to support municipalisation. Legislation passed in 1916 allowed local authorities for the duration of the war to establish banks to receive payments made by employers on behalf of their employees to aid the war effort. The opportunity was taken up by only Birmingham City Council but proved sufficiently successful for the scheme to be renewed through a Private Act in 1919 that created a savings bank dedicated largely to receiving savings from local residents and lending money for mortgages.[35] The Birmingham Municipal Savings Bank was both popular and successful, and enthused several Labour-held authorities to frame private Bills to secure such powers. All such applications were refused,[36] even though the policy had a Conservative supporter in Neville Chamberlain who praised the Birmingham Savings Bank as an effective means of encouraging thrift and home-ownership. In 1928 a Private Bill sponsored by Bristol Corporation was supported by Chamberlain,[37] but was challenged by the Treasury, concerned that municipal banks could not guarantee their liquidity if faced with mass withdrawals of savings. Churchill observed to Chamberlain in a Treasury memorandum:

> It will be, in practice, impossible to prevent all kinds of incompetent Town Councils from endeavouring to run Banks and from using deposits improperly for municipal expenditure. Many socialistic Town Councils would only be too delighted to operate on these lines.[38]

Chamberlain and Churchill agreed to refer their differences to a joint-departmental committee which ruled against the idea, arguing that this was an activity that could just as well be conducted by the private and voluntary sectors and there was, therefore, no justification for local authority involvement in the activity.[39]

The ending of the local Poor Law

The conflict between the Poplar Board of Guardians and, later, with other Poor Law boards precipitated a more general concern that the system was out of control and ineffectual. Higher levels of unemployment in the late 1920s, the General Strike of 1926 and the subsequent prolonged miners strike led to increasing levels of outdoor relief being paid at differential rates by boards of guardians. In strongly Labour areas guardians were inclined to subsidise strikers through outdoor relief payments and were, therefore, seen as prolonging industrial action. In contrast, some Conservative guardians interpreted the rules for poor relief to able-bodied workers so stringently that the Ministry of Health had to ask them to at least give help to the families of striking workers. These problems led Chamberlain to conclude that the system of poor relief should be placed under national rather than local control.[40] The first step in this direction was the Local Government Act of 1929 which abolished boards of guardians and transferred their responsibilities to county councils and county boroughs. The Act also administratively separated the granting of poor relief from the many social service, educational and health functions that had been attached to Poor Law administration. Relief for the able-bodied destitute was to be administered by statutory public assistance committees of the counties and county boroughs. In order to equalise provision of poor relief, payment would be subsidised not only by the rates but by the Exchequer.[41] Functions such as the education of the poor and health care of the destitute were transferred to other branches of the local authorities. In the context of health, this represented a considerable consolidation of local authority responsibility and the creation of a more uniformly administered health service at the local level. Despite its Conservative origins the 1929 Act in many of its aspects was welcomed by the Labour Party and was seen by the Webbs as a vindication of many elements of the minority report of the 1909 Poor Law Commission.

Poor relief did not remain for long under local government control. The formation of the National Government in 1931 brought Neville Chamberlain to the office of Chancellor of the Exchequer with an undiminished enthusiasm for placing the administration of poor relief outside the day to day control of local politicians. The Cabinet agreed that assistance for the unemployed was too costly a service for local government[42] and

> resulted in unequal treatment in different localities and subsequent discontent, strained the finances of local authorities and entailed severe pressure on those elected members of Local Councils involved in public assistance as to threaten a shortage of suitable candidates for these bodies, and a consequent deterioration of local government in many districts.[43]

In 1934 the Unemployment Act transferred administration of relief to a national Unemployment Assistance Board separate from direct ministerial control although questions on its conduct could be directed to the Minister of Labour. Even in Cabinet this was seen to be replicating Chadwick's strategy of creating an ad hoc national authority that would not be subject to close parliamentary scrutiny.[44] The members of the new Board, who were inclined to distribute poor relief uniformly around the country and apply the means test of qualification for assistance, generated such intense opposition that the Board, like the Poor Law Commission nearly a 100 years earlier, was soon to fall under closer central government control. The development of assistance for the poor, however, lies outside the scope of this book. Responsibility for social security in terms of basic subsistence, which had been the cornerstone of eighteenth-century community government, had become a matter of national responsibility to be dictated under uniform arrangements.

Although direct assistance to the poor had transferred to central government, local authorities in the 1930s retained considerable interest in health care and social services through their Poor Law and public health responsibilities. The city of York, for example, had control over hospitals for mental health, infectious diseases, tuberculosis and maternity, and shared responsibility for hospitals treating other ailments.[45] Manchester in the 1920s was responsible for over 1,000 hospital beds.[46] In 1942 outside of the larger cities there were 155 joint hospital boards that had a strong element of local government control constituted under the Public Health Acts of 1875 and 1936.[47] Local governments therefore, as in the case of housing, had assumed much of the responsibility for hospital care of the last resort for those unable to afford better quality provision. From a national perspective, the service they provided was necessarily variable and patchy, with some larger authorities offering sound facilities while in smaller towns and rural areas health care provision could be less accessible and of indifferent quality. Local authorities also retained considerable responsibility for the care of children and the elderly, and this formed the basis of their social service powers.

Finance and the decline of the dual state

The expansion of services in the late nineteenth century sharpened the long-established concern that unless Exchequer grants to local authorities were increased, under the rating system higher local expenditure would have to be funded by the wealthier property owners. There had never been widespread confidence in the assigned revenue system established by Goschen as an effective means of funding the expansion of services, and with unrest among local authorities as to how those revenues were to be distributed. A Royal Commission, chaired by Balfour, was established in 1896 to review local finance. Before the Commission had seriously begun work Salisbury's Government made a substantial concession to the

Central Chamber of Agriculture and the heirs of Massey Lopes by halving the Poor Law rate on agricultural land and reducing the district rate by three-quarters on the grounds that land was a raw material and goods passing through businesses were exempt from the rates.[48] The Commission which had reported in 1901 recommended that certain services conducted by local authorities were to be regarded as local as they benefited predominantly only residents in specific communities while other services had a much wider national impact and could be undertaken on behalf of central government.[49] It was thought that the latter services should be funded by national grants rather than the rates.[50] There was, however, no agreement on how national funds were to be allocated, and a minority report advocated the removal of the assigned revenues. The divisions ensured that no immediate action was taken on the report, but the problem of funding remained.[51]

Despite the lack of action on the 1901 report, the increase in the number and scale of the tasks undertaken by local government rapidly undermined the assigned revenue scheme. It was easier for ministers wishing to enhance national provision through local government to set up a grant to induce local authorities to take seriously their proposed requirements. Between 1896 and 1925 at least seventeen grants to local authorities were established for specific purposes, including the substantial housing grants of 1919 and for items such as mental health or the registration of electors.[52] Existing grants for education were further increased in 1902 and 1906. The spirit of assigned revenues, nevertheless, had some life yet as in 1909 part of the revenue from motor and carriage licensing was given to local authorities for highway construction,[53] but in 1910 the Government showed its lack of interest in assigned revenues by placing limits on the income to be paid from this source. In 1914 an Inquiry into local taxation established by Lloyd George recommended the abolition of assigned revenues and reaffirmed the Balfour Commission's view that central government should fund local authority services that had national impact.[54]

During the inter-war years growth in the social service functions of local authorities and the drift away from profitable activities continued to shift local government finances towards increased dependence on central sources of revenue rather than local funding. The consequence of such changes was a dramatic acceleration in the expenditure of local authorities after 1918, alongside a flattening of the revenue that they could raise from their own resources. Expenditure in Britain by local authorities rose from £147 million in 1919 to £416 million by 1939,[55] even though there was a decline in the cost of living, due to the Depression, which will have more than compensated for population increase.[56] The increase in spending on the services controlled by local authorities in 1939 was, however, somewhat greater than these figures suggest if allowance is made for the transfer of most Poor Law expenditure, especially assistance to the unemployed, from the local to the national Exchequer in 1934. The services that most strongly account for the change are education, which has always been the largest source of local expenditure following the disappearance of most of the Poor Law responsibilities, and housing, which started from a negligible level of expenditure in 1918 to become a substantial item of local government activity by 1939. The considerable growth of expenditure also involved roads and highways.[57]

A rapid expansion in service provision relegated the assigned revenue stream to insignificance. In 1919 23 per cent of revenue expenditure was funded by grants, but by 1939 this had risen to 39 per cent.[58] A major new stream of grant aid accompanied the development of public-sector housing, and further funding was given to mental health and education services. The financial issues arising from the confrontation with Poplar's guardians also motivated the Conservatives, and particularly Neville Chamberlain, to reform the funding system to overcome the problem of poorer authorities. In the 1929 Local Government Act Chamberlain peacefully laid the assigned revenues to rest by establishing a Treasury block grant to local authorities. The block grant was calculated on the basis of population, but built into the formula were weightings that would give more grant to local authorities with higher unemployment and larger numbers of children, and to county councils with a greater mileage of roads in proportion to their population. The grant was recalculated every three years.[59] The block grant replaced some smaller grants but did not displace separate payments for housing and education, and there remained at least forty-three grants for special purposes in 1934.[60] The reforms established but did not resolve fully the problems of local finance, although, perhaps guided by Poplarism, they established the principle, the absence of which blighted many inner cities in the USA, that poor authorities must be given outside help if they were to maintain an efficient local government system.

Although sensitive to the need for more equity in grant allocation, the Conservative dominance in the inter-war years, along with a decline in the profitablity of farming, completed the chain of events initiated by Sir Massey Lopes to shift the burden of local taxation from farmers on to general taxation or the domestic rate-payer. In 1923 rates on agricultural land were reduced to 25 per cent and were removed entirely by the 1929 Act which also decreased rates for railways and industry to only 25 per cent of their full assessed value.[61] Effectively this was a concealed subsidy to business at a time of economic depression, as the loss of revenue for local government was made up by further Exchequer grants. Arguments favouring a decreased rate revolved around the considerations that most businesses made far lighter demands on local authority expenditure than did domestic rate-payers, the rate was a fixed cost on any business regardless of its profitability and, as many businesses manufactured materials for other businesses, the rate had an accumulated effect on the price of finished goods.[62]

The increased costs of local government also created pressures for reform of the rating system, which had not substantially evolved since the mid-nineteenth century. In rural areas, the parish was still responsible for levying the Poor Law rate from which counties and boroughs drew a precept. In addition, a general district rate was levied by authorities that had inherited separate systems of rate collection from former improvement commissions and sanitary authorities. Addison had drawn up legislation for a more uniform rating system that required the Inland Revenue to make uniform valuations throughout the country. Changes in government and hostility to the centralisation implied by the use of the Inland Revenue delayed further action, until Chamberlain radically restructured the antiquated system in 1925 through the Rating and Valuation Act,[63] which removed the responsibility for rate collection from the parish overseers to the boroughs and the districts from which the Poor Law unions and counties had to precept their share of the rates.[64] Valuation of property for rating was removed from the Poor Law unions and assigned to 343 area assessment committees[65] composed of representatives of the guardians and local councillors,[66] as Chamberlain could not muster sufficient support for using the Inland Revenue for the purpose. The proposal, viewed from the perspective of the twenty-first century, appears to be a logical resolution of an antiquated system, but it marked an important shift in opinion from the Acts of 1888 and 1894 concerning the role of the parish as a significant tier of local government. Parishes were now being recognised as wholly minor elements of the local government system, with almost no serious executive powers.

The inclusive professional authorities

During the inter-war years local government was losing much of its capacity to be innovative but at the same time was being based on increasingly large units that on account of their size were more inclined to implement all their services in-house on a bureaucratic professional basis dominated as much by its officer core than by its councillors. Appendix 1 puts the expansion in context by indicating how the boroughs which were upgraded to county boroughs extended their powers. The increasing size and the changing functions of local government were also, for large authorities, accompanied after 1914 by a rapid growth in expenditure by local authorities, as shown in appendix 2.

The assumption that the authority implemented as well as devised policy for the services for which they had responsibility emerged as a facet of the battles waged over municipalisation of utilities in the late nineteenth century. A central issue concerned the extent to which a large authority contracted-out construction and repair of housing and other public works. The LCC pioneered the creation of a local authority works department in 1891 to undertake its own building operations rather than contracting-out to private firms. Pressure to establish such a system came from a federation of building trade unions which demanded, successfully, that all contractors employed by the LCC should pay union rates.[67] The idea was enthusiastically championed also by John Burns, who set up a similar direct labour department in the Battersea vestry.[68] The LCC works department became a substantial undertaking, but was plagued by scandals that were grist to the mill of the Moderates' contention that dubious book-keeping hid losses on contracts.[69] In 1907 when the Moderates took control of the Council the works department was wound up, only to re-emerge in 1934. In Sheffield a direct works department was created in 1901 with all-party support due to the lack of competitive bids from the private sector. As the concern registered losses, the Conservatives wound up the venture in 1905 and it was not revived until 1926 when Labour gained control of the authority.[70] A Conservative–Liberal alliance gained a majority on the Sheffield Council in 1932 and began running down the works department, only for it to be revived and strengthened by taking in smaller departmental direct labour units when Labour regained control in 1934.[71] The works department subsequently became a major fixture in the authority, although never to the extent that every building contract was awarded to it. In general, large authorities subject increasingly to Labour control were increasingly partial to operating all local functions on an in-house basis by the 1930s.

Although predominantly in-house service delivery was established in the larger authorities, this was arguably as much a function of the tendency for a bureaucracy to expand its influence for the benefit of its members as much as it was an expression of socialist concern for municipalisation. During the inter-war period local authority staff and workers fought strenuously for better and more uniform pay and conditions in accord with their status in society. In 1918 the general secretary of NALGO, Levi Hill, seized on the development of 'Whitley Councils'[72] to press for a body that would bring together local government workers and employers in securing, on the one hand, nationally recognised conditions of service and, on the other, pre-eminence for NALGO as the representative of white-collar local government staff. In 1920 a Whitely Council for local government was established for England and Wales, another for Scotland, but once common pay-scales had been agreed the LAAs, under pressure from their members, repudiated the proposals.[73] The idea was resurrected by the third Onslow report[74] which received evidence from E. D. Simon, the influential former Mayor of Manchester, Graham Wallas[75] and W. A. Robson,[76] each of whom argued, from rather different perspectives, that there should be graduate recruitment to an administrative class of local government officers. Evidence from both the CCA and the AMC was consistent in a desire to recruit staff on their own terms and continue to select non-graduates to the highest position if they saw fit to do so. The Onslow Commission considered the issue too complex for the two

Associations to deal with and recommended that it be referred to a further Inquiry, which, under the chairmanship of Sir Henry Hadow, in 1934 published a report, not fully implemented until after 1945, recommendg that each local authority have a system of graded posts and salary-scales compatible with those of authorities of a similar kind and size.[77] All posts should be widely advertised and patronage removed by devices such as a requirement that candidates disclose any relationship with councillors or senior officers. Entry should be subject to competitive examination for more junior posts and more senior posts should not be open solely to local government employees. All authorities should have pension schemes. Hadow also anticipated the Maud and Bains reports suggesting that administrative ability be given as much regard as professional competence.[78]

The goal of common working conditions was left to evolve through the development of a number of advisory provincial Whitely Councils, covering some but not all parts of the country. These were brought together by 1936 into a national council that was national in name only.[79] The war brought uniformity to fruition through legislation requiring national arbitration for labour disputes. The LAAs, using Bolton Council as the test case, challenged in the High Court trade union insistence that the legislation applied to local government.[80] The case was a victory for the unions and paved the way for NALGO to gain government support to bring together the LAAs and the unions to forge a national Whitely Council. This was established in 1943, and by 1946 it had produced a common pay-scale for local government officers and workers, and agreements on conditions of service. Local authorities were, however, still able to determine the pay and conditions of chief officers outside the nationally agreed arrangements.[81] The creation of national conditions of service led to a Local Government Examinations Board to supervise common entry tests for recruits to the local government service and the Government also created the somewhat ineffectual consultative Local Government Manpower Committee in 1951.[82]

Central–local relationships in the 1930s

Keith-Lucas and Richards observe that 1930s were 'a relatively peaceful period for central–local relationships',[83] although the calm belied significant changes in attitudes and working practices within larger local authorities that formed the basis for further, if gradual, evolution. The disasters of the 1929 Labour Government and the defection of McDonald and Snowden led to a temporary collapse of Labour control in many of their heartland authorities. These developments brought to the remnants of the party a greater concern to rebuild support by cautious Fabian progressive New Liberalism. Lansbury's brief occupancy of the party leadership was brought to an end by the more pragmatic unions. The danger of Labour councillors taking on the Government, as in the case of Poplar or West Ham, was effectively over. The differences, such as they were during the decade, between Labour authorities and the Government were managed by negotiation. Herbert Morrison, who had become leader of the LCC in 1934, persisted in reconstructing Waterloo Bridge by ignoring parliamentary votes opposing capital grants for the scheme until it became evident to the Conservative Government that unless it co-operated with the LCC and Morrison it would face considerable popular dissent for delaying necessary traffic improvements in the capital.[84] Labour leaders could take the cue that success required firmness of purpose that stopped short of illegality.

The more settled framework for local government prompted government ministers to intervene with consolidating and modernising measures rather than major restructuring to shift the balance of influence between centre and periphery. Following the Poor Law abolition Arthur Greenwood, Minister of Health in the minority Labour Government, established a Committee under the chairmanship of Lord Chelmsford[85] to keep under review the need to consolidate local government and public health measures. The Committee, in its first report in 1933, made many relatively minor recommendations to remove what were viewed as archaic practices and to ensure greater uniformity in the regulations affecting local government. The proposals were taken forward in the 1933 Local Government Act which, although making no major change to the structure and procedures of the local government system, brought together many more disparate laws and precedents in forming the most defined Act relating to the constitution of the system until 1972. In terms of new legislation the Act determined issues ranging from the role of local authority chairs, the eligibility of individuals with an interest in an authority's activities to stand for office, the appointment of freemen of a borough to arrangements for borrowing and the creation of by-laws. The detailed Act gives the impression that local government was a highly regulated body concerned with the minutiae of its own internal procedures as much as with service delivery and the social and economic development of its community.

Effectively it was the first decade in which a new framework for intergovernmental relations had become consolidated in Britain. From the first years of the twentieth century until the fall of the Labour Government in 1931, a number of pressures that had their origins in changing liberal thinking in the nineteenth century and the consequences of democratisation had created the conditions under which central government assumed a much closer and more detailed interference in the activities of local government. New Liberal thinking prompted governments to establish social welfare policies on a large scale and the Liberal politicians who shaped the system had no confidence in the capacity of local authorities to implement their visionary projects. The growth of the Labour Party as a consequence of universal suffrage created fears among Conservatives that socialist urban local governments might, if unrestrained, be a trojan horse for collective ownership of the means of production and the redistribution of wealth. They, therefore, placed in train the means to restrain ideologically unsound local governments. The outcome of the battles of the 1920s between Labour authorities and the predominantly Conservative central government was legislation that made attempts, to take on the centre through unlawful actions, a far more hazardous procedure. Underlying these trends, as discussed in chapter 9, was the erosion of a sense of local pride, at least among business elites who looked increasingly to central rather than local government to secure their interests. The idea that there was a dual polity in which local and central government had their separate spheres of action and responsibility had almost wholly disappeared by 1930. As the exchanges between Morrison and Lloyd George and Mond show, for the Labour Party it was the responsibility of the State to fund local authorities to enable them to help carry forward the national task of securing the reduction of poverty, provision of social welfare and social equality.

The 1930s was not only a decade in which local authorities became institutionalised as more of an agency for undertaking central services but also as bureaucracies that implemented these services in-house through professional officers, who often could determine the direction of an authority more adroitly than its councillors. The decade was thus beginning to develop from within the larger authorities that ethos of the post-war years in which local government was an area of rather grey, cautious, administrative activities generating little innovation or excitement among its citizens and as such was out of touch with popular interests.

Notes

1 Lipman, *Local Government Areas 1834 –1935* (Oxford: Blackwell, 1949), pp. 168–9.
2 *Ibid.*, p. 170.
3 *Ibid.*, pp. 178–9.
4 *Ibid.*, p. 187.
5 That borough was Aston, which had been absorbed into Birmingham.
6 Lipman, *Local Government Areas 1834–1945*, p. 188.
7 Keith-Lucas and Richards, *History of Local Government in the Twentieth Century*, p. 200.
8 *First Report of the Royal Commission on Local Government: Constitution and Extension of County Boroughs*, Cmd 2506 (London: HMSO, 1925).
9 The Local Government (County Boroughs and Adjustments) Act, 1926: 16 & 17 Geo. V, c. 38.
10 Ministry of Housing and Local Government, *Local Government: Areas and Status of Local Authorities in England and Wales*, Cmnd 9831 (London: HMSO, 1956), p. 4, para. 4.

11 The Local Government (County Boroughs and Adjustments) Act, 1926: 16 & 17 Geo. V, c. 38.
12 Lipman, *Local Government Areas 1834–1945*, pp. 185–6.
13 *Ibid.*, p. 200.
14 *Second Report of the Royal Commission on Local Government: Local Authorities, Their Constitution, Relations, Areas and Functions*, Cmd 3213 (London: HMSO, 1928).
15 Lipman, *Local Government Areas 1834–1945*, p. 200.
16 *Ibid.*, p. 200.
17 *Ibid.*, p. 207.
18 R. Ottewill, 'Redrawing the boundaries: politics and outcomes of the county review process in Surrey 1929–1933', *Southern History*, 26 (2004), pp. 100–27.
19 H. V. Wiseman (ed.), *Local Government in England 1958–1969* (London: Routledge & Kegan Paul, 1970), p. 11.
20 Keith-Lucas and Richards, *History of Local Government in the Twentieth Century*, p. 203.
21 Robson, *Government and Misgovernment of London*, p. 294.
22 Robson, *ibid.*, pp. 294–313, provides a comprehensive if acerbic account of the failed Commission.
23 Finer, *Municipal Trading*, p. 58.
24 For example a series of articles written by London law professor John Macdonnell denouncing municipal trading appeared in *The Times* between August and December 1902; see also L. Darwin, *Municipal Trade* (London: John Murray, 1903).
25 *Attorney General v. Manchester*, 1906, 1, ch. 643; Street, *Treatise on the Doctrine of Ultra Vires*.
26 Young, *Local Politics and the Rise of Party*, pp. 86–7.
27 W. G. Towler, *Socialism in Local Government* (London: George Allen & Sons, 1908), p. 11.
28 *Ibid.*, p. 11.
29 Darwin, *Municipal Trade*; Towler, *Socialism in Local Government*.
30 G. B. Shaw, *The Common Sense of Municipal Trading* (London: A. Constable & Co., 1904).
31 Finer, *Municipal Trading*, p. 62.
32 For example, after 1920 all applications to sell milk, coal or bricks were refused, although some authorities were allowed to sell ice and could also manufacture products from household waste: NA, HLG 68/20, 1 Nov. 1929.
33 *Ibid.*
34 Finer, *Municipal Trading*, p. 147.
35 The measure formed part of the – Private – Birmingham Corporation Act 1919: 9 &10 Geo. V, c. 65.
36 HLG 68/20, 1 Nov. 1929, Inter-departmental correspondence on a Bill to extend municipal powers lists ten local authorities who had unsuccessfully presented Bills to secure municipal banks.
37 NA, HLG 51/45, 2 Feb. 1926, Chamberlain to Churchill; see also Chamberlain, *Neville Chamberlain Diary Letters*.
38 HLG 51/45, 16 Feb. 1926, Churchill to Chamberlain.

39 J. A. Chandler and P. Lawless, *Local Authorities and the Creation of Employment* (Farnborough: Gower, 1985), pp. 176–8.

40 P. Thane, *Foundations of the Welfare State* (London: Longman, 2nd edn, 1996), p. 174.

41 *Ibid.*, p. 174.

42 NA, CAB 27/501 Reports, Proceedings and Memoranda of the Cabinet Committee on Unemployment Insurance, 3rd meeting: Memorandum from the Chancellor of the Exchequer (Neville Chamberlain), 2 Dec. 1932.

43 CAB 23, 7th meeting, 25 Jan. 1933.

44 CAB 27/501, 3rd meeting: Memorandum of Dissent from the Minister of Labour, 12 Dec. 1932.

45 J. B. Morrell and A. G. Watson (eds), *How York Governs Itself* (London: George Allen & Unwin, 1928), pp. 155–6.

46 E. D. Simon, *A City Council from Within* (London: Longmans, 1926), p. 19.

47 *The Local Government Manual and Directory* (London: Charles Knight & Co., 1942).

48 Keith-Lucas and Richards, *History of Local Government in the Twentieth Century*, p. 139.

49 A. J. Balfour (chair), *Final Report of the Royal Commission on Local Taxation*, Cd 638 (London: HMSO, 1901).

50 J. J. Clarke, *A History of Local Government of the United Kingdom* (London: Herbert Jenkin, 1955), p. 232.

51 Keith-Lucas and Richards, *History of Local Government in the Twentieth Century*, p. 142.

52 Clarke, *History of Local Government of the United Kingdom*, p. 234.

53 Keith-Lucas and Richards, *History of Local Government in the Twentieth Century*, p. 143.

54 *Local Taxation*, Cd 7315 (1914) (Kempe Committee); see also C. D. Foster, R. A. Jackman and M. Perlman, *Local Government Finance in a Unitary State* (London: George Allen & Unwin, 1980), p. 46.

55 G. Rhodes, 'Local government finance 1918–1966', in *Report of the Royal Commission on Local Government Finance* (London: HMSO, 1976) (Layfield report), Appendix 6, p. 154.

56 The cost of living index was 4 per cent lower in 1939 than in 1914, while population had increased by an estimated 5 million: B. R. Mitchell (ed.), *International Historical Statistics 1750–2000: Europe* (Basingstoke, Palgrave, 5th edn, 2003).

57 Keith-Lucas and Richards, *History of Local Government in the Twentieth Century*, pp. 126–30; Finer, *English Local Government*, p. 383.

58 Rhodes, 'Local government finance 1918–1966', p. 154.

59 J. H. Burton, *The Finance of Local Government Authorities* (London: Charles Griffen, 1934), pp. 189–98.

60 *Ibid.*, pp. 202–5.

61 The Rating and Valuation (Apportionment) Act, 1928: 18 & 19 Geo. V, c. 44, made a distinction for rating purposes between agricultural land, business property and freight transport systems which meant in effect railways and this was followed up in the Local Government Act, 1929: 19 & 20, Geo. V, c. 17, with the actual reductions.

62 Hansard, vol. 218, cols 194–222, 6 June 1928, provides an exchange of

views between Snowden and Harold Macmillan; Finer, *English Local Government*, p. 409.

63 The Rating and Valuation Act 1925: 15 & 16 Geo. V, c. 90.

64 Rhodes, 'Local government finance 1918–1966', pp. 106–7.

65 Keith-Lucas and Richards, *History of Local Government in the Twentieth Century*, p. 137.

66 C. Oakes, *Wright and Hobhouse on Local Government and Local Taxation in England and Wales* (London: Sweet & Maxwell, 6th edn, 1928), p. 213.

67 S. Pennybacker, *A Vision for London 1889–1915* (London: Routledge, 1995), pp. 99–114.

68 *Ibid.*, p. 105.

69 *Ibid.*, pp. 136–48.

70 H. Keeble-Hawson, *Sheffield: The Growth of a City (1893–1926)* (Sheffield: Northend, 1968), pp. 306–7.

71 A. Thorpe, 'The consolidation of a Labour stronghold, 1926–1951', in Binfield *et al.* (eds), *History of the City of Sheffield 1843–1993*, vol. 1, pp. 85–118.

72 These were formed at the instigation of the Committee chaired by J. H. Whitely MP, established in 1916 to secure conciliation arrangements to lessen the number of industrial strikes.

73 Spoor, *White-Collar Union: 60 Years of NALGO*, pp. 80–9.

74 Lord Onslow (chair), *Final Report of the Royal Commission on Local Government*, Cmd 3436 (London: HMSO, 1929).

75 Graham Wallas strongly advocated a system of national exams to determine recruitment similar to that which had been evolved for higher entrants to the Civil Service.

76 *Ibid.*, p. 125, para. 403; Robson was particularly concerned about the tendency of councillors to nepotism.

77 Ministry of Health, *Report of the Departmental Committee on Qualifications, Recruitment, Training and Promotion of Local Government Officers* (London: HMSO, 1934) (Hadow report).

78 *Ibid.*, the secretary to the Committee was the young Evelyn Sharpe.

79 Spoor, *White-Collar Union: 60 Years of NALGO*, pp. 129–30.

80 K. P. Poole, *The Local Government Service in England and Wales* (London: George Allen & Unwin, 1978), p. 19.

81 Spoor, *White-Collar Union: 60 Years of NALGO*, pp. 222–44.

82 Poole, *Local Government Service in England and Wales*, p. 19.

83 Finer, *English Local Government*, p. 165.

84 B. Donoughue and G. W. Jones, *Herbert Morrison: Portrait of a Politician* (London: Weidenfeld & Nicolson, 1973), pp. 203–6.

85 After his death the chair was taken by Lord Addington.

8

War and social democracy

Undermining the dual-polity ethos of the nineteenth century opened the door to an insidious encroachment of central controls and manipulation of local government services and structure by central government. During the 1930s a general mood of modernisation and streamlining attached to economies of scale pervaded radical thinking in relation to service provision. The major utilities – gas, electricity and water – along with transport such as the rail services were viewed as national rather than local concerns that needed to be supplied under central rather than local guidance. Modernisers during the Second World War began preparing for a major restructuring of service provision and the organisation to supply those services. The post-war Labour Government carried forward these values. Without serious thought as to their effect on local government itself, these attitudes further reorientated the functional role of local government back to the predominantly social service-orientated functions of the Poor Law parish of the eighteenth century as opposed to the provider of profitable services and infrastructure as in the nineteenth century.

The impact of war

Local government was not viewed as an agency particularly suited to national defence needs, even by Neville Chamberlain. In the gloomy months after the Munich Agreement his Government rather quietly established fourteen regions, each under the control of a commissioner, a senior civil servant who would co-ordinate civil defence work and act as an intermediary between central and local government.[1] As invasion became a real possibility these commissioners were also viewed as potential governors of their areas in case of the fall of central government.[2] Although established as a new regional entity in the political system, the commissioners, in practice, made relatively little impact on the working relationship between local and central government, although they created a precedent for enthusiasts for regional government in post-war reconstruction.

The exigencies of war obliged both private and public agencies such as local government to operate under a framework of commands and regulations from central government that would have been unacceptable in times of peace. Churchill directed ministers following a cabinet debate on planning authorities 'to compel recalcitrant or obstructive authorities to do what is necessary in the larger interest'.[3] Labour former mayors Clement Attlee, as Deputy Prime Minister, and Morrison, as Home Secretary, in Churchill's coalition Government were involved in ensuring this was implemented. Prior to the the Second World War the Government had created a framework for civil defence and air-raid precautions, co-ordinated by the regional controllers.[4] Morrison supervised their work and controlled many of the functions of local government from his office, regardless of any sympathy he harboured for local autonomy. Local authorities, such as the London Borough of Stepney, that failed to effectively deal with the emergencies of bombing were placed directly under the control of a regional commissioner.[5] The 1,688 local authority fire services were seen from Whitehall to be too diverse in their structure and equipment to deal effectively with bombing raids and, after serious failures to co-ordinate services following an attack on Plymouth in April 1941, Morrison reluctantly arranged for the nationalisation of the fire service for the duration of the war.[6] Scarcity of resources and manpower ensured that house-building in both the public and private sectors was at a standstill. Non-essential services were run with temporary, often female, labour, as workers and professionals volunteered for the armed services. Local governments were, however, given new responsibilities geared to the war effort. In 1941 an Order was issued to allow local authorities to supply catering for public air-raid shelters and this was soon developed into the British Restaurants scheme that permitted local authorities to establish cafés to provide nutritious inexpensive meals for workers. By 1945 there were 1,479 British Restaurants operated by local authorities, of which about half ran at a profit.[7]

Local government reform

Churchill was not opposed to modest post-war social developments and was aware that promises of a better future were a sound morale booster, but his attention was directed more to military strategy and foreign policy. As Paul Addison observes 'reconstruction could not come about through Churchill. But gradually it flowed around and past him, like a tide cutting off an island from the shore.'[8] The coalition Government provided opportunities for Labour and advanced Liberal activists with a vision of a more equitable society. Local governments' lack of capacity to deal with emergencies created by bombing added further grist to the mill of the growing numbers of politicians, civil servants and academics who believed that if local government was to be efficient it had to be based on large units. As in the First World War, a Ministry of Reconstruction was established to collate and co-ordinate post-war plans and inspire forward thinking. The

Minister of Health in the 1929 Labour Government, Arthur Greenwood, was installed as its political head, although he saw his role more as a co-ordinator of the activities of departmental ministers.[9] His most serendip-itous appointment was that of William Beveridge as chair of a Committee, established at the request of the trade unions, to look into the inadequa-cies of social security. The outcome was the Beveridge Report, which, so far as the development of local government was concerned, was not particularly good news.[10] The report showed a complete indifference to the institution as the basis of social reform. Beveridge, in line with the views he had developed when earlier he had sought solutions to unem-ployment, conceived of social reform as a national issue requiring equal treatment for all. This he considered too large a task for inefficient small local authorities staffed by individuals of lesser accomplishments than those operating within the Civil Service.

Soon after taking over the co-ordination of reconstruction Greenwood recruited Sir William Jowitt, the under-employed Labour Solicitor General, to consider the broad issue of the machinery of sub-national government.[11] His brief was translated into a request to review the poten-tial peace-time role of the newly established regions but this soon came to be a review of the structure and functions of local government as such.[12] Jowitt took relatively little time in researching and preparing the first draft of his report consulting largely with regional commissioners and internally with leading officials in government departments.[13] The first version of his report, delivered in August 1941, argued that, while regional government based on war-time structures would be inappropri-ate in peace time, there was a strong case for major reform of local government structures. His arguments were similar to those used earlier by Robson and Cole. Urban areas needed to be looked at as single communities and there was insufficient recognition of the community of interests between towns and their rural hinterlands. Some local authori-ties were too small for the functions allocated to them. It was essential to establish 'settled principles' for the allocation of local authority responsi-bilities.[14] Jowitt recognised that it was easier to see the system's defects than to devise a remedy for its problems, but suggested that there should be a 'substantial reduction' in the number of local authorities through the amalgamation of smaller counties and districts and of 'all the authorities within the area of a large urban centre into a single authority of the county or county borough type'. Some borough and district functions also were be transferred to the counties. The proposed changes would, he argued, have the advantage of ensuring that local government areas would be financially more viable and capable of raising funds from the rates so as not to over-tax the poorer areas. The system would also ensure that essential trading services could remain under local government control, although for certain activities it may be necessary to revert to the unsatis-factory expedient of joint boards.[15]

The Jowitt report did not please the ministries with local authority interests. John Maud,[16] Greenwood's permanent secretary, who, twenty-nine years later, as chair of a Royal Commission, was to recommend a not dissimilar structure for local government, showed no enthusiasm for the issue of county borough and borough amalgamations, reminding Jowitt that any wider discussion on reform must involve the LAAs.[17] Jowitt and Greenwood communicated the report to the LAAs for comment and, although supposedly a secret document, it immediately became the subject of press comment. The Ministry of Health received numerous largely hostile reactions from local authorities ranging from county boroughs to parish councils.[18] The LAAs' opinions reflected their specific interests. The AMC was generally favourable and supported a structure based on a single tier of authorities with an urban centre that embraced its rural hinterland.[19] The CCA required the retention of the counties but thought it 'evident that many existing authorities ... are out of tune with modern conditions and can neither provide nor be expected to provide adequately the local services now required'.[20] Unsurprisingly the rural and urban districts found little to their liking in the proposals.[21] The Ministry of Reconstruction attempted to rescue the plan by suggesting that change would occur only gradually and probably after the war. They also pressed, with the backing of the AMC, for a royal commission on the structure of local government, arguing that an enquiry during a time of war aided with a spirit of co-operation, would be more successful than in peace time.[22] However a consensus had emerged among established Whitehall departments maintaining

> that the 'democratic' basis of the existing system was its greatest strength and that any proposals for reform must command the greatest possible measure of assent among local authorities and the general public and it should safely be said that it was futile to hope for a programme of reform which would command a large measure of agreement.[23]

Churchill ended further speculation about a substantive restructuring, observing that while there may be a case for reform it was a controversial issue that would unnecessarily divert attention from the war effort.[24]

Although ambitious ideas for the construction of a single-tiered system of local authorities had been sidelined, the demands of many county boroughs for expansion remained a volatile issue. Henry Willink, a Conservative, appointed Minister of Health in November 1943, brought a new impetus to the issue. He was fully aware that once the war ended county boroughs would be demanding change by forwarding private bills to secure their expansion into the surrounding counties. In order to avoid such expensive piecemeal growth Willink proposed the creation of a commission with delegated power to recommend changes to county and county borough boundaries. The idea was acceptable to the LAAs and the proposal formed the central element in a 1945 White Paper.[25] Although

Leo Silkin for the Labour Party demanded a far more fundamental restructuring of local government, the Commission became a reality through an Act later in the year.[26] Pressure from Attlee[27] to reform local government in London prompted Willink to establish in April 1945 a small Departmental Committee chaired by Lord Reading to look into the issue,[28] but both the LCC and the London boroughs refused to provide any but factual evidence to the inquiry. The Committee was dissolved by the incoming Labour Government in view of its lack of progress[29] and possibly a measure of obstruction from Herbert Morrison.[30]

Pressures to restructure local government during the war years had produced only the ill-fated 1945 Boundary Commission. The inability of Jowitt and Greenwood to press for at least a royal commission to restructure the system may have rested on the need to concentrate on the war effort, although this did not curtail other substantive reforms such as in education. In part, the Ministry of Health was opposed to the upstart Ministry for Reconstruction muscling in on their territory and the longest serving war-time Minister of Health, Ernest Brown, a Liberal, was concerned not to embark on major reforms in war time since this would depress enthusiasm within local authorities as there was no chance of agreement on new structures among those authorities.[31] The conflict between the LAAs together with the implicit Conservative and Labour divisions between urban and rural authorities formed a political stumbling-block for the coalition Government. Nevertheless, the Jowitt proposals and other reforms in health services and town and country planning demonstrate that within the Civil Service and among some Labour politicians the belief that local government was based on too many units to be efficient and to attract capable officers and members was gaining in strength.

Reconstruction of services

While wholesale reform of local government was not a possibility, piecemeal changes affecting several important locally provided services came about through the social reforms permitted by Churchill. Local authorities had gained a considerable role in primary and secondary health care but began losing much of their hold on medical services as peacetime approached. Prior to the publication of the Beveridge report, the Ministry of Health announced that it would create a comprehensive hospital service freely available to all.[32] Initially it was thought that local government should continue its role in provision of last-resort hospital care, but there was also a strongly held view that, as constituted, local government would not be an acceptable basis for such a service. John Maud observed in 1943 that many county councils and county boroughs were financially too weak and too small to help operate a comprehensive national medical service and would attract inferior medical staff. Doctors, he noted, hated any idea of incorporation within the local government system. Rural areas had to be incorporated into an administrative unit centred on an urban area for the purposes of an effective health service.

Maud's reluctant preference was for joint boards even though he recognised that 'it would, of course, be a complete reversal of the development of the last half-century to start establishing ad hoc authorities on the lines of the old Boards of Guardians or School Boards'.[33] Willink published a health White Paper[34] recommending that local authority and voluntary hospitals would retain their organisational independence but be subject to planning boards composed of local authority and medical interests at a ratio of approximately 60 to 40. Local authorities were to have all-purpose health committees dealing with home helps and maternity services, with a sub-committee for mental health. Health centres, as distinct from individual GPs surgeries, were to be located in areas designated by local authorities.[35] The proposals were criticised by the doctors who observed that the voluntary hospitals would object to any local authority control,[36] while numerous local authorities and the AMC argued that they were perfectly capable of running their own health services.[37] Such complaints played into the hands of Bevan, who later rejected local authority control of health services.

The substantive reform of the education system that culminated in the 1944 Education Act had its origins in the 1920s following the Hadow[38] and Spens reports[39] that had been widely supported but never effectively implemented. In 1940 senior civil servants, with the support of the newly appointed President of the Board of Education, R. A. Butler, prepared a Green Book to guide their deliberations on a post-war structure for education. The plans, supposedly for governmental internal use only, were soon widely known and like the Beveridge report created considerable interest.[40] The momentum for change led to a White Paper in July 1943 and the subsequent 1944 Act which established the central framework for the organisation of the English and Welsh education system until 1988. The Board of Education was established as a ministry with powers, albeit worded rather loosely, to oversee the education system as a whole. The school-leaving age was raised to 15 so that all children in State schools were to progress to secondary schools and, following intelligence tests, the more able would receive academic grammar-school education.[41]

As far as local authorities were concerned the most divisive proposals in the White Paper were plans to remove responsibility for education from the Part 3 authorities created under the 1902 Act.[42] Larger boroughs and urban districts had to give up any interest in education to the county councils and county boroughs, and even smaller counties and county boroughs were being advised to merge their education committees. There was a widely held view in Whitehall that the system of administering education was too complicated and involved too many under-resourced smaller authorities.[43] This view was promulgated against the background of the Jowitt Inquiry which had recommended in 1943 that the number of LEAs should be reduced to 315.[44] Objections from dispossessed authorities led to a compromise in which some larger non-county boroughs received divisional executive status that gave them administrative powers delegated by an LEA. In a few cases boroughs could receive even further powers as excepted districts. Some 171 divisional executives and a few excepted districts were created but their powers remained limited as they had no ability to raise their own funding and were financed wholly by their sponsoring LEA.

Wartime reconstruction also gave opportunities to enthusiasts of town planning. In 1940 the Barlow Inquiry into the distribution of industry had argued that existing planning controls were inadequate and that stronger central government controls were required, although demonstrating little consensus on how this was to be achieved.[45] The initiative was taken by the Ministry of Works and Buildings under its Minister Sir John Reith, the dour but able founder of the British Broadcasting Corporation, who saw his role as not only securing construction and maintenance of government property but also spearheading planning for the post-war reconstruction of devastated towns and cities. His ambition immediately put him at odds with the Ministry of Health that had responsibility for planning. A compromise was reached that the Ministry of Health would retain responsibility for existing planning regulations and Reith's department would consider the longer term town and country planning needs of the country.[46]

Reith quickly established two inquiries, the Uthwatt Committee,[47] concerned with the financial gains and losses consequent on major planning decisions, and the Scott Committee,[48] to look at the use of land in rural areas. Their reports along with the earlier Barlow report established much of the thinking behind the town and country planning policies of the Attlee Governments. Reith was not content, however, with sharing powers with the Ministry of Health and campaigned for a separate ministry for town and country planning. The Cabinet duly transferred the planning powers of the Ministry of Health to Reith's department, but two weeks following this decision Reith was dismissed from the Government in a ministerial reshuffle probably due fears communicated to Churchill concerning his un-Conservative attitude to the building industry.[49] The new Minister for Works had little interest in planning and shifted the responsibility out of his department.[50] As it was thought that the Ministry of Health was sufficiently overloaded already, the Cabinet accepted Reith's original idea and created a Ministry of Town and Country Planning, which came into being in February 1943. The Ministry, which was not represented in the Cabinet, was responsible only for England and Wales, leaving the Scottish Office and local governments in Scotland to retain their policy-making powers in this area. It required a further Employment Policy White Paper in 1944 to determine that the new

Ministry's responsibilities were not to extend to housing or the location of industry. The Ministry thus became, in its first manifestation, a body largely concerned to co-ordinate the activities of several government departments.[51]

During the war elections, whether to central or local government, were suspended but measures had to be made, once victory seemed likely, to at least revise the electoral register for peace time. The reformist ideals within the coalition Government turned also to wider considerations on the franchise and plans were developed to remove remaining anomalies in the electoral system. One of the most substantial concerned the arrangement, which had persisted since the time of Lord John Russell, that the local franchise was vested in a property qualification. To qualify for the local franchise, citizens had to have a permanent address in a local authority area. Itinerant citizens, such as anyone in military service, although allowed to vote nationally, could not choose a local councillor. The anomaly was resolved in 1945 through the Representation of the People Act that made the local franchise identical to the national franchise by enabling those without a residential qualification to nominate the locality in which they intended to vote.[52] The Labour Government in 1948 removed the further anomaly of plural voting by ending the qualification for local voting based on ownership of business property.[53]

The Attlee Government

The unexpected success of the Labour Government in the 1945 election gave the party for the first time an opportunity to advance its policies, although the economic climate was hardly propitious for launching major reforms. Reconstruction had established the basic thinking concerning the welfare state and the health service to the extent that had Churchill won the 1945 election it is probable that there would have been new arrangements made for social security, health and energy production, although it is also likely that the Conservatives would have left far greater control of welfare provision in the hands of local authorities.

The majority of Labour MPs and ministers were less inclined to value localism over uniform national solutions to policy problems. The party contained few like Toulmin Smith who valued localism as a virtue that enhanced individual freedom. Many Labour leaders harboured a sense of a dual polity only in the recognition of a sphere of low politics that would divert their interest from the high politics of the economy and foreign policy. Hugh Dalton, a central figure among up-and-coming Labour leaders, had never stood for local government office. He 'did not ... believe in spending more time in his constituency than was absolutely necessary'.[54] Dalton was one of many MPs with no framework of local loyalties or ties to a patron–client structure that could bind the national to the local political system. Not surprisingly, when in 1951 he became

Minister for Local Government and Planning, he records in his diary that given the probability of a Tory election victory 'I can't pretend in these conditions, to get up a really driving interest in my new Department'.[55] The condescension of some leading Labour politicians to local government was rooted in an ethos that developing a more open, classless, egalitarian and prosperous society required policies and planning that could not be dealt with at the local level. Attlee in 1937, outlining in *The Labour Party in Perspective* the policies and principles of the Labour Party, mentions local government only to affirm his credentials as a former mayor and alderman,[56] and for dealing with 'the distressed areas', by observing that 'so long as the burden of Public Assistance in the Special Areas continues to be borne exclusively by the authorities in those areas, the local rates will be out of all proportion to the capacity of the district'.[57] In the remainder of the book local government gets hardly a mention. Attlee proposed that once in power the party would 'initiate measures in every department of Government designed to fit in with a general plan'.[58] It may be assumed Attlee believed that, when necessary, local government should adhere to this view.

Attlee's choice for Minister for Health was, controversially, the left-wing firebrand Aneurin Bevan, whose selection helped to balance a right-leaning Cabinet with a powerful orator who could secure support for the Government from left-wing backbenchers. Bevan was also a tenacious politician who might be able to steer through crucial and controversial policies on the health service and housing. He was not selected as an individual with a concern for local government *per se*. Bevan had been a councillor for the Urban District of Tredegar and for Monmouth County Council, where he was not infrequently at odds with more conservative Labour colleagues, and was later to observe that 'some of those Councils stewed in their own juice for so long they became rancid'.[59]

The Cabinet was nevertheless not devoid of members who believed that local government had a key role in the welfare democracy to be constructed by the Labour Government. Herbert Morrison, leader of the LCC from 1934 to 1940, was so attached to his local authority that he 'resented criticism of it as criticism of himself'.[60] Chuter Ede, the Home Secretary, who had served as a county alderman for Surrey and on Epsom Urban District Council, also showed a strong affinity with local interests. These cabinet ministers were, nevertheless, far from being enthusiasts for a dual polity. In particular the ethos of equality, at least of opportunity, which permeated the party could not tolerate administrative systems that allowed social provision to be different in one part of Britain from another. Neither Morrison nor Ede opposed the argument that in relation to productive services such as gas and electricity, national control was more efficient than local control. Moreover, as will be clear from Morrison's debate with Bevan on the structure of the health service, he could articulate only a very vague defence of local interest and was unable to formulate support for local government based on robust principles.

Nationalisation

Many nationalisation policies were concerned not with transferring privately owned industry into public control but with rearranging public responsibility from elected sub-national governments to nationally established boards. In particular, gas and electricity nationalisation, and to some extent hospitals, fell largely into this framework. Hennessy[61] observes that 'prior to the election of the Attlee Government, public ownership had been a staple of socialist thinking for generations', although as Morgan notes of Clause IV of the party's Constitution, 'until 1945, the meaning of this commitment in practical terms was most uncertain. In the 1920s Labour made little of the subject.'[62] Both writers concur that only Herbert Morrison had a clear blueprint as to how industries could be nationalised. Based on his experiences as leader of the LCC, Morrison saw public corporations following the same model as obtained in the private sector. They would seek profits under the hierarchical control of a chief executive responsible to a board of directors representing the owners of the business but, unlike private firms, the owner was the Government which appointed boards of directors to be responsible to a government minister. Morrison had developed his ideas on nationalised corporations partly through his experience of municipal electricity supply in London[63] and then during his tenure as Minister of Transport in the 1929 Labour Government seized the opportunity to take London bus and underground companies into public ownership. LCC control of the public transport was, he thought, impracticable given that the size of the area concerned would involve joint local authority boards which would be composed of indirectly elected councillors. Such a situation 'cannot be guaranteed to attract the best municipal ability'.[64] He proposed an arrangement for national control of public transport in the London conurbation through the creation of a public company whose directors were to be appointed by the minister. The fall of the McDonald Government in 1931 brought his Bill to an end before it had passed all its stages, but the successor National Government revived the idea with amendments, not wholly to Morrison's taste, making the appointment of the board subject to a wider group of London trustees.[65]

The 1945 Government established a Ministerial Committee on the Socialisation of Industries, chaired by Morrison, to steer nationalisation with each appropriate government department undertaking detailed work on particular bills. Nationalisation of gas and electricity emerged from pre-war debate and inquiry. Concern over the fragmented system for electricity generation and the technical possibility of establishing a national grid for distribution had prompted Morrison in the 1920s to advocate a municipal joint authority for the generation of electricity in London, but by the end of the decade he was arguing for a national solution to the problem.[66] In 1926 the Conservative Government created a Central Electricity Board for power generation and the National Grid, managed largely by businessmen, leaving local authorities and the few private companies in operation to concentrate on electricity supply to the consumer. However, pressure for uniformity remained. In 1938 the McGowan Committee proposed that there should be a major reduction in electricity undertakings.[67] The Government accepted the conclusions but shelved further action in view of the international situation. During the war a Committee created under the auspices of the Ministry for Reconstruction reported in December 1943 on the need for national consolidation of the industry, although no action was taken before to the Churchill coalition came to an end. In July 1946 Minister of Power Shinwell proposed to the Cabinet that all assets of public and private electricity ventures should be transferred to a National Electricity Board that would be accountable to, and appointed by, the government. The Board would be responsible for planning the service, but that supply would be delegated to a number of subordinate regional electricity boards. Shinwell noted the role of local authorities in establishing the electricity industry,[68] but recognition of local interest in practice took the form of the Minister's appointment of a few local government representatives to the regionally based boards. In 1947 Shinwell turned to the gas industry which had also been subject to a number of inquiries concerned with national consolidation of the many scattered and predominantly urban undertakings. As the industry was not technically equipped for a nationwide distribution grid, responsibility for gas production and distribution was placed in ten regional boards and the national organisation was given to a less powerful board. As with electricity, local authorities were given little interest in the nationalised industry.[69]

The national health service

Bevan brought to the Labour Cabinet much of the predisposition of ministers in the coalition Government, civil servants and doctors to by-pass local government in the creation of a national health service. Bevan at the outset rejected local government control over the service. In his first presentation on the issue to Cabinet he stated that local authority hospitals 'run ... in the general surroundings and atmosphere of the Poor Law system and their general hospital service as a whole is of questionable efficiency'.

> A few local authorities run a good hospital system. The great majority are not suited to run a hospital service at all under modern conditions. Areas are usually too small for the needs of specialised services; the present demarcation of town and country in local government is inconsistent with the right

arrangement for hospital responsibilities; the ordinary local authority cannot attract and maintain the quality of expert officers needed for organising modern specialist services.[70]

His paper also argued that the costs of the service could not be borne by the rates without heavy subsidy from the Treasury and that the rating system was in any case an inequitable tax as between local areas. Finally, 'Local Government ... is already overloaded – and a new nation wide hospital and consultant service is too big and unsuitable to put upon it'.[71] The possibility of new, ad hoc, elected local government structures to run the service was rejected as unlikely to attract electoral support and would produce 'a hotch potch of local government areas and rating', while joint local authority boards were also an unsuitable alternative as these would be removed from direct electoral control, were unpopular with local authorities and would be unlikely to attract the right members to serve on them.[72] He also rejected the Willink White Paper suggestion that voluntary hospitals should remain under the control of their existing managers since they would be dependent on public funds for 70–90 per cent of their activity and that, apart from the teaching hospitals, many were not particularly efficient. Bevan concluded that it was necessary to place both the voluntary and local authority hospitals under a national service that would be organised into ten regional boards which would also devolve operational activities to smaller district boards. Membership of the boards would include people of local and general experience to represent the public interest, with an admixture of medical and other experts.[73]

In Cabinet Herbert Morrison challenged the Minister for Health's proposals as far as they concerned local government and suggested that, for all their faults, a system of control through joint boards would be the appropriate way forward. Morrison did not deny that national control might be more efficient for the health service but was concerned that the loss of these services alongside the proposed removal of gas and electricity and 'probably passenger transport and possibly water ... would risk ... major damage to the fabric of local government'.

> It would be disastrous if we allowed local government to languish by whittling away its most constructive and interesting functions and we must not blind our eyes to the fact that to deprive the local authorities of public health responsibilities would be a very serious thing from this point of view.[74]

He also objected to the excessive centralisation in the hands of the Minister for Health and added that Bevan's proposals would be more difficult to pass due to local authority opposition and could result in the Labour Party losing votes at the next municipal elections. Bevan replied that Morrison had already conceded the argument for greater efficiency through centralised management and that delay to his Bill would be more probable if the voluntary hospitals thought that they were to be taken over by local authorities. On the issue of the loss of local authority powers in general, Bevan adopted a view that suggests a significant difference in outlook concerning the status of local government as compared to Morrison's position. The Minister for Health reiterated his complaint that local authorities were already too dependent on central government subsidies and that this would greatly increase if funds had to be provided from them to run hospitals.[75] For Bevan local government should be financially autonomous and be more distant from the State whereas for Morrison, as indicated in his exchange with Lloyd George when mayor of Hackney, local government could administer services independently under the broad control of central government.

The outcome of the debate was a clear victory for Bevan.[76] Only the Home Secretary, Chuter Ede, gave much support to Morrison's view:

> He saw considerable objection ... to the transfer of hospital services from the major local authorities who had a good record in hospital administration, and he feared any such step would make it more difficult to attract the right type of persons into local government.[77]

Addison, now Labour's Minister for the Dominions, had long fought for a national health service and broadly welcomed Bevan's plans without discussing the role of local government. Attlee clinched the debate by commenting that the differences between the Minister of Health and the Lord President were not as great as they appeared since he thought that 'doubtless the people on the Minister of Health's district committees and the Members of Joint Boards would probably be the same whichever system was applied'. He also observed that as much of the funding would also come from the Exchequer and thus implied national control was for this reason acceptable.[78]

Housing and town planning

Bevan inherited a need to construct 750,000 new houses to make up for damage during the war and an estimated further 500,000 to deal with slum properties.[79] The war had created serious economic barriers to achieving this aim, as raw materials were in short supply and there was a shortage of skilled labour as many craftsmen still serving in the armed forces. Bevan kept his building targets initially at a modest figure and, to avoid criticism, took care that they were not made public. He resisted the blandishments of the Conservative opposition and the building trade to allow market forces, through private builders, to make good the housing stock, insisting that only through firm regulation over the types of dwelling to be built could the Government house the homeless. Thus, the Ministry of Health discouraged private building for home ownership and concentrated all building resources on the rented sector. Bevan saw local government as the principal means of facilitating, under strict central controls, such a programme and rejected moves from within the Ministry of Works, which had been responsible for some rebuilding work during the war, to establish a central housing corporation to work alongside the local authorities in building and renting houses. His objections to a fully nationalised programme probably stemmed from suspicions that if housing were left to other departments or agencies, the private sector would be able to intrude into the building programme with much less regulation and divert housing policy away from the needy to the middle-class home purchaser.[80]

Bevan's policy greatly boosted the importance of housing in the remit of local authorities and a number of funding reforms to aid local government housing initiatives were set out in an Act of 1946.[81] The increased government subsidy to local authorities for the capital cost of building new houses for rent also allowed them to borrow more for the purpose.[82] The policy also gave a major stimulus to local authority direct works departments where the council itself took responsibility for the design and construction of new properties. Bevan was relatively successful in achieving the construction of council housing and by 1949 had met the need for 750,000 new homes, many of them more spacious than built by his predecessors, to replace those lost through war damage.[83] The Ministry of Health regulated and approved the types of dwelling that were to be built and, through the Town and Country Planning Ministry, where they could be built. Bevan and his civil servants drew up regulations concerning the size and facilities for council houses and specified much higher standards than previously, although these were not maintained by the Conservatives.[84] Local authorities were, therefore, to some extent agencies building and servicing rented accommodation as required by their 'customer', the Minister of Health. Growth was, however, seriously arrested by the economic crisis that hit the Labour Government in 1947. The housing programme was a major casualty of the ensuing cutbacks and the rate of building was almost halved for the remainder of Labour's administration. This setback opened the way for Harold Macmillan to gain prominence as the housing Minister who achieved building targets in the early 1950s.

Attlee retained the Ministry of Town and Country Planning as it had been established during the war, although he did not provide a place in the Cabinet for its Minister, Lewis Silkin. The Ministry, charged with developing a more robust and comprehensive system of building and planning controls, had inherited the legacy of the Scott and Uthwatt reports and the ambitions of Lord Reith. Silkin drafted a Bill in 1946 that became the 1947 Town and Country Planning Act, requiring all building developments to be subject to local authority planning approval and enacted a workable scheme for compensating those who had lost value for land not designated for building development. A particular issue of contention was the tier of local authority to be responsible for the new regulations. This had been a district function but, argued Silkin, having regard to the inefficiency of many District Councils and to the special arrangements that could be made for joint planning authorities even if the preparations of plans was made a function of the County Councils and County Boroughs, the majority of the Sub-Committee considered that planning functions should be taken out of the hands of the County Districts and given to the County Councils.[85]

Whether motivated by inter-departmental rivalries or a concern that district councils should have some powers, Bevan objected to this proposal and succeeded in keeping planning powers at a more local level, arguing that the districts were capable of fulfilling this function and needed to link this role with their powers over housing and sanitation.[86]

Grassroots local government fared less well in relation to the creation of new towns. The idea was anticipated in the garden city developments of the late nineteenth century and was floated by a number of academics and architects, who in turn influenced progressive Labour leaders such as Dalton.[87] The Government quickly approved the principle of decentralising housing outside London and establishing a green belt around cities.[88] A Committee under the chairmanship of Lord Reith[89] was established to study the issue of dispersing populations from the slums of larger cities to new beginnings in new towns. In general the Cabinet[90] accepted the majority of proposals for new towns, as proposed by the Reith report, and responsibility for their development was assigned to the Ministry of Town and Country Planning.[91] Reith argued that local authorities would themselves be able to sponsor new town construction but, not untypically for the Attlee Government, this was overruled as local authorities were not considered to have the capacity to buy the land and plan or construct new houses or industrial sites.[92] The services for the new towns would be a local authority responsibility and once constructed the development corporations of new towns would be wound down, their communities reverting to local government control.

Silkin's Ministry further demonstrated its predilection for larger local authority areas in the creation of national parks. From the beginning of the century there had been demands to establish planning structures both to preserve areas of outstanding scenic beauty and to facilitate greater public access to open areas of the countryside kept private by landowners.[93] Under pressure from interest groups such as the Council for the Preservation of Rural England and the National Trust, a Committee had been formed in 1931 under the chairmanship of Addison which reported strongly in favour of national parks. Labour favoured the idea and Hugh Dalton observed in 1936 that 'Britain has lagged badly behind. National Parks are found in nearly every civilised country but our own.'[94] The Dowler[95] and Hobhouse[96] reports established by Silkin concluded that national parks should be established under the control of a national commission which would give planning powers for designated areas to an ad hoc authority rather than the local authorities. The Ministry did not accept this recommendation, following strong local authority objections, and the central co-ordinating agency was purely advisory.[97] The resulting Act[98] gave planning powers to the local authorities in the areas to be designated national parks, but where a park covered several local authorities joint boards or co-ordinating advisory boards were established that left the final decisions to the relevant constituent local planning authority.[99]

Finance

The Attlee Government inherited a system of funding local government devised by Neville Chamberlain that had within it elements of redistribution of income to poorer rather than wealthier areas through weighting of the grant allocation formula. The Attlee Government continued to build on this structure rather than attempt any radical overhaul of the system. In the 1948 Local Government Act Bevan augmented Chamberlain's system for calculating the block grant through an equalisation grant paid to counties and county boroughs with a lower than average rateable value to bring them up to the grant income they would have received had they had an average rateable value.[100] Bevan did not, however, set about reforming the finance structures put in place by Chamberlain to de-rate agriculture and industry and the Government tended to increase rather diminish local authority dependence of specific grants.

The Attlee Government also substantially modified the finances of local authorities through its restructuring of their functions. The nationalisation of gas and electricity services removed responsibility for functions that for many large cities provided a substantive income. The tasks acquired were in general activities that could not generate income and required further subsidy from the rates or from central government. Compensation was paid to authorities that surrendered their gas or electricity businesses to the nationalised system,[101] but the sums received were never in the medium, let alone the long, term seriously factored in to the funding arrangements for local authorities. The Labour administration preferred to make up the shortfall through the allocation of more substantive grant aid as opposed to increasing the rates.

Restructuring

There were few within the Attlee Government, perhaps only Chuter Ede, who did not believe that some reform of boundaries and tiers was necessary. Electricity, gas and, for Bevan, water needed to be assigned to national or regional bodies. A national health service similarly could not be designed to fit existing local government boundaries while Town and Country Planning also prompted debate on regional structures. The means to secure structural change, the Boundary Commission established by the coalition Government, was, however, wholly inadequate for the challenges set by the 1945 Government. The five-person Commission was approved by Bevan but its chair and vice-chair – respectively Sir Trustram Eve, who had experience of chairing commissions on war damage, and Sir John Maud – had already been selected by Willink. The Commission worked industriously, but as it could alter only the *boundaries* of authorities, rather than the arrangement of tiers or functions, its members became frustrated with their inability to resolve either the tensions between county and county borough or the widespread feeling that many authorities were too small to be efficient. The Commission's second report, in 1947, stated that no worthwhile restructuring of local government was possible simply by changing boundaries as opposed to establishing new structures and reallocating functions.[102] Trustram Eve recommended, among other things, that the Government create a watered-down version of county councils, with the boroughs having education powers but still being subject to county control on other matters. The proposal brought protests from the county councils and, most vigorously, the county boroughs, which complained directly to Bevan.[103] The Minister was not happy that the Commission was making the running on reform and chose to make no comment on the proposal let alone act on it. Bevan was also being pressed by Morrison to discuss with him how they were to respond to the Commission's proposals, with a warning that any major restructuring of local government was out of the question during that Parliament.[104]

It was not until 11 March 1949 that Bevan indicated publicly that the time was not right for legislation to restructure local government. By this point the Commission's relationship with the Minister had all but broken down. The Commissioners had drafted their report for 1948, in which they suggested extensive boundary changes and in its conclusion also pressed for much greater powers:

> In view of this huge recasting of the substance of the main local government services – which is presumably intended to stand for many years – it seems scarcely possible to argue now that it is either premature or inopportune to reshape the machine.[105]

They recommended that they be given powers to undertake what would have been a complete recasting of the local government system, dividing England and Wales into single-tier authorities in urban areas and having a two-tier system for rural areas.[106] Bevan was not unsympathetic to the Commissioners' position,[107] but unknown to them he had already decided to move the agenda for local government reform out of their hands by creating a Royal Commission to review the whole system. Bevan informed Morrison that he was particularly worried about leaks of information and subsequent opposition from the LAAs were he to discuss issues of reform in a wider context:

My difficulty is that I have to stall until after the election. I feel that if we have to circulate papers discussing reform of local government over a wide circle of Ministers, it is bound to become known in the local government world that we are considering the matter so there will be pressure on us to disclose our intentions and embarrassing accusations will be made which may ruin the whole electoral position.

I think we should therefore have an informal and un-minuted discussion amongst a few Ministers who are most concerned with the question so that we can review our tactics in the light of the whole political position.

Morrison added the hand-written comment in the margin to the latter paragraph: 'I am inclined to agree.'[108]

Bevan's preferred means for change, a royal commission, was put to the Cabinet in April. He argued that the many changes to the function of local government since the nineteenth century ensured that any alterations to the local government system had to be substantive and would generate opposition, but these changes were not urgent.[109] Bevan's ideas did not please Morrison who countered with a paper arguing that a royal commission was unlikely to reach a clear solution to the problem if composed of local government representatives but the alternative – a commission composed of unprejudiced, impartial minds – would have insufficient knowledge of local government to make a sound judgement. He also argued that a commission would be unlikely to report until 1953, which would be late on in a second term of office. A better path would be for the Government itself to decide the issue or at least determine clearly what it was that a commission should consider.[110] A further and some-what ambiguous paper by Silkin gave initial broad support to Bevan, but then suggested a less formal arrangement than a royal commission may be a better strategy.[111] The differing positions on local government reform were debated in Cabinet on 12 May 1949. Morrison added to his earlier paper, with the endorsement of Silkin, that restructuring of local govern-ment in London was urgent and recommended that the Boundary Commission be asked to look at this issue. The Cabinet was more supportive of Morrison's view that the Government had sufficient under-standing of the problem to make a decision and should not evade that responsibility. A royal commission would be clearly a delaying tactic and Bevan's strategy presumed that the Government would last another five years. Attlee resolved the debate in Morrison's favour by stating that a Cabinet Committee should be convened to discuss the underlying princi-ples for local government to enable officials to create detailed plans. The first task of the Committee would be to determine the future of the Boundary Commission.[112]

Attlee had a meeting with the chair and vice-chair of the Boundary Commission on 24 May, and Trustram Eve and John Maud came away optimistic about the continuation of their role;[113] but at the first meeting of the Cabinet Committee on local government on 31 May, it was clear that there was no support for its continuation. Ministers agreed that the Commission required further powers to make a serious impact on the structure of local government, and since the Commissioners had told Attlee that they would not suspend their proceedings while the Government deliberated what to do, the best course was to suspend their activities.[114] When Trustram Eve was informed of this decision he felt betrayed by the Government and in forthcoming years wrote columns in the press as a local government expert that were highly critical of the Labour Party.[115] Bevan formally announced the Government's intention to end the Commission on 27 June and, to the annoyance of the county boroughs, the system for reviewing local authority boundaries reverted to that of review by county councils.[116]

Following the decision to remove the Commission, the Cabinet Committee on Local Government began to consider whether there was common ground among its members concerning the future shape of local government.[117] It was agreed that 'local government could not retain its vitality if the work entrusted to it was dull and lacking in interest', and that the transfer of functions had indeed diminished that vitality, but there 'were few functions which would more appropriately be exercised by small units'.[118] At least one member also raised the possibility of local authorities receiving enabling powers and Bevan was asked to investigate the issue. Another member suggested all-purpose single-tier authorities of populations ranging from 50,000 to 60,000 taking in both urban and rural areas.[119] While this had support, in that it would remove what was seen as the nineteenth-century urban–rural divide, there were counter-arguments to the effect that while single-tier structures might be applicable to predominantly urban areas, it was still appropriate to retain two-tier structures for more rural areas. There was a further suggestion that smaller 'neighbourhood' authorities could be created to look after local amenities. The quandaries expressed in relation to provincial England applied also to London. Doubts were expressed whether the London boroughs should be retained but if the LCC were the only local authority in London only a fraction of its inhabitants would participate in local government. The suggestion was made that the small neighbourhood authority, if it were shown to be workable for the rest of the country, might have some application in London.[120]

Bevan proposed at the next meeting that the country should be served by all-purpose authorities with populations of at least 50,000, creating around 300 authorities. Their boundaries should be centred on urban areas which took in their rural hinterlands, and a scheme was developed to ensure that 80 per cent of those authorities would not extend farther than 10 miles from their centres of government. The idea was received with polite interest but also reservations over problems that might arise for the functional interests of particular departments. The Minister for Education observed that this would increase the number of education authorities when the trend was towards fewer and larger LEAs. Silkin also argued that the proposed size of the authorities was insufficient for effective planning. Bevan was asked to consider such issues in preparing a sounder proposal.[121]

By the third meeting, which was delayed until November, Bevan had worked up a firm plan for restructuring local government based on his earlier ideas, but with the addition of smaller neighbourhood councils to provide local amenities through funds distributed by the principal authorities.[122] Less than favourable papers were tabled by the majority of ministers affected by the proposal. Bevan had already given up the fight by the time he arrived for the meeting and 'doubted whether the matter could be carried much further at the present stage. He thought it would be unreasonable to ask his Department to put further work into the subject when there was no prospect of decisions being reached before the General Election.'[123] Attlee agreed, but suggested, perhaps to further dim the declining star of Bevan as a reforming minister, that the Cabinet Committee might as well discuss the issue since members present might wish to enlarge on their views. The subsequent discussion, while of no practical importance, is of interest in revealing the extent of differences within the Labour leadership on the purpose and nature of local government. The Ministers for Education, Transport and Agriculture, and the Home Secretary, probably primed by departmental interests, each tabled a paper raising concerns that the Bevan plan would increase the number of local authorities dealing with their areas of interest, and only Silkin provided any support for the plan. The majority in this group, however, broadly supported single-tier authorities and presumably wanted even larger and less local units than suggested by Bevan. The exceptions in this group were Chuter Ede and Minister of Agriculture Tom Williams. The Home Secretary strongly opposed major reform, arguing:

> The historic units of English local government are the parish, deriving from the manor, and the county. There is local patriotism attaching the individual to both, varying in intensity but quite well marked in both cases ... Historic association is not lightly to be disregarded and there are sometimes historic antipathies which have to be borne in mind when considering new groupings.[124]

Enlarging on this view to the Committee, he remarked that 'the village green would be well looked after locally, but would be neglected by an authority which was twenty miles away'. Chuter Ede also roundly condemned any single-tier solution, maintaining: 'In some of the present large towns, the councils may be un-wieldy in size, but the lower authority in the two tier system enables a very large number of people who have limited means, both of time and money, to participate.'[125] Unlike other departmentally minded ministers, Chuter Ede supported a case made out in the reports of the Local Government Boundary Commission for smaller police authorities.[126] Williams strongly supported Chuter Ede, expressing concern 'about the violent treatment of long established local government boundaries' and stating that 'it was necessary to balance considerations of efficiency against the loss of valuable training grounds for local administrators'. Moreover, he did not care for the establishment of neighbourhood councils on the lines proposed, as 'the acid test of local responsibility was the power to levy a rate'.[127] Morrison was strangely silent at the meeting, but may well have seen that others could destroy Bevan's reformist ambitions for local government without his intervention. The meeting accepted the view that further reform of the system was impossible and would fail to muster any consensus within the Cabinet.

Not only were Bevan's plans for restructuring local government defeated in Cabinet but he was also being rebuffed on his proposals for the water services, which became one nationalisation of municipal services too many for the Labour Government. Bevan proposed the idea to the Cabinet in March 1950 to resolve a long-running concern about the quality of water supplies in rural areas. Reform, it was argued, required a substantial reduction in the number of statutory water undertakings in England and Wales to ensure that the large schemes that must be designed and implemented during the next few years were properly co-ordinated.[128] Bevan proposed the creation of 50–60 water authority districts, which would be managed by engineers and be subject to the Ministry of Health. Local government would, therefore, have almost no involvement in the proposed system. The idea was widely criticised in Cabinet. The Scottish Office argued that since almost all water services in Scotland were under local authority control, there was no need for any system of nationalisation to be introduced simply to bring Scotland into conformfity with what was proposed for England. Morrison was particularly opposed to the idea, arguing that local authorities had great pride in their water services and would strongly object to the removal of yet another of their major responsibilities. The Cabinet Committee concluded that there was also no public enthusiasm for the initiative and that in 'the interest of good local government the bias should be against further transfers of services from local authorities to the state'.[129] The Cabinet accepted that private water undertakings should be nationalised but there was no enthusiasm for Bevan's plans, and he was asked to reconsider his ideas for the industry.[130]

In January 1951 Bevan was moved to the Ministry of Labour and the local government element of the Ministry of Health was merged with the Ministry of Town Planning that had been allocated to Hugh Dalton after the 1950 general election. Health, initially a non-Cabinet department, was henceforth separated from any close connection with local government. Housing remained connected with local government and thus was transferred to the new Ministry of Local Government and Planning, and while the housing civil servants at first felt they were being taken over[131] they were soon to find themselves in a lead position when the Conservatives came into office in October 1951.

Both Jowitt and Bevan had put the issue of restructuring local government, a system which had emerged but fifty years previously, on the political agenda, and it is probable that the majority of the Cabinet agreed in principle with a predominantly single-tiered system of large local authorities. Members had failed to develop their ideas, partly due to the weight of more pressing government business, but resistance from the CCA and the districts and the hostility of a few senior Cabinet members such as Morrison and Chuter Ede also played a part. However, as with the genesis of many of the major restructurings of local government in the last 200 years, the possibility of change is tabled many years before circumstances ensure that the proposals are carried thorough in practice. Over the fifty years that followed, Bevan's ideas were increasingly established as the structural basis of local government in Britain.

Notes

1 2 & 3 Geo. VI, c. 76.
2 NA, CAB 117/ 213, Draft of Jowitt report, 25 Aug. 1941.
3 NA, CAB 65/ 51, Cabinet, 9 April 1943.
4 Responsibility was assigned to Sir John Anderson as Privy Seal and, later, Home Secretary: Donaghue and Jones, *Herbert Morrison: Portrait of a Politician*, p. 285.
5 *Ibid.*, p. 286.
6 NA, CAB 65/43 WM 96 (44); Donaghue and Jones, *Herbert Morrison*, pp. 294–5.
7 NA, HLG 51/940–2.
8 P. Addison, *The Road to 1945: British Politics and the Second World War* (London: Pimlico, 1994), p. 126.
9 K. Young and N. Rao, *Local Government Since 1945* (Oxford: Blackwell, 1997), pp. 9–10.
10 W. H. Beveridge, *Social Insurance and Allied Services*, Cmd 6404 (London: HMSO, 1942).
11 NA, CAB 117/213, Chrystal to Greenwood, 7 Jan. 1941.
12 CAB 117/213.
13 Young and Rao, *Local Government Since 1945*, p. 22.
14 NA, CAB 117/213, Jowitt report, draft of 11 Oct. 1941, p. 22.
15 *Ibid.*, pp. 28–32.
16 John Maud, before the war Master of Birkbeck College in London, was drafted into the Civil Service initially on the staff of the Regional Commissioner's team and then as a Regional Commissioner; but after a spell in the Ministry of Food became deputy and then permanent secretary in the Ministry of Reconstruction, and later was permanent secretary for Education and Fuel and Power. He subsequently was High Commissioner in South Africa before returning to academic life in 1963.
17 NA, HLG 43/973; the issue concerned merger of local education services in

the county and city of Cambridge. Maud was, however, aware that change was necessary to facilitate the development of an integrated health service: HLG 42/973, John Maud to Sir Alexander Maxwell, 19 April 1943.

18 NA, CAB 117/217; HLG 43/969.

19 CAB 117/217, AMC report on the reorganisation of local government.

20 *Ibid.*, County Councils' Association, Local Government Reform (final report), 18 Feb. 1943, p. 5, para. 17.

21 *Ibid.*, Urban District Councils' Association, Reorganisation of Local Government Memo; and Rural District Association Memorandum of the Executive Council in the place of Rural Districts in Local Government.

22 NA, CAB/117/217.

23 NA, HLG 43/973, Memorandum on present position on local government reform, 13 Feb. 1943; the term democratic is in quotes in the original text.

24 Hansard, vol. 392, cols 195–6, 22 Sept. 1943, Response to a parliamentary question.

25 Ministry of Health, *Local Government in England and Wales during the Period of Reconstruction*, Cmd 6579 (London: HMSO, 1945).

26 The Local Government (Boundary Commission) Act, 1945: 9 & 10 Geo. VI, c. 38.

27 NA, HLG/43/1167, Paper of 1 Aug. 1946.

28 *Ibid.*, Willink to Reading, 12 April 1945.

29 *Ibid.*, Reading to Bevan, 12 April 1946; Bevan to Reading, 12 May 1946.

30 NA, HLG/43/1167, Paper of 1 Aug. 1946 provides a resumé of the fortunes of the Reading Committee and indicates that Morrison was aware of the issue but showed no support for the study.

31 NA, CAB 117/218.

32 T. H. Marshall, *Social Policy* (London: Hutchinson, 4th edn, 1975), p. 83.

33 NA, HLG 42/973, John Maud to Sir Alexander Maxwell, 19 April 1943.

34 Ministry of Health, *A National Health Service*, Cmd 6502 (London: HMSO, 1943).

35 NA, MH 77/30 A.

36 MH 77/30 B.

37 MH 77/81.

38 Board of Education, *The Education of the Adolescent* (London: HMSO, 1926 (Hadow report).

39 Board of Education, *Report on Secondary Education* (London: HMSO, 1938) (Spens report).

40 Young and Rao, *Local Government Since 1945*, pp. 40–3.

41 K. Jones, *Education in Britain, 1944 to the Present* (Cambridge: Polity Press, 2003), pp. 14–23.

42 These were authorities that under Part 3 of the 1902 Education Act could operate elementary schools and were mainly larger urban districts and non-county boroughs.

43 S. J. Curtis, and M. Boultwood, *A History of English Education Since 1800* (London: University Tutorial Press, 4th edn, 1966), pp. 200–1.

44 NA, HLG/43/973.

45 Board of Trade, *Report of the Royal Commission on the Distribution of Industrial Population*, Cmd 6153 (London: HMSO, 1940) (Barlow report).

46 J. B. Cullingworth, *Town and Country Planning in Britain* (London: George Allen & Unwin, 6th edn, 1976), p. 34.

47 Ministry of Works and Building, *Report of the Expert Committee on Compensation and Betterment*, Cmd 6386 (London: HMSO, 1942 (Uthwatt report).

48 Ministry of Works and Building, *Report of the Committee on Land Utilisation in Rural Areas*, Cmd 6378 (London: HMSO, 1942) (Scott report).

49 I. McIntyre, *The Expense of Glory: A Life of John Reith* (London: Harper Collins, 1994), p. 265.

50 A Conservative, Lord Portal.

51 Cullingworth, *Town and Country Planning in Britain*, pp. 34–7.

52 B. Keith-Lucas, *The English Local Government Franchise* (Oxford: Basil Blackwell, 1952), p. 76; the Representation of the People Act, 1945: 8 & 9 Geo. VI, c. 5.

53 Keith-Lucas, *English Local Government Franchise*, p. 77; the Representation of the People Act, 1949: 11 & 12 Geo. VI, c. 65.

54 B. Pimlott, *Hugh Dalton* (London: Jonathan Cape, 1985), p. 176.

55 H. Dalton, *The Political Diary of Hugh Dalton, 1918–40, 1945–60*, ed. Ben Pimlott (London: Jonathan Cape, 1986), p. 515.

56 C. Attlee, *The Labour Party in Perspective* (London: Left Book Club–Gollancz, 1937), p. 7.

57 *Ibid.*, p. 197.

58 *Ibid.*, p. 176.

59 M. Foot, *Aneurin Bevan*, vol. 1: *1897–1945* (London: MacGibbon & Kee, 1962), p. 85.

60 Edith Summerskill quoted in Donoghue and Jones, *Herbert Morrison*, p. 189.

61 P. Hennessy, *Never Again: Britain 1945–51* (London: Jonathan Cape, 1992), p. 198.

62 K. O. Morgan, *Labour in Power 1945–51* (Oxford: Clarendon Press, 1984), p. 94.

63 Donaghue and Jones, *Herbert Morrison*, pp. 124–5.

64 NA, CAB 24/206 CP 305 (29), Report of the Committee on London Traffic, 7 Nov. 1929.

65 Donaghue and Jones, *Herbert Morrison*, pp. 140–50, 187–8.

66 *Ibid.*, pp. 123–4.

67 Ministry of Transport, *Electricity Distribution* (London: HMSO, 1936).

68 NA, CAB 129 CP 217, 11 Oct. 1945.

69 CAB 129 CP 124, 14 April 1947.

70 CAB 129 CP 205, 5 Oct. 1945, p. 2.

71 *Ibid.*, p. 2.

72 *Ibid.*, p. 3.

73 *Ibid.*, p. 4.

74 CAB 129 CP 227, 12 Oct. 1945.

75 CAB 129, CP 231, 16 Oct. 1945.

76 CAB 128, 40th meeting, 11 Oct. 1945, p. 2.

77 *Ibid.*, 43rd meeting, 18 Oct. 1945.

78 *Ibid.*

79 Young and Rao, *Local Government Since 1945*, pp. 55–6.
80 M. Foot, *Aneurin Bevan*, vol. 2: *1945–1960* (London: Davis-Poyner, 1973), p. 72.
81 The Housing (Financial and Miscellaneous Provisions) Act, 1947: 9 & 10 Geo. VI, c. 48.
82 Foot, *Aneurin Bevan*, vol. 2, p. 75.
83 *Ibid.*, p. 86.
84 I. Cole and R. Furbey, *The Eclipse of Council Housing* (London: Routledge, 1994), p. 98.
85 NA, CAB 129 CP 311, 31 July 1946.
86 CAB 128, 76th meeting, 1 Aug. 1946.
87 H. Dalton, *Practical Socialism in Britain* (London: Routledge, 1935), p. 274.
88 NA, CAB 132/2, Lord Privy Seal's Committee, 15 Feb. 1946; this was Morrison's Committee to co-ordinate domestic policy.
89 Ministry of Health and Ministry Town and Country Planning, *New Towns Committee: Interim Report*, Cmd 6759 (London: HMSO, 1946) (Reith report).
90 NA, CAB 129 CP 142, 8 April 1946, on the New Towns Bill.
91 The New Towns Act, 1946: 9 & 10 Geo VI, c. 68.
92 NA, CAB 129, CP 142, 8 April 1946, p. 1.
93 Cullingworth, *Town and Country Planning in Britain*, p. 179.
94 Dalton, *Practical Socialism in Britain*, p. 286.
95 Ministry of Town and Country Planning, *National Parks in England and Wales*, Cmd 6628 (London: HMSO, 1945) (Dowler report).
96 Ministry of Town and Country Planning, *National Parks (England and Wales)*, Cmd 7121 (London: HMSO, 1947) (Hobhouse report).
97 The National Parks Commission, which in 1968 became the Countryside Commission.
98 The National Parks and Access to the Countryside Act, 1949: 12, 13 & 14 Geo. VI, c. 97.
99 Cullingworth, *Town and Country Planning in Britain*, p. 181.
100 The Local Government Act, 1948: 11 & 12 Geo. VI, c. 26.
101 Minutes of the AMC General Purposes Committee, 2 Feb. 1950.
102 *Local Government Boundary Commission Report, 1947* (London: HMSO, 1948).
103 Young and Rao, *Local Government Since 1945*, p. 91.
104 NA, CAB 124/758, Memorandum from Lord President of the Council, March 1949.
105 *Local Government Boundary Commission Report, 1947*, para. 76.
106 *Ibid.*, para. 72.
107 NA, CAB 124/758 Bevan to Morrison, 14 March 1949.
108 *Ibid.*
109 CAB 129/34 CP 82, 8 April 1949.
110 CAB 129 CP 101, 4 May 1949.
111 CAB 129 CP 102, 9 May 1949.
112 CAB 128, 15th meeting, 12 May 1949.
113 Young and Rao, *Local Government Since 1945*, p. 94.
114 NA, CAB 134/470, Minutes of the 1st meeting of the Cabinet Committee on Local Government, 31 May 1949.

115 Young and Rao, *Local Government Since 1945*, p. 95.

116 NA, HLG 43/994, 27 June 1949.

117 The Committee which met on three occasions, 31 May, 13 July and 24 November 1949, was chaired by Attlee and had as members Morrison, Bevan, Silkin, Lord Chancellor Jowitt, Home Secretary Chuter Ede, Minister for Education Tomlinson, Minister for National Insurance Griffiths and parliamentary secretary for pensions C. J. Simmons; at the final meeting Minister for Agriculture and Fisheries Williams and Minister for Transport Barnes were also present.

118 NA, CAB 134/470, Minutes of 1st meeting, 31 May 1949.

119 The Minister is not named in the minutes.

120 NA, CAB 134/470, Minutes of 1st meeting.

121 *Ibid.*, Minutes of 2nd meeting, Cabinet Committee on Local Government, 13 July 1949.

122 *Ibid.*, LG (49) 3, Memorandum from the Minister for Health, 14 Oct. 1949.

123 *Ibid.*, Minutes of 3rd meeting, Cabinet Committee on Local Government, 24 Nov. 1949.

124 *Ibid.*, LG (49) 9, Memorandum from the Home Secretary, 15 November 1949.

125 *Ibid.*

126 *Ibid.*

127 *Ibid.*, LG (49) 7, Memorandum from the Minister for Agriculture and Fisheries, 16 Nov. 1949.

128 CAB 129 CP 54, 29 March 1950.

129 *Ibid.*

130 CAB 128, 28th meeting, 4 May 1950.

131 E. Sharpe, *The Ministry of Housing and Local Government* (London: George Allen & Unwin, 1969), pp. 15–16.

9

'Modernising' the system 1951–79

The incoming Conservative Government of 1951 had no developed plans for reforming local government. The Butskillist common ground between the Conservative and the Labour Party encompassed a tacit consensus on the structure and functions of the system as it had developed into a more service-orientated approach since 1945. Underlying this common outlook also ran an undercurrent of modernising zeal that had propelled Jowitt, Willink and, later, Bevan to consider the restructuring of the system into larger units. During the 1950s and 1960s this was to become an increasingly engrained value in the changing leadership of both parties, driving an eventual recasting of the late nineteenth-century system into a structure that, as its proponents thought, fitted a commuting rather than community-based generation.

Macmillan at Housing and Local Government

During the first years of the Churchill Government local government became in effect a ministry for housing. Churchill allocated the Ministry of Local Government and Planning to Harold Macmillan in order to fulfil the latter's ambitious pledge made at the 1950 Conservative Party Conference to build 300,000 new houses a year.[1] Macmillan immediately renamed his charge the Ministry of Housing and Local Government (MHLG), and during most of his two years in office concentrated on housing by ending the restraints on private building and encouraging local authorities to build more homes.[2] Despite Treasury constraints on spending, the pledge was sufficiently important to enable Macmillan to initiate a period of expansion in local authority budgets. Macmillan was concerned in the longer term to develop private sector housing and shift the balance of provision away from the Labour Party's concentration on the public sector. A White Paper published in 1953 proposed amending legislation to allow both private and public sector landlords to increase rents, provided their houses were in good repair, in order to encourage private landlords to maintain older properties and ensure that buying houses was a more attractive option.[3] The required legislation was enacted in 1954.[4] Rents, Macmillan argued, should be connected to rateable values for houses, but therein lay a further problem, in that the formula for revaluation established under the 1948 Local Government Act was considered unworkable.[5] To pay for housing, Chancellor of the Exchequer R. A. Butler allowed local authorities to borrow some of their funds from banks or stock options on the grounds that borrowing from the private sector as opposed to the Public Works Loans Board (PWLB) would be more costly for local authorities and would reduce their enthusiasm for capital spending.[6] Doubtless, not a few Conservatives realised the arrangement might also benefit private sector banks. By 1960 the Board had become a less significant source of capital for local government as the banks and the investing public came to regard local authorities as a financially secure source for long-term investment.

By 1954 Macmillan was becoming increasingly concerned about a groundswell of irritation among home-owners concerning the rates and the possible increases that might follow the planned rates' review. A revaluation of rates scheduled for 1952 was postponed[7] and a new system of valuation under the control of the Inland Revenue was introduced the following year.[8] Local authorities were also threatening to raise rates to pay for expansionist policies in housing, education and roads. A further difficulty was the continuing quarrels between county and county boroughs as larger boroughs sought county status. The Minister decided to initiate a preliminary debate on all of these issues in a paper he entitled 'Operation Round-Up' with the subtitle 'A comprehensive system of local government: *A poor thing but mine own*'. In reality the ambitious Minister was setting the future agenda, observing that there would probably be insufficient time to deal with his ideas before the next election, but 'even if the Cabinet think it more prudent, after viewing the collection, to have it dusted and put away, it will be useful for my successors to leave it properly catalogued'.[9] On the reform of local government structure Macmillan was more prudent than Bevan, recommending the retention of two-tier systems of local government, modest expansion of larger boroughs to county borough status and the removal of some of the smaller boroughs and districts.[10] His financial proposals were more radical and led to the introduction of a general grant, the phasing out of many block grants and a realigning of the rating system.[11] The paper was assigned to a Cabinet Committee, which did not come to a conclusion until 1955, by which time Macmillan had moved on to be replaced by Duncan Sandys.

Financial reforms

The problem of funding was perhaps the most serious issue concerning local government for the Conservatives. Increasing numbers of specific grants for new services and the expansion of social and infrastructure programmes ensured that the burden of paying for local services was falling increasingly on the tax-payer rather than the rate-payer. The payment of rates had been concentrated since 1929 on the domestic resident and on shopkeepers following the de-rating of industry and agriculture, but redressing the balance would create inevitable hostility from farmers and businesses. Increasing payments from the Exchequer, however, would oblige ministers to intervene more closely in local authority activities if they wished to restrain spending. There was no thought prior to the Thatcher Government of curbing local authorities' capacity to set rates, and hence any centrally managed controls over revenue would have to apply to either general or specific grants. In 'Operation Round-Up' Macmillan viewed specific grants as a national charge and suggested that 'it would be much better to work back to the partnership system between Central and Local Government, which is best expressed by fifty per cent grants for the various services and to have a modified system of general grants'. With regard to rates, he thought that 'the time has come to end the "de-rating" of industry. This is the only way, other than dangerous "fancy schemes" (like local income tax) which can help substantially.'[12] Macmillan also hinted at the possibility of rating agricultural land and, in an appendix to his paper, observed that 'the total abolition of agricultural rating has forced many of the counties to become largely reliant upon the Exchequer'.[13] In order to make such a scheme palatable he proposed reductions in government subsidies for council-house building and changes to the equalisation grant.

Following Macmillan's initiative, Duncan Sandys launched an extensive inquiry into local government finance.[14] Ministers accepted their civil servants' recommendation that reform should be 'directed to increasing the independence and financial responsibility of local authorities, not to relieving the rate payer'.[15] Sceptical ministers argued that greater independence may mean more extravagant local authorities but the Treasury representative Henry Brooke, who before becoming an MP had been leader of the Conservatives on the LCC, observed that 'if local authorities were not to be the financial partners of central government they would merely be its agents'.[16] Fanning the embers of dual-polity values, Brooke maintained: 'Local authorities would undoubtedly exercise greater prudence in financing services which they would be required to sustain out of their own resources', claiming that 'extravagance in local government was often due to the imposition of national standards where they were not required by local opinion'.[17]

Ministers endorsed, without apparent debate, a civil service report rejecting new forms of local taxation such as a local income tax and decided to raise further funds locally by re-rating industry and possibly land. The Board of Trade objected to a further cost on business activity and the Minister of Agriculture adamantly opposed re-rating for farmland. The final conclusion was a compromise of a 50 per cent rate on industry and the re-rating of farm buildings. The main beneficiary of re-rating was the Treasury, as the extra funds were to be clawed back by the Exchequer in grant reductions. Greater local autonomy would be secured by replacing many specific grants with a general grant. Sandys proposed the creation of a general grant which should account for nearly two-thirds of grant aid rather than one-sixth as had previously been the case. The changes modified the contentious equalisation grant set up by the Labour Government. Objections from the Ministries of Education and Health that they would be unable to control local spending on their services without specific grants[18] were overridden by the Treasury's belief that economies could be secured if local authorities had to sustain themselves on their own resources.[19]

The agreed financial package was announced in July 1957[20] and where necessary put into practice within the 1958 Local Government Act.[21] This proved to be but a brief return to the principle that local authorities were responsible for raising their own funds. The Macmillan and Douglas Home Governments were dogged by fears in relation to the revaluation of rateable property in 1963 over the electoral impact of a rise in the value in middle-class areas. The Government appointed an Inquiry under the chairmanship of Professor R. G. D. Allen to assess the impact of the rates on individuals with differing levels of income and, in the interim, cast around for measures to decrease the rate demands on voters for the following year.[22] It was eventually agreed, contrary to decisions during Sandys's study of local government finance, to transfer further funds from the Treasury to the block grant to resolve the situation.[23] To what extent ministers were fully aware of the dangers of shifting responsibility for local services to themselves is not clear from committee debates, but it is evident that Conservative ministers, discussing the issue away from narrow interests of departmental control, generally saw value in a partnership arrangement in which the local authorities shouldered at least half the burden of paying for services and in consequence would be more prudent in their use of resources. Nevertheless, ministries, such as Education, which had developed policies that were implemented by local governments were unwilling to relinquish their fiscal powers to steer local policy.

Restructuring local government

As well as resolving financial problems, the Conservatives had to deal with the unresolved issues of local government structure. In 1954 Luton forced the pace by sponsoring a Private Bill to gain county borough status, but Macmillan had shelved immediate resolution of the problem by announcing he would not support the Bill, although he was prepared to review the status of boroughs, county boroughs and counties. The LAAs, realising that they needed to reach some agreement on reform if they were to have any influence over their future, suggested to Sandys that he could chair a number of meetings between their officers and members to thrash out some form of agreement on the way ahead. Sandys seized the opportunity and presented ministers with a draft proposal for restructuring of local government, outside of London, in England and Wales.[24] The process for altering status and boundaries should be given to a Local Government Commission. Applications for county borough status would normally not be considered for populations of less than 125,000 in conurbations and 100,000 elsewhere. Authorities could apply for extensions to their boundaries and counties could make recommendations on the boundaries of districts and boroughs within their borders, although a borough could not be demoted other than with the agreement of a minister. The agreement was less clear on the redistribution of functions between different types of authority, although it was suggested that some of the functions yet to be determined could pass from counties to districts and boroughs with populations over 60,000 and that 'all functions should be exercised at the lowest administrative level consistent with efficiency and economy'.[25] In reality, the LAAs were still unable to agree on the issue, but hoped Sandys would broker a deal on their behalf.

Ian Macleod, then Minister of Health, observed that 'it must be regarded as remarkable, almost an incredible achievement to reach an agreement at all on such a subject ... no subject is more explosive than this and none will raise more controversy however carefully the White Paper be worded'.[26] The Conservative Government viewed the LAAs as weighty and influential interest groups which it was advisable not to offend. The predominantly Conservative CCA was viewed with respect and its leading members had sufficient informal links with Conservative MPs through County Conservative Associations to be an influential force.[27] Much discussion took place in the Cabinet Committee on the need to ensure that any statement made on the proposed reforms would be seen to have derived from the LAAs themselves. Following the 1955 election, Duncan Sandys remained in post to pursue his strategy. Although there was still no accord on the redistribution of functions, there was sufficient agreement on other issues to facilitate publication of a White Paper in July 1956[28] announcing the establishment of a Local Government Commission. Several ministers had questioned whether it would die the death of the abortive 1945 Boundary Commission, but Sandys believed that during the time it took for the Commission to be established agreement would be reached on functions.[29] Such an agreement never materialised as the county councils refused to relinquish powers to urban authorities. Following inconclusive negotiations with the LAAs, Sandys secured Cabinet agreement to establish his own solution in a White Paper published in May 1957[30] proposing a range of services that could be delegated on request to any urban district or borough with a population exceeding 60,000. These included education services granted to the existing excepted areas, some social service functions, weights and measures and public health inspection. The 1958 Local Government Act put into practice the proposals for the Boundary Commission's functions and the reforms of local finance.[31]

The Boundary Commission for England, chaired by Sir Henry Hancock, adopted a framework of piecemeal and gradual change acting largely as a quasi-judicial arbiter between conflicting claims and counter-claims by local authorities and their associations. Long-demanded upgrades of boroughs like Luton and Cheltenham to county borough status were granted and also additions to the boundaries of several county boroughs. The West Midland conurbation was reorganised to create six county boroughs and the Isle of Ely and the Soke of Peterborough, which had the status of separate counties, were merged with the counties, respectively, of Cambridgeshire and Huntingdonshire. A few recommendations were, however, rejected by the Government, including, most controversially, the merger of Rutland with Leicestershire. A parallel Commission for Wales was less successful, proposing a reduction of the 13 counties to 7 and the demotion of Merthyr Tydfil to borough status, but securing Government approval only for extensions to the boundaries of Newport and Cardiff.[32] The Welsh proposals nevertheless pointed the way to reorganisation in the 1970s.

Root and branch: the restructuring of London

The 1956 and 1957 White Papers had side-stepped the issue of London's structure by retaining the *status quo* in Middlesex to the annoyance of large boroughs in north London. The boroughs of Ealing and Illford had pressed several times for county borough status, but to concede such an arrangement would severely diminish the status of Middlesex. Only vague promises were made to consult further on the issue. Irresolution changed to purposeful action when Macmillan appointed Brooke as Minister for Housing and Local Government. Henry Brooke had retained his interest in the affairs of the capital's Conservative party since becoming an MP[33] and set about the reform of the metropolis with an eye towards party advantage by replacing the Labour stronghold of the LCC with an arrangement that might be far more propitious for Conservatives. It was, argued Brooke, absurd that the Boundary Commission was considering the structure of local authorities in conurbations in England to the exclusion of the largest of them all. It was unlikely, however, that they could resolve the problem of London through the Boundary Commission as no agreement among the Middlesex authorities was probable. The issue was best tackled by a root-and-branch review undertaken by an independent inquiry with some clout. Brooke favoured giving the review royal commission status because 'it will have to be extremely pertinacious to get the facts as local authorities will not look beyond their own boundaries'.[34] The area to be studied would be defined by the confines of the greenbelt around the conurbation, and was in effect the boundaries of the Metropolitan Police.[35]

The Royal Commission was announced in July 1957 and in November Sir Edwin Herbert, a solicitor with no close interest in local government, was appointed as its chair. The other members also had no direct experience of working in local government, although several members had much experience working with the system.[36] The Commission followed standard procedures of inviting evidence from interested organisations, which yielded predictable responses. Boroughs such as Illford and Harrow pressed their case for county council status, while Middlesex defended its integrity.[37] The AMC advocated larger single-tier London boroughs whereas the CCA supported the *status quo*.[38] The LCC, as did London's Labour party, opposed any substantive change to its county council status, fearing that any wider representative body for London would be Conservative. The London Municipal Society speaking for the Conservative interest criticised the conduct of the LCC and, following policies that could be traced back to Lord Salisbury, showed no enthusiasm for the creation of a powerful upper-tier authority, preferring the delegation of greater powers to London boroughs. After a rethink, perhaps following contacts at ministerial level, they began to favour a stronger greater London council.[39]

The Commission set a standard for future studies in its use of research by commissioning a more impartial academic view. It was influenced particularly by William Robson, who had formed a Greater London Study Group, which favoured the creation of a single authority for greater London, although the group was divided on the role of sub-units, with Robson favouring a smaller number of populous London boroughs in contrast to a faction led by David Donnison that proposed a larger number of smaller authorities.[40]The Commission's report issued in October 1960 advocated a root-and-branch overhaul of London government along broadly the lines suggested by the Greater London Study Group.[41] It recommended the creation of a conurbation-wide Greater London Council (GLC) to be responsible for strategic planning, transport, fire services, housing and education standards. The implementation of many of these services would be in the hands of a tier of 51 London boroughs with populations ranging from 100,000 to 250,000, apart from the City of London which was to remain unchanged. Their size was regarded by the Commission as the smallest possible to adequately discharge local functions such as refuse collection and housing. The creation of fewer but larger London boroughs was rejected on the grounds that there was a need to retain a sense of local representation.

The report was well received by most members of the Government. Brooke accepted the need for the 'greater' strategic authority but argued the case for some forty London boroughs, as 'boroughs over a quarter of a million population are not the best units of local government. They inevitably tend to become bureaucratic – and the larger they are the more remote the councillor.'[42] Other cabinet members preferred larger authorities and finally Brooke had to compromise by accepting thirty-two London boroughs.[43] There remained serious objections from the Ministry of Education to a GLC with strategic responsibility for education, as such an arrangement had not worked in Middlesex and would not work in London as a whole. The Ministry maintained that an education authority should cater for a population of at least 320,000 and in central London it would be necessary to have even larger units of administration, as the borders between authorities would be highly artificial barriers in the minds of parents seeking the best schools for their children.[44] The compromise emerged that the GLC would have no responsibility for education and that some form of joint board would be created to serve the interests of education in the centre of London. A sub-committee under the chairmanship of Lord Hailsham resolved the issue by proposing that the old LCC Education Authority would continue as the Inner London Education Authority for a five-year trial period, while the outer boroughs would be education authorities in their own right.[45]

Before drafting the Bill to restructure London government, Charles Hill, who had succeeded Brooke at the MHLG had to resolve several issues of detail. The exact boundaries of the GLC had to be determined and a number of Conservative authorities in the commuter-land of deepest Surrey argued for their exclusion from the conurbation. Discreet but effective pressure through local MPs was applied and districts such as Epsom were removed from the scheme.[46] While the number of authorities had been agreed by the Cabinet, drawing up the boundaries required some adroit manoeuvring before a scheme could be devised to create the minimum of opposition from existing councils and local interests. The system of determining the new structures for London was a top–down process rather than one emanating from local initiatives. The MHLG began the process by drafting a plan that was circulated for consultation in December 1961. This was discussed in a series of conferences presided over by one of a team of four town clerks, drawn from local authorities outside of London, who reported their proposals to the Minister for his final approval.[47]

The Bill was the most controversial measure tabled by the Government during the parliamentary session of 1962–63. The Labour Party was pushed strongly in the direction of outright opposition by, the now, Lord Morrison of Lambeth who, supported by other prominent Labour MPs for London, at every opportunity argued that the whole scheme was a Tory device to destroy the LCC solely because it was a Labour stronghold.[48] There was little public support for Morrison's orchestrated opposition to change[49] and the Bill became an Act on 31 July 1963, requiring the new system to be implemented on 1 April 1965. By that time Labour had taken power but made no effort to overturn an arrangement that was well on the way to completion. The fears of Morrison that the Conservatives had rearranged London in their own electoral interests were not to materialise since in April 1964 Labour gained control of the GLC in the first elections for the new structure and the following month won control of twenty of the London boroughs.[50]

The Labour Government 1964–70

The Conservatives had entered office in the 1950s with no strong modernising agenda, but left power having initiated a major root-and-branch reform of local government in London. During the first years in office, Macmillan attempted to resolve the quarrels between county and county borough and ensure that the growing burden of social costs for which local government had increasing responsibility could be paid for by the local authorities themselves. Brooke inclined towards medium-sized London boroughs and did not value large authorities that could lose touch with their communities. By the end of their thirteen years in office, there were, however, elements entering the Conservatives' ranks who were changing the ideology of the party on the role of the State in general and, as a minor element of such thinking, of local government. A more impatient view was shown by Keith Joseph, the final Minister for HLG in the Conservative's long stay in office, who pressed the Boundary Commission to recommend changes to smaller counties, arguing that

> the re-organisation of local government was an essential part of the policy of modernisation; progress in a number of fields was impeded by the existence of antiquated and inefficient units of local government.
>
> It was important to the development of the Government's policies in relation to housing transport and the social services to abolish small units of local government, which were incapable of providing the specialist and other services necessary to maintain the standards achieved elsewhere.[51]

Keith Joseph and Richard Crossman, the first Minister for HLG in Wilson's Labour Government, may have differed in relation to social welfare provision but not in their lack of reverence either for tradition or for viewing local government as an agency of the State. Crossman, like many of Labour's leaders during the 1960s, including Harold Wilson, was drawn to the view that equality meant ensuring that the working class had opportunities to receive a middle-class lifestyle. They were, like the evolving New Right of the Conservative Party, fully aware of the appeal of a 'modern' lifestyle that involved for the lower-middle and the skilled working classes home-ownership and, crucially, a family car. A modern world was not based on a neighbourhood community but on communities at a distance. Working men and women could commute to work using their own transport and their leisure hours, when not fixed indoors to the television, meant days out to the country, the shopping-centre of a large town or, for the more affluent including many a Labour MP such as Crossman, from London flat to weekend rural retreat. Localism was becoming, therefore, irrelevant. As Labour MP and academic John Mackintosh remarked of local government, 'it is generally accepted that its structure has not changed enough to keep up with the changing patterns of travel to work, shopping and holiday areas'.[52]

The 1964 Labour *Manifesto* highlighted the need for modernisation of the nation's economy following what was in its view 'thirteen wasted years' of Conservative rule. There was a pressing need to restore British pre-eminence in industry and technology by 'mobilising the resources of technology under a national plan'.[53] Almost nothing in the document suggested that local authorities, as opposed to a nebulous vision of regions, were to have any part in this modernising vision.[54] Despite the relatively scant attention given to local government in the *Manifesto* of 1964, the Wilson Government initiated major reforms of the system. A survey by the MHLG at the request of Cabinet Secretary Sir Burke Trend highlighted eleven major initiatives by 1969 involving local government reforms and raised serious concerns about the capacity of the Labour administration to reconcile all their inter-linking elements.[55] The first tasks facing the new Minister of HLG initially made Crossman, much like Macmillan, predominantly a minister of housing. The party had committed itself to building 400,000 houses a year. Chancellor of the Exchequer Jim Callaghan raised serious concerns about the cost of an expansive housing policy, but Crossman argued that by using modern building methods it was possible to create housing estates much less expensively than in the past. Harold Wilson, an enthusiast for modern technology, decisively supported Crossman, who raised tower blocks in their multitudes.[56]

A further initiative was the Seebohm Committee, established in 1965 in response to serious concerns over standards of childcare.[57] A separate study that reported in 1966 had been established for Scotland.[58] The Seebohm report was published in July 1968 on the same day as a Green Paper on the restructuring of the health service. Seebohm argued that all personal social services should be consolidated as a local government responsibility at county and county borough level under major committees, each of the same weight as an LEA and controlled by a director of social services whose appointment would be subject to central government approval. In principle the idea was much to the taste of Whitehall and the report's recommendations were approved by the Cabinet, though the Government reserved decision on when to implement the proposal while the local government system and the health service were being reconstructed.[59]

Throughout the Blair governments Labour has displayed much management-driven enthusiasm for what has been termed 'joined-up' government. In practice governments since the 1830s have been tinkering with the machinery of governance to join up disparate elements of the system that need to be co-ordinated in view of pressing policy problems. The LGB, for example, was created to merge those elements of central government overseeing both the issue of sanitation and the amelioration of poverty. The Seebohm Report is an essay in joining up elements of government in a sector attracting considerable critical attention. Similarly, the Willink Royal Commission in 1962 had recommended that police forces for efficiency should cover populations of at least 250,000.[60] A Police Act in 1964 gave the Home Secretary powers to amalgamate smaller police forces. As Labour Home Secretary, Roy Jenkins began to rigidly implement this recommendation and in 1966 reduced the number of police forces from 117 to 49 by amalgamating county borough with county council forces or by joining together the police authorities of neighbouring county boroughs.[61] The change pre-empted the Redcliffe-Maud report's enthusiasm for linking town with country.[62]

The joined-up enthusiasm of the Wilson governments which trailed their modernisation and anti-traditional credentials with a passion equal to New Labour's committed them to restructuring central government on the basis of a smaller number of strategic government departments whose ministers would have an overview of previously rather disparate but, nevertheless, interlinked departments. A consequence of this strategy would be the creation of the Department of the Environment (DoE), by joining the MHLG with Transport and Public Building and Works, to which was given a broadened remit of ensuring a more habitable environment, especially in relation to water supply. The proposal of the department, made in 1969, was retained by Edward Heath and the DoE came into being in October 1970.[63]

Finance 1964–70

By 1964 the principal difference between the Conservatives and Labour on the issue of local government lay largely in Labour's distaste for the rate system, which it saw as a regressive tax. The Government was, therefore, inclined to shift the payment for local services from the rate-payer on to the Exchequer and thus secure greater equality in local funding. Callaghan observed that in shifting the balance of the rate burden they should leave 'as much independence as possible to local authorities',[64] but that could be achieved only by funding local authorities from more progressive central taxation. In practice serious discussion of the dangers of decreased independence among local authorities scarcely entered Labour's deliberations in the Cabinet or its committees. Finance was the most prominent issue in the Labour Manifesto relating to local government. The rate was viewed 'as a tax which falls heavily on those with low incomes'[65] and greater reliance would, therefore, be placed on funding local government from the Exchequer, following an investigation of alternative systems of local government finance. In February 1965 Crossman received the long-awaited report of the Allen Committee which confirmed that the rate was a regressive tax, particularly for one- or two-person households, and that there were serious inequalities in the capacities of local authorities to raise rates. Only one-fifth of local authorities raised more than half of the total rate fund.[66] Following a manifesto commitment to provide rate rebates for poorer householders, the policy was accepted in June, despite the Chancellor's wish for at least a delay to this expensive commitment.[67] Crossman succeeded in getting an Act through Parliament that allowed domestic rate-payers on low incomes to apply for rebates, with the Treasury paying back most of the revenue that was otherwise lost to local government.

Rate rebates were intended by Crossman to be simply a short-term measure until he could devise a more substantial reform of local government funding,[68] but radical change proved to be more difficult to engineer than Crossman had anticipated. Although some form of local income tax was seen by Harold Wilson as preferable to the rating system,[69] the Civil Service continued to condemn any alternative to the system, arguing that the only other means of raising sufficient funds were a local sales tax, an employment tax or income tax. The first two were ruled out as creating economic tensions between authorities, should they charge different rates of tax on sales or employment. A local income tax was also unsuitable as it would be difficult to collect at source due to the need to factor in the place of residence of an employee.[70] Moreover 'tax on personal incomes and business profits would seriously inhibit the freedom of the Central Government in operating in the same fields' and would frustrate the capacity to use income tax to implement economic policies consistently throughout the country.[71] Callaghan's acceptance of the finding of 'official studies' that 'there was no alternative to the rating system as a major source of independent finance for local authorities' meant that the Government had to consider a scheme that relied on central taxation for limiting calls on the rates.[72] A White Paper published in February 1966 was regarded as something of an interim measure.[73] It was agreed that grants would be calculated on the assumption that they would only rise in line with increases in the GDP and that departments would calculate how much extra was needed to support an expansion of services. If local authorities wished to raise more on top of this then they would have to increase the rates above the centrally planned levels. Assuming expansion in services, the arrangement was expected to decrease the proportion of income accruing from the rates. The Government would also relieve pressure on the rates by providing half the cost of permitted capital expenditure. The general grant was recast as the rate support grant in a form that would facilitate redistribution to poorer local authorities. Despite the inevitable pressure from the Ministries of Education and Health for a specific grant to allow them greater control over local services,[74] only the police and the highways were to be funded by specific grants.

Restructuring the local government system

Crossman reflected in his diary:

> When I first became Minister of Housing I started with the usual ideas that were taught me, and in my very first speech I said that the one thing that one couldn't possibly have was the reform of local government because no sane politician would undertake it ... Then as I travelled round the country I became more and more aware, week by week, as so often happens, that what I was told by all the local government politicians and civil servants was untrue. In sober fact the time was ripe for a total and radical reform of local government because the people in local government, the officials as well as the councillors, were aware of their own inanity and inadequacy.[75]

This mood was accentuated by the slow legalistic process of the Boundary Commission reviews which Crossman thought meant 'accepting the war between county councils and the county boroughs as endemic in our national life'.[76] He endeavoured to get the local government section of his department to develop ideas on restructuring, but such initial efforts to restart the reform process were opposed by Dame Evelyn Sharp, the permanent secretary to the MHLG, who considered that the Boundary Commission was the best option open to them.[77] Crossman publicly announced the possibility of an inquiry on local government restructuring to the AMC Conference on 21 September without consulting his permanent secretary[78] who, although by no means pleased, was obliged to support his initiative. For Harold Wilson, who seems to have been initially indifferent to the idea, the clinching factor in its favour was that proposals for restructuring local authority boundaries in Lancashire would have had led to a reduction in safe Labour constituencies in the very area in which several cabinet members and the Prime Minister himself held their seats.[79]

The proposal to establish a Royal Commission was agreed in Cabinet without serious opposition. Crossman's breakthrough succeeded partly because he faced a Cabinet which had few champions of local authorities. He quotes Wilson telling him:

> You have got nobody like Herbert Morrison, Chuter Ede or Nye Bevan ... who really is an authority on local government. In this Cabinet there isn't a single person of that quality and that's why you have been getting away with murder.[80]

Crossman argued his case in a paper which rehearses familiar themes that the size of local authorities bore no relation to their function and that in the nineteenth century urban governments had been divided from their rural hinterland prompting the running battles between counties and county boroughs that had to be brought to an end.[81] The suggestion that an inquiry was unnecessary, as relevant government departments could conduct their own studies, met with little support on the grounds that the task was so complex it required careful consideration of local authority opinion.[82] It was also accepted that the Scottish Office would conduct a parallel Inquiry into local government within the Province. A senior Scottish judge, Lord Wheatley, was appointed to chair their inquiry. The Welsh Office, which had only recently been created in response to nationalist pressures, explained that it was already preparing for reform; it was agreed that the Welsh Inquiry should continue alongside, but distinct from, the English Inquiry.

The precise terms of the Royal Commission were agreed in May and were to involve the whole of England with the exception of London, given its recent major restructuring. It was also agreed not to include issues relating to the allocation of functions as between central and local government. An essential concomitant of the Commission was the winding up of the Boundary Commission. Crossman faced difficulties in finding a suitable chair for the Inquiry. Harold Wilson suggested Sir Norman Chester, then Warden of Nuffield College, Oxford, but Sir Mathew Stevenson, who had replaced Evelyn Sharp as permanent secretary to the department, had 'made it clear that he wants to have John Maud … Moreover, if I am not going to be at the Ministry in two and half years' time when the report is produced and Steve is, it's only fair for him to have the person he wants.'[83]

The members of the Redcliffe-Maud[84] Commission were appointed predominantly on the recommendation of officials. Unlike the Herbert Commission, there was strong representation of local authority members and officers from counties and county boroughs, but significantly the Commission had no representative of rural and urban districts, the boroughs or the parishes. Expert opinion from outside local government came from Dame Evelyn Sharp, Mr Reginald Wallis, a retired senior Labour Party official, and Derek Senior, a respected *Guardian* correspondent on town and country matters. Members were likely to accept the basic premiss that local government was based on too many small and unequal units and needed restructuring into fewer larger authorities.[85] The Commission was the most thorough, to that date, of post-1945 inquiries, meeting on 181 occasions, receiving over 2,000 witnesses and consuming more funds than any preceding study.[86] Maud built on the Herbert Commission's pioneering use of academic research, appointing a research team led by L. J. Sharpe of Nuffield College, Oxford.

The main report was radical but, given the weight of official and academic opinion concerning the structure of local government, predictable. The Commission accepted that the local government system was based on too many units of disparate size and with functions which bore little relevance to urban growth in the twentieth century. A survey commissioned for the Inquiry asked respondents in their own homes to name the area where they found themselves most at home. A majority of the respondents named a very small area of a few streets or a hamlet. The conclusion derived from this information was that a sense of community was usually grounded in areas that were too small to form the basis of a viable local authority and, therefore, such a concept as 'community' could not be used as a basis for determining local government structure. Such a question can be misleading since respondents may answer differently according to whether they are asked in their homes or in more distant locations. It is symptomatic of the overwhelming presumption in favour of larger authorities that the Commission accepted the view that 'community' was not a factor on which they could found a reformed local government structure.[87] It was accepted that larger local government units could, as in the older Bevan plan, be based on urban centres united with their rural hinterlands.

The solution was, therefore, to divide England into 59 single-tier authorities with populations ranging for the most part between 250,000 and 1,000,000 which centred wherever possible on a large town that was to serve as the hub of its surrounding suburbs and rural districts. Three large conurbations, the West Midlands, Greater Manchester and Merseyside would be two-tier structures in which strategic functions such as planning and transport would be assigned to an upper-tier metropolitan county, while metropolitan districts would provide education, social and housing services. In minor notes of dissent two Commissioners advocated a slightly larger number of districts, while the county education official Jack Longland suggested slightly fewer. The idea of regions was cautiously accepted, with a proposal of eight indirectly elected provincial councils having rather ill-defined advisory powers on land use, economic development and major services such as education and social care. The single-tier structure was slightly assuaged by proposals to retain elected parish councils or town councils based on former boroughs that would not have significant powers to provide services but would 'watch over the particular interests of communities in city town and village throughout England'.[88] The only major note of dissent came from the journalist Derek Senior, who penned a minority report advocating a two-tier system of local government based on upper-tier city regions which would take over planning and education functions, with smaller districts responsible for the remaining services.[89] While Senior's proposals arguably made more geographical sense than the main report, they were more complex and did not vary from the basic assumption that the existing map of local government should be torn up and replaced by a much smaller number of larger units that embraced town and country as a single unit.

Redcliffe-Maud's outline of his proposals was broadly welcomed by the Cabinet in March 1969. The Senior Report was to be viewed as a critique of the majority report but henceforward received little attention. The

Cabinet's local government sub-committee did not see the report as an issue of great urgency, as it could not be debated before the end of that parliamentary session.[90] The Cabinet accepted that view, but some ministers clearly had reservations considering that its implementation 'would necessitate a great deal or work and be likely to draw ... complaints from local interests and was not worth undertaking unless they believed that the quality of local government would be improved as a result'.[91] However by 18 June, Wilson had requested the Civil Service to speed up consideration of the report so that a white paper could be issued by October and legislation in the next session of Parliament.[92] Crossman argues that Wilson's haste was motivated by his concern to justify the Government's strategy of setting up the inquiry in order to forestall potential changes to constituency boundaries.[93] Despite holding two other meetings, the local government sub-committee did not get round to discussing reform until its September meeting, which considered the Wheatley report and the conclusions of the Welsh Office on restructuring, although greater urgency had entered its deliberations as it put in train a three-month period for consultation, which drew immediate criticism that the time allowed was too short.

The Wheatley report, published in September 1969, accepted a diagnosis of the ills of local government in Scotland similar to that of the Maud report for England: 'At the root of the trouble is the present structure of local government. It has remained basically the same for forty years when everything around it has changed.'[94] The Commission arrived at a solution to the problem far more akin to Senior's than to Redcliffe-Maud's. Scotland should be divided into 7 large regions which would be responsible for major services such as education, police, social services, transport, major roads and overall strategic planning, with a further tier of 37 districts to deal with more local services such as housing, environmental health, recreation and local planning. Proposals for local government restructuring in Wales had been on the table since the publication of a White Paper of 1967 recommended a two-tier structure based on 5 counties, each of which was divided into 36 districts.[95] The counties would be responsible for major services such as education, social services and strategic planning, while housing and refuse collection became the principal tasks for the districts. In south Wales the three county boroughs of Cardiff, Swansea and Newport were to remain unchanged. There would finally be an advisory Council for Wales as a whole. Despite constant pressure from the Welsh Office the proposals were not discussed until the findings of the Redcliffe-Maud Inquiry were known. The two-tier system, in contrast to England, could, as in Scotland, be justified on the grounds that it was better suited to a predominantly rural area. The MHLG objected to the idea on the grounds that if the two-tier system was possible in rural Wales it would provide a strong argument for rural areas in England to seek a similar arrangement. Although not brought into the discussion, such reasoning applied also to the Wheatley proposals. The Cabinet requested the Welsh Office to think again,[96] but later in October accepted the view that Scotland and Wales were sufficiently different to accept a two-tier structure but could not accept the retention of county boroughs, and obliged the Welsh Office to conduct a further Inquiry into the structure of local government for Glamorgan and Monmouthshire.[97] The outcome of that Inquiry led to a proposal to form three unitary authorities, Monmouthshire, and East and West Glamorgan, with a joint police authority.[98]

Apart from the issues of structure, a wholesale reform of local government initiated debates on a raft of related issues. The Cabinet Committee agreed to remove aldermen from the local government system, decided that councillors should receive expenses including compensation for loss of earning, but not a salary, and debated, without any clear resolution, the extent to which local authorities could be given powers of general competence.[99] A further issue concerned the relationship of local government with the NHS. The Government had suggested in a Green Paper[100] that hospitals and the executive councils which managed the general practitioners' services be merged under one agency with the local government managed ambulance and health-visiting services. The Green Paper left open the possibility that the more unified NHS could be included as part of a reformed local government structure. The Redcliffe-Maud report hinted that this was possible[101] and the Senior memorandum of dissent referred to and favoured this arrangement.[102] However, the Civil Service in 1966 had shown a strong antipathy to such an idea[103] and there was little enthusiasm for the proposal among ministers. The Cabinet Committee for reorganisation never seriously discussed the issue.[104] Crossman, now Minister for Health and Social Services, managed to use the antipathy of the doctors to incorporation into the local government system as a bargaining counter with both the local authorities and the BMA to ensure a compromise on Seebohm. If the doctors accepted that local government would retain personal social services as a co-ordinated service then he would resist any attempt to force the NHS into the reformed structure of local government.[105] All sides settled for an arrangement that maintained a health service not subject to effective local controls and a system of social services weakly linked, and often in conflict, with the health services.[106]

As the Government's proposals for a Bill based largely on the Commission's reports began to take shape, opposition to single-tier governance from many local authorities began to take shape. The most intense hostility came from the rural districts which in 1969 launched a campaign supported by posters urging 'Don't vote for R. E. Mote'.[107] By November 1969 the CCA, which had initially shown some support for a single-tier structure, joined forces with the Rural and Urban District Associations to favour a scheme in which there would be a two-tier local government system throughout the country. Their view would emerge in the form of the proposals that Peter Walker put into place by 1974. The AMC was hopelessly divided on the issue, with the smaller boroughs desperate to defend their status within a two-tier structure and the county boroughs, especially those under Labour control, far from averse to a single-tier solution.[108] The main body of the AMC resolved to accept a two-tier arrangement but the larger authorities dominating its executive attempted to work against the views of the majority.[109] Despite the mixed response from local governments, the Labour Government issued a White Paper on the new structure for England in February 1970 promising legislation for the 1971–72 Parliament.[110] The changes to the Redcliffe-Maud proposals were relatively slight, with the addition of two metropolitan areas covering West Yorkshire and the Southampton–Portsmouth conurbation. In the metropolitan areas education was to be a county rather than, as suggested by the Commission, a district responsibility. The White Paper promised consultations on issues such as the electoral systems and the size of councils, councillors' allowances and reduction in central controls over local authorities, including an element of general competence, but there was to be no further discussion on the basic structure of the system or the division of functions between local authorities.

The 1972 Local Government Act

The best laid plans for local government devised by the Civil Service and the Labour Party came to nothing, with victory for the Conservative Party in the general election of June 1970. Neither Peter Walker, the shadow minister of HLG, nor his predecessor Geoffrey Rippon believed that the issue required urgent action on their part as it was widely accepted among the party elite that reform had been initiated by the Labour Party as a cynical ploy to delay constituency boundary changes and that once the Commission issued its report the Government would refuse to take the matter further.[111] Peter Walker, although eventually regarded as rather 'wet' by Mrs Thatcher, was, like Keith Joseph, in the vanguard of the new generation of business-minded Conservatives who could be seen as constituting a break from the traditional landowning leadership cadre of the party. Before the 1970 general election the party arranged a series of meetings for Conservative council group leaders on the Redcliffe-Maud report. Peter Walker came to the first national consultative meeting having made up his mind as to the advisability of local government reform and in his opening address urged the assembled 'knights of the shire' to consider the report, not from a parochial point of view or because of sectarian support for a specific type of authority, but from a strategic stance on the overall future of local government.[112] His words of wisdom found little resonance among the Conservative leaders and in his closing speech to the assembled company he berated them for their insular approach:

One or two speakers used phrases as 'we don't think local government is that bad as it is'. In reality the public is not enthused by the present system of local government. I am facing an audience riddled with vested interest ... if somebody came from the moon and created a new place called Britain and they recommended for us a system of local government as it is today, we would certainly consider that they needed their heads looking at.[113]

Reform, he argued, presented an opportunity to devolve power from central government which could only be achieved with larger more professional authorities. In this respect Walker's vision for local government could be accepted by Robson or Cole or later Labour-inclined academics such as John Mackintosh.[114]

The meetings for Conservative council group leaders demonstrated to Walker the intense hostility within the party rank and file to a single-tier system. Sir Frank Marshall, the Conservative leader of Leeds City Council, encountered similar hostility when he attempted to justify elements of the Redcliffe-Maud report at the 1969 Conservative Party Conference.[115] Walker felt obliged to meet grassroots hostility at least half way by recommending that any restructuring by the Conservative Party would involve a two-tier structure, although the urban and rural districts and the smaller boroughs would be retained even though merged into larger units. In February 1970 Walker gained shadow cabinet approval for a policy statement that committed the party to supporting a 'sensible measure of local government reform' which would ensure devolution of power from central to local government and would keep a lower tier of district councils in all areas of the country. There was little interest in the matter among Conservative fellow-leaders and Walker's policy was agreed with but drafting amendments[116] to form part of the party's 1970 electoral manifesto.[117]

The Civil Service found that Peter Walker had effectively done much of the preparation for restructuring the local government system during the months preceding the general election. His main departure from Redcliffe-Maud was the concession to grassroots Conservatives that there should be 'lower tier authorities outside the metropolitan area, to discharge such functions as can more democratically and without loss of efficiency and confusion be discharged on a smaller scale'.[118] The tasks to be assigned to the small-scale authorities included housing administration. Thus, the counties were to be reprieved, but urban and rural districts and smaller boroughs merged into larger district authorities. The metropolitan two-tier areas suggested by Redcliffe-Maud were to be retained, with roughly the same distribution of powers for a larger number of conurbations. However, they were to take in less of their rural hinterland so as to confine Labour-controlled industrial areas within tightly drawn boundaries that prevented them from dominating predominantly rural Conservative hinterlands. At the community level 'in rural areas parish councils are flourishing bodies'[119] and should therefore be retained, but Walker kept an open mind on urban community councils. He saw no role for larger provincial councils at least in context of local government services. Walker's ideas were was far from the Civil Service ideal. The minutes of the official committee demonstrate the members' resignation to the Secretary of State's view, 'if there was to be a two tier system of local authorities over the country and if, as was agreed, a system of provincial and local councils on the lines proposed by the AMC was ruled out ...'.[120] The permanent secretaries could at leat be assured that the kite flown by Redcliffe-Maud that the new local government structure could incorporate the NHS had been ruled out by the Government without further discussion.[121]

The Conservatives' adoption of a two-tier system for England removed the problems of inconsistency confronting the Wilson Government over two-tier structures in Scotland and Wales. The Heath Government accepted the broad outline of the Wheatley proposals but was concerned to tone down the extent of its leaning towards large-scale units. Walker required a larger number of district councils with greater powers including responsibility for housing. He also increased the number of regions and insisted that the Islands of Orkney and Shetland should, due to their remoteness, be unitary authorities rather than part of the Highland Region.[122] The two-tier formula proposed by the Welsh Office was also accepted, but not the unitary scheme for Glamorgan. It was finally agreed to divide Glamorgan into the three counties within which would be second tier district authorities.[123]

Although the Conservatives had established through Peter Walker's initiative a framework for legislation, many issues of significance remained to be resolved. Early wrangling concerned the importance of the non-metropolitan districts in England. Walker suggested that housing in England should be a predominantly upper-tier responsibility as opposed to the situation in Scotland and Wales, but was obliged to relent and give housing to the districts.[124] There was also debate on the allocation of libraries, weights and measures, and building regulations. Mrs Thatcher, as Minister for Education, showed a surprising proclivity towards the districts and community democracy, suggesting that the larger LEAs could suffer from being too remote and that districts with populations over 250,000 could be LEAs. The idea was not adopted.[125] Early in the discussions the possibility of a south Hampshire metropolitan area was dropped, as this would undermine Conservative Hampshire while metropolitanising the Labour strongholds of South Yorkshire and Tyneside emerged as favoured strategies.[126] Walker had accepted the idea of retaining as far as possible existing county boundaries but was prepared to make exceptions largely for political gain. Thus, new counties were created for Teeside and the Bristol conurbation which removed predominantly Labour enclaves from otherwise strongly Conservative counties, while other claimants to form the basis of a new county, such as Milton

Keynes, were kept within the old county framework for fear their exclusion would make a county like Buckinghamshire too small to be viable.[127] Some anomalies had to go, however, and despite heroic resistance Rutland became a district within Leicestershire.

The issue of local councils was resolved by retaining the parishes with their existing powers and responsibilities. Boroughs and urban districts which were to disappear could petition for parish or town council status and, if a town council, to designate its chair with the dignity of being the mayor. One element of controversy concerned Redcliffe-Maud's proposal for the removal of alderman. Few in the Labour Party had any objection to this strategy. Conservatives were divided on the issue,[128] with some ministers regretting that the proper function of aldermen, to attract into local authorities people of ability who had no wish to stand for election, was never practised and that powers should be given to co-opt members to council sub-committees to secure this goal.[129] It was also argued that aldermen created some stability in policy making and protected councils from violent swings in policy due to changes in Party control.[130] Democratic sensibilities prevailed and the Cabinet accepted the removal of institution.[131]

In opposition, Walker with shadow cabinet support[132] had placated grassroot Conservative suspicions of the Maud proposals by stating: 'I want it to be a reform that shifts power from Whitehall to local government.'[133] In practice, neither Labour nor Conservative politicians warmed to Maud's suggestions that local authorities should have powers to spend money for the benefit of their citizens subject only to the wishes of their electors and restrictions that might be necessary in the interests of national economic policy.[134] The ill-defined proposal which could, if interpreted generously, have given substantial powers of general competence to local authorities was given little support by either party, partly under the prompting of civil service concern that extended powers could be used to undermine central government policy. The Cabinet agreed without substantial debate to make no mention in the White Paper of powers of general competence.[135] The Bill provided, under Section 137, power to raise but half a pence in the rate poundage for activities beneficial to an authority but not specifically allowed under legislation. The discussion on general competence took place alongside a study by civil servants on lessening controls over local government. A large number of unnecessary and obsolete controls were identified but the controls that most concerned local authorities were not even considered.[136] The exercise cleared away dead wood, but did nothing to decrease local dependence on central tutelage. For example, the Minister concerned with industrial development complained in 1972 that the limited powers given to local authorities to provide loans to industry might distort government powers concerning the location of industry and should, therefore, be curtailed. Maudling as Home Secretary responded that it was important to 'leave room for local enthusiasm and initiative' and that the powers were seldom used; but he also added that if they were used significantly they could always look at the issue again.[137] In effect some appearance of independence was fine as long as it did not infringe on central policy.

The proposals for local government reorganisation were officially announced in a White Paper published in February 1971[138] and work immediately began on preparing a Bill for implementing reorganisation in England and Wales that received its second reading in November 1971. The complex Bill was subject to numerous minor amendments,[139] perhaps the most substantial being a concession to Henry Brooke, the instigator of the Herbert report, to raise the half pence in the pound limit to two pence for spending on activities not specifically sanctioned by legislation.[140] Much time was spent in the debates on the White Paper and the Bill over routine appeals from MPs concerning the integrity of the local authorities in their constituencies rather than on matters of general principle.[141] A number of wealthy commuter towns, such as Wilmslow, originally scheduled to be incorporated into the higher taxed metropolitan areas, were also able to remain within a non-metropolitan county. The Bill passed all its stages by September to become the 1972 Local Government Act, and continued, despite many amendments, to be the founding constitution for local government in England and Wales until the end of the century.[142] Reform proposals for Scotland were delayed until the next session of Parliament. A White Paper[143] had been published in February 1971, but the Bill was not debated until December 1972, and received the Royal Assent the following October. The changes came into effect from May 1974.

The 1974 Wilson Government inherited the task of implementing the 1972 Local Government Act. As in the case of the reorganisation of London, the Government was unwilling to change the structures inherited from the Conservatives. The Minister in charge of local government, Anthony Crosland, left the changes to take their course but his successor in the Callaghan Government, Peter Shore, was under increasing pressure from larger cities to unwind some elements of the 1972 Local Government Act by granting to former county boroughs, such as Leicester, Hull and Nottingham, that had been demoted to district status, a return of many of the powers that had been ceded to county councils. The Government produced in January 1979 a White Paper[144] which supported the view that 'some of the county services in the shire areas are run at a level which is too remote from the people who are actually affected by them'.[145] The White Paper suggested that district councils could propose to the Government that they should take up further services, although it was made clear that only areas with a population of over 100,000 could expect a transfer of powers and that in respect to education this would be considered only for the 9 largest former county boroughs. The White Paper was, however, published too late in the ailing Government's tenure to be put into practice.

Nationalism and regional devolution

While the Redcliffe-Maud Commission deliberated the restructuring of local government, the Wilson Cabinet became increasingly worried about the growth of nationalist parties and, in 1968, determined to show some public concern for Welsh and Scottish demands for independence by establishing a Royal Commission to consider the relationship between the constituent parts of the United Kingdom. The Commission published its findings in 1973, providing a majority report in which several members had reservations over specific points and a minority report.[146] In the majority report all but one Commissioner proposed that Scotland should have its own directly elected Parliament and an Executive able to legislate on a range of domestic policies including the structure of local government, policing and education. A majority also accepted that Wales should have an Assembly and an Executive with fewer powers than were to be devolved to Scotland, although three members thought that the Welsh Assembly should be advisory only. Devolution of legislative powers to English regions was rejected although a majority favoured the creation of advisory regional councils based on the existing economic planning regions. The proposed English regions would be appointed largely by local authorities, along with a smaller group of government appointees, and would make representations to central government on policies for their region including the operation of nationalised industries. Two members advocated elected English regional councils.

The Heath Government saw no reason for action on these proposals and simply called for further public debate on the issue. The party that had consistently opposed Irish Home Rule remained unsympathetic to regional devolution and nationalist parties had made little headway in the 1970 election. The Civil Service was also strongly opposed to the idea, with the Treasury fearing it would loose further controls over spending and its capacity to steer the national economy, while many departments overseeing specific functions were opposed to losing their powers over particular services. Neither the Scottish nor the Welsh Office warmed to a policy that would effectively render them redundant.[147]

Harold Wilson did not share the Conservative's dislike of devolution but, since many Labour MPs had serious reservations about the idea, the party did not mention devolution in its Manifesto for the February 1974 election. The result of the election, however, showed significant advances for nationalists which renewed Labour leaders' fears that they needed to steer this movement to their advantage or risk promoting a trend that could sweep away their strongholds in Scotland and Wales. The Wilson Government in response issued a White Paper in September proposing devolution for Scotland and Wales and committed the party to take the policy further in its *Manifesto* for the October election. Winning a narrow majority over all other parties in the Commons obliged the Wilson

Government to set out its policies[148] in a White Paper.[149] The subsequent Bill promised devolution of a range of domestic functions, including local government, to a Scottish Parliament and a Welsh Assembly. Legislation faced difficulties in the Commons as many Labour backbenchers were hostile to the idea and several Scottish and Welsh MPs feared for their status as British representatives.[150] Wilson's resignation and his replacement by Callaghan did little to rally Labour backbench enthusiasm for the Bill. As the proposal ground its way through its committee stage encumbered by over 1,000 amendments 22 Labour MPs defied their Whips to prevent closure of the committee stage which ensured it failed to complete its progress through the Commons.[151]

As soon as the Bill appeared to have been consigned to oblivion electoral defeats conspired to raise from the dead the issue of devolution. Labour lost its overall majority and required the support of the Liberals, who made its revival a central requirement to keep the Government in power. Devolution had been rooted within the ethos of the Liberal Party since Gladstone's stance on Home Rule and Lloyd George's belated attempts to give Ireland its own government.[152] As a party of the Celtic fringe with its traditional core support among nonconformists in rural Wales, Scotland and south-west England, preservation of electoral support reinforced this policy. The revived Bill was similar in most respects to its predecessor. The Liberals secured some changes to the Bill, such as referenda to gain acceptance for the constitutional change and a fixed block grant to provide a degree of financial autonomy to the devolved systems. The Act passed in 1978 and the referenda in Wales and Scotland took place in March the following year, but in Wales the proposals were defeated while in Scotland, although a small majority of those voting approved devolution, the numbers in favour were nowhere near the required 40 per cent of eligible voters. The Labour Government could at least claim to have tried to establish devolution, although its support of the idea was at best equivocal and insufficient to will the means to secure the creation of Scottish and Welsh Assemblies. Two months later the incoming Thatcher Government removed the issue of devolution from its political agenda.

The Labour Party in 1969 had deferred any decision on English provinces until the Commission on the Constitution published its report,[153] and when the document arrived with no strong enthusiasm for regionalism neither the Heath Government nor Wilson in opposition gave any support to the idea. However, the suggestion was taken up with enthusiasm by the National Executive Committee (NEC) of the Labour Party which in 1974 published a document whose main thrust was to restore elected democracy to 'the wide expanse of governmental and public service decision making' that lay outside the electoral system. [154] A year later the NEC published a discussion document on the regions, observing that, while the Labour Government was following up the issue of Scottish and Welsh devolution, it would take up the task of consulting with the party on English regionalism.[155] The party held a series of regional conferences for its members on the possibility of establishing English regions, receiving a somewhat mixed response. In Yorkshire, for example, the meeting was dominated by Labour council leaders raising concerns about potential loss of power to their cities if the policy was pursued.[156] Despite such doubts, the NEC went on to incorporate the idea of English regions in a policy programme published in 1976. Among other features, the elected regions would incorporate the regional health authorities. The proposals were subject to a further consultation document in 1977,[157] but despite these promptings the Government never took the bait offered by the party machine.

Finance yet again 1970–79

By the late 1960s local government was being shaped not only be structural change but also by the economic problems that beset both the Wilson and the Heath Governments. High rates of inflation exacerbated by the oil crisis and labour unrest following nearly two decades of growth in public sector finance culminated in economic crisis. Heath's initial response was to cut taxes by reducing unnecessary public expenditure, and made local government services a particular target.[158] The rate support grant announced in November 1970 reduced funding to local authorities in respect to their estimated need.[159] Cut-backs on specific local government services fell on relatively small but, nevertheless, controversial items. Secretary of State for Education Mrs Thatcher speculated about charging for public libraries but the tradition of a free service obliged her to drop the dead donkey.[160] However, increasing school meals' charges and abandoning free school milk were pushed forward despite attracting widespread criticism. The Heath Government also attempted to resolve the perpetual dilemma of whether to finance local government through the rates or from the Exchequer by seeking means to increase locally raised taxes.

In parallel with the reform of local government structure, the Government initiated yet another review of local government finance. Conservative ministers considered that in order to reduce their extravagance local authorities themselves should raise a substantial proportion of their income. As in earlier reviews the Civil Service blocked long-term strategies for finding alternative sources of local government income by continuing to argue that no system was viable other than the rating system. Ministers had to accept that the rate was to be the main source of local taxation, but saw some merit in attaching a local sales tax to the incoming value-added tax or to 'super-rate' business. Further ideas canvassed included the re-rating of agriculture or, shades of the poll tax, charging rates partly on the basis of the number of adults at one address.[161] The politically more plausible ideas, which were floated in a subsequent Green Paper, included local income tax, higher rates for businesses or transferring motor vehicle licence fees to local authorities, but none of these ideas made further progress.[162] Peter Walker also floated a strategy to 'equalise the burden of the rates on households with comparable earnings in comparable households' by developing an index to adjust the rate for each county in line with this aim. It was thought that the system would decrease rate rises in London and the north of England and result in higher charges in wealthier areas. There was to be a similar balancing of the non-domestic rate which would also become a higher proportion of the total rate earnings in most parts of the country.[163] The Minister's proposals were not greeted with enthusiasm by his colleagues, who may have seen them as unnecessarily egalitarian. The ideas were dropped soon afterwards when in December 1972 Geoffrey Rippon replaced Walker as Secretary of State for the Environment.[164]

The Labour governments that emerged from the two 1974 elections with a just-workable majority were beset by problems of inflation and industrial unrest that would have felled even the most robust of governments backed by a united party. Among the many consequences of the unprecedented rate of inflation was a huge rise in local authority budgets. Rate demands in 1974–75 rose by an average 25 per cent. The Government mitigated the increases in rates by further support from the Exchequer, to the extent that by 1975–76 grants amounted to 66.5 per cent of total local authority income.[165] Local authority spending was to be given no real term growth as it had exceeded its planned allowance the previous year.[166] As Secretary of State for the Environment, Crosland told the local authorities: 'The party is over.'[167] In line with many of his predecessors, he accompanied efforts to deal with immediate financial problems by establishing a Committee to resolve structural dilemmas. The Inquiry chaired by Sir Frank Layfield issued a lengthy, if rather circumspect report in 1977, arguing that the Government should choose either to place the burden of funding at the local level by supplementing rates with a local income tax or on central government through higher grants and reduced reliance on the rates.[168] On balance the Inquiry favoured the local option, although it was recognised that income tax could only be levied by one tier of the local government system, the counties. The Government issued a non-committal Green Paper[169] on the subject but by 1977 was not in a strong position to push forward Layfield's proposals and, given Inland Revenue and Civil Service hostility to local income tax, the proposals were not developed further.

Crosland was able, at least, to restructure the relationship between local government and the centre, establishing by statute a Consultative Council on Local Government Finance (CCLGF). The CCLGF met as a single body only once or twice a year but it was divided into a wide range of sub-committees attended by civil servants and LAA officials to trash out the details concerning the demands for funding for particular services and the funding the Government could concede.[170] The CCLGF created a formal mechanism for determining levels of local authority expenditure that brought representatives of the LAAs in much closer contact with ministers and, more importantly on a day-to-day basis, civil servants, by amalgamating a raft of ad hoc discussion groups that had previously aided the process of determining grant allocations. Although electorally an unspectacular move, it was arguably the most successful reform of the local government system of the 1974–79 Labour governments.

Local government at low ebb

During the 1970s several factors conspired to lower the status of local government. The first of these was serious corruption. The use of local public office for personal benefit by securing contracts, nepotism and, later, manipulating planning permission had been practised within some local authorities since their creation. The issue re-emerged in the sensational bankruptcy of the successful architect John Poulson who was found to have worked closely with T. Dan Smith, leader of Newcastle City Council and chair of the Northern Economic Development Council, perhaps the most widely recognised local politician of his day. They had bribed local councillors, officers and civil servants to accept contracts from Poulson's architectural and building interests. A number of prominent councillors were convicted of corruption and implicated Home Secretary Reginald Maudling, who resigned. The 1974 Wilson Government established a Royal Commission under the chairmanship of Lord Salmon to investigate standards of conduct in public life. The Salmon report did not find corruption to be endemic in local authorities but recommended that councillors register their business interests and establish more effective procedures to oblige councillors to reveal conflicts of interest.[171]

More insidious were the continuing pressures to loosen local authority control on some central services. The nineteenth-century local authority initiatives to supply water and sewage services were a particular casualty. The Central Water Advisory Committee had been established by the 1945 Water Act to aid radical consolidation of the many river, water and sewage authorities from these bodies to form a small number of regional water agencies.[172] The Committee had proposed to the Government further radical consolidation,[173] which was favoured by the Civil Service[174] although not by all Conservative ministers.[175] For the sake of efficiency as favoured in Whitehall, the interests of larger agencies won the argument, and in 1973 the Water Act established seven unelected water authorities, based on water drainage areas, which had no connection with other regional boundaries.[176] In Scotland water supply remained a joint local authority responsibility.

The issue of housing, which more than any other local government issue had divided Labour and the Conservatives between 1945 and 1979, became a source of bitter controversy during the Heath Government. Walker devised a strategy to further the Conservative predilection for home ownership, subsidising council-house rents for only the poorest in society, while all other tenants were to pay a 'fair rent' based on the cost of the house on the commercial rented market, saving the Treasury some £280 million by 1975.[177] In July 1971 the Government published its White Paper *Fair Deal for Housing*[178] which confirmed the intention to remove the previous system for determining council-house rents on the basis of rentable value if it were in the private sector. Tenants unable to pay higher rents were to be protected by a rent-rebate scheme that was to be administered by the local authorities under regulations set by central government. The proposals, which were strenuously opposed by the Labour Party, became law in the 1972 Housing Finance Act.[179]

On taking office in 1974 Crosland was obliged through left-wing pressure to lessen the privatising impact of the Heath Government's legislation and repealed[180] the measures that had created the greatest opposition, although the Government reserved the right to prohibit excessive rent rises for specific types of housing rather than for individual authorities.[181] Crosland did not favour a return to fully subsidised local authority housing and began reviving the rather minor third sector for housing provision, the housing associations. The Minister also signalled a major policy change from funding large-scale slum clearance and estate development in the public sector by encouraging urban renewal through the refurbishment of run-down properties, including the many ageing pre-war council estates. In 1975 Crosland initiated a major review of housing policy which reported in 1977 when Peter Shore had become Secretary of State for the Environment. Cole and Furbey observe that 'the Housing Policy Review was the last opportunity to stake a claim to a distinctive public sector housing in Britain operating on different principles to the private market'.[182] The report suggested, however, that rented accommodation should decline in favour of private ownership and confirmed a transition within the Labour Party to defer to the popularity of owner occupation. The Government also armed itself with further controls on council-house construction by establishing a Housing Investment Programme that specifically allocated capital funding for house-building and improvements by local authorities.

The image of local government was further undermined by the growth of left-wing militancy among councillors. During the Heath Government a growing spirit of defiance against cuts in services prompted the first attempts since the 1920s among left-wing local authorities to defy central legislation. 'Maggie Thatcher, milk snatcher' not only became a catchy refrain in radical circles but minded six left-wing Scottish and Welsh local authorities to continue illegally to provide free school milk. The threat of surcharge was needed to deter them. A few London boroughs also continued to supply milk through discretionary payments, against the spirit of the legislation.[183] Even before the Government's policy on council rents came into force in August it was clear that a large number of housing authorities were preparing to defy the legislation. By the end of September the Government was aware of 14 local authorities that were threatening not to implement the proposal.[184] By November only 8 English and 5 Welsh authorities were opposing the Act, although they had been joined by 22 Scottish local authorities, including Glasgow.[185]

The Government allowed the measures developed by Chamberlain in 1929 to take their course. Defaulting authorities were reported, usually by Conservative interest groups, to the district auditor who then investigated the charges and, if he or she found them to be valid, imposed orders that could include surcharging the councillors and officers supporting unlawful action. One by one the intransigent authorities backed down, leaving the solitary urban district of Clay Cross, near Chesterfield, in defiance. The radical Labour authority was dominated by the three brothers Skinner[186] who continued to hold out against the policy. The Heath Government brought in a Commissioner in October 1973 to take charge of the district's housing policy. Their actions were endorsed by Crosland following the change of Government in 1974. The defiant Labour councillors were surcharged, made bankrupt and disqualified from office, but by that time the Urban District had ceased to function with the implementation of the 1972 Local Government Act.[187]

Paralleling the emergence of militancy among left-wing councillors was growing militancy among local authority trade unions which was being exacerbated by the growing pace of inflation. The threat of local government workers' strikes over pay overshadowed the 1970 election.[188] The Heath Government had to respond to wage demands immediately on taking office.[189] Its initial action was to place responsibility on local authorities to deal with those demands while at the same time giving no grounds for expecting additional funding to meet any increases in wages that might be awarded. Faced with record levels of inflation, public sector unions, just as much as those in the private sector, were increasingly inclined to strike to achieve their demands. Although Callaghan's Government agreed with trade union leaders a prices and incomes policy that began to bring down the rate of inflation, it was at the cost of a real decline in living standards for many of the poorer paid local authority workforce. When the unions refused to co-operate with a further government limit on pay rises many local government workers joined the widespread unofficial strikes. The disruption to services such as refuse collections and burials caused by the striking council workers presented a field day for those in the Conservative press hostile to left-wing councils and the Government, and led to the myth of the 'winter of discontent'.

The travails of the Wilson and Callaghan governments were conducted within a polarising society as the Labour Party became increasingly divided between militants on the Left, Old Labour social democrats and the precursors, such as Crosland, of Blair's New Right. The divisions translated into growing militancy and enthusiasm for redistributive socialist policies in several urban authorities, such as Liverpool, Sheffield and the GLC, that were, after 1979, to become the local socialist movement. Paradoxically, given the reported mayhem created by the absence of local authority workers, it may be suggested that the press should have realised the importance of the low-paid and underrated municipal worker. In reality it created an atmosphere of public opposition to local authorities in general, and to militant trade unions and councils in particular, that did much to create the groundswell of public opinion in support of the Thatcher Government's onslaught on local government as an institution.

Notes

1 H. Macmillan, *Tides of Fortune 1945–55* (London: Macmillan, 1969), p. 363.
2 *Ibid.*, p. 377.
3 Ministry of Housing and Local Government, *Houses: The Next Step*, Cmnd 8996 (London: HMSO, 1953).
4 The Housing Repairs and Rents Act, 1954: 2 & 3 Eliz. II, c. 53.
5 Macmillan, *Tides of Fortune*, pp. 445–50.
6 NA, CAB 128, 85th Cabinet meeting, 14 Oct. 1952.
7 The New Valuation Lists (Postponement) Act, 1952: 1 Eliz. II, c. 4.
8 The Valuation and Rating Act: 1 & 2 Eliz. II, c. 42.
9 NA, CAB 129/67, C (54) 111, 'Operation Round-Up', 24 March 1954.
10 *Ibid.*, p. 2.
11 *Ibid.*, pp. 3–4.
12 *Ibid.*
13 *Ibid.*, p. 6.
14 T. Travers, *The Politics of Local Government Finance* (London: Allen & Unwin, 1986), p. 8.
15 NA, CAB 134/1260, Home Affairs Sub-Committee on Local Government Organisation and Finance 1956, 2nd meeting.
16 *Ibid.*
17 *Ibid.*
18 CAB 134/HP (LG) (56), 6th meeting.
19 CAB 128, 7th Cabinet meeting, 5 Feb. 1957.
20 Department of the Environment, *Local Government Finance (England and Wales)*, Cmnd 209 (London: HMSO, 1975); Scottish Office, *Local Government Finance in Scotland*, Cmnd 6208 (London: HMSO, 1975). Differences in the Scottish proposals related to the rating of nationalised industries and the equalisation grant.
21 The Local Government Act, 1958, 6 & 7 Eliz. II, c. 55; and the Local Government and Miscellaneous Financial Provisions (Scotland) Act, 1958: 6 & 7 Eliz. II, c. 64.

22 NA, CAB 128, 15th meeting, 27 Feb. 1963.
23 *Ibid.*, 58th meeting, 3 Oct. 1963; and CC (63) 59, 8 Oct. 1963.
24 CAB 134/1005, 24 Feb. 1955, Proposals for Local Government Reorganisation.
25 *Ibid.*, p. 3.
26 CAB 134/1005 LG (55), Memorandum 2.
27 From their creation the LAAs usually appointed as president or vice-president an MP who would be sensitive to their interests.
28 Ministry of Housing and Local Government, *Local Government Areas and Status of Local Authorities in England and Wales*, Cmd 9831 (London: HMSO, 1956).
29 NA, CAB 134 HP (LG) (56), 1st meeting.
30 Ministry of Housing and Local Government, *Local Government Functions of County Councils and County District Councils in England and Wales*, Cmnd 161 (London: HMSO, 1957).
31 Local Government Act 1958: 6 & 7 Eliz. II, c. 55.
32 J. Stanyer, 'The local government commissions', in V. H. Wiseman (ed.), *Local Government in England 1958–1969* (London: Routledge & Kegan Paul, 1970).
33 G. Rhodes, *The Government of London* (London: Weidenfeld & Nicolson, 1970), p. 18.
34 NA, CAB 129 C 152, 2 July 1957.
35 *Ibid.*
36 They included Sir John Wrigley, a former deputy permanent secretary of the MHLG, and two academics, Vice-Chancellor of Leeds University Sir Charles Morris and W. J. M Mackenzie, Professor of Government at the University of Manchester.
37 Rhodes, *The Government of London*, pp. 33–6.
38 *Ibid.*, pp. 36–8.
39 *Ibid.*, pp. 47–8.
40 *Ibid.*, pp. 51–62.
41 Herbert Commission, *Report of the Royal Commission on Local Government in Greater London 1957–60*, Cmnd 1164 (London: HMSO, 1960).
42 NA, CAB 129, CP 85, 26 June 1961.
43 CAB 128, 39th meeting, 6 July 1961.
44 *Ibid.*, and CAB 129 CP (61) 85, 26 June 1961.
45 CAB 128 C 65, 23 November 1961; CAB 128 CC (62) 29, 1 May 1962.
46 Rhodes, *The Government of London*, pp. 124–6.
47 *Ibid.*, pp. 143–53.
48 Donaghue and Jones, *Herbert Morrison: Portrait of a Politician*, pp. 557–9.
49 F. Smallwood, *Greater London: The Politics of Metropolitan Reform* (Indianapolis, IN: Bobbs-Merrill, 1965), pp. 166–7.
50 Rhodes, *The Government of London*, pp. 223.
51 NA, CAB 128, 48th meeting, 25 July 1963.
52 J. Mackintosh, *The Government and Politics of Britain* (London: Hutchinson, 1970), p. 160.
53 Labour Party, *Lets Go with Labour for the New Britain: The Labour Party's Manifesto for the 1964 General Election* (London: Labour Party, 1964), p. 3.
54 *Ibid.*, p. 11.

55 NA, CAB 164 703, 18 Sept. 1969; these initiatives were; the Redcliffe-Maud and Wheatley reports; the Welsh reorganisation proposals; the Crowther (Kilbrandon) Commission; the Seebohm report; the Green Paper on NHS reorganisation, the Holroyd Committee on fire service reorganisation; the Maud report; the Mallaby report; Parliamentary Boundary Commission reports; and the Beeching report on assize and quarter session courts.

56 R. H. S. Crossman, *The Diaries of a Cabinet Minister*, vol. 1 (London: Hamish Hamilton–Jonathan Cape, 1975), p. 169; NA, CAB 128, 12th meeting, 25 Feb. 1965.

57 Home Office (and other Departments), *Committee on Local Authority and Allied Personal Social Services 1967–1968*, Cmnd 3703 (London: HMSO, 1968) (Seebohm report).

58 Scottish Office, *Social Work and the Community: Proposals for Reorganising Local Authority Services in Scotland*, Cmnd 3605 (London: HMSO, 1966).

59 NA, CAB 128, 33rd meeting, 16 July 1969.

60 H. Willink (chair), *Royal Commission on the Police*, Cmnd 1728 (London: HMSO, 1962).

61 *The Times*, 18 May 1966, p. 4.

62 B. Wood, *The Process of Local Government Reform* (London: George Allen & Unwin, 1976), p. 48.

63 F. Stacey, *British Government 1966–1975* (Oxford: Oxford University Press, 1975), pp. 83–5.

64 NA, CAB 129 CP 125, Memorandum on Local Government Finance from the Chancellor of the Exchequer, 14 Sept. 1965.

65 Labour Party, *Manifesto for 1964*, p. 13.

66 Ministry of Housing and Local Government, *Report of the Committee of Inquiry into the Impact of Rates on Households*, Cmnd 2582 (London: HMSO, 1965) (Allen report), paras 345 and 347.

67 Crossman, *Diaries of a Cabinet Minister*, vol. 1, p. 250.

68 *Ibid.*, p. 620.

69 NA, CAB 128, 2nd meeting, 20 Jan. 1966.

70 Pay as You Earn, which was a relatively new device in the 1960s.

71 NA, CAB 134/1948, Memorandum of the Official Local Government Finance Committee, GLF (0) (65) 2.

72 CAB 134/1947, Cabinet Committee on Local Government Finance, 1st meeting, 14 June 1965.

73 Ministry of Housing and Local Government, *Local Government Finance in England and Wales*, Cmnd 2923 (London: HMSO, 1966).

74 NA, CAB 128, 48th meeting, 16 Sept. 1965.

75 Crossman, *Diaries of a Cabinet Minister*, vol. 1, p. 439.

76 *Ibid.*, p. 65.

77 *Ibid.*, pp. 64–5.

78 *Ibid.*, p. 331.

79 *Ibid.*, p. 441; the Commission that reviewed constituency boundaries always ensured that constituencies did not cross local authority boundaries and hence always followed up local authority boundary change with a revision of constituency boundaries.

80 *Ibid.*, p. 440.

81 NA, CAB 129, CP 6, 21 Jan. 1966.
82 CAB 128, 2nd meeting, 20 Jan. 1966.
83 Crossman, *Diaries of a Cabinet Minister*, vol. 1, p. 491.
84 John Maud, on being made a baron, took the title Lord Redcliffe-Maud.
85 Wood, *The Process of Local Government Reform*, pp. 41–3.
86 T. J. Cartwright, *Royal Commissions and Departmental Committees in Britain* (London: Hodder & Stoughton, 1975), p. 259.
87 Lord Redcliffe-Maud (chair), *Royal Commission on Local Government in England, 1966–1969*, 3 vols, Cmnd 4040 (London: HMSO, 1969), vol. 1, p. 60.
88 *Ibid.*, p. 5.
89 *Ibid.*, vol. 2, *Memorandum of Dissent by Mr D. Senior*, Cmnd 4040–1.
90 NA, CAB 134/2978, 1st meeting, 25 March 1969.
91 CAB 128, 23rd meeting, 10 June 1969.
92 CAB 134/2975, Official Committee on Local Government Reorganisation, 3rd meeting, 18 June.
93 Crossman, *Diaries of a Cabinet Minister*, vol. 3, pp. 515–16, 592
94 Report of the Royal Commission for Local Government in Scotland, *Reform of Local Government in Scotland*, Cmnd 4150 (London: HMSO, 1969) (Wheatley report), p. 1, para. 2.
95 MHLG, *Local Government in Wales*, Cmnd 3340 (London: HMSO, 1967).
96 NA, CAB 128, 46th meeting, 8 Oct. 1969.
97 CAB 128, 51st meeting, 23 Oct. 1969.
98 CAB 134/2980, 3rd meeting.
99 CAB 134/2978, meeting (on alderman) 10 and 11 Dec. 1969; meeting (on general competence) 10 and 17 Dec. 1969.
100 Department of Health and Social Security, *The Administrative Structure of the Medical and Related Services in England and Wales* (London: HMSO, 1968).
101 Redcliffe-Maud report, vol. 1, pp. 92–4; the report pointed out that a previous report on financing health care in 1956 from the Guillebaud Committee had rejected local authority control of the service due to the antiquated structure of local government.
102 Redcliffe-Maud report, vol. 2, pp. 66–72.
103 NA, CAB 134/2971, 1st meeting, 22 June 1966; HLG/120 1349, Draft paper to the Ministerial Committee on Social Services, 29 Oct. 1969.
104 CAB 134/2978, throughout 1969.
105 Crossman, *Diaries of a Cabinet Minister*, vol. 3, pp. 499, 572.
106 NA, HLG 120/1349, Letter from Mr Osmotherly to Mr Hannigan, 26 Jan. 1971. Agreement was not, however, reached on the numbers of local authority representatives on the Health Boards.
107 Wood, *Process of Local Government Reform 1966–1974*, p. 78.
108 K. Isaac-Henry, 'The Association of Municipal Corporations and the County Councils' Association: a study of the influences and pressures on the reorganisation of local government 1945–1972', Ph.D thesis, University of London, 1980, pp. 133, 142–3.
109 Wood, *Process of Local Government Reform*, pp. 75–82.
110 Department of Local Government and Regional Planning, *Reform of Local Government in England*, Cmnd 4276 (London: HMSO, 1970).

111 Conservative Party Archive (CPA), CCO 500/34/6, 3 July 1969.
112 *Ibid.*
113 *Ibid.*
114 Mackintosh, *The Government and Politics of Britain*, pp. 159–63.
115 Isaac-Henry, *The AMC and the CCA*, p. 159.
116 CPA, LCC/1/12/19, Minutes of Leader's Consultative Committee, 4 Feb. 1970.
117 Conservative Party, *A Better Tomorrow* (London: Conservative Party, 1970).
118 NA, CAB 134/3178, Memorandum 2, Local Government Reform in England: Memorandum by the Minister of Housing and Local Government, 10 Aug. 1970.
119 *Ibid.*
120 *Ibid.*, Official Committee on the Reorganisation of Local Government, 1st meeting, 13 Aug. 1970.
121 CAB 134/3176 1st meeting of the Ministerial Committee on Regional Policy and the Environment Sub Committee on the Reorganisation of Local Government, 19 Nov. 1970.
122 CAB 134/3176, Memorandum 3, 2 Oct. 1970.
123 *Ibid.*, Memorandum 2, 28 Sept. 1970.
124 *Ibid.*, 2nd meeting, 25 Nov. 1970.
125 *Ibid.*, 3rd meeting, 2 Dec. 1970.
126 *Ibid.*, 4th meeting, 8 Dec. 1970.
127 Wood, *Process of Local Government Reform*, pp. 106–7.
128 NA, CAB 134/3441, Walker to the Ministerial Committee on Regional Policy and the Environment Sub-Committee on Reorganisation of Local Government, 1st meeting, 8 March 1971.
129 CAB 134/3439, Ministerial Committee on Regional Policy and the Environment (RE 71), 2nd meeting, 21 Jan. 1971.
130 CAB 134/3441, 1st meeting, 8 March 1971.
131 CAB 134/3439, 8th meeting, 8 July 1971.
132 CA, LCC/1/2/19, Minutes of Leader's Consultative Committee, 4 Feb. 1970.
133 CA, CCO 500/34/6, Concluding address to Conference of Conservative Group Leaders, 3 July 1969.
134 Redcliffe-Maud report, vol. 1, p. 84.
135 NA, CAB 134/3176, 6th meeting, 17 Dec. 1970.
136 CAB 134/3178, 3rd meeting, 23 Sept. 1970.
137 CAB 134/3561, Ministerial Committee on Regional Policy and the Environment, 4th meeting, 5 July 1972.
138 DoE, *Local Government in England: Government Proposals for Reorganisation*, Cmnd 4584 (London: HMSO, 1971).
139 Wood, *Process of Local Government Reform*, p. 149.
140 NA, CAB 134/3561, 6th meeting, 13 Sept. 1972. Brooke was by this time in the House of Lords.
141 Hansard, vol. 837, cols 1278–403, 19 May 1971; vol. 846, cols 227ff., 16 Nov. 1971.
142 The Local Government Act, 1972: Eliz. II, c. 70.
143 Scottish Office, *Reform of Local Government in Scotland*, Cmnd 4583 (London, HMSO, 1971).
144 DoE, *Organic Change in Local Government*, Cmnd 7457. (London: HMSO, 1979).

145 *Ibid.*, p. 5.
146 *Report of the Royal Commission on the Constitution 1969–1973*, Cmnd 5460 (London: HMSO, 1973) (Kilbrandon report). The original chairman of the Commission, Lord Crowther, died during the Inquiry and was replaced by Scottish judge Lord Kilbrandon, and the report of the Inquiry is referred to in this book by the latter's name .
147 R. Rose, *The Territorial Dimension in Government* (Chatham, NJ: Chatham House, 1982), pp. 191–2.
148 B. Castle, *The Castle Diaries 1974–1976* (London: Weidenfeld & Nicolson, 1980), pp. 281–3.
149 Lord President of the Council, *Our Changing Democracy: Devolution to Scotland and Wales 1975–76*, Cmnd 6348 (London: HMSO, 1975).
150 Rose, *The Territorial Dimension in Government*, p. 193.
151 *Ibid.*, p. 194.
152 Party leader David Steel indicates the importance of this ethos in *A House Divided* (London: Weidenfeld & Nicolson, 1980), p. 92.
153 NA, CAB 128, 60th meeting, 11 Dec. 1969.
154 Labour Party, *Bringing Power Back to the People* (London: Labour Party, 1974).
155 Labour Party, *Devolution and Regional Government in England* (London: Labour Party, 1975).
156 Observation by the author.
157 Labour Party, *Regional Authorities and Local Government Reform* (London: Labour Party, 1977).
158 Conservative Party, *A Better Tomorrow*.
159 *The Times*, 27 Nov. 1970, p. 4d.
160 NA, CAB 128, 16th meeting, 14 Sept. 1970.
161 CAB 134/3176, 5th meeting, 16 Nov. 1971.
162 DoE, *The Future Shape of Local Government Finance*, Cmnd 4741 (London, HMSO, 1971).
163 NA, CAB 134/3561, Sub-Committee on Regional Policy and the Environment, 1972, 4th meeting.
164 *Ibid.*, 5th meeting, 26 July 1972.
165 Travers, *Politics of Local Government Finance*, p. 41.
166 Municipal and Public Services Journal, 8 Aug. 1975, p. 1015.
167 In a speech to a Local Government Conference in Manchester, May 1975: K. Jefferys, *Anthony Crosland* (London: Richard Cohen Books, 1999), p. 184.
168 F. Layfield (chair), *Local Government Finance: Report of the Committee of Inquiry*, Cmnd 6453 (London: HMSO, 1976).
169 DoE and Welsh Office, *Local Government Finance*, Cmnd 6813 (London: HMSO, 1971).
170 J. A. Chandler, *Public Policy Making for Local Government* (London: Croom Helm, 1988), pp. 48–50.
171 Lord Salmon (chair), *Report of the Royal Commission on Standards of Conduct in Public Life*, Cmnd 6524 (London: HMSO, 1976).
172 The Water Act, 1945, 8 & 9 Geo. VI, c. 42.
173 NA, CAB 134/3439 (RE 71), 9th meeting of the Ministerial Committee on Regional Policy and the Environment, 15 July 1971.

174 *Ibid.*, 13th meeting, 2 Nov. 1971.
175 Particular opposition came from the Secretary of State for Wales but he was quickly browbeaten into accepting a single water authority for the Principality: *ibid.*, 14th meeting, 9 Nov. 1971
176 The Water Act, 1973: Eliz. II, c. 37.
177 NA, CAB 128, 25th meeting, 1 Oct. 1970; CAB 128 CM (70), 29th meeting, 15 Oct. 1970.
178 The DoE's *Fair Deal for Housing*, Cmnd 4728 (London: HMSO, 1971), put a revival of the Bill as a central requirement
179 The Housing Finance Act, 1972: Eliz. II, c. 47; a parallel Act for Scotland was the Housing (Financial Provisions) (Scotland) Act, 1972: Eliz. II, c. 46.
180 The Housing Rents and Subsidies Act, 1975: Eliz. II, c. 6.
181 Young and Rao, *Local Government Since 1945*, pp. 166–7.
182 Cole and Furbey, *The Eclipse of Council Housing*, p. 73.
183 NA, CAB 128, 53rd meeting, 4 Nov. 1971.
184 CAB 128, 43rd meeting, 19 Sept. 1972.
185 CAB 128, 46th meeting, 25 Oct. 1972
186 David, Graham and Dennis; the latter had left the Council when elected MP for Bolsover and was to become a perpetual and sharp backbench critic of faltering Labour leaders.
187 D. Skinner and J. Langdon, *The Story of Clay Cross* (Nottingham: Spokesmen Books, 1974).
188 'NALGO threaten strikes over pay that might affect poll clerks', *The Times*, 20 May 1970, p. 2c.
189 For example, *ibid.*, 10 Nov. 1970, p. 5a, on the dustmen's strike.

10

Professionalism and alienation

The 1972 Local Government Act and its Scottish counterpart were the culmination of continuous pressures throughout the twentieth century for change in terms both of the size of local authorities and of their inclusivity and professionalism. These changes had been envisaged by leading academic writers such as Cole since the 1920s and, later, Robson and Chester, and were grist to the mill for many reform-minded New Liberal and Labour politicians. While suspicious of the larger Labour-controlled municipal and county boroughs, many Conservatives after 1950 also were willing to tread this path. Underlying these values were social and economic trends such as improved transport, the creation of national mass media and competitiveness among political parties which began to eclipse local as opposed to centralised management of services and economic development, and arguably decreased the relevance of local government as an institution central to each individual's well-being. Leading business interests began to forget notions of civic pride and voters saw less need to involve themselves with local politics. The trend was accompanied by major restructuring of both the internal operations of local bureaucracy and, over a longer time-span, the evolution of the political decision-making process of the local authority and the composition of its membership.

Management of local government

Prior to the 1972 Local Government Act the larger authorities had developed into inclusive organisations undertaking as many services in-house as was possible. The Act consolidated the process. As late as 1974 smaller district authorities might still retain a local solicitor as their part-time town clerk and use the manager of their local bank as their financial officer, contracting many of their services to private businesses. Typically, in the Urban District Council of Stocksbridge, on the outskirts of Sheffield, the authority's chief officer, the town clerk, had been as late as the 1940s the local solicitor, while the treasurer was the manager of the local branch of a national bank. Small authorities were reliant on external contractors or other authorities for service provision and could lean heavily on the private sector for capital developments. The Borough of Glossop made £75,044 in capital payments for amenities such as parks between 1867 and 1939, of which £47,426 had been donated by benefactors.[1] The co-operation between private sector benefactors and other public service providers in such small communities was, therefore, similar to the practices of many small city communities in the USA today.[2]

The apparent enabling behaviour of the smaller authorities was in most cases a function of necessity rather than inclination. During the inter-war years even relatively small borough councils and numerous urban districts of some size supplied as many of their own services as possible. Glossop fought a protracted legal battle with Manchester City Council between 1935 and 1951 over the right to capture water on the local moors. There appears to have been no thought let alone any move in this conflict towards some partnership between the two authorities concerning water supply.[3] The tendency of local authority councils in Britain was that if resources were available to implement as well as to provide services, then the authority should do so. Since the largest and most widely recognised authorities, in many cities reinforced by Labour majorities, aspired to run almost all their services in-house, it seems probable that many smaller authorities, in a climate that was turning against their continuation, also followed this trend, where possible, in order to project an image of self-sufficiency and importance. From a public-choice perspective, many town clerks and borough surveyors were eager to enhance their chances of promotion to larger authorities by increasing the range of their responsibilities.

Dame Evelyn Sharp, who had serious doubts concerning the capability of councillors and officers, was probably influential in persuading both the Minister, Keith Joseph, and the LAAs to jointly set up two departmental Inquiries into local government staffing.[4] John Maud[5] chaired an Inquiry into how 'in the light of modern conditions local government might best continue to attract and retain people (both elected representatives and principal officers) of the calibre necessary to ensure its maximum effectiveness' and George Mallaby was appointed to look at the recruitment of local government officers.[6] Both committees were strongly influenced by the innovation in the 1960s of larger authorities who were adopting management ideas from the private sector by using prominent business consultancy firms to review their structures. These included Hull, Liverpool and Stockport.[7] Organisationally, the committees were influenced by a few high-profile experiments in restructuring policy machinery led by Newcastle-on-Tyne which had appointed, in effect, a chief executive officer. A number of authorities, such as the LCC, Bedfordshire and Basildon Urban District Council, had also formed more centralised policy management committees to co-ordinate their work.[8]

The Maud Committee, although set up in 1964 supposedly to deal with staffing in local government, concerned itself with spearheading these advances in local government decision-making machinery. The Inquiry was particularly critical of the tendency of councillors to implement rather than devise policy and hence to take over tasks that were the province of officers. A further concern was the lack of co-ordination within the committee structures of most local authorities. The solution to these problems proposed by the Maud Inquiry was arguably ahead of its time and anticipated Blair's cabinet structure, although some of this concern perhaps missed the point that political factors were increasingly holding together local authorities as corporate organisations. It was recommended that the number of committees be drastically reduced to around six and that they report to a small policy committee of councillors who would, if they approved a committee's proposals, pass it to the council for ratification.[9] The policy committee would be advised by a single dominant officer, the chief executive, who would chair a parallel co-ordinating committee of chief officers.[10] The idea was widely criticised by both local authorities and weighty academics such as Norman Chester as demeaning the power of the majority of councillors while cramming many different services into too few committee boxes.[11] More controversially and, perhaps deliberately overlooked, were parallel recommendations that central government should reduce controls over local authorities and allow them greater financial autonomy.[12] Given the progress of the Redcliffe-Maud Committee, which had been appointed by the time Maud presented these findings, the Labour Government and the Civil Service could shelve serious consideration of them until after the Royal Commission had completed its work.

Maud's ideas were, nevertheless, widely accepted by more managerially inclined politicians and academics. Greenwood and Stewart published an influential study on corporate management in support of such developments.[13] As restructuring became a reality under the Heath Government, the Maud initiative was revisited by a DoE Inquiry established in conjunction with the LAAs to devise ideas for the management of the post-1974 local authorities. This Committee,[14] chaired by the county secretary for Kent, M. A. Bains, was composed of local authority clerks and a manager from the private sector, but had no civil service representative. The result was a far less radical but more acceptable framework for restructuring divisive committee structures. The Bains report recommended that local authorities reduce the number of committees, but not as drastically as had been suggested by Maud. The strategy of a local authority should be co-ordinated by a policy committee, which would not be able to overrule committee decisions although some strategic committees, such as finance and personnel, might report to it. There should, as Maud suggested, be a chief executive – as opposed to the town clerk – who would be the co-ordinating manager for the authority, and not necessarily a lawyer. Although six years earlier Maud had received little enthusiasm from local authorities, almost all the post-1974 authorities immediately adopted the

Bains recommendations. The capacity to make such a radical change was in part made possible by the creation of new authorities following the 1972 Local Government Act, but it also reflected the impact of post-Maud academic and political proselytising on the need for more co-ordinated management in local government.

The larger local authorities that came into being in 1974 were fully professionalised and the remaining pockets of non-Weberian part-time management had retreated to all but the parish and community council. Almost all the post-1974 authorities appointed chief executives rather than maintain the office of town or county clerk and established a management committee of senior officers, under the chief executive's control, to co-ordinate the activities of departments. As the senior paid official in the authority the chief executive worked closely with council leaders or senior committee chairs. Below the office of chief executive the post-1974 local authorities were staffed by professional senior officers in departments that generally formed themselves into pyramidal hierarchies of officers, below which remained the established junior grades of clerks, craftsmen and labourers. In this context little had changed in local government structures in relation to pre- and post-1974 authorities, save that all authorities were larger and all tended to conduct a far greater extent of their tasks in-house rather than through outside contractors. Even the smallest districts were employing a considerable number of staff and could be regarded as complex, if largely hierarchical, structures.

Parallel to Maud's Inquiry, the Mallaby report recommended graduate entry into the higher echelons of local government and the creation of degree courses in public administration to service that need.[15] Although the local authorities had given way on their retention of local conditions of service, many of the ideas within the Hadow report made little immediate impact. It was not until the 1960s that trends in education were undermining the practice of recruiting staff largely from school-leavers who would learn their profession in-post. Following the Robbins report[16] and the creation of more university places, the most able school-leavers were more likely to go on to university rather than be attracted to the town hall and then grind on through night-school to pass professional examinations. By 2000 the expansion of higher education had ensured that the majority of entrants to the officer ranks of local government were graduates either already specialised in a specific service need or aiming, through post-graduate training, to obtain professional qualifications.

The growth of party control

Throughout the nineteenth century local politics was being transformed through the insidious growth of party influence. This trend was not so much a consequence of any potential in party central offices to direct the activities of their rank and file supporters on a local authority as it was a reflection of attitudes, in part stimulated by an increasingly national media, to see local electoral contests in terms of referenda on the fortunes of the national government rather than on local community issues.[17] In rural areas and especially district authorities councillors maintained their independence well into the nineteenth century. Many of these independent members were Conservatives, but especially in Scotland and Wales it could not be assumed such local activists were covert Tories.[18] Particularly where district or parish elections were concerned, councillors often considered that party politics should not be part of the local decision-making process. The restructuring of 1974 was an important catalyst for change within districts from non-partisan to party political contest.[19] The proportion of non-party local authorities had by the mid-1980s diminished to the extent that only 4 per cent of local authorities had councils in which none of the members declared a party affiliation and but 14 per cent, largely in rural areas of Wales and Scotland, had a majority of independents.[20] Not only was there a decline in independent members but also in localised parties. In the 1930s contests were frequently fought by local rate-payer candidates who were affiliated neither to Labour nor to the Conservative Party. Rate-payer parties have sporadically emerged and declined in subsequent decades, but have never subsequently been a dominant political movement.[21]

The trend towards national party dominance is also reflected in the increasing number of contested local authority elections. In the newly created county and district councils in the late nineteenth century many seats in county and district authorities attracted but one candidate. Lee observes that in the early years of Cheshire County Council, 'once selected a councillor had a very good chance of representing his division, frequently unopposed until either his retirement or death'. One ward did not have a contest until 1922.[22] In some towns which had a strong majority for one party the number of uncontested seats during the first half of the nineteenth century was likely to be high. In Guildford only 37 per cent of possible ward elections were contested between 1898 and 1914; but between 1919 and 1920 this number rose to 66 per cent and by the 1960s almost all seats were contested, often with at least 3 candidates in the field.[23] Even before the 1974 reorganisation and the creation of larger authorities there was an increase in the number of both partisan and contested elections stimulated by the Conservative Party, which used an unaccustomed majority following local elections in 1967 to take control of almost all senior committee chairs on the AMC. Its action precipitated the structuring of the LAAs on much more rigid party lines and had the knock-on effect of further reinforcing party control in individual authorities.[24] By the 1980s only 4 per cent of local authorities had more than a third of their seats elected without a contest and in 75 per cent of all local authorities all seats were contested.[25] By 2003 in England and Wales only 6 per cent of local elections were not fought between rival candidates, and of these by far the largest number were in district authorities.[26]

The growing tendency during the nineteenth century for most elections to be contested and for candidates to declare their political affiliation reflects in part concern among the national parties to secure a presence in both local and national political life. As the parties and the national media increasingly viewed local elections as referenda on the popularity of the party in government, they became more concerned to control the local political process. The pattern of party discipline was set nationally, with the Labour Party requiring from 1930 that councillors must predetermine their policy and remain unified within the council chamber.[27] The Conservative and the Liberal Party gave a much freer reign to local political leaders and did not insist on unity until after 1945. Until the late 1940s Conservatives, Liberals and non-socialist Independents followed the pattern of the LCC 'Moderates' by creating electoral coalitions to fight against Labour candidates. The rate-payers' movement emerged in the 1920s as a covert front in London for the Conservative Party and local rate-payer groups affiliated to the National Union of Rate-Payers which initially was heavily subsidised by Conservative interests. By the 1930s local rate-payer leaders increasingly resented interference from the Conservative Party and became far more independent, but this also cut them off from potential funding and after party political life resumed in 1945 had few affiliating local groups.[28] From 1920 to 1930 the party of the Right in Sheffield was a Conservative–Liberal alliance called the Citizens' Party, which from 1930 to 1948 evolved into the Municipal Progressive Party.[29] Even in smaller towns such as Guildford non-Labour activists coalesced in 1924 into a Town Association which finally gave up the ghost in 1958.[30] The widespread, although by no means universal, incidence of local anti-Labour coalitions came to an end, partly when the Liberals reached their electoral nadir in the 1950s but also because the Conservative Party nationally urged through its Local Government Committee that party members should fight for Conservative values of economy and for lower rates.[31]

The growth of party politics in local elections is to be attributed not only to national party concern to infiltrate all levels of political activity but reflects also the disappearance of *Gemeinschaft*[32] from politics as local authorities became larger at the expense of community ties and voters from urban backgrounds infiltrated rural areas. Studies of rural areas in the 1950s[33] show that local people were reluctant to discuss politics with interviewers and when pressed might observe that 'they voted for the Conservatives because "we all do"'.[34] In areas where one party was likely to predominate local political activists could see no sense in involving themselves in the expense of a futile gesture and until mass parties began to subsidise elections there was little motivation to generate a contest unless the outcome was genuinely uncertain. The absence of elections also reflected the close links between the leaders and the electorate of a small community and it was possible effectively to operate a process in which the favoured candidate emerged as a consequence of informal soundings among opinion-formers in the community and the realisation among potential rivals that any challenge to the growing consensus would be futile and perhaps in the long term damaging to them personally.[35] Deference to the local squire was in many areas a further crucial factor, but such attitudes did not always explain non-contests as in some strongly socialist mining areas the community might select candidates whose chances of victory were so secure that no contest was in practice worth the expense. The tendency by the 1980s for most elections to be contested may not, therefore, be simply translated as a greater commitment to local democracy but to a decline in the close community ties that could ensure electoral outcomes emerged by consensus among villagers who communicated with each other.

The impact of parties on local policy-making

Although the major parties increasingly felt it expedient to fight all electoral contests and that their candidates make clear their allegiance, the importance of the party machine as a source dictating local policies, at least until 1974, varied widely between local authorities. Birch found in 1950s Glossop that neither the Conservatives nor the Liberals held party group meetings of councillors and that while the Labour party held such meetings their councillors commonly took opposite sides in debates.[36] In Lancashire the Labour group of the Borough of Middleton demanded a far stricter adherence to the central party's rules than did the County Boroughs of Manchester or Salford.[37] George Jones observed that in Wolverhampton the Labour group councillors 'voted together not because they were coerced, but because they were in most cases in agreement with each other'.[38] In rural areas party discipline was even less in evidence, at least until the 1974 reorganisation. Although elections to Cheshire and Devon County Councils had been organised along party lines from 1888,[39] the opposing party groups quickly formed working agreements to select in turn the county chair and aldermen and even to determine which, if any, seats were contested.[40] The rise of the Labour Party cut across this consensus but, with the decline of the Liberals from 1920, until their revival in the 1960s, Conservatives in all but a few counties could regard the Labour opposition as an isolated and containable threat. Many county councils up to 1974 refused to declare officially the party compositions of their membership.[41] Under such circumstances there was little need for a strongly whipped party caucus.[42] In urban and rural districts where elections were fought on party lines the councillors, once elected, were probably even less inclined to subject themselves to a rigid framework of party discipline. Newcastle-under-Lyme Rural District Council, at least until the mid-1960s, had Labour members, but they never met as a Labour group.[43] Although local party groups of councillors were, and still remain, relatively independent of control by the national party leadership, they began to organise themselves into far more disciplined and hierarchical structures after the 1974 reorganisation. The practice of rank and file members taking their own line in council was far less a feature of local decision-making as newly restructured lower-tier councils covering wider areas than the previously smaller boroughs and districts adopted from the outset a much more adversarial stance.

The development of organised party machines within local authorities was much enhanced after 1918 with the trend, initiated within Labour parties, to replace the mayor as the political voice of the council with the leader of the majority party.[44] The office of mayor subsequently becomes the symbol of the 'dignified element' of the local constitution, a figure who is the ceremonial representative of the town, and usually for the duration of his or her one year in office a politically neutral figure who thus can also chair the full council meeting. Party leaders arguably existed in substance if not in name during the nineteenth century. Few could, for example, dispute the pre-eminence of Joseph Chamberlain in his active years as a Birmingham councillor and alderman. In Sheffield William J. Clegg and, after his death in 1915, his son Sir William Clegg could be referred to as in effect the leader of the Liberal councillors.[45] As in the national Labour Party, prominent politicians who held the office of chairman of the party group were referred to as the leader and determined the chief spokespersons for the party group, and, if the party had a majority, therefore the committee chairs. The small group of councillors supporting Labour on the LCC were forged before 1914 into a group by Harry Gosling, who was seen as leader of the party group from 1919.[46] In Sheffield Cecil Wilson, a former Liberal and manufacturer, became leader of the Labour group in 1922, to be followed by Ernest Rowlinson who dominated Sheffield politics during the inter-war years.[47] The initiative to form regular party group meetings of Labour councillors in Glasgow was taken by Patrick Dollan, who took the role of secretary to the group following his election in 1913 and had become the undisputed leader of Glasgow City Council by the time the party secured, with the Independent Labour Party, majority control of the authority.[48] By the 1930s the authority of the council leader was well established particularly within the Labour party in the larger authorities. Herbert Morrison, who was reaffirmed as leader of the Labour group on the LCC following its electoral victory in 1935 giving them for the first time control of the Council, in consultation with three other prominent party members, determined which council members became committee chairs.[49] Morrison subsequently came to be regarded as the dominant figure in the LCC, directing its policies with a prominence almost parallel to the influence of the elected mayor of the GLC some seventy years later.[50] The evolution of the disciplined party group and the position of group and council leader did not, however, necessarily elevate a single individual to dominance of party or council policy. Leaders are only as successful as factions among their party colleagues on the council will permit. In some cases rival factions elected leaders as compromise figures who sought to reconcile differences among their colleagues rather than dictatorially impose their policies. George Jones observes that although post-1945 Labour and Conservative members on Wolverhampton Borough Council established more formal and regular party group meetings, their leaders were less dominant than the principal politicians of either party in the 1920s and 1930s.[51]

The variable level of party discipline within local authorities reflects the absence of strong lines of control between the national party organisations and local government party machines. Labour, the Conservatives and the Liberals built up local government sub-committees and held regular local government conferences as part of their national consultative apparatus, but these agencies, as indicated by Peter Walker's efforts to convince the 'knights of the shire' to accept radical reform, served as consultancy fora rather than as command structures. Apart from the heavy-handed recourse to expulsion from the party, there was no formal apparatus in any of the major British parties to allow national leaders to instruct locally elected politicians as to the party policies they must adopt in the council chamber.[52] Expulsions of errant councillors are rare and often involve, as with the removal by the national Labour Party of communists in the 1920s or militants in the 1980s, broader issues of ideology as opposed to particular local policies. Gyford and James illustrate patterns of co-operation between local party leaders and the leadership in the Conservative Party but also hostility between local leaders and the national party in, for example, the differences between South Yorkshire councillors and the Labour Government over transport subsidies. In general, they point to a detachment between many councillors and their national party machinery.[53]

Councillors

The emergence of the Labour Party to become by the 1920s the major opposition to the Conservatives had profound effects on the composition of urban local governments. The development effectively displaced the Gladstonian industrial leaders from pre-eminence in big city politics. In Sheffield, for example, in 1910 there were 25 council members who were directors of industries or involved in commerce and a further 14 who were professionals, whereas by 1930, although there were 23 more seats on the council, only 9 members were industrialists or in commerce and 9 were professionals.[54] The arrival of working-class Labour councillors in large numbers destroyed the town halls as gentlemen's clubs and, for many local patricians, the whole character and value of local political activism. Manufacturers were unlikely to be enthusiastic about having to share the ornate committee rooms and councillors' library with individuals who might well be their ill-paid employees. Neville Chamberlain noted:

> The policy of the Socialists is definitely to capture local government in the towns and as soon as they begin to get really aggressive I expect the better men will clear out.[55]

Working-class members of local authorities faced a particular problem in sustaining themselves financially as councillors, given that no payment was available for loss of wages incurred as a result of devoting some of their earning hours to council duties. Nineteenth-century tradition dictated that gentlemen should have sufficient funds at their disposal to undertake public duties without need of further support, apart from social honour. In essence, such an arrangement, despite the arrival of democracy, was upheld by Conservatives who wished to discourage working-class councillors. Stanyer notes that up to 1914 only one working-class member even stood for membership of Devon County Council.[56] G. D. H. Cole recognised that 'councils of almost all types have too high a proportion of elderly retired members'.[57] A minor concession to greater participation was secured in the 1933 Local Government Act which allowed county councils to reimburse their members' travelling expenses. Mayors and chairs of councils could also receive expenses for extending hospitality to dignified visitors to their authority. Scottish county councillors since 1929 had enjoyed much better conditions of service and could statutorily be paid travelling and subsistence expenses, and also be compensated for loss of salary when engaged in council work.[58]

In 1946 the Labour Government reviewed how councillors could be recompensed for their services,[59] but despite the advantages for working-class members the Committee firmly rejected the possibility of paying councillors by reaffirming the principles of civic virtue:

> The health of this democracy depends upon the fact that large numbers of men and women give their time and trouble to all sorts of voluntary work, and it is from such public-spirited people that the members of public author-ities should be recruited. Such voluntary work must involve sacrifice, and indeed would lose its savour if it did not: sacrifices of some other interests and hobbies, and also of income, or of chances of increasing income.[60]

However, by 1948 the Labour Government had ensured that councillors in England and Wales received expenses for travel and subsistence when engaged on council business, and there was some recompense for loss of earnings. The Maud Inquiry agreed that councillors should not receive a salary but argued for a more simplified system of expenses and compen-sation for loss of earning,[61] while the Redcliffe-Maud Inquiry suggested that leading councillors might receive greater compensation, given their work-loads and responsibilities.[62] During the policy debates for the restructured system, Michael Heseltine proposed a flat-rate allowance for all councillors attending local authority business,[63] and this was accepted in the 1972 Local Government Act.[64] The issue was soon revisited by the next Labour Government with an Inquiry chaired by Derek Robinson which proposed that councillors should receive a small annual payment and that higher special responsibility payments could be given to more senior councillors.[65] The Widdecombe report[66] went further by arguing for a flat-rate salary for councillors in particular types of authority, with higher payments for those having key responsibilities. It was not until 1995 that action was taken on the issue to allow local authorities to pay councillors what was in effect an annual salary, and the Local Government Act 2000 has firmly established the salaried framework by ensuring that payments can also include pension contributions.

A further issue that tended to skew representation on local authorities largely in the Conservative local business interest was the principle that no citizen could stand as a councillor for any authority that employed him or her. Effectively this prevented teachers or dustmen from becoming local authority representatives, even though property developers or representatives of local businesses, who might have far more to gain from membership, were free to become councillors. Although subject to some debate prior to the Thatcher Government, the Labour Party made no changes to this arrangement. Following the Widdicombe report in 1989 the Thatcher Government made eligibility rules even tighter by preventing senior local government officers in one authority from being able to stand in another so as to prevent a developing system of neighbouring authorities employing each other's leading politicians.[67]

Councillors remained unrepresentative of the population at large even after the reforms of the Attlee Government made it easier financially for working-class wage-earners to be active in local government, since the council chambers remained predominantly the preserve of men rather than women and also, following the increase in immigration from the West Indies and the Indian sub-continent in the 1950s, a steadfastly white Anglo-Saxon preserve. A survey of councillors for the Maud report found that only 12 per cent of councillors were women and the proportion rose only marginally from then until 1986 when research for the Widdicombe report yielded the higher figure of 19 per cent.[68] During the 1990s, however, the situation improved considerably: although falling far short of parity with men, women in 2003 accounted for 27 per cent of councillors.[69] Councillors tended also to be older than the population at large, with forty nine percent over 55 years of age[70] but were, nevertheless, better educated, with 22 per cent being graduates compared with five per cent, in 1986, of the British population.[71]

The disappearance of the upper-middle-class Liberal manufacturers from the council chamber may not be wholly a result of the emergence of the Labour Party. The merger of businesses to form joint-stock companies operating on a national and, later, an international stage may have had a significant impact on the changes in the backgrounds of the city councillors. In the nineteenth century industrialists, like Joseph Chamberlain, owed their prosperity to the success of an enterprise based wholly in one community. The enterprise of Nettlefold & Chamberlain, manufacturing a sizeable income for Joseph Chamberlain, was located in Birmingham and drew its labour from the locality. Local businessmen realised that the success of their company was bound up with the success of the community in which it was based. Acquiring for the city efficient and relatively cheap gas, water and electricity supplies and an effective system of elementary education could give a manufacturer a competitive edge over rivals within a community less well endowed with inexpensive utilities. More enlightened businessmen also realised that a healthy, well-housed labour force would facilitate greater profitability for their enterprise than if they were situated in a community with poor sanitation. The philanthropy of the Cadburys, Titus Salt or Lord Lever in constructing model communities was based not only on humanitarian values but on sound commercial sense.

As companies merged with other firms to become part of a national network whose many shares were bought and sold on the stock market, the importance of the infrastructure of a specific location in giving a firm a competitive edge came to be of much less importance. Businessmen gaining profit from shareholdings in several companies or in a business with multiple manufacturing and distribution outlets will not seek to resolve problems of infrastructure or of the social well-being of labour by applying to an array of specific local authorities but will seek national solutions from central government. By the 1980s research for the Widdicombe Inquiry reported that legislation requiring local authorities to consult with business interests on the rates was ineffectual due in part to the 'often hostile and combative attitude of some businessman'.[72] The close links between businessmen and the local authority that typified urban local governments at their zenith at the beginning of the nineteenth century had been replaced by indifference or even hostility. The efforts of the Thatcher and Blair governments to break up the inclusive authority by creating partnerships may, however, be reversing this trend.

In rural areas where the Labour Party was not a serious threat to the established pattern of politics the decline of the local notable, in the form of the squire or the rural professional, was a more gradual process. County landowners retained an interest in local government rather longer than did the urban industrialist, but by 1945 they were probably a dominant interest in few authorities. Lee's study of Cheshire argued that the economic slump of the late 1920s and its effect on agriculture undermined the predominance of country-house society and led to the decline of landowners' interest in local government.[73] From 1889 to 1941 2 of the 4 chairmen of Cheshire County Council were landowners and the founding chair was a prosperous Liverpool merchant, but the post-war representatives were drawn from trade and manufacturing.[74] Stanyer finds similarly that Devon County Council evolved between 1946 and 1972 from a local government led largely by landowning social leaders to one in which middle-class professionals predominated.[75] Lee concludes for Cheshire as a whole that by the mid-nineteenth century 'the county society of social leaders was replaced by a community of public persons in which the leading members and Chief Officers of the County Council were the principle personalities'.[76]

After 1918 the rise of the Labour Party and the working-class voter led to an increasing chorus from the Right that 'councillors are not what they were'; Bright and Addison's comments noted in earlier chapters suggest that, like *Punch*, they never were. A waspish critic of the local government system, Eugene Hasluck, in 1936 offered a thirteen-page tirade against councillors, which concluded:

> Taken as a whole the average local council is a poor thing: Were the members left to undertake the duties of supervising the details of local administration, in the same way as the old Parish Overseers ... there would be chaos in a very short time in most areas.[77]

Harris observed in 1939 that while Hasluck's view may not be wholly justified 'it cannot be denied that that many people ... are seriously disturbed about what they consider to be the deterioration in the type of member'.[78] These concerns continued after 1945 and contributed to the disposition of national politicians and the Civil Service to reform local government. Dame Evelyn Sharp in 1962 stated that 'what is wrong' with local government is that 'not ... enough really able people are interested to-day in local government. I do not think enough people from business, from industry, from agriculture, from the professions are going into it.'[79] Many of these complaints reflect the rise of the Labour Party and emergence of working-class councillors, and a concomitant reduction in the numbers of what Clements termed 'local notables'[80] standing as councillors and aldermen. While the local industrialist and leading professionals such as solicitors certainly declined as local authority representatives, the criticism of lower quality reflects more Neville Chamberlain's aversion to representatives of the lower classes. As Stanyer eloquently observes, it is a denigration of the values of democracy to suggest that the change marks a decline in capability within local authorities.[81] The higher educational achievements of councillors compared with those of the population as a whole in recent surveys suggests that members of local authorities are not incompetent, while reference to the capabilities of, for example, Birmingham councillors prior to the arrival of Joseph Chamberlain in the 1870s might also indicate that in the nineteenth century not every councillor was an honest and innovative representative.

The relationship between citizen and councillor

An issue of central contemporary concern is the apparent growing indifference of voters to local government. Electoral turnout in boroughs during the 1920s was between 50 and 55 per cent, but this seems to have fallen to around 45 per cent in the 1930s[82] and by the 1970s was often dipping below that level.[83] Voting turnout was probably always higher in non-metropolitan district elections and between 1973 and 1978 was on average 42 per cent in England[84] and 52 and 53 per cent in Wales and Scotland.[85] Restructuring local authorities into larger units does not appear to have resolved the issue of low turnout, which fell as low as 39 per cent for English districts in 1980 and a nadir of 31 per cent in 1998, recovering to 41 per cent in 2004. In metropolitan districts a low point of a 25 per cent turnout was reached in 1998 and, as in the district elections, recovered to 41 per cent in 2004.[86] The reluctance to vote in local elections cannot, however, be attributed to a lack of interest in local politics. A survey of public attitudes in 2005 showed that 81 per cent of respondents were interested in local issues compared with 77 per cent interested in national issues and 66 per cent in international issues.[87] It might be inferred that the structure of local politics and decision-making rather than the issues is the problem.

Since the 1960s detailed electoral and public attitude surveys have suggested that, at least by this date, those who bothered to vote viewed the local electoral contest in terms of a plebiscite on the standing of the parties nationally. Butler and Stokes in their survey of voting behaviour in the 1960s argued that over 90 per cent of electors with a party attachment voted for that party locally as well as nationally[88] and Newton in 1972 found that less than 10 per cent of the variance in local election results in Birmingham was the consequence of local factors.[89] Dunleavy in 1980, adding further survey evidence to those factors, argued that national political values dominate local electoral outcomes.[90] Some caution is needed in the interpretation of these findings since it may be argued that in a relatively partisan society it can be expected that there would be little variance between electors' choices of candidates for local and national elections. Few voters who supported, for example, higher taxation and better public services in the 1970s would rationally have voted Labour nationally and Conservative locally.

Since the late 1970s the growth of the Liberal Democrats and of the Scottish and Welsh Nationalists as parties of protest has greatly complicated the predictability of local election results and can create circumstances in which local events may make a substantive difference in local electoral results. Sheffield was controlled by the Liberal Democrats between 1999 and 2003 despite national increases in the Labour vote and in Liverpool the popular reaction against the militant faction ensured that Labour has ceased to hold on to power in the city despite the popularity of the Blair Government from 1997 to 2005. A further consequence of the emergence since the 1970s of parties to rival the Conservatives and Labour is the growing incidence of 'hung' local authorities in which no party has overall control. As Leach and Stewart demonstrate, this situation has led to many authorities developing a range of coalition alliances to secure effective governance.[91] By the 1980s the dominance of two-party competition during the preceding five decades was very much in the past.

How far there has been a decline in popular understanding of the role of local government and in familiarity with local councillors that might parallel the decline in the nineteenth century of voting turnout cannot easily be determined due to lack of evidence of popular attitudes pre-1945. Enthusiasts for larger authorities from the mid-1930s claimed that the bigger authorities would attract more capable and charismatic leaders who would gain wider publicity and be recognised by voters. Such thinking has been since the 1990s a substantive argument in favour of directly elected mayors. There has, however, always been a plausible argument that the smaller the authority and the greater the ratio of councillors to citizens the more likely there is to be familiarity between the councillor and his or her electors. The merits of the small authority were expressed in a memorandum from the Urban District Councils' Association to the Jowitt Inquiry in 1942:

> The urban district councillor lives among the people he is trying to serve and has a fairly intimate knowledge of the matters the council is dealing with. He is not entirely dependent upon officers' reports. His knowledge is first hand. Also he can gather local opinion. On the other hand a county councillor is often discussing matters arising in regard to areas distant from his own and of which he cannot have the same knowledge as the man on the spot.[92]

This argument may go some way to explain the disparity in voting turnout between British local authorities and those of West European nations, as is shown in appendix 3.

Communication with the electorate after 1974 was not so much through personal contact on the street but through more formally arranged surgeries. In exchange, it may be argued, councillors were probably becoming more professional and obliged to devote far more of their time to council duties, but it is questionable how much this involved work in the community rather than in the town hall. A close relationship between local authorities and business interest groups had probably been eroded prior to 1950 with the dominance of Labour councillors in most cities. Newton's study of Birmingham in the 1970s showed that of over 4,000 potential interest groups in Birmingham only 30 per cent had frequent links with the City Council,[93] while Dearlove's parallel study of the London Borough of Kensington and Chelsea argues that the successful interests are those such as the Chamber of Commerce favoured by the majority Conservative councillors.[94] These studies can be interpreted as showing that by the time of local government restructuring in 1974 local authorities were, just as with central government, closely reliant on the co-operation of larger voluntary associations or representatives of business and trade unions.

A further factor that has not enhanced public understanding of local government is the development in Britain of a dominant national press centred in London, and 'north of the border' in Glasgow, which tends to reflect on local issues largely in terms of their importance for central government. The trend to a national press has been at the expense of the provincial daily paper and, more latterly, an evening press that reported the activities of each local authority and was an important outlet for councillors to express their views. While most parts of the country still retain a weekly press, even those journals are tending to cover wider areas and are not flourishing in terms of their circulation. Despite such changes, and the poor turnout in elections, citizens have generally been supportive of the institution of local government. Research for the Widdicombe Inquiry found that over 70 per cent of citizens considered that local authorities 'ran things very or fairly well'.[95] It may be suggested that local government remains a respected institution, but is increasingly seen as a remote, if efficient, institution that delivers uncontroversial services rather than a body determining policy for, and with the involvement of, local people.

The councillor and Parliament

Although local councillors were becoming more distant from the communities that they represented and arguably more professional, after 1974 they were probably no closer to securing influence within national government. W. J. M. Mackenzie observed in the 1950s that British MPs had shown little concern over the erosion of local powers and that the numbers of MPs in the House of Commons with local authority experience was less than the proportion of national representatives with local government experience in the USA and France.[96] Rejoinders to Mackenzie's argument suggest that he underestimated the numbers of MPs with local authority experience.[97] As table 10.1 shows, the link between MPs and local government in terms of experience at some time in their career has grown steadily during the twentieth century.

Experience is not the same as continued joint membership of a local authority and Parliament. There has been a steady decline in the numbers of MPs who remain as local councillors. In 1889 there were 131 Peers and 87 MPs who were also county councillors, but this had declined by 1950 to 54 Peers and 20 MPs, and between 1960 and 1975 dropped dramatically to 10 Peers and 6 MPs.[98] By 1991 only 5 MPs were also councillors, of whom 3 represented Northern Ireland seats while the 2 representatives

Table 10.1 *Number (and percentages) of MPs with local government experience (LGE) as councillors or aldermen*

	1911[a]	1931	1951	1971	1981	1991	2003	2006
MPs with LGE	164	182	222	266	292	315	370	351
	(29)	(30)	(36)	(43)	(46)	(49)	(56)	(54)
MPs without LGE	396	433	403	458	343	322	289	295
	(71)	(70)	(64)	(57)	(54)	(51)	(44)	(46)
Total	560	615	625	624	635	637	659	646

Note: [a]Excluding Irish MPs.
Source: Dod's Parliamentary Companion for relevant years.

of English constituencies had been elected the previous year in by-elections.[99] In January 2006 there are 18 MPs who are still local authority members, of whom 8 are Conservatives, 4 Labour, 4 Liberal Democrats and 2 Northern Ireland Democratic Unionists;[100] this does not, however, suggest an upsurge in the interest linking local and national politics as 16 of these members were first elected in 2005.[101] In recent decades almost all newly elected MPs who were councillors have either immediately resigned from their local authority or simply have not stood again when eligible for re-election as councillors.[102]

This trend to an extent has been prompted by the political parties themselves which have not in recent decades encouraged joint-office holding,[103] but it may also relate to the broader change in attitudes to local government itself. In the 1990s interviews with Sheffield MPs who had been very active in local politics, principally as councillors, showed that all of them had left behind local activism and would pass on any questions relating to local government to a councillor rather than investigate the matter personally. As one Sheffield MP observed about leaving the City Council, 'I was glad to be out of it'.[104] The MPs, moreover, argued that it would be impossible to undertake the volume of work required as a councillor alongside service as an MP, and they appeared to have little or no interest in, or even conception of, the patron–client role of some French Deputies.[105]

The assumption that serving on a local authority would necessarily prompt an MP to defend local interests is also scarcely justified. As shown in earlier chapters, MPs with local authority experience post war have been just as inclined to reduce as to defend local powers. Morrison presided over the nationalisation of municipal enterprise such as gas and electricity and though he and Chuter Ede may have scuppered Bevan's plans for unitary authorities, it must be borne in mind that Bevan himself had local authority experience. More recently, the tenure of the former leader of Lambeth Borough Conservatives, John Major, at Number 10 did little to alleviate the parlous state of local authorities in the early 1990s.

Former Conservative leaders of the London Borough of Wandsworth who became MPs, Beresford and Chope, did much to shape the Thatcher Government's enabling strategies.

The power of Parliament lies not so much in its backbench MPs but among the MPs who are leaders of the majority party and form the membership of the Government; as table 10.2 shows, however, MPs with local government experience have always been underrepresented in the Cabinet. Previous experience within local government has also never been a significant qualification for the bequest of responsibility for its guidance within the Government. Of the 21 cabinet ministers who since 1945 have been responsible for overseeing local government only 6 have served as councillors. Ambitious young politicians may, at least in this policy sector, heed the advice of Gilbert and Sullivan's Ruler of the Queen's Navy and 'never go to sea'.

Over the twentieth century Britain lost the characteristic tendency to patron–client links between central government and the localities that has been so significant in the modernisation of local government in Europe and the USA to embrace new technologies and yet retain small, community-based, local structures. In the nineteenth century, even after the formation of the county councils' local notables, there were many elite leaders who dominated their local councils and at the same time defended their position in Parliament. Even in urban areas prominent politicians, such as Joseph Chamberlain or J. B. Firth, used their influence in government to shape a local government system in which they retained some interest. By the twenty-first century, for an ambitious politician local government service may be a stepping-stone to power, but it is rarely a central interest as distinct from a means to an end. The politics of many a city council in recent decades has been littered with aspiring MPs who gain a position on the local authority but, after failing to secure nomination as an MP, resign their membership.

While links between local government and parliamentarians are not particularly strong, the process of electoral competition among the major parties during the nineteenth century has had an increasing powerful influence over the extent to which central government may concern itself with the local delivery of services. Gladstone or Salisbury[106] would not have dreamt of staking the claim of their party to be returned as the

Table 10.2 *Cabinet members (CMs) with Local Government Experience (LGE)*

	1911	1931	1951	1971	1981	1991	2003	2006
CMs with LGE	3 of 20	9 of 20	7 of 17	2 of 18	3 of 20	3 of 20	12 of 23	8 of 21

Note: Data for MPs as in table 10.1.
Source: Cabinet membership data from D. Butler and G. Butler, *Twentieth-Century British Political Facts 1900–2000* (Basingstoke: Macmillan, 8th edn, 2000).

Government with reference to improvements in health care or education within boroughs, counties or districts. In the 1920s and 1930s the manifestos of Labour, the Conservatives or the Liberals did not make promises concerning improvement in service quality for tasks operated by local government. After 1945 competition for support in the context of the changing functions of local government, popular demands for better welfare services and the erosion of a dual-state mentality ensured that the major parties increasingly made promises to improve services delivered locally by compelling local governments to follow centrally determined directives. The Conservatives' pledge in their 1951 *Manifesto* to build 300,000 houses, which was not reflected in any corresponding promise in the Labour Manifesto, is, perhaps, a landmark in inter-party competition, highlighting the value of promising central command of locally provided functions.[107] These insidious changes culminate in the debates of the early twenty-first century between the parties concerning the delivery of successful schools, improved rented housing, community policing or even enhanced provision for the arts.

Notes

1   A. H. Birch, *Small Town Politics* (Oxford: Oxford University Press, 1959), p. 138.

2   Ostrom, Bish and Ostrom, *Local Government in the United States* (San Fransisco: CA, Institute of Contemporary Studies Press, 1988).

3   Birch, *Small Town Politics*, pp. 126–9.

4   Poole, *Local Government Service in England and Wales*, p. 19; Young and Rao, *Local Government Since 1945*, pp. 220–1. Dame Evelyn had been Secretary to the Hadow Inquiry and, later, in Silkin's Ministry of Town and Country Planning was the official in charge of new towns' policy.

5   Ministry of Housing and Local Government, *The Management of Local Government* (Maud report), vol. 1 (London: HMSO, 1967), p. iii.

6   Sir George Mallaby was formerly Commissioner for the Civil Service and thus in charge of recruitment.

7   H. Elcock, *Local Government: Politicians, Professionals and the Public in Local Authorities* (London: Methuen, 2nd edn, 1986), p. 241.

8   Maud report, pp. 28–9.

9   *Ibid.*, pp. 48–51.

10   *Ibid.*, pp. 47–8.

11   Young and Rao, *Local Government since 1945*, pp. 221–2.

12   Maud report, pp. 68–89.

13   R. Greenwood and J. D. Stewart, *Corporate Planning in Local Government* (London: Charles Knight, 1974).

14   Department of the Environment and Local Authority Associations, *The New Local Authorities: Management and Structure* (Bains report) (London: HMSO, 1972).

15   Ministry of Housing and Local Government, *Staffing of Local Government* (Mallaby report) (London: HMSO, 1966).

16 Lord Robbins (chair), *Report of the Committee on Higher Education*, Cmnd 2165 (London: HMSO, 1963).

17 K. Young, 'Party politics in local government: an historical perspective', in *Report of the Committee of Inquiry into the Conduct of Local Authority Business* (Widdicombe report), Cmnd 9797, Research Volume 4 (London: HMSO, 1986), pp. 81–105, p. 100, notes how Lord Woolton as Party Chairman in 1948 urged the Conservative faithful to rally to local elections as '[i]n April and May 1949 we shall have a miniature general election in the country'.

18 W. Grant, *Independent Local Politics in England and Wales* (Farnborough: Saxon House, 1977), p. 3.

19 *Ibid.*, p. 2; P. Lynch, *Scottish Government and Politics* (Edinburgh: Edinburgh University Press, 2001), p. 213.

20 S. Leach, C. Game, J. Gyford and A. Midwinter 'The political organisation of local authorities', in Widdecombe report, vol. 2 (London: HMSO, 1986), p. 37.

21 In Barnsley since the 1970s, for example, rate-payer candidates have been a significant force in local politics and, on occasion, have won a considerable number of seats on the Council: see election results since 1979 online at www.barnsley.gov.uk/elections/previous-results.doc.

22 J. M. Lee, *Social Leaders and Public Persons* (Oxford: Oxford University Press, 1963), p. 59.

23 R. Ottewill, 'The changing character of municipal election 1835–1974', *Local Historian*, 34:3 (2004), pp. 159–78.

24 J. Gyford, 'The politicisation of local government', in M. Loughlin, D. Gefland and K. Young (eds), *Half a Century of Municipal Decline* (London: George Allen & Unwin, 1985), p. 86.

25 Leach *et al.*, 'The political organisation of local authorities', p. 41.

26 Local Government Chronicle Elections Centre, University of Plymouth, online at www.plymouth.ac.uk/researchcover/rcp.asp?page=52&pagetype=G

27 Labour Party, *Annual Report* (London: Labour Party, 1930), pp. 12, 298, on the adoption of model standing orders for Labour groups.

28 Young, 'Party politics in local government: an historical perspective'.

29 A. Thorpe, 'The consolidation of a Labour stronghold'.

30 Ottewill, 'The changing character of municipal election 1835–1974'.

31 K. Young, 'Party Politics in Local Government: An Historical Perspective', pp. 100–1; J. Gyford and M. James, *National Parties and Local Politics* (London: George Allen & Unwin, 1983), pp. 22–7.

32 The term coined by the German sociologist F. Tönnies expresses social relationships based on personal knowledge of individuals, in contrast to *Gesselschaft*, a relationship where individuals treat one another on an impersonal, machine-like basis.

33 R. Frankenberg, *Village on the Border* (London: Cohen & West, 1957); W. M. Williams, *The Sociology of an English Village: Gosforth* (London: Routledge, 1956); J. Littlejohn, *Westrigg* (London, Routledge, 1963).

34 Williams, *Sociology of an English Village: Gosforth*, p. 175.

35 The author observed in 1970 an arrangement of Welsh farmers to decide among themselves who would be nominated for their local community council. On one occasion an unwise English settler got herself nominated

separately from the local arrangement and occasioned an election, which she lost.

36 Birch, *Small Town Politics*, p. 119.
37 J. G. Bulpitt, *Party Politics in English Local Government* (London: Longmans, 1967), pp. 100–1.
38 G. W. Jones, *Borough Politics* (London: Macmillan, 1969), p. 184.
39 J. Stanyer, *A History of Devon County Council* (Exeter: Devon Books, 1989), pp. 30–1; Lee, *Social Leaders and Public Persons*, pp. 60–3.
40 Lee, *Social Leaders and Public Persons*, p. 64; Stanyer, *History of Devon County Council*, pp. 90–2.
41 Lee, *Social Leaders and Public Persons*, p. 222.
42 Stanyer, *History of Devon County Council*, p. 63.
43 F. Bealey, J. Blondel and W. P. McCann, *Constituency Politics* (London: Faber & Faber, 1965), p. 339.
44 J. Garrard, *Leadership and Power in Victorian Industrial Towns* (Manchester: Manchester University Press, 1983), pp. 64–5, gives a useful illustration of the centrality of the mayor in nineteenth-century town politics.
45 H. E. Mathers, 'Sheffield municipal politics 1893–1926: parties, personaliries and the rise of Labour', Ph.D thesis, University of Sheffield, 1979, pp. 126–7.
46 B. Donoghue and G. W. Jones, *Herbert Morrison* (London: Weidenfeld & Nicolson, 1973), p. 87; H. Gosling, *Up and Down Stream* (London: Methuen, 1927), p. 107.
47 Mathers, *City of Sheffield, 1993–1926*, p. 72.
48 H. Carr and W. Knox, 'Patrick Dollan', in W. Knox (ed.), *Scottish Labour Leaders 1918–1939* (Edinburgh: Mainstream Publishing, 1984), p. 96.
49 Donoghue and Jones, *Herbert Morrison*, p. 191.
50 *Ibid.*, pp. 197–210.
51 Jones, *Borough Politics*, p. 204.
52 J. Gyford and M. James, *National Parties and Local Politics* (London: George Allen & Unwin, 1983), p. 195.
53 *Ibid.*, pp. 126–51.
54 *Sheffield Telegraph* Year Books and *Sheffield Red Guide* Year Books.
55 Chamberlain, *Neville Chamberlain Diary Letters 1921–27*, vol. 2, p. 424.
56 Stanyer, *History of Devon County Council 1888–1989*, p. 86.
57 Cole, *Politics of Local and Regional Government*, p. 247.
58 Ministry of Health and Scottish Office, *Report of the Inter-Departmental Committee on Expenses of Members of Local Authorities*, Cmnd 7126 (London: HMSO, 1947) (Lindsay report).
59 *Ibid.*, pp. 5–19.
60 *Ibid.*, p. 22, para. 21.
61 Maud report, vol. 1, p. 146, para. 524, and Appendix D, pp. 167–74.
62 Redcliffe-Maud report, vol. 1, p. 128, para. 504.
63 NA, CAB 134/3441, 1st meeting, 8 March 1971.
64 Local Government Act, 1972, Clauses 173–8.
65 Department of the Environment, *Report of the Committee on the Remuneration of Councillors* (Robinson report), Cmnd 7010 (London: HMSO, 1977).
66 Widdicombe report, pp. 125–35, paras 6.80–117.

67 Local Government and Housing Act, 1989: Eliz II, c. 42.
68 J. England, 'The characteristics and attitudes of councillors', in *The Conduct of Local Authority Business,* vol. 2 (London, HMSO, 1986), p. 19; see also J. Barron, G. Crawley and T. Wood, *Councillors in Crisis* (Basingstoke: Macmillan, 1991), p. 32.
69 Local Government Chronicle Elections Centre, University of Plymouth, online at www.plymouth.ac.uk/researchcover/rcp.asp?page=52&pagetype=G.
70 England, 'Characteristics and attitudes of councillors', p. 24.
71 *Ibid.,* p. 32.
72 Widdicombe report, vol. 2, chapter 7: 'The local authority and the public'.
73 Lee, *Social Leaders and Public Persons,* pp. 91–109.
74 *Ibid.,* p. 179.
75 Stanyer, *A History of Devon County Council 1888–1989,* pp. 80, 88.
76 Lee, *Social Leaders and Public Persons,* p. 212.
77 E. Hasluck, *Local Government in England* (Cambridge: Cambridge University Press, 2nd edn, 1948), p. 57; the critique is not revised for the second edition.
78 G. M. Harris, *Municipal Self-Government in Britain* (London: P. S. King, 1939), p. 57.
79 E. Sharp, 'The future of local government', *Public Administration,* 40 (autumn 1962), pp. 375–86.
80 R. V. Clements, *Local Notables and the City Council* (London: Macmillan, 1969).
81 J. Stanyer, *Understanding Local Government* (London: Fontana, 1976), p. 278.
82 S. Davies and B. Morley, *County Borough Elections in England and Wales 1919–1938,* vol. 1: *Barnsley–Bournemouth* (Aldershot: Ashgate, 1999), p. 654.
83 T. Byrne, *Local Government in Britain* (Harmondsworth: Penguin, 1981), p. 107.
84 P. Dunleavy, *Urban Political Analysis* (Basingstoke: Macmillan, 1980), pp. 135–40.
85 W. Miller, 'Local electoral behaviour', in Widdecombe report, vol. 3, chapter 2, p. 111.
86 Local Government Chronicle Elections Centre, Univeristy of Plymouth, online at www.plymouth.ac.uk/researchcover/rcp.asp?page=52&pagetype=G.
87 Electoral Commission and Hansard Society, *An Audit of Political Engagement 2* (London: Electoral Commission and Hansard Society, 2005), p. 23.
88 D. Butler and D. Stokes, *Political Change in Britain* (London: Macmillan, 1969), p. 39.
89 K. Newton, *Second City Politics* (Oxford: Oxford University Press, 1976).
90 Dunleavy, *Urban Political Analysis,* pp. 135–40.
91 S. Leach and J. Stewart, *The Politics of Hung Authorities* (Basingstoke: Macmillan, 1992).
92 NA, CAB 117/217, Urban District Council Association Memoranda on the Reorganisation of Local Government, 17 July 1942.
93 Newton, *Second City Politics,* p. 61.
94 J. Dearlove, *The Politics of Local Policy in Local Government* (Cambridge: Cambridge University Press, 1973), pp. 166–7.

95 Widdecombe report, Research Volume 3: *The Local Government Elector*, p. 40, table 3.1.
96 W. J. M. Mackenzie, 'Local government in Parliament', *Public Administration*, 29 (1951), pp. 345–56.
97 D. E. Butler, 'Local government in Parliament', *Public Administration*, 31:1 (1953), pp. 46–7; B. Keith-Lucas, 'Local government in Parliament', *Public Administration*, 33:2 (1955); C. Mellors, 'Local government in Parliament – 20 years later', *Public Administration*, 52:2 (1974), pp. 223–9.
98 Keith-Lucas and Richards, *A History of Local Government in the Twentieth Century*, pp. 98–9.
99 Dod, *Dod's Parliamentary Companion* (London: Dod, 1991); Municipal Journal, *Municipal Year Book* (London: Municipal Journal Ltd, 1991).
100 Dod, *Dod's Parliamentary Companion* (London, Dod, 2006); Municipal Journal, *Municipal Year Book* (London, Municipal Journal Ltd, 2006).
101 The two members who retain their position on a local authority since 2001 are the DUP husband and wife team of Peter and Iris Robinson.
102 In 1991 145 MPs and in 2006 221 MPs with local government experience ceased to be councillors a year before or three years after being elected to Parliament: Dod, *Parliamentary Companion* (1991, 2006).
103 Interview with Alan Whitehead, MP.
104 J. A. Chandler and J. E. Kingdom, 'MPs and local government: the case of Sheffield', paper presented to the Political Studies Association Annual Conference, University of Nottingham, 1999.
105 *Ibid.*
106 Salisbury's manifesto for the 1900 election makes no mention of domestic policies whatsoever and is concerned specifically with colonial issues.
107 Conservative Party, *Manifesto 1951* (London: Conservative Party, 1951), in F. W. S. Craig (ed.), *British Election Manifestos 1900–1974* (London: Macmillan, 1975), p. 172.

11

Thatcher and Major

'It looked for a time as if local authorities might be cut right back to rubbish collection and street lights – the kind of services they could reasonably be expected to provide out of money they could raise themselves.'[1] Sarah Hogg's summary of the state of inter-governmental relations at the end of Thatcher's reign is indicative of the decline in trust between central and local government during the Thatcher and Major administrations. It is probable that in 1979 the incoming Conservative Government had no such consequences in mind. Kenneth Baker observes that 'successive Conservative Governments, could not agree what the role of local government should be. Margaret did not have much time for local councils, which she expected to be the agents of central government.'[2] The 1979 Conservative *Manifesto* makes no comment on policy in relation to local government as a whole, although local services are discussed in promises to promote council-house sales, in relation to wasted spending by direct labour schemes and that eventually the party would get rid of domestic rates.[3]

The Selsdon programme that preceded the Heath Government in 1970 was the first serious manifestation of New Right values within Conservative governments, but it remained a minority view. With the failure of Heath's Government the party elite warmed to the new strategy. New Right theory is not necessarily inimical to local as opposed to central government. The founders of the US Constitution, Madison and Jefferson, envisaged a state in which power at the centre was dispersed so as to allow no one individual or interest to dominate policy-making.[4] Alongside a separation of powers at the centre, this could be achieved through the system of subsidiarity that allowed communal needs to be provided by the smallest unit affected by a joint need. These values remain entrenched in much New Right thinking in the USA.[5] Thatcher, as Gamble observes, was New Right only in respect of economic policy, but remained a centralist Tory in her attitude to the 'strong state'.[6] New Right policy for the Thatcher Government meant that public services should be transferred to the private sector and that welfare services should be reduced to a minimum necessary to prevent destitution among the deserving poor. Fashionable monetarism also committed the Government to ensure that the money supply was kept within limits compatible with economic growth, and at a time of relatively high inflation this required reductions in public spending. The Thatcher and Major governments, however, assumed that Downing Street, aided by Whitehall, would determine national policy and that all elements of British government would be subordinate to what they saw to be the national interest. This view was confirmed by the Widdicombe report which clearly laid down the principle that in 'Great Britain Parliament is sovereign ... all current local authorities are the statutory creations of Parliament and have no independent status or right to exist'.[7]

The Local Government Planning and Land Act

Michael Heseltine, as Secretary of State for the Environment, had no doubt about his part in pursuing cost-cutting and privatisation policies even if this was not necessarily from a purely ideological New Right stance. Immediately on taking office he outlined his ideas to his permanent secretary over a lunch outside the confines of Whitehall and handed over notes written on the back of an envelope that were headed with his concern to established better managerial practices in his department and also to cut the number of staff. These issues were perhaps more of an obsession to Heseltine than was reshaping local government. In terms of policies, council-house sales were first on his list, followed by local government finance and controls, the latter not necessarily implying more of them.[8] An immediate priority for the incoming Government was to cut public expenditure. Heseltine was fully prepared for his department and local government to share in the Government's zeal to secure lower inflation. He announced in July 1979 cuts to local authorities that amounted to a 5.5 per cent reduction in the funds promised by the outgoing Labour Government.[9] Although, due to the Labour Party's unpopularity, the Conservatives controlled all three of the English LAAs, they were not so buoyed up by their party's national success that they were inclined to accept such heavy cuts without complaint.

With enthusiasm, and some naiveté in his understanding of local government, Heseltine launched into drafting a Bill designed to fit local government to the new ideology and to resolve in one blow many problems at a pace that could but astound the plodding progress of local government financial reform since the days of Harold Macmillan. A first version of the Bill, published in December 1979, was so cumbersome and full of holes that it had to be withdrawn and resurrected as the Local Government Planning and Land Bill No. 2, which secured the Royal Assent in November 1980.[10] The Act, while concerned with greater financial constraints and efficiency, was not in itself wholly hostile to the *raison d'être* of local government and promised the removal of some 300 detailed controls over local authorities.[11] A system of block grants was to combine the needs and resources element of the preceding system of rate support grants. This proposal was uncontroversial, since Layfield had suggested a less cumbersome assessment procedure by unifying these elements and the Labour Party had shown support for the idea in a Green Paper.[12] The sting in Heseltine's formula was a mechanism that penalised local authorities which proposed to spend more than the Government's assessment of their financial requirements under their block-grant calculations by setting an annual threshold of overspend that would trigger penalties in the form of progressively higher reductions in grant as spending increased. Heseltine probably thought this would not be a wholly effective control but could go some way to restrain local spending.[13] In Scotland, Secretary of State Malcolm Rifkind piloted legislation that allowed him to directly order rate reductions and selectively applied the ruling to a number of left-wing councils, for example the Lothian Region.[14] In addition to the Government's attempts to constrain revenue spending, the Act changed the system of capital expenditure by setting limits on spending rather than borrowing to allow them to closely control actual rather than intended developments. However, the Government also gave local authorities more freedom to determine how they used their capital by allowing them to vire between the five functional blocks of capital expenditure.[15]

The strategy fulfilled a central aim of the Macmillan years in ensuring that grants were much reduced as an element of local authority expenditure, falling from 58 per cent of their total spend in 1980–81 to 47 per cent by 1985–86.[16] However, any hopes within the Government that the Act would serve to decrease local spending were soon shattered. While most local governments reluctantly trimmed their budgets, a few found that they could raise rates by unprecedented bounds without creating an electoral backlash. Sheffield increased rates by 47 per cent in 1980 and 37 per cent in 1981 without losing voters,[17] while Stirling and Dundee in 1981 more than doubled their rate demands.[18] A number of local authorities secured further funding in the middle of their financial year by raising a supplementary rate. Even before local authorities announced their budgets in 1981, the Government brought in a further device for restraining local spending by setting an expenditure target based on a lower figure than their real spending the previous year. The target was calculated on a different basis from the grant-related expenditure needs. It was proposed that clawing back rates could be based on excessive spending over the target figure and would be even more severe than had been initially announced.[19] Legislation was necessary to establish the new arrangement and, despite the complexity of the 1980 Act, a further Bill was introduced in November 1981 that proposed not only extra penalties for overshooting target spending but also direct constraints on higher rate expenditure by requiring any local authority wishing to charge more in rates than a limit to be set by Government to submit its proposals to a local referendum. It soon became apparent that the mechanisms for establishing local referenda would be costly and complex but also would set a precedent for their frequent use. The idea was dropped and a modified Bill introduced to secure the target and related penalties arrangement, along with proposals to remove the capacity of local authorities to set a supplementary rate during the financial year.[20] Some concessions were made to local authorities through an amendment that ensured that the Government had to announce how it would penalise local authorities when announcing the rate support grant, rather than being able to demand cuts after the funding for the forthcoming year had been officially announced and budgets subsequently determined.[21] The Act,[22] passed in July 1982, was operated with increasing severity but without restraining high spending authorities. The Government countered by changing each year the exact mechanism through which it determined targets and penalties, until they replaced the unsuccessful formula in 1984.[23]

The Government further fortified a cost-cutting regime for local authorities by radically restructuring the system for external audit. Heseltine came to believe that 'the relationship between council officer and auditor might have become too comfortable after years of friendly familiarity'.[24] Layfield had specifically criticised the system that allowed local authorities to appoint their favoured private auditors and had suggested that auditors should be fully independent of both central and local government.[25] Changes to the audit system were brought to fruition in the 1982 Local Government Finance Act[26] which established the Audit Commission as the agency overseeing the appointment of auditors to review local authority accounts. An important innovation required the Commission to review not only whether money was spent legally but also secured value for money. Under its first Director, John Banham, the Commission quickly developed into an influential agency for regulation and also for its research and advice on the effectiveness of local authority services. Its views, however painful at times, became widely respected.[27]

The beginning of privatisation: DLOs, housing and regeneration

In addition to its financial measures the 1980 Local Government and Planning Act required local authority Direct Labour Organisation (DLOs) to obtain and accept tenders from the private sector for substantial contracts, and to make a surplus over a three-year period. Heseltine was forwarding established Conservative antipathy to a practice the party had condemned from the beginning of the twentieth century, rather than initiating the later strategy of privatisation and the enabling authority. The measures, however, were built on prior work that had been conducted by civil servants.[28] Following a growing number of claims that some DLOs in large cities such as Glasgow were grossly inefficient due largely to deference to trade union influence[29] CIPFA had recommended in 1969 that DLOs contract out at least some of their services.[30] The Labour

Party, mindful of possible scandals, had also suggested that DLOs should be run profitably.[31]

The 1980 Local Government Planning and Land Act further reflected Heseltine's zeal to by pass local government in favour of the private sector by creating Urban Development Corporations (UDCs) to take over the planning powers of local authorities within a designated area and place these in an ad hoc un-elected Corporation which would receive substantive Government financial support to radically develop the area in order to bring in new private sector investment. The UDC policy during the first Government of Mrs Thatcher was applied to the docklands area of London and the Liverpool docklands. Urban rioting in the summer of 1981 which decimated much of Toxteth gave added impetus to this initiative and Heseltine sought out[32] the role of Minister responsible for Liverpool and spent a fortnight in the City trying to bring together potential private sector developers and local government to resolve the problems of inner city decline.[33] The Government also created by 1984 twenty Enterprise Zones where controls on industrial development could be relaxed and funds made available from central government for business start-ups.[34]

The most successful privatisation policy of the Thatcher Governments that directly concerned local government was the sale of council housing. The policy was not new as the Conservatives had encouraged sales during the Heath Government as part of their 'fair rents' policy. The march of right-wing Conservative thinking led to a Manifesto commitment to ensure that the sale of housing was not an option. Immediately on taking office Heseltine informed local authorities they could sell houses at a discount of one third of their cost and provide applicants to buy with 100 per cent mortgages.[35] This was but a measure prior to legislation to compel sales. The party had in opposition anticipated a fight with left-wing authorities on an issue that had in the past generated some of the most heated central–local differences since 1945:

> we briefed a barrister from outside government to assume that he had been retained by a dedicated Marxist council, committed at any unlawful price to frustrate the right to buy. It was a valuable exercise. Loopholes were found and closed.[36]

The subsequent 1980 Housing Act alongside a similar Act for Scotland[37] gave the majority of council tenants with three or more years occupancy the right to buy their homes with the support of generous discounts on the market value of the property. The 'right to buy' was strengthened by withdrawal of subsidies for rents, thus sharply increasing the cost of council housing for those not entitled to rebates. Legislation in 1984 further increased the level of subsidies and reduced the residency qualification to two years.[38] The Government also began reducing the approvals to build new houses and re-directed most of the income from house purchases to refurbishing the existing stock. The Act was strongly opposed by most Labour Authorities. The city of Norwich was the only housing authority that refused to sell houses but their intransigence was brought to an end by the Government using its powers to appoint a commissioner to take over their housing stock and manage sales for the city.[39] The policy was popular with tenants but was not the runaway move to owner occupier capitalism that the Conservatives may have hoped. By 1987 approximately a sixth of council houses had been sold but these were not unexpectedly mostly semi-detached properties in more affluent estates. Local authorities were increasingly left to manage the far more burdensome stock of flats and decaying houses on run down estates. Further reductions in the capacity of local authorities to use the receipts of council house sales even for maintenance also ensured that the remaining houses were declining in quality.[40] Effectively the policy was forcing local authorities to be the supplier of last resort housing to the poorest sector of the population who had no alternative accommodation.[41]

Local socialism

The sharp swing to new right policies that brought Mrs Thatcher to power fuelled the revival of left-wing idealism which had been prefaced by rebellions over council-house rents and school milk during the Heath Government and during the Labour administration culminated in the 'winter of discontent'. The leftward move was associated with a significant shift in the occupational and educational basis of the Labour Party whose membership was becoming disproportionately middle class and better educated.[42] The loss of Labour control in many metropolitan strongholds in the late 1960s swept aside an ageing guard of more conservative Labour councillors and brought the educated young professionals into leading positions in local authorities.[43] The entry of educated younger militants into the party was reflected in a revival of interest in Marxist ideas and the militant English radicalism of Paine and the Chartists, and was also accompanied by influential academic studies showing how Labour councils had come to reflect the values and interests of big business.[44] The radical younger politicians in some cities benefited from power vacuums that had built up in many urban Labour parties. This was a consequence not so much, as Hindess suggested, of the middle-class entrants shifting the less educated working class from party organisations,[45] but of the older generation ceasing to encourage new members into the Party for fear that they would challenge their dominance of the spoils of office.[46] Thus, in cities such as Liverpool it was possible for Marxists to infiltrate a party machine consisting of a handful of elderly members and take control of ward, constituency and even city Labour parties.

Local socialism was characterised by different strands of radicalism in specific urban centres and cannot be classed as a clearly co-ordinated social movement. Liverpool was in May 1983 captured by Militant.[47] Lambeth under the leadership of Ted Knight had its own variant of left wing radicalism. The majority of local socialist councils, such as the GLC under Ken Livingstone or Sheffield as led by David Blunkett, were more within the broad church of the Labour Party, deriving inspiration from Tribune stalwarts such as Tony Benn and Michael Foot. Local socialist authorities had, however, the common characteristic that they were prepared to challenge the decline of their services and the Government that had created the malaise. Although politically a passing phase, local socialism has left a valuable legacy. Economic development was put on the menu of central local authority functions. Concern for the local economy that had been central to the municipalisation policies of the late nineteenth century had seriously declined. Efforts to revise local economies with support from central government led to the development areas of the 1930s, but these efforts had declined with post-war economic growth.[48] As the 1950s boom relapsed into the 'stop–go' economy of the 1960s some councils such as Bradford[49] experiencing accelerating de-industrialisation interested themselves in relatively modest attempts to attract new industry to their areas using private sector marketing techniques. The *laissez faire* policies of the early Thatcher administrations towards 'lameduck' industries gave little encouragement to socialist authorities to pursue conventional capitalist marketing techniques when the Government was withdrawing subsidies to steel or coal, generating mass unemployment in their communities. The new generation of local Labour leaders looked to more socialist alternatives for facilitating business development, including regeneration through subsidising workers co-operatives, establishing sheltered workshops for start-up businesses and schemes to buy local products. Several authorities also sought to regulate local businesses by insisting that any firm in receipt of local funds or under contract to the council must recognise trade unions and trade ethically.[50] Finance was inevitably the problem for developing serious regeneration. Apart from modest funds raised through Section 137 of the 1972 Local Government Act, local government had few powers to support businesses directly. Much discussion, though little action, centred on how local authorities might be able to use their pension funds to invest in local business.[51] Sheffield established the first council sub-committee dedicated to economic redevelopment,[52] while the GLC under Livingstone created a Greater London Enterprise Board to preferentially fund co-operative business start-ups.[53]

Local socialist authorities also began pioneering schemes to redistribute income to poorer sections of their communities by subsidising public services. The policy was particularly easy to purse in relation to transport. South Yorkshire County Council and the GLC began policies to provide high levels of support for their transport services through subsidies from the rates, despite opposition from the Labour Government, and some local bus services were even run free of charge.[54] Liverpool under Militant control attempted to put much of its effort into building council houses in order to provide labour for the unemployed and ensure low-cost tenancies.[55] A further avenue of innovation concerned social exclusion and the accommodation of social diversity.[56] Under the leadership of Ken Livingstone the GLC attempted to forge a winning coalition from excluded minority interests such as racial groups, homosexuals and the disabled.[57] Local authority employment, particularly in inner London boroughs, was transformed from a predominantly white male preserve to a sector where women and citizens of Asian or West Indian descent would be welcomed as employees. Councils also put much greater effort into publicity aimed at undermining discriminatory attitudes, throwing themselves open to lampooning and misrepresentation by the right-wing tabloids, coining the epithet 'Looney Left'.[58] Decentralisation of service provision from the town hall, a policy as much initiated by the Liberals,[59] was also taken up as a key initiative of local socialism.[60] Islington under the leadership of Margaret Hodge established twenty-four local fora to deal with the majority of their services, other than education, and one-stop shops providing the decentralised services which were open to community residents.[61]

The 1984 Rates Act and its consequences

Mrs Thatcher in 1974 had proposed a review of the rating system and the possibility of rate-capping,[62] and remained throughout her tenure in office one of the most enthusiastic seekers after the elusive alternatives to the rates. The failing system of penalties and targets had been for many ministers little more than a stop-gap arrangement until a formula could be reached in the long-standing quest to find an alternative to the rates. The possibility of rate-capping had already been established in Scotland, at least in theory, by the Wilson Government under legislation[63] which allowed the Secretary of State for Scotland to reduce grant to authorities thought to be spending excessively. Scotland therefore required fewer measures than did England and Wales to further control expenditure. However, the powers had never been used, partly because they required parliamentary approval to be put into force.[64] Cuts in the rate support grant in 1981 led to a number of Labour-left-controlled Scottish authorities, with Lothian and East Stirling Districts in the vanguard, to raise their rates dramatically. An Act paralleling English legislation was, therefore, pushed forward to give powers to reduce grant to Scottish authorities at the discretion of the Secretary of State for Scotland.[65] This was further fortified in 1982 by legislation that allowed the Secretary of State to reduce grant or to compel high-spending local authorities to reduce their rates, or else to settle for a combination of those alternatives.[66] In the following year, action was taken to reduce the grants of seven Scottish local authorities, and in the next few years these powers were in continual use against increasingly intransigent Labour districts.[67]

From 1981 Leon Brittan, as Secretary of State for the Treasury, seconded Mrs Thatcher's enthusiasm for curbing local government spending by radical changes to the system of finance. Heseltine, far more cautious, was soon trading blows behind the scenes with Brittan over local government finance, to the displeasure of Mrs Thatcher.[68] Pressure from the Right obliged Heseltine and his deputy Tom King to undertake a departmental review of local authority funding which, published as a Green Paper,[69] poured cold water on the alternative measures for raising local revenue. Thatcher was furious at such a lame result and established a Cabinet committee, chaired by William Whitlaw, to look into the issue, but after a year of deliberation that august body came to the same conclusions as its predecessors. An official committee suggested the possibilities for rate-capping, which then became much favoured by Brittan.[70] Heseltine and Tom King, his successor at the DoE, believed such a measure could be an unconstitutional constraint on what was an ancient privilege of local government.[71] As an alternative they suggested that by abolishing the troublesome GLC and the MCCs, among the worst Labour offenders, they could alleviate the problem. In the run-up to the 1983 general election Brittan's view suddenly found favour as Mrs Thatcher sought to include in the *Manifesto* some measures which, at least in her mind, would convince voters that her Government would resolve the problem of spendthrift Labour authorities. To Heseltine's chagrin, not only was abolition of the GLC and MCCs part of the Conservative's 1983 *Manifesto* but so was the proposal for rate-capping.[72]

Following the 1983 election, Patrick Jenkin was appointed Secretary of State for the Environment with the task of implementing rate-capping and abolishing the GLC and MCCs. The assault on the rates began with a White Paper, published in August 1983, which continued to defend the rates as the best method of raising local finance, despite the widely canvassed alternatives of local income tax, a sales tax or even the emerging idea of a poll tax. However, the Government's responsibility for the economy and the rapid rise in local government expenditure obliged them to take powers to control rate rises.[73] It was proposed that the Government should be able either to generally set limits to the level of rate collected by local authorities or to do so selectively by placing limits for specific types of local authority. A Bill followed in December despite widespread opposition from the LAAs, including the Conservative-controlled county councils and a number of Conservative MPs.[74] It was argued that the Government was destroying a bastion that guaranteed the traditional independence of local government and that rates were not a seriously unpopular tax or an excessive burden for local businesses.[75] The Government's majority, although seriously reduced in some crucial votes, was sufficient to ensure that the Bill gained the Royal Assent by the summer of 1984.[76]

The latter stages of the rate-capping Bill were being goaded through Parliament against a background of confrontation between the Government and the ruling, militant-dominated, Labour group of Liverpool City Council over the funding settlement for 1984–85. Popular support for Liverpool's plight returned Militant Labour to power in the city in 1984 with an increased majority and a greater determination to confront the Government by refusing to set a rate.[77] Patrick Jenkin felt it politically expedient to negotiate with Liverpool's councillors, and in July 1984 made what he thought was a deal to increase grant support to the City Council, provided the Militant councillors maintained a low-key response to their success. The councillors, however, appeared on the council offices' steps with clenched-fist salutes of victory,[78] humiliating Patrick Jenkin and ensuring that ministers had no inclination to make further concessions to left-wing councillors.

As soon as the Bill was passed, the Government announced that it would cap rate rises in local authorities that budgeted to spend more than 20 per cent of their grant-related expenditure and 4 per cent above the expenditure guidelines set for the authority.[79] This formula resulted in sixteen Labour-controlled authorities facing capping,[80] along with Brent, where there was no overall control, and the Conservative Portsmouth Council. The capped Labour authorities had anticipated their fate and had already met in July to co-ordinate their response, deciding on non-compliance by either setting a deficit budget or refusing to set a budget at all.[81] Liverpool's humiliation of Patrick Jenkin was a significant factor in emboldening the capped authorities to take on the Government. The challenge was also set against the background of the miners' strike and the possibility that Arthur Scargill and the National Union of Mineworkers could break down the Government's stance against militant trade unionism. Liverpool, which was prudently excluded from the capping constraints, also joined the dissenting authorities and thus extended its successful campaign of confrontation over the previous year's settlement by proposing to set no rate in protest at the paucity of its grant allocation.[82] For Kenneth Baker, who replaced Jenkin in September 1985, the central fight was against Liverpool's Militant councillors. As he observed of Mrs Thatcher, 'one thing she could not stomach was making a "U" turn'.[83]

Neither Patrick Jenkin let alone Mrs Thatcher were willing to make concessions to the Labour authorities and, in view of Militant's betrayal of confidence in Liverpool the previous year, had no confidence that any deal was possible other than complete subjection to the legislation. They were supported by the Labour Party, now under Neil Kinnock's leadership, which recognised the long-term dangers of allowing local authorities to defy the law both in terms of popular opinion and also their own chances of controlling local authorities if ever they regained power.[84] The capped Labour authorities in November confirmed their intention not to set a rate and rejected suggestions from the Labour front bench that they should settle for whatever concessions they could gain from the Government.[85] Many of the Labour council groups, in anticipation of being surcharged, began to establish funds to aid those who were to lose substantially by their actions. Confrontation continued until March 1985, interspersed with meetings with Patrick Jenkin when the GLC, ILEA and the metropolitan counties were set to breach legal rules if they failed to precept a rate. Splits occurred between GLC leader Ken Livingstone and his deputy that showed weaknesses in local socialist solidarity, and given that these authorities were also facing their battle against abolition it was agreed by the remaining authorities that they should set legal rates in order not to further undermine their struggle for existence.[86] At this point Basildon, Brent and Leicester also dropped out of the fight, and by mid-April only eight authorities remained defiant. Faced with imminent surcharging, after it had passed the May deadline, Sheffield City Council gave up the fight when a sufficient number of Labour backbench councillors voted with the opposition to push through a legal rate. Further authorities capitulated in May and early June, effectively leaving only Liverpool and Lambeth standing out against setting a rate. Both authorities gave up the struggle, Liverpool on 14 June and Lambeth on 3 July.[87]

Subsequently, Liverpool and Lambeth, which had prolonged the illegal action, were taken to court by the district auditor, where they were surcharged and the defiant councillors disqualified. Militant councillors in Liverpool, nevertheless, were able to continue to take on the Government by threatening to set an illegal rate in the following financial year, 1986–87, but Kenneth Baker and Mrs Thatcher were agreed in giving no concessions to the authority and risking unpopularity by allowing, if necessary, the city's finances to collapse.[88] In the run-up to the new financial year Liverpool City Council was forced to issue redundancy notices to employees in case of funding defaults and then made a balanced budget at the last minute to secure continued payment of its workforce.[89] In March 1987, following unsuccessful appeals to the House of Lords, Liverpool's surcharge and disqualification for the previous year's defiance became effective and the Militant threat was finally broken. The national Labour Party succeeded in expelling several Militant councillors from the party in October 1986. Labour regained control of the city, following an opposition interregnum, in the 1987 elections, but with sufficient non-Militant Labour members to end any further attempts at confrontation by the authority.[90]

Abolition of the GLC and the metropolitan county councils

The decision to abolish the GLC and the MCCs had emerged within the Cabinet sub-committee chaired by Whitelaw as part of the strategy to curtail high spending by authorities. The metropolitan authorities were particularly vulnerable as there had also been considerable friction between the metropolitan counties and districts over the allocation of some services, such as museums and art galleries, or planning in the first few years of their brief existence, which may have helped behind the scenes to enable the Government to press ahead with abolition, despite the popular campaigns in their favour. According to Patrick Jenkin, some Labour leaders of metropolitan districts maintained informal contact with the Government and one leading Labour politician had assured Jenkin that the districts could absorb the duties of the MCCs within two days.[91] There were stronger arguments for retaining an authority for London as a whole, which was, following the abolition of the GLC, the only major European capital city not subject to a strategic elected council. Antipathy to the GLC and its populist leader Ken Livingstone became an increasingly important motive for abolition. Kenneth Baker,[92] who as Minister of State for Local Government inherited responsibility for steering the Bill through Parliament, cites Livingstone's success in developing high-spending but popular policies of transport subsidies and support for minority groups as the reason behind abolition. Mrs Thatcher's lack of empathy with the worth of local representation is illustrated by her put-down of a Conservative backbencher advocating the need of a voice for London:

> My dear Phillip, there is no such thing as a voice for London. Why should Londoners be especially represented when people from Birmingham, Liverpool and Manchester manage without it. Lorries come from the South-West and the North and they have just as much of an interest in road planning in London as Londoners.[93]

The abolition of the GLC and the MCCs was given substance in a White Paper in 1983.[94] The functions of the GLC were to be transferred to the London boroughs, apart from the fire service which was to be the responsibility of an agency that, paralleling the Metropolitan Police, would be directly answerable to the Home Office. London's transport had been subject to an earlier announcement proposing the creation of a non-elected Transport Board. The White Paper stated that further consideration would be given to the future of the ILEA. The police, fire and transport functions of the MCCs were to be transferred to joint boards composed of councillors selected, in proportion to their party representation from the metropolitan districts while more minor responsibilities such as economic regeneration or museums would become the responsibility of the metropolitan districts.

The Government gave a higher priority to the Rates Bill and delayed legislation on GLC abolition to the 1984–85 parliamentary session, but required an interim 'paving' Bill to cancel the scheduled 1985 elections to the threatened authorities, replacing the outgoing councillors with members appointed by the metropolitan district authorities. Disaffected

Conservatives in the House of Lords forced the Government to keep the elected councillors in office until the date of abolition, in April 1986. The difficulties faced by the Bill reflected the success of the GLC, under Ken Livingstone, and the MCCs, co-ordinated by leader of West Yorkshire County Council John Gunnell, in stirring up popular opinion against abolition.[95] From County Hall, facing the Houses of Parliament across the Thames, Livingstone directed an expensive but highly visible campaign to demonstrate the effectiveness of and the popular support for the GLC. Opinion polls showed that throughout the abolition campaign a majority of Londoners favoured retention of the GLC.[96] The MCC's campaign also gained attention of – and later retribution from – the Government by using posters of ministers photographed in an unfavourable light. The AMA refused to talk to the Government about the Bill[97] but, following an uneasy passage through the Commons and the Lords, it became an Act in July 1985.[98] The GLC and the MCCs, created only twelve years previously by the Conservatives, were brought to an end on 1 April 1986.

The Government had shown it was capable of resisting any pressure from local government to act unlawfully although much time and effort had to be exerted to resist local authority pressure. Fortified by the weakening of local government following the collapse of the rates confrontation, Thatcher's administration set about alleviating its remaining fears concerning local authorities' capacity to resist central authority by pushing ahead with a number of legislative changes which, to use Rhodes's power dependence metaphor,[99] aimed at altering the 'rules of the game' of inter-governmental relations so as to further weaken the resources held at the local level to challenge the centre. In February 1985 the Government appointed barrister David Widdicombe to chair an Inquiry into the political role of local government. The immediate remit of the Inquiry was to provide evidence to enable the Government to prevent local authorities from politically challenging future governments through mass publicity campaigns. The Committee faithfully produced an interim report that criticised such practice.[100] Legislation was pushed through Parliament preventing local authorities from politically campaigning against the Government.[101] The Act which remains in force sustains the view, reinforced in the full Widdicombe report, that local government is constitutionally subordinate to Parliament and has no right to voice publicly opinions contrary to those of the State.[102] A further 1985 Act compelled local authorities to release information to the public on a scale that brought a shudder to ministers and civil servants at the very thought of its application to their own Whitehall deliberations.[103] The full report, published in June, was, however, far from the damning exposé of local authority corruption and inefficiency that many right-wing publications had suggested. Widdecombe argued that local democracy was essential to secure effective local policy-making, that party government was an inevitable and indispensable part of the decision-making process and that while in many ways improvements could be made to the systems of accountability the basic structure of local decision-making should remain as it had been established.

The enabling authority

Having browbeaten the local authorities to conform to central policies, the Thatcher Government could without serious opposition include local governments in their broad schemes to 'roll back the frontiers of the state' in favour of the private sector. The resultant policies, collectively termed the 'enabling' philosophy by its proponents,[104] had their genesis in the resurrection of *laissez-faire* liberalism in the early twentieth century with the Austrian School and its economist luminaries such as von-Mises and Hayek, who argued that redistributive transfers of resources through taxation and welfare payments made the poor dependent on the State and undermined the entrepreneurial spirit that drove forward economic and social progress.[105] In the 1970s such views were mixed with theories of the ungovernable state according to which the bureaucracy that had been built up to sustain the welfare state was so vast and cumbersome that it was becoming impossible to control. Finally the New Right public-choice economists of the Virginia School – Tullock, Niskanen and Buchanan – gave academic substance to the view that any publicly funded bureaucracy if isolated from competition would expand to become far larger than was necessary.[106] These ideas provided an intellectual justification for a policy that had long been harboured by the Conservative right wing that government should retreat as far as possible from providing services and ensure that private competition could supply public needs. A significant tranche of the consequently privatised national industries was made up of those developed predominantly by local authorities for gas, water and sewage, and electricity that had been nationalised by the Attlee Government.

Few Conservative authorities were standard bearers of the new-right policy. The London Borough of Wandsworth began to develop a policy for contracting out services to the private sector against competition within the local authority in the early 1980s largely as a means of breaking down local trade union controls over their in-house street-cleansing and refuse-collection services.[107] Two-thirds of the contracts in Wandsworth were secured by the private sector once the borough adopted this strategy.[108] As a New Right strategy unfolded in Wandsworth, it rested, according to borough leader Paul Beresford, on the three pillars of efficiency, a vigorous sales policy and high-capital investment in run-down facilities paid for by receipts from sales.[109] The Conservative Government, was, however, to undermine the capacity of local authorities to use capital from housing sales to reinvest in new services. New Right policies were also embedded in the London Borough of Westminster under the leadership of Lady Porter, although her zeal was diverted into questionable strategies in terms of economy and efficiency. Westminster sold 2 cemeteries at a nominal sum of 6 pence to developers[110] and, most damagingly for Lady Porter's peace of mind, council houses on the understanding they would be occupied by wealthy home-owners who were likely to vote Conservative and bolster the party's vote in the borough. The planned sale of housing for political reasons eventually prompted the district auditor to surcharge the offending Westminster councillors. Only a few Conservative local authorities enthusiastically followed the example set by Westminster and Wandsworth. Solihull had pioneered local management of schools and Southend the privatisation of refuse collection,[111] while Kent County Council dabbled in the possibility of semi-privatising education through issuing parents with vouchers to be redeemed in private as well as State schools. In 1988 Bradford Metropolitan District Council was gained by the Conservatives under the leadership of Eric Pickles who vigorously pursued sales of council houses and cuts in education services, but the leader's motives reflected more the businessman style of Michael Heseltine and he showed no interest in or knowledge of New Right theory.[112]

During the first Thatcher Government privatisation had been applied to DLOs and council housing not because of a clear strategy on local government but in order to pursue policies that had for some time been an element of the Conservative's agenda. Following the 1983 election the only serious privatisation imposed on local authorities was the deregulation of bus routes to allow private transport initiatives to compete on the same routes as municipal undertakings. The policy was steered by Nicholas Ridley, who as Minister for Transport set about undermining the increasingly imitated policy initiated by South Yorkshire County Council and later the GLC of subsidising bus fares from the rates. The Callaghan Government had not favoured such policy[113] and the Conservatives had even less enthusiasm for public transport as a social service. Conservatives legally challenged the right of local authorities to subsidise fares, being successful in the case of London Transport but not in respect of the MCCs.[114] Thwarted by the courts, Ridley decided on legislation and in the 1986 Transport Act not only made subsidies from the rates to public transport undertakings unlawful but also removed regulations established in the 1930s giving bus companies a monopoly on their routes.[115]

Having faithfully pursued Thatcher orthodoxy in the Ministry of Transport, Ridley was promoted to Secretary of State for the Environment in May 1986, where he further developed the enabling strategy. The policy broke with the tradition that wherever possible services were to be provided in-house. Influenced in part by Wandsworth and Westminster, Ridley drew up legislation that obliged all local authorities to compete with the private sector.[116] Competition would be secured by requiring the public providers to tender for services on an equal playing field with private contractors, with the contract awarded to the lowest credible bid. The Act applied compulsory competitive tendering (CCT) to a range of non-professional services that included refuse collection, school meals, vehicle, buildings and ground maintenance, with the possibility that further legislation could widen the range to encompass professional services. The Audit Commission was given the task of policing the procedure to ensure that hostile local authorities did not rig the contracts or the bidding procedures to favour their own in-house provision. Initially the impact of CCT was not as dramatic as had been hoped by the Government as the majority of contracts were awarded in-house. British firms were not geared up for public service which, due to local authority efficiency and low cost to the customer, were unlikely to secure high profits. However the threat of receiving opposing contracts was sufficient to force most local authorities to review how they could cut costs and secure greater efficiencies in service provision. The service most quickly colonised by private sector provision was refuse collection for which the lead contractors were subsidiaries of large French businesses with long-established experience in the field of supplying local governments.

Following the 1987 general election the Government began stumbling towards a strategy of introducing competition into such services that could not be privatised outright by engineering market-based competition in which the citizen is the customer. The strategy undermined local authority influence over a range of services. Kenneth Baker created quasi-market competition within the school system by placing parents in the role of consumers in the 1988 Education Reform Act.[117] LEAs lost their power over the curriculum, their capacity to determine admissions' policy for schools, their day-to-day controls over the management of schools and their capacity to determine a school's income. Parents were also given the power to remove schools wholly from LEA control.[118] The enabling philosophy in the context of social services followed a report from Sainsbury's former executive Sir Roy Griffiths[119] that led to the NHS and Community Care Act of 1990, which required social services departments to become purchasers of private care either from themselves or more preferably from the private sector and plan a social care strategy with the District Area Health Authorities and local family practitioner committees.[120] The demand was a rather rare essay on behalf of the Conservative Government to secure more 'joined-up' working between agencies but in practice the Act led to a rapid expansion in private sector provision of homes for the elderly and a consequential reduction in the numbers of council-operated residential homes and directly employed care workers.

The undermining of local authorities' role in housing during the post-1987 Thatcher and Major years followed a broadly similar trend of encouraging local consumers to opt out of local government control. A White Paper of 1987 stated that the local authorities would be confined to a strategic role in housing, identifying areas of need and finding means

through which other agencies could remedy deficiencies in supply.[121] The
Housing Act of 1988 followed up this strategy by allowing tenants in a
local authority estate to vote to transfer the housing stock to an independent trust funded by central government or co-operative management
schemes run by the tenants.[122] Tenants preferred to remain with their
local authority and only six Housing Action Trusts came into being
despite the substantial subsidies offered by the Government to participat-
ing local authorities.[123] The following year the Local Government and
Housing Act restricted further capital funding to local authority housing
schemes and with the threat of forced transfers of stock many local
authorities began co-operating with housing associations. CCT for
housing management also encouraged this trend. A number of largely
Conservative authorities in the south east transferred under this regime
the whole of their housing stock to housing associations. More generally,
local authorities established new housing through arrangements that gave
a housing association responsibility for building and maintaining the
property and the local authority responsibility for allocating tenants. By
1999 more than 325,000 council houses involving 86 local authorities
were transferred to housing associations.[124] The strategic enabling role
for local authority housing was thus emerging although not exactly along
the lines planned by the Conservative Government.

The creation of UDCs and Enterprise Zones had removed many aspects
of economic regeneration and the associated planning powers from local
authorities, but slowly the Government had to accept that local government should have at least a strategic role in economic development and
this was first formally recognised in the 1989 Local Government and
Housing Act.[125] The Act was designed to remove the capacity of local
authorities to engage in such development without private sector co-operation. Local economic development agencies could not have a majority of
council representatives on their boards. Agencies such as the Greater
London Enterprise Board set up initially under GLC control were obliged
to become much more detached organisations. In addition the Act
removed powers of local authorities to finance local business on the
grounds that they accepted planning agreements including recognition of
trade unions.

The poll tax

Mrs Thatcher might have been well advised, following the success of the
Government in outfacing the local socialist authorities over rate-capping, to
reconsider her enthusiasm for removing the rating system altogether. Further
deliberations on local government finance following the 1983 general election had been set in train within the DoE following an Audit Commission
report severely critical of the system of block grants and the difficulties over
implementing rate-capping.[126] A revaluation of the rates in Scotland also

provoked hostile reactions from Scottish Conservatives.[127] Patrick Jenkin decided to rescue the growing accumulation of disasters by yet a further Whitehall Inquiry, led by Kenneth Baker, into the restructuring of local government finance,[128] which concluded that a poll tax supplementing the rates could ensure that every citizen was directly exposed to locally generated increases in local taxation.[129] Baker obtained the idea from William Waldergrave, his ministerial colleague at the DoE, who was in turn sold the idea by Lord Rothschild, formerly head of Heath's Central Policy Review staff.[130] An essential element of the scheme was to undermine the principle of rate rebates and ensure that even the poorest in a community had to pay at least some proportion of locally raised taxes.

A package of proposals was presented in March 1985 to a meeting of ministers and advisors at Chequers. The ideas included the principle of what was then named the 'residents charge' and that the business rate should be set by government. It was also mooted that local government should be restructured on unitary lines and be elected on an annual basis. The restructuring proposals were dismissed immediately as too complex, but the taxation ideas were almost unanimously accepted.[131] The only dissent came from the Treasury representative whose principal, Nigel Lawson, although not present at the meeting, was much alarmed at the decision to apply a new direct tax on citizens at the same time as he was planning to simplify and reduce income tax.[132] The momentum in favour of the proposals was sufficient to override Lawson's reservations. In January 1986 the Cabinet agreed the publication of a Green Paper[133] proposing that the tax, officially named the 'community charge', would be slowly tapered in by 1990 as the rating system was gradually phased out. The two ministers most likely to object were Lawson, who kept quiet over the issue, and Michael Heseltine, who resigned from the Cabinet during this meeting over his feud with Leon Brittan that culminated in the Westland affair. The Green Paper was given, unlike many other Conservative proposals for local government, a rather long consultation period and it was expected that legislation would be developed after the expected general election in 1997. However, the Scottish Office urged more immediate implementation in Scotland as that would be likely to return many wavering Scottish Conservative voters back into their fold. Against the counsels of their civil servants, Scottish ministers ensured that the proposal became the last major legislation enacted before the 1987 election.[134] Following amendments at the committee stage, rather than a gradual tapering in of the charge, the Act[135] was to be applied all at once, and every adult resident in a household was liable to pay the charge rather than the householder.[136]

The poll tax did not occasion much controversy during the 1987 election campaign, thus emboldening Nicholas Ridley to follow the Scottish example and remove the tapering arrangement in order to introduce the tax as an immediate replacement for the rate. Ridley believed the average community charge would amount to the relatively low sum of £200 per person and later could not understand why in practice it was more than double this amount.[137] The necessary legislation was introduced into the Commons in December 1997 and was immediately attacked on its Second Reading by prominent Conservative backbenchers, including Heseltine. The central battle took place at the report stage when Michael Mates, a close associate of Heseltine, tabled an amendment which would vary the tax paid by each citizen in relation to their capacity to pay. The proposal had been rejected by the Government largely due to Treasury concern that this would turn the charge effectively into a local income tax, which was for them an even more challenging idea than the poll tax.[138] The Government rejected the Mates amendment but with a greatly reduced majority and the Bill passed all its stages by July 1988. The Act not only abolished the domestic rate and installed the community charge but also transferred the power to set the business rate to central government. Less than 20 per cent[139] of local authorities' income was then subject to their discretion and even this was bound to the DoE's powers to cap the community charge if it exceeded the guidelines for local expenditure. It was not, however, these restraints that most exercised the minds of either Conservative or Labour opponents of the Bill, let alone the general public, but the abolition of rebates. Every citizen had to pay a contribution and while this was reduced to 20 per cent of the full charge for students and those on income support, the consequence of the legislation was that groups which had been exempt from the rate were now personally liable to pay a local tax.

Popular opposition to the poll tax in Scotland began spilling over into civil disobedience when the tax became first due for payment from April 1989. It had also become clear that the charge levied on each individual was to be higher than government estimates. Both the Scottish National Party and the Militant faction supported non-payment, while the Labour Party resolutely condemned the tax but urged payment on the grounds that citizens should not break the law. Estimates from Scottish urban authorities of the numbers defaulting on payment were by September 15–20 per cent of residents and the sums being paid were insufficient to cover local authority costs. The Scottish Office responded by adding a few marginal groups to the list of those exempt from the tax but it was becoming clear that a significant minority of residents were prepared to refuse payment and that this would be sufficient to make the tax unworkable if repeated in England and Wales.[140]

Anticipating difficulties in implementing the poll tax in England the following year, Nicholas Ridley attempted to throw Treasury money at the problem by easing poll-tax demands. Lawson as Chancellor of the Exchequer had long feared this happening but had to concede a far higher increase in the block grant. In July an early announcement of the grant settlement suggested that the average poll tax for each individual in

England and Wales would be £275. The extra funding did little to alleviate the growing opposition to the tax. In July 1998 Ridley was replaced
by Chris Patten whose immediate reaction was to seek yet more subsidies
from the Treasury as it was becoming clear that the proposed cost of the
tax to many households bore little relation to the Government's estimate.
He obtained only a fraction of what he felt was needed. When the grant
settlement was put before the House of Commons the Government's
majority was reduced to only thirty-six. Conservatives were all too aware
of the loss of electoral support for their party and the demoralisation
experienced among many rural Conservative authorities.[141] In April 1990
the governing Conservative councillors in West Oxfordshire District
resigned from the party in protest.[142]

Opposition to the poll tax spilled on to the streets in early 1990 as
Militant and Socialist Workers' Party groups began organising public
rallies against the tax. The confrontation had been preceded in Scotland
by 'can't pay, won't pay' civil disobedience. Peaceful demonstrations
broke into violence on 31 March 1990 as the tax became due for
payment. A march in central London ended in politically motivated
violence, with attacks on shops and the burning of buildings. Although
condemned by parliamentary parties it was clear that there was a huge
sense of public indignation at such an inegalitarian tax, and in retrospect
even Mrs Thatcher concluded:

> Because of the size of the bills now being sent out, the new system had the
> very same law abiding decent people on whom we depend for support in
> defeating the mob – protesting themselves.[143]

The Government's reaction to the riots was to use both the carrot and the
stick. Patten announced his intention to cap the community charge for
twenty councils but also established a review of both the poll tax and,
given protests from companies at the larger than expected demand, the
business rate. As studies in Whitehall on how to rescue the situation began
in earnest, Mrs Thatcher's hold on her party began to crumble. Heseltine
called for greater transitional relief for hard-hit poll tax payers and the
adoption of a tax on residents banded in terms of income. Mrs Thatcher
showed no appetite for turning and appointed Michael Portillo as the
minister charged with defending the tax. In July, following the Whitehall
review, Patten was obliged to confirm the retention of the poll tax but put
forward a scheme of higher transitional relief for those facing the greatest
increases in payment and also a regime for announcing in advance a
capping of the tax below £400 for all local authorities.[144] The poll-tax
disaster adding to the deterioration in Conservative electoral support had
by this stage wholly undermined the confidence of senior party members
to retain power with Mrs Thatcher still at the helm. In October long-
nurtured grudges could be assuaged and knives were unsheathed. Striking
the first blow Heseltine precipitated a leadership contest to unseat the

incumbent although, like Cassius, he was unable to profit from the deed with the highest office.

After failing to beat John Major to become Prime Minister, Heseltine had to settle for a return to the Cabinet in his former position of Secretary of State for the Environment. The appointment reflected the Government's intention not to continue with the tax. Heseltine initiated a ministerial Inquiry into alternatives to the tax and delegated much of the detailed work to Michael Portillo, who remained Minister for Local Government. Major himself kept an eye on the proceedings through Sarah Hogg, the head of his policy advisory unit.[145] At the official level new ideas were tabled in a working party bringing together DoE officials who had slaved to try and make the idea work alongside a strong Treasury representation. While the Government was careful not to rule out abolition of the poll tax entirely, there was little support for a flat-rate system in the working group although the view that the level of local taxation on a household should reflect the number of residents remained an acceptable principle for the planners. In the run up to the 1992 general election, John Major sought to mitigate public non-payment of the poll tax for the forthcoming year, obliging Chancellor Norman Lamont to announce in his budget speech of 1991 a 2.5 per cent rise in the rate of VAT to fund a £450 reduction in the poll tax.[146] In March the Cabinet debated four alternatives: a return to the rating system; a continued heavily subsidised poll tax; a banded property tax with an added poll tax element; or a banded property tax.[147] The latter suggestion received greatest support and was worked up into a complex scheme based on regional variations and the numbers living in a property that would have retained the poll tax registers. John Major demanded a less complex and politically more popular scheme.[148] The final solution, which became the council tax, charged differing levels of rate for eight bands of property based on their estimated capital value, with a reduced charge for any household consisting of a single adult occupant. Effectively, the Government decided on a modified and scaled rating system. The review did nothing to diminish central controls on local authorities' funding as the Government reserved the right to cap the council tax. The legislation was hastened through Parliament in time to be on the statute book before the 1992 general election.[149]

The poll tax generated the most ferocious campaign of civil disobedience and rioting on any measure relating to local government perhaps since the anti-Poor Law riots of 1837. It was, however, an issue not about local government *per se* but rather a revolt against a Government prepared to roll back deeply engrained popular values concerning justice and equity in relation to taxation. The poll-tax demonstrations were never in favour of the local government system and many of those involved in riots or who refused to pay will have viewed local government as much as central government as part of the system upholding injustice. Mrs

Thatcher by the late 1980s may have mistaken the temper of the British populace but she and her ministers had at least learnt how to tightly control and cowe even the most potentially radical of local governments. The drafting of the 1988 Local Government Finance Bill with regard to penalties for councillors or officials who refused to administer the tax was watertight, so that no local authority sought openly to undermine the charge, and, in order to remain solvent, local authorities were obliged to pursue defaulters with the threat of sequestration of property or imprisonment for non-payment. The learning curve on how to control local government is illustrated by the example of the failure of the 1980 Local Government Planning and Land Act compared with the 1988 Act in terms of local government compliance and of the readiness of left-wing authorities to carry the flame of rebellion in 1985 and their refusal to do so in 1990.

The Major governments

John Major began his political career as a councillor in the London Borough of Lambeth, but he appears to have been at best indifferent to local government as an institution. Major had appointed Michael Heseltine to bury the poll tax but also conceded that a condition of his rival's acceptance of an office that he had occupied earlier in his career would be to allow him to review the structure, organisation and finance of local government with a view to a complete reshaping of the system.[150] Heseltine outlined his reformist intentions to the House of Commons in March 1991 as encompassing, in addition to the council tax, restructuring the internal management and policy-making mechanisms of local government and the two-tier structure of the system.[151] Reform of finance and the development of a single-tier structure for the system had been for decades under intermittent discussion and review, as had the need for more corporate organisation of local authority services but no attempt had been made to reform decision-making mechanisms or the role of councillors which was, to use Stewart's phrase, 'one of the dominant assumptions' concerning local government.[152] It was not until the Audit Commission in 1990 published a critique of the system entitled *We Can't Go on Meeting Like This* that reform of this central aspect of local authority organisation had been seriously suggested.[153] Heseltine's roots lay within his businessman's values more than in the New Right ideology and he warmed to the idea of a local government equivalent to a chief executive who could set a vision for the company and steer this idea to fulfilment. Crick observes that Heseltine's reform ideas were shaped by his experience in 1981 of studying at first hand urban deprivation in Liverpool and also by his understanding of the role of the mayor as chief executive in France and the USA.[154]

Heseltine's ideas for restructuring political leadership in local authorities closely mirrored the policy that would be adopted by the first Blair Government. He proposed that a local authority should be subject to a directly elected mayor supported by a small cabinet of senior committee chairs who would direct specific services. The proposal was floated in the 1991 discussion document *The Internal Management of Local Authorities*, but gained little headway.[155] There appears to have been little or no support for these ideas within the Cabinet. It was widely thought by rival ministers that the creation of directly elected mayors would create a monstrous regiment of Ken Livingstons to further challenge the Government.[156] Backbench MPs were worried that elected mayors would eclipse their own local political standing and civil servants were concerned that elected mayors and council majorities culled from distinct political parties would create policy deadlock.[157] Michael Howard, who succeeded Heseltine as Secretary of State for the Environment after the 1992 election, kept alive some debate on the issue in a working party with a broad membership, including local government representatives, which suggested that backbench councillors should concentrate more on representing their electors so as to allow their leaders to concentrate on strategy.[158] The working party floated the idea that these aims might be achieved by a cabinet-style leadership or perhaps an independent executive elected separately from the council, and hence the possibility of an elected mayor. An opinion poll in the *Municipal Journal* in June 1996 reported that 70 per cent of those questioned supported such an idea.[159] The idea of change in policy-making structures was, therefore, slowly gaining headway and began to be seized by groups, such as the Commission for Local Democracy established in 1993 by journalist Simon Jenkins to rescue local government from humiliation at the hands of Conservative governments.

A second element in Heseltine's restructuring agenda, to complete the long march towards single-tier authorities, came to the fore as soon as his scheme for elected mayors collapsed. The proposal, which will certainly have been more to the taste of civil servants if not the Cabinet, was accepted in a White Paper that pointed to a single-tier arrangement as the way forward, following the creation of a Boundary Commission. Existing single-tier authorities, the London boroughs and the metropolitan areas were not, therefore, to be included in the review. Guidance to the Commission, nevertheless, required consultation with local opinion and the retention of two-tier structures if supported by the public. The Commission was also instructed not to assume that local authorities had to provide all their services in-house. Legislation gave the Secretary of State for the Environment powers to implement the Commission's proposals.[160] Heseltine chose as chair of the Commission John Banham who had been one his most successful patronage selections as the first Controller of the Audit Commission and had since moved on to be Director General of the CBI. Banham was far from an ideal choice to pursue a single-tier solution. His later views on local government structure suggested large strategic authorities determining service policy which would then be implemented by a single executive at a neighbourhood level, subject to accountability from up to three elected local councillors for that area. The local councillors would also liaise with elected advisory parish and town councils.[161]

The Commission divided its members into teams of two, each of which was assigned to study reform in a group of adjacent counties. Commissioners initiated a three-stage process in which they canvassed public and local authority views, often using opinion-polling, then drew up proposals for change and, finally, reviewed local comments on their ideas before making a firm recommendation to the DoE. The earliest uncontroversial report was implemented by 1995 to create a single-tier county authority for the Isle of Wight. There was also little dispute, except from the condemned authorities themselves, about abolishing the unpopular counties, formed in 1974, of Cleveland, Avon and Humberside. However, the process, which in terms of sounding-out local opinion was much in advance of previous top–down approaches, produced, as might be expected, very differing proposals for local government in differing areas. The second tranche of studies established the principles behind Labour's 1979 White Paper *Organic Change* by returning several cities that in 1974 had lost their county borough status to a similar single-tier arrangement. A new structure was added to the local government bestiaries, the unitary authority, which was created for cities such as Leicester, Nottingham, York and Derby at the expense of their shire counties. The counties of Worcestershire and Herefordshire, unhappily married since 1974, were returned to their former status, although now as unitary authorities with no lower-tier districts. Major inconsistencies seemed to emerge as the process unfolded. In Derbyshire, for example, although the major city of Derby gained unitary status, the remainder of the county was left intact as a two-tier arrangement, while in Berkshire it was decided that extracting Reading and Slough as unitary areas would render the County Council unviable, and hence the more rural areas in the county were also designated as unitary areas. From the point of view of local opinion the conclusions of the Commission have not, however, been seriously challenged, but the resulting pattern is far from the simple single-tier map that had, at least in the 1970s, been sought by civil servants.

The inconsistencies involved in the process led to serious tensions between the Government and the Commission. By 1993 Michael Howard's successor John Gummer found the whole process an unnecessary distraction and petitioned John Major to wind up the exercise.[162] Major instead asked Gummer to demand more unitary authorities but a legal challenge to the presumption in favour of unitary authorities was successfully made in the courts by Derbyshire County Council[163] and Banham showed little enthusiasm for changing his procedures. He was replaced in March 1995 by another ex-Audit Commission chair Sir Derek

Cooksey, who wound down the Commission by establishing a further eight unitary authorities. A consequence of these changes was to induce the several English LAAs in 1997 to merge into single Local Government Association (LGA).

While the restructuring of local government in England proceeded on the basis of public consultation, the Scottish and Welsh Offices paralleled Heseltine's initiative but not his methods. In each region restructuring was undertaken by the Government Office as an in-house exercise. Ian Lang at the Scottish Office and David Hunt followed by John Redwood at the Welsh Office supported the least complex and bureaucratic option of single-tier systems. A choice of 13, 20 or 24 unitary authorities was suggested for Wales, while for Scotland a White Paper in 1993 proposed abolition of the regions and amalgamation of the districts, to leave 25 single-tier authorities, and the continuation of the 3 island councils.[164] In both countries the existing local authorities bitterly contested the proposals and their representative associations for some time refused to co-operate with the process but without gaining serious concessions from the Government.[165] A late concession to Scottish opinion came in the debate on the restructuring Bill, four districts being added. In Wales the 8 counties were abolished and replaced by 23 unitary districts, with the majority concentrated in populous south Wales. In Scotland the regions were similarly abolished and succeeded by thirty two unitary authorities divided, as in Wales, into areas of roughly similar population, ensuring that in rural areas such as the Scottish Highlands districts cover vast areas and many small but widely separated communities. In April 1996 the proposals were put in place.[166] The arrangements for Scotland and Wales arguably represent the ideal for the Civil Service –and not a few politicians in Conservative and Labour ranks – of an apparently simple single-tier arrangement based on relatively few populous authorities. However, below the surface of the Scottish reforms the framework is far more complex and led, as Wilson and Game observe, to the creation in the former Strathclyde Region of an additional thirteen non-elected joint agencies.[167]

Furthering the enabling authority

With the exception of Heseltine, the policy-makers within the Major Government with responsibilities for local government were little interested in reform of the institution *per se* rather than ensuring that their functions could be delivered more efficiently by the application of stiff private sector competition was rather their concern. The idea of an enabling authority initiated by Nicholas Ridley and publicised as the way forward in securing better services, secured also New Right values of shifting responsibility for service delivery to the private sector. The White Paper *Competing for Quality*[168] advocated an extension of CCT to professional services, and this was consummated in the 1992 Local Government Act.[169] Tasks to be contracted out in the first wave included financial services such as collecting council tax dues or providing rent rebates, legal and technical services such as IT provision. The assault on financial services drew strong criticism from professional bodies such as CIPFA and the Government twice postponed the date when some of the white-collar services had to be subject to competition. Attempts to make local authorities more sensitive to the citizen as consumer were enshrined in Major's 'big idea', the Citizen's Charter. Services not readily subject to competitive market forces were to be subject to government-approved criteria for efficient delivery that were established as promises to citizens who then had rights to complain if standards were not maintained. The policy was not new and had been anticipated by some local authorities, such as York City Council and Lothian Region.[170] Most local authorities responded by publishing targets for service delivery that were required by central government departments and inspectorates, and many also got into the spirit of conformity by applying for Charter Marks that recognised good practice in the context of the Citizen's Charter as a whole.[171]

Following some fifteen years of New Right government, local authorities, particularly in Conservative-held areas, were warming to the policy of contracting out. Even for strongly held Labour authorities the policy could be seen as a way of easing their levels of debt and the strains of operating a service on a shoestring with no intermediary body to share at least some of the blame. The broad enabling philosophy was also being pursued through the continued hollowing-out of local responsibilities by the creation of ad hoc public-private partnerships or public trusts to manage established services. In education provision there is every possibility that had the Major Government continued in power after 1997 the whole of this sector would have been removed from local government control. The 1992 Further and Higher Education Act removed all further education colleges, including sixth-form colleges from local authorities by placing them under the national Further Education Funding Council. The Major Government provided additional financial inducements for schools to opt out. The 1993 Education Act created a Funding Agency for Schools (FAS) to act as the intermediary agency between government and opted-out schools.[172] The FAS could assume some LEA functions if more than 10 per cent of children in an LEA were attending opted-out schools and once 75 per cent of all pupils had transferred, the FAS could assume all the responsibilities of the LEA.[173] LEAs in April 1997 were subjected to inspection by OFSTED, the more arms' length replacement for the nineteenth-century corps of Her Majesty's School Inspectors created by the Major Government in 1992.[174]

Police services were also further distanced from local controls during the Major period following on from a number of amalgamations of smaller forces under the Thatcher Government that had reduced the number of police authorities in Britain to fifty-one. Under the 1994 Police and Magistrates Courts Act Home Secretary Michael Howard restructured police committees with the intention of giving local authority representatives a minority role, but following the Lords' amendments their representations was reduced to a bare majority of 9 out of 17 members, with 3 JPs and the remaining 5 members appointed by the Home Secretary.[175] The process probably caused many a nineteenth-century gentleman JP to rotate in his grave, but it further pushed the police service along the road to being effectively a national rather than local force. Changes in powers had, however, already whittled away the responsibilities of the police committees to issues largely of the supply of premises and equipment rather than of operational responsibility. The use of police in the miners strike in areas such as South Yorkshire, where police committees were generally sympathetic to the miners' cause, illustrates the impotence of local representation to channel policing in directions that find no sympathy at the national level.

The development of local agencies was further embedded in strategies for urban development initiated by Michael Heseltine in 1991 in the form of the City Challenge, in which local authorities were required to competitively bid for government funding for re-development schemes which would require matching funds to be put into the project by private sector developers.[176] In most cases the development schemes were initiated and steered by local authorities but embedding a strong private sector interest also required the development of ad hoc bodies with representatives from both public and private sectors to promote the bids and when successful to implement the schemes. The City Challenge initiative was merged with other development schemes in 1994 into a Single Regeneration Budget (SRB) which was administered through the regional government offices that were created by merging local overseeing functions in nine English regions that had previously been handled by individual central government departments. The SRB allowed local authorities or private and voluntary sector organisations to make bids of varying size for development projects but the arrangement retained the requirement that the bidding agencies should match government funding and required the private sector to be partners in development projects.[177] The SRB framework further reinforced the need, initially prompted in the 1988 Housing and Local Government Act, to establish joint ad hoc development bodies that included not only local authority representatives, but local chambers of commerce and the Training and Enterprise Councils (TECs) which had been formed outside the orbit of local government as local public agencies to plan for further education and business training needs.

Local authorities were, as a result of the enabling initiatives and restrictions, becoming more fragmented. In the sector of economic development local authorities were sponsoring agencies in partnership with other private sector organisations to pursue initiatives that they would be either legally or financially unable to sponsor themselves. Sheffield, for example, created arms' length companies, which were not under local authority control, to build sports facilities, initially to host the 2001 World Student Games. Regeneration of local industry was fostered by Sheffield Forward, a partnership between the council and business interest.[178] Expense was reduced by placing a number of museums under the care of trusts that were not wholly under local authority control.

New public management

As the years of Conservative government under Thatcher and Major progressed, local authorities began gradually to transform themselves in line with New Right thinking through the insidious adoption of management values and ideas culled from the private sector. The view established by the Conservatives within a generally supportive media that public sector provision, whether in central government, the nationalised industries or the local sector, was necessarily less efficient than provision in the private sector, given the absence of a profit motive, fostered the adoption of private sector management techniques in relation to local governance. By the mid-1980s the term 'administrator' was being replaced by the term 'manager'. The managerial revolution in the public sector was also a move to loosen the grip of the specialist professional on services intended to prevent self-proclaimed experts in the field monopolising policy-making to their own advantage rather than that of the citizen. Emphasising private management techniques the citizen was also increasingly referred to as a 'customer' and democratic councils were urged, despite the theories of pluralism, to become closer to their customers.[179] The development of what became known as 'new public management' (NPM) established that officers had to be far more conscious of the costs of their service and their provision of value for money outputs.[180] The pressure to win contracts under CCT put the need to secure value for money at a premium. CCT required certain officers to serve as customers and draw up contracts to set out the needs of the local authority and a separate group to act as the contractors who bid for the services. Many service departments therefore were divided into customer and supplier teams who were not permitted to communicate with each other in relation to the drawing up and processing of bids for contracts, becoming focused on ensuring economies at worst or value for money at best. At senior levels in some local authorities, such as Kirklees, the professional former chief officer for each department was pushed further down the decision-making hierarchy by a small collective of senior managers to serve as generalist managers of the professional whose task was to implement the manager's policy. At the most extreme the London Borough of Brent restructured the authority by breaking up its departmental structure into a large number of service-delivery units which bid for contracts from small centralised teams of officers setting and monitoring contract delivery.[181] The pattern ensured in most authorities that private sector business skills were to be more prized than was sensitivity to public interest.

Behind the rhetoric of efficiency created by NPM was a more serious undermining of the idea of local government. The approach tended to be based on an argument that the rationale for local authorities was to deliver necessary services as efficiently and as at as low a cost as possible to the public, and that so long as people received services to their satisfaction they had little or no interest in the mechanics of how this was to be achieved. They became customers to the public sector supplier and ideally had redress against poor quality through government's ensuring that they had alternative sources of supply, as in the 1988 legislation on education. The Government ceased to entertain the possibility that a rationale for local government might be as the representative of the co-operative values of a community which should determine which services they wished to provide for themselves and to what standard. With the defeat of local socialism this view was put to flight and local government after 1984 settled into a slow decline in terms of politicisation. While the Blair Government may have removed the more aggressive private sector monopolisation of service provision that was being built into the New Right concept of local government, the more insidious private sector managerial values are still strongly entrenched in Blairism.

Notes

1 S. Hogg and J. Hill, *Too Close to Call: Power and Politics – John Major in No. 10.* (London: Warner, 1995), p. 58.
2 K. Baker, *The Turbulent Years: My Life in Politics* (London: Faber & Faber, 1993), p. 111.
3 Conservative Party, *The Conservative Party General Election Manifesto* (London: Conservative Party, 1979).
4 A. Syed, *The Political Theory of American Local Government* (New York: Random House, 1966).
5 Ostrom, Bish and Ostrom, *Local Government in the United States.*
6 A. Gamble, *The Free Economy and the Strong State: The Politics of Thatcherism* (Basingstoke: Macmillan, 1988).
7 Widdecombe report, p. 45, para. 3:3.
8 M. Heseltine, *Where There's a Will* (London: Hutchinson, 1987), p. 15.
9 T. Travers, *The Politics of Local Government Finance* (London: Allen & Unwin, 1986), pp. 81–2.
10 The Local Government Planning and Land Act, 1980: Eliz. II, c. 65.
11 Travers, *Politics of Local Government Finance*, p. 83.
12 *Ibid.*, p. 84.
13 *Ibid.*, pp. 86–7, 95.
14 A. Midwinter, *The Politics of Local Spending* (Edinburgh: Mainstream Publishing, 1984); Local Government (Miscellaneous Provisions) (Scotland) Act, 1981.

15 Travers, *Politics of Local Government Finance*, pp. 140–1.
16 *Ibid.*, p. 133.
17 D. Blunkett and J. Jackson, *Democracy in Crisis: The Town Halls Respond* (London: Hogarth Press, 1987), p. 154.
18 Midwinter, *The Politics of Local Spending*, p. 35.
19 Travers, *Politics of Local Government Finance*, pp. 104–6.
20 The Local Government Finance (No. 2) Bill, 1982.
21 Travers, *Politics of Local Government Finance*, p. 111.
22 The Local Government Finance Act, 1982: Eliz. II, c. 32.
23 Travers, *Politics of Local Government Finance*, pp. 125–9.
24 Heseltine, *Where There's a Will*, p. 36.
25 DoE, *Local Government Finance: Report of the Committee of Inquiry* Cmnd 6453 (London: HMSO, 1976) (Layfield report), pp. 94, 98.
26 The Local Government Finance Act 1982: Eliz. II, c. 32.
27 J. Kelly, 'The Audit Commission: guiding, steering and regulating local government', *Public Administration*, 81:3 (2003).
28 K. Walsh, *Public Services and Market Mechanisms* (Basingstoke: Macmillan, 1995), p. 119.
29 D. A. Langford, *Direct Labour Organisations in the Construction Industry* (Aldershot: Gower, 1982), p. 24, critically discusses a number of these studies which in many cases emanate from New Right interest groups and 'think tanks'.
30 K. Walsh, 'Competition and service in local government', in J. D. Stewart and G. Stoker (eds), *The Future of Local Government* (Basingstoke: Macmillan, 1995), p. 32.
31 Labour Party, *Building Britain's Future: Labour's Policy on Construction* (London: Labour Party, 1977).
32 Heseltine, *Where There's a Will*, pp. 135–6.
33 *Ibid.*, pp. 136–9; Crick, *Michael Heseltine*, pp. 222–7.
34 Created under the Local Government Planning and Land Act, 1980, para. 79 and Schedule 32; Chandler and Lawless, *Local Authorities and the Creation of Employment*, p. 223.
35 Crick, *Michael Heseltine*, p. 199.
36 Heseltine, *Where There's a Will*, p. 89.
37 The Housing Act, 1980: Eliz. II, c. 51; the Tenants' Rights (Scotland) Act, 1980: Eliz. II, c. 52.
38 I. Cole and C. Furbey, *The Eclipse of Council Housing* (London: Routledge, 1994), p. 197; the Housing and Buildings Control Act, 1984: Eliz. II, c. 29.
39 Announcement in *The Times*, 4 January 1981, p. 1d; and report on the appeal, *ibid.*, 26 January 1982, p. 3a.
40 Cole and Furbey, *The Eclipse of Council Housing*, pp. 198–200.
41 *Ibid.*, p. 198.
42 I. Gordon and P. Whitely, 'Social class and political attitudes: the case of Labour councillors', *Political Studies*, 27:1 (1979), pp. 99–113; P. Whitely, *The Labour Party in Crisis* (London: Methuen, 1983).
43 J. Gyford, *The Politics of Local Socialism* (London: George Allen & Unwin, 1985), pp. 25–6.
44 Studies included M. Castells, *The Urban Question* (London: Edward Arnold, 1977); C. Cockburn, *The Local State* (London: Pluto Press, 1977);

P. Dunleavy, *Urban Political Analysis* (Basingstoke: Macmillan, 1980).

45 B. Hindess, *The Decline of Working Class Politics* (London: Granada, 1971).

46 D. Green, *Power and Party in an English City* (London: George Allen & Unwin, 1981), pp. 24–34.

47 M. Crick, *The March of Militant* (London: Faber & Faber, 1986).

48 Chandler and Lawless, *Local Authorities and the Creation of Employment*, pp. 11–19.

49 *Ibid.*, p. 44.

50 *Ibid.*, pp. 165–8.

51 R. Minns and J. Thornley, *State Shareholding: The Role of Local and Regional Authorities* (London: Macmillan, 1978); Chandler and Lawless, *Local Authorities and the Creation of Employment*, pp. 227–8.

52 Blunkett and Jackson, *Democracy in Crisis*, pp. 108–42.

53 K. Livingstone, *If Voting Changed Anything, They'd Abolish It* (London: Fontana, 1987), pp. 148–9.

54 Blunkett and Jackson, *Democracy in Crisis*, pp. 70–82; A. Clarke, *The Rise and Fall of the Socialist Republic: A History of the South Yorkshire County Council* (Sheffield: Sheaf Publishing, 1987), pp. 37–8, 42–3.

55 P. Taafe and T. Mulhearn, *Liverpool: A City that Dared to Fight* (London: Fortress Press, 1988).

56 Gyford, *The Politics of Local Socialism*, pp. 48–52.

57 Livingstone, *If Voting Changed Anything, They'd Abolish It*, pp. 229–45.

58 G. Philo, 'Television, politics and the rise of the New Right', in G. Philo (ed.), *Glasgow Media Group Reader*, vol. 2 (London: Routledge, 1995), pp. 218–49.

59 Tower Hamlets under Liberal Democrat control similarly divided the borough into seven communities, although when the party lost control of the borough the incoming, less radical, Labour leadership swept the innovation aside.

60 C. Fudge, 'Decentralisation: socialism goes local?', in M. Boddy and C. Fudge, *Local Socialism?* (Basingstoke: Macmillan, 1984).

61 U. Kahn, 'Neighbourhood forums: the Islington experience', *Local Government Policy Making*, 16:2 (1989), pp. 27–33.

62 M. Thatcher, *The Path to Power* (London: Harper Collins, 1995), p. 247.

63 The Local Government Scotland Act, 1966: Eliz. II, c. 51.

64 Travers, *Politics of Local Government Finance*, pp. 136–7.

65 Local Government (Miscellaneous Provisions) (Scotland) Act, 1981: Eliz. II, c. 23.

66 Midwinter, *Politics of Local Spending*, p. 41.

67 A. Midwinter and C. Monaghan, *From Rates to the Poll Tax* (Edinburgh: Edinburgh University Press, 1993), pp. 45–6.

68 Crick, *Michael Heseltine*, p. 215.

69 DoE, *Alternatives to the Domestic Rates*, Cmnd 8449 (London: HMSO, 1981); Travers, *Politics of Local Government Finance*, pp. 112–25, provides a good summary of the Green Paper.

70 D. Butler, A. Adonis and T. Travers, *Failure in British Government: The Politics of the Poll Tax* (Oxford: Oxford University Press, 1994), p. 37.

71 Crick, *Michael Heseltine*, p. 215; Butler, Adonis and Travers, *Failure in British Government*, p. 37.

72 Crick, *Michael Heseltine*, p. 216.

73 Proposals for rate limitation and reform of the rating system, Cmnd 9008.
74 These included Edward Heath and former Environment Secretary Geoffrey Rippon.
75 Hansard, vol. 57, Second Reading of Rates Bill, 17 Jan. 1984: Cunningham, cols 176–82; Heath, cols 184–7.
76 Travers, *Politics of Local Government Finance*, pp. 152–64.
77 M. Parkinson, *Liverpool on the Brink* (London: Hermitage Policy Journals, 1985), pp. 59–105.
78 *Ibid.*, p. 107.
79 *The Times*, 25 July 1984, p. 1g.
80 The Labour authorities were predominantly local socialist and included the GLC, ILEA, South Yorkshire and Merseyside, nine London Boroughs, the Metropolitan District of Sheffield, and Basildon and Leicester.
81 Blunkett and Jackson, *Democracy in Crisis*, p. 170.
82 Travers, *Politics of Local Government Finance*, p. 170.
83 Baker, *The Turbulent Years*, p. 105.
84 Blunkett and Jackson, *Democracy in Crisis*, p. 168.
85 *Ibid.*, pp. 170–1.
86 *Ibid.*, p. 175.
87 *Ibid.*, p. 181.
88 Baker, *The Turbulent Years*, p. 109.
89 Neil Kinnock made much of this incident at the 1985 Labour Party Annual Conference in which the actions of Militant and Liverpool Council were disowned by the party: P. Kilfoyle, *Left Behind* (London: Politico's, 2000), pp. 141–2.
90 Taafe and Mulhearn, *Liverpool: A City that Dared to Fight*, pp. 488–91.
91 Interview with Patrick Jenkin; Chandler, *Public Policy Making for Local Government*, p. 166.
92 Baker, *The Turbulent Years*, pp. 98–102.
93 *Ibid.*, p. 103
94 DoE, *Streamlining the Cities*, Cmnd 9063 (London: HMSO, 1983).
95 Chandler, *Public Policy Making for Local Government*, pp. 195–70.
96 *The Times*, 6 March 1985; at no time did support for retention of the GLC drop below 60 per cent of Londoners.
97 Chandler, *Public Policy Making for Local Government*, p. 166.
98 The Local Government Act, 1985: Eliz. II, c. 51.
99 The latest version of this theory is in Rhodes, *Control and Power in Central–Local Relations*.
100 DoE, *Interim Report of the Inquiry into the Conduct of Local Authority Business* (London: HMSO, 1985).
101 The Local Government Act, 1986: Eliz. II, c. 10.
102 Widdecombe report, pp. 45–7.
103 The Local Government Access to Information Act, 1985, Eliz. II, c. 43.
104 Ridley uses the term in the 1988 pamphlet *The Local Right: Enabling, Not Providing* (London: Centre for Policy Studies, 1988).
105 Most succinctly stated by F. A. Hayek, *The Road to Serfdom* (London: Routledge, 1944).
106 W. A. Niskanen, *Bureaucracy and Representative Government* (Chicago, IL: Aldine Atherton, 1971).

107 P. Beresford, *Good Council Guide: Wandsworth 1978–1987* (London: Centre for Policy Studies, 1987), pp. 21–4.

108 *Ibid.*, p. 9.

109 *Ibid.*

110 *The Times*, 7 Jan. 1987, p. 8a.

111 I. Holliday, 'The Conservative Party in local government 1979–1997', in G. Stoker (ed.), *The New Politics of British Local Governance* (Basingstoke: Macmillan, 2000), p. 176.

112 K. Smitham, 'The new urban Right: a study of Bradford City Council 1998–1990', BA dissertation, Sheffield Hallam University, 1991.

113 Blunkett and Jackson, *Democracy in Crisis*, p. 72.

114 Livingstone, *If Voting Changes Anything, They'd Abolish It*, pp. 217–28.

115 The Transport Act, 1985: Eliz. II, c. 67.

116 The Local Government Act, 1988: Eliz. II, c. 9.

117 The Education Reform Act, 1988: Eliz. II, c. 40.

118 K. Jones, *Education in Britain 1944 to the Present* (Cambridge: Polity Press, 2003), p. 131.

119 Department for Health and Social Security, *Community Care: Agenda for Action in 1988* (London: HMSO, 1988) (Griffiths report).

120 Department of Health, *Caring for People: Community Care in the Next Decade and Beyond*, Cm 849 (London: HMSO, 1989); the National Health Service and Community Care Act, 1990: Eliz II, c. 19.

121 Department of the Environment, *Housing: The Government's Proposals*, Cm 214 (London: HMSO, 1987).

122 The Housing Act, 1988: Eliz. II, c. 50.

123 P. Malpass, *Housing Associations and Housing Policy: An Historical Perspective* (Basingstoke: Macmillan, 2000), pp. 191–2.

124 *Ibid.*, p. 237.

125 The Local Government and Housing Act, 1989: Eliz. II, c. 42.

126 Audit Commission, *The Impact on Local Authorities' Economy: Efficiency and Effectiveness of the Block Grant Distribution System* (London: HMSO, 1984).

127 A revaluation due for England had been vetoed by Mrs Thatcher on account of the political hostility that might result, but she had left the Scottish Secretary of State to independently continue with revaluation north of the border: Butler, Adonis and Travers, *Failure in British Government*, pp. 61–5.

128 *Ibid.*, pp. 41–6.

129 Baker, *The Turbulent Years*, pp. 120–1.

130 N. Lawson, *The View from No. 11* (London: Bantam Press, 1992), p. 570.

131 Butler, Adonis and Travers, *Failure in British Government*, pp. 70–87; Baker, *The Turbulent Years*, pp. 124–5; N. Lamont, *In Office* (London: Little, Brown & Co., 1999), p. 43.

132 Lawson claims that he had never favoured a tax 'which had been notorious throughout the ages': Lawson, *The View from No. 11*, p. 561.

133 DoE, *Paying for Local Government*, Cmnd 9714 (London: HMSO, 1986); the Green Paper was published in a new more populist style with colour charts and photographs.

134 Butler, Adonis and Travers, *Failure in British Government*, pp. 101–4.

135 *Ibid.*, pp. 70–87; Baker, *The Turbulent Years*, pp. 124–5; Lamont, *In Office*, p. 43.

136 The Abolition of Domestic Rates, etc. (Scotland) Act, 1987: Eliz. II, c. 47.
137 N. Ridley, *My Style of Government* (London: Harper Collins, 1992), p. 130.
138 Butler, Adonis and Travers, *Failure in British Government*, p. 119. Local Government Finance Act 1988: Eliz. II, c. 41.
139 J. A. Chandler, *Local Government Today* (Manchester: Manchester University Press, 3rd edn, 2001), p. 56.
140 Butler, Adonis and Travers, *Failure in British Government*, pp. 134–6.
141 *Ibid.*, pp. 141–7.
142 A. Travis, 'Poll tax fears leave Prime Minister cold', *Guardian*, 2 April 1990, p. 4.
143 M. Thatcher, *The Downing Street Years* (London: Harper Collins, 1995), p. 661.
144 Butler, Adonis and Travers, *Failure in British Government*, pp. 165–6.
145 Crick, *Michael Heseltine*, p. 368.
146 J. Major, *John Major: The Autobiography* (London: Harper Collins, 1999), p. 218. The move was highly convenient for creating maximum publicity for the Government created problems for local authorities who had already prepared their poll-tax demands for dispatch the following month to their residents.
147 Butler, Adonis and Travers, *Failure in British Government*, p. 174.
148 Crick, *Michael Heseltine*, p. 368.
149 Local Government Finance Act, 1992: Eliz. II, c. 14.
150 Crick, *Michael Heseltine*, pp. 362–3.
151 Hansard, vol. 188, cols 410–15, 21 March 1991; vol. 189, cols 901–3, 23 April 1991.
152 J. D. Stewart, *The Nature of British Local Government* (Basingstoke: Macmillan, 2000), p. 43.
153 Audit Commission, *We Can't Go On Meeting Like This: The Changing Role of Local Authority Members*, Management Papers No. 8 (London: Audit Commission, 1990).
154 Crick, *Michael Heseltine*, pp. 370–1.
155 Heseltine trailed the idea in the House of Commons in March 1991 but made no mention of it when he announced the formation of the Commission to restructure local government in April 1991: Hansard, vol. 900, col. 401, 21 March 1999 and col. 901, 23 April 1999; Young and Rao, *Local Government Since 1945*, p. 226.
156 Crick, *Michael Heseltine*, p. 371.
157 *Ibid.*
158 DoE, *Community Leadership and Representation: Unlocking the Potential*, report of the Working Party on the Internal Management of Local Authorities in England (London: HMSO, 1993).
159 J. E. Kingdom, 'Centralisation and fragmentation: John Major and the reform of local government', in P. Dorey (ed.), *The Major Premiership* (Basingstoke: Macmillan, 1999), p. 56.
160 The Local Government Act, 1992: Eliz. II, c. 19.
161 J. Banham, *The Anatomy of Change: Blueprint for a New Era* (London: Weidenfeld & Nicolson, 1994), p. 78.
162 S. Leach, 'The strange case of the Local Government Review', in J. D. Stewart and G. Stoker (eds), *Local Government in the 1990s* (Basingstoke:

Macmillan, 1995), p. 62.

163 Kingdom, 'Centralisation and fragmentation: John Major and the reform of local government', p. 51.

164 Welsh Office, *Local Government in Wales*, Cm 2155 (London: HMSO, 1993); Scottish Office, *The Structure of Local Government – Shaping the Future: The New Councils*, Cm 2267 (London: HMSO, 1993).

165 Leach, 'The strange case of the Local Government Review', p. 54.

166 The Local Government (Wales) Act, 1994: Eliz. II, c. 19; the Local Government, etc. (Scotland) Act, 1994: Eliz. II, c. 39.

167 D. Wilson and C. Game, *Local Government in the United Kingdom* (Basingstoke: Palgrave, 3rd edn, 2002), p. 78.

168 Treasury, *Competing for Quality: Buying Better Public Services*, Cm 1730 (London: HMSO, 1991).

169 The Local Government Act 1992: Eliz. II, c. 19.

170 N. Barnett and S. Harrison, 'The Citizen's Charter in local government', in J. A. Chandler (ed.), *The Citizen's Charter* (Aldershot: Dartmouth, 1996), pp. 2, 139–42.

171 *Ibid.*

172 The Education Act, 1993: Eliz. II, c. 35.

173 P. Dorey, 'The 3Rs – reform, reproach and rancour: education policies under John Major', in P. Dorey (ed.), *The Major Premiership* (Basingstoke: Macmillan, 1999), pp. 148–50.

174 The Education Act, 1997: Eliz. II, c. 44, Sections 38–41.

175 Kingdom, 'Centralisation and fragmentation: John Major and the reform of local government', p. 61.

176 Crick, *Michael Heseltine*, p. 374.

177 Announced by John Gummer, Secretary of State for the Environment: Hansard, vol. 251, cols 517–18, 4 Nov. 1994.

178 J. A. Chandler, 'Regenerating South Yorkshire: how the public sector dominates business partnerships in Britain', in N. Walzer and B. Jacobs (eds), *Public–Private Partnerships for Local Economic Development* (Westport, CT: Praeger, 1998).

179 The term coined originally by T. Peters and R. Waterman in their influential study *In Search of Excellence* (New York: Harper Collins, 1982).

180 Of the many definitions of this disparate movement, among the most representative is that of C. Hood in 'A public management for all seasons', *Public Administration*, 69 (1991), pp. 3–19.

181 P. Curwen, M. Hunt, J. A. Chandler and R. Turner, *Charging for Services: Approaches to Price Setting in Local Authorities* (London: Local Government Management Board, 1995), p. 41.

12

New Labour

How new is New Labour? As the tenor of this book indicates, there are no instant revolutions in British government, rather a gradual evolution of ideas towards eventual change either through legislation or differing patterns of political and social behaviour. Apart from restructuring the machinery for decision-making within local authorities many New Labour initiatives were established elements of the party's policy before Tony Blair assumed the leadership. Labour governments in recent times have married these initiatives to many of the trends towards the enabling authority and the formation of ad hoc local trusts and agencies begun under the preceding Conservative administrations. The hollowing out of local government begun by Thatcher and Major has continued, but with a rather different emphasis as the implementation of many core local authority services are distributed to ad hoc agencies in the form of trusts and community-based local strategic partnerships (LSPs). Understanding local government under New Labour also requires an appreciation that its agenda does not emerge from a unified ideology and that within the Blair leadership are many voices and opinions which may exert contradictory approaches to policy. There is a tendency in any government for ministers to pursue their particular enthusiasms with little reference to other developments. In the context of such diffuse statements of New Labour values as is the 'Third Way' there is much scope for developing specific and uncoordinated ideas and policies. If, however, there is a precedent for Blair's policies, it is, as Samuel Beer has argued, in the liberalism of Lloyd George[1] and this, as is argued in this book, began the decline of the dual polity.

Labour in opposition

Michael Foot's leadership signalled the ascendancy of left-wing values and policies, which if they were to follow traditional Labour emphasis on equality could be expected to keep local government in a position firmly subordinate to the centre of government. The Labour Left was obliged, however, to accept policies that would give local authorities a greater measure of independence, partly in reaction to the attempts of Thatcher and Heseltine to subvert local discretion. The eclipse of Labour's parliamentary Right also gave socialist politicians based in local government, such as David Blunkett, Ken Livingstone and the Militant group, a far stronger voice in national party policy than at any time since the party's formation. In 1983 David Blunkett became the first constituency representative who was not an MP to be elected to the National Executive Committee of the party since 1947 and set about establishing a much stronger sub-committee on local government within the party machine.[2] The 1983 *Manifesto* promised the development of powers of general competence that allowed local authorities to undertake any activity unless expressly forbidden by statute and acknowledged the role of local authorities to 'implement comprehensive local plans, covering economic, social and environmental policies'.[3] Controls imposed by the Conservatives over local spending would be repealed. Council workers would be given more of a voice in determining local policies. Commitment to devolution for Scotland remained, although not for Wales. Despite the devolutionary rhetoric, Foot's leadership cannot be seen as a wholesale relaxing of control of local policy from the centre. The party promised a redefinition of central–local relations 'as part of the application of realistic minimum standards' although there were no clear plans as to how this aim should be imposed.[4] Local government would be reformed to create as far as possible unitary authorities, and health and water authorities would be subject to a greater measure of local accountability. For the first time since the Ullswater Commission the status of the City of London was raised as a political issue with a promise to absorb the institution 'into the democratic system of local government'.[5]

Labour policy towards local government under Kinnock's leadership began to evolve many of the characteristics that fully emerged during Blair's first term as Prime Minister. The demise of local socialism following its defeat over rate-capping and the abolition of the GLC and the MCCs gave the parliamentary party the opportunity to reassert authority over the party in London and in the major industrial cities. Membership of the Militant faction was made incompatible with party membership by 1986. Effective curbs on local socialist activity by the Thatcher Government and the absence of support from the Labour front bench ensured that the brief period in which local Labour leaders could gain more attention than the party's national leadership was at an end. However, a number of the social democrat, as distinct from the neo-Marxist, leaders of the local socialist movement were able to retain substantive positions at the national level of the party, although their ideas were beginning to be tempered by the demands of national leadership. In 1987 a consultative paper reiterated the Redcliffe-Maud enthusiasm for a local government structure based largely on single-tier district authorities, emphasised the need for regional authorities and, reflecting the Webbs, that local authorities should be compelled to provide minimum standards of service.[6] Minimum standards appeared in the 1987 Labour *Manifesto* as a commitment to a quality commission[7] but the idea of single-tier authorities and regional authorities in England did not feature in the election proposals.

The *Manifesto* and the consultative paper also took up several local socialist initiatives, such as enhancing the capacity of local authorities to develop their local economies.[8] This, however, represented a considerable retreat from the ideas of general competence that had been floated in 1983. Proposals for Scottish and Welsh autonomy, and a greater London authority, and the idea of Regional Development Agencies (RDAs) also became prominent features of party policy. The ideas developed in 1987 remained largely intact for the election *Manifesto* of 1992[9] which resurrected the idea of single-tier, 'most purpose', local government units to be based largely on district authorities, or in some cases a single county, and opened up the possibility of English regions. The *Manifesto* again raised the possibility of giving local authorities a power of general competence, but this was subject to even further restraints. Proposals such as that of the quality commission remained in place. The party led by Neil Kinnock thus viewed local government as the creature it had known in the 1970s and paid little attention to the many developments imposed by the Conservatives or initiated by local authorities themselves during the 1980s. Decentralisation was at best simply noted by the Kinnock leadership, but not strongly encouraged let alone expanded into a central strategy for ensuring that local authorities were closer to the people. Labour policies in opposition continued to advocate large, preferably unitary, local authorities delivering all their services in-house, rather than more fragmented bodies giving leadership and co-ordination to a wide range of public and private service agencies.[10]

Influences on New Labour

The emergence to the fore of Tony Blair, following the sudden death of John Smith, ushered into power a new generation of politicians eager to show that the party had broken with its Old Labour past. Blair quickly popularised his leadership under the mantra of New Labour as an alternative route between the New Right's inequitable policies on competition and the top–down, all-inclusive egalitarianism of Old Labour. Blair himself had no direct local government experience. His more detailed ideas on policy as laid out in a collection of speeches issued prior to the 1997 election extend to no more than four disparate pages.[11] This suggested that, while many authorities were competent, not all harboured the highest standards and so required modernisation.[12]

Within the diffuse ideology of the Third Way, Blair, nevertheless, places considerable emphasis on community, 'We all depend on collective goods for our independence; and all our lives are enriched – or impoverished –

by the communities to which we belong.'[13] As a student at Oxford, Blair was impressed by the writings of John Macmurray[14] who argued, rather unfashionably in the 1930 and 1940s, the importance of the community in shaping the lives of individuals and that self-actualisation cannot be achieved without working in accord with society. Such a view when applied to the political system of the nation encapsulated a concern for increasing public participation within the political system to secure civic engagement with the political process outside the old institutional structures.[15] Low turnout in elections showed that the old local government arrangements were failing to engage the citizen. Reform was needed not just for local government but for local governance and Blair seems to be fully prepared to jettison old institutions and allow new ad hoc stakeholder community fora to flourish. However, juxtaposed with the rhetoric of community participation there is in Blair's values a harder edge of managerialist leadership. Individuals and organisations are empowered only as long as they are seen to be successful:

> 'Intervention in inverse proportion to success' is the philosophy underpinning our educational reforms. Ministers have been given tough powers to intervene in the case of failing schools and education authorities, but they are increasing the autonomy of the majority doing a good job. We are applying the same principle to the NHS and local government.[16]

Underlying this attitude is the continued growth of the ethos of omnicompetence within and towards national governments. Central to the Blair leadership's campaign for votes was the promise to improve public services whether or not controlled directly by central government. Having staked its reputation on improving services, the Government could scarcely risk trusting this task to other agents, such as local authorities who might even be elected and run by political opponents. Having claimed they would improve public services, failure in this context could not easily be blamed on others and hence for New Labour, even more than the preceding Conservative administrations, it has become impossible not to treat local governments as agencies whose capacity to deliver local services cannot be viewed as solely a local matter. For the Blair administration, successful innovation by local authorities is to be encouraged but failure requires the intervention of central government.

Tony Blair's was not the only voice within New Labour. In his first years in office the Prime Minister leant for ideas on local government on ministers who had significant involvement in local politics such as David Blunkett and Frank Dobson. National prominence in local government does not, as this history shows, necessarily result in increased concern for local authorities once the local politician steps into a ministerial role, but it can place within Government a sufficiently powerful group of politicians to block any steps to wholly recast the system. Deputy Prime Minister John Prescott also brought into the policy-making arena a strong view on the need for regional government. These concerns were recognised when the DoE was divided, in May 2002, to allow Prescott to establish an Office of the Deputy Prime Minister (ODPM), which took over the tutelage of local government, responsibility for the proposed regional assemblies, planning and housing, leaving the DoE to look after issues of sustainable development, pollution and water. The ODPM became an organisation that, perhaps even more than the former LGB, dedicated in the main to local authority matters. A government department built around an individual could not be sustained. Following the 2005 general election, with Prescott's regional policy in tatters and his political authority on the wane, Blair created within the framework of the ODPM a minister of cabinet rank for Communities and Local Government, and installed in the post one of the rising stars of New Labour values, David Miliband. In less than a year the ODPM was replaced by the Department for Communities and Local Government with another Blair loyalist, Ruth Kelly, as Secretary of State.

Many of the policies relating to local government brought in by the 1997 Government, including devolution for Scotland and Wales, RDAs in England and 'best value', had been staple elements of Labour policies since the 1980s. The new leadership, however, continued a gradual retreat from the enthusiasms of the Foot leadership, especially the idea of powers of general competence. Local authorities would be given new powers but with major constraints on their use. The strong commitment to establish a largely single tier of 'most purpose' local authorities also wavered, partly under the impact of Heseltine's partial move to unitary authorities and partly because it was thought that further major change was unlikely to receive great enthusiasm from local authorities which in the last two decades scarcely had time to absorb one structural change when another was on its way. Pressure from Peter Mandelson to develop city regions made little headway with other Labour leaders and particularly the sector led by John Prescott which was supporting regional councils.[17]

The New Labour leadership, however, generated a significant change through its concern to restructure the internal decision-making of local authorities. The idea of a strong leadership through a popular and clearly identifiable local figurehead became an increasingly plausible strategy for reform in a society increasingly enthused by managerial solutions to social problems. The concept was taken up most enthusiastically by the Commission for Local Democracy, a campaign set up by in 1993 and sponsored by a number of groups concerned at the decline of local authority influence, including UNISON[18] and the *Municipal Journal*. The Commission, chaired by former editor of *The Times* Simon Jenkins, published over the following two years detailed studies, largely by academics, on ways to improve the standing of local government, and in its final report made forty-three recommendations for reform.[19] Some of the proposals, such as the development of powers of general competence, the return of former functions, an end to rate-capping and local powers to set the business rate, made little impression on the Labour Party. The Commission's ideas on reshaping the committee structure of local government were, however, comprehensively taken up by New Labour interests. As in the past in relation to the ideas of Cole or Robson the Labour leadership took from academic deliberations only what it wanted to hear.

The change of government in 1997 was marked by an immediate transformation in the relationship between central and local government. An immediate and widely welcomed move was to sign, a month after the general election, the European Charter of Local Self-Government[20] which had been created by the Council of Europe to establish the right of local governments to conduct a substantial number of activities for their communities and to allow citizens to participate in decisions affecting their locality. It may be questioned whether the size of local authorities in Britain and the Blair Government's lack of interest in developing stronger small authorities fully conform to such a measure, but given that the Thatcher and the Major Government would have nothing to do with the document, signing the Charter signalled that the Blair Government fully recognised that local government had a significant role in its vision for Britain. Many larger local authorities had by 1997 opened up offices in Brussels and also appointed their own staff to deal with European Union issues. Local authorities, especially in urban areas, could be cautiously optimistic that the new regime in Whitehall would reverse the decline in local powers and funding. The new Government expected co-operation from local government and did not view the local system as a necessarily antagonistic interest. Prior to the 1997 elections meetings had taken place between the LAAs and the Labour leaders over possible reforms and agreement had been reached on a framework for replacing CCT with 'best value' (BV).[21] John Prescott as Secretary of State for the Environment announced his intention to establish regular meetings between himself and local government leaders to improve central–local relations and attended with Gordon Brown the first LGA Conference following the change of government. There was but one fly in the soothing ointment, however, in that the Chancellor refused to increase public spending for local authorities, although he had relaxed spending on council housing,[22] but this was the first occasion a Chancellor had addressed the LGA since Geoffrey Howe had told the Association that Mrs Thatcher was to cut the rate support grant.[23]

Devolution

Following such a lengthy gestation of policy the Blair Government could implement its ideas on local government immediately, with little need for lengthy internal discussions with the civil service on the way ahead. Local and regional government issues were also towards the top of the party's

action list, not because they were necessarily the most important objectives for the Government, but because they were not particularly expensive policies. The prudent Chancellor Gordon Brown was determined to
retain low levels of public spending during the first years of the administration to build up the resources with which to expand services through
higher expenditure in the lead up to the next election.

The Government pressed ahead with policies not requiring substantial
expenditure with sufficient dispatch to be able to publish White Papers on
Scotland and Wales within two months of coming to power.[24] They
proposed the creation of a Scottish Assembly and an Executive that would
be given powers to legislate and implement policy on the issues that had
been previously managed by the Scottish Office. A Welsh Assembly and
Executive would be delegated the power to make executive orders within
the framework of Westminster legislation. A referendum in Scotland was
favourable to an Assembly with limited tax-raising powers and the subsequent Scotland Act received the Royal Assent in November 1998.[25] In
Wales a referendum favoured devolution by less than 7,000 votes on a 50
per cent turnout. Given the Government's policy favouring devolution,
the narrow win was sufficient to ensure the establishment of the Welsh
Assembly and Executive.[26]

The Scottish and Welsh Assemblies provide a new dimension in
central–local relations. From May 1998 the Scottish Assembly was able
on its own initiative to determine the size, tiers and functions of local
authorities in the Province and also how much revenue it can raise
through the rates in addition to any funds it received in grants direct from
the UK Government. The Scottish government can also determine policy
for education, social services, housing and the police, as well as services
for the health sector or water supply that could potentially be merged
back into the local government system. The Welsh Assembly has more
limited powers. The structure or system of finance for local government
in Wales could not be changed without, at least, the acquiescence of
Westminster and Whitehall. However, the Welsh Assembly can propose
primary legislation to central government, and, as structuring the local
government system in Wales is a task that since its creation had been jealously guarded by the Welsh Office, it is presumed that the Welsh
Executive would be likely to be given free range in this sector.[27]

Most members of the Blair Government expected, at least in the short
term, to see Scotland and Wales under the control of New Labour acolytes.
The first elections to the Regional Parliaments and Assemblies took place the
following May. In Scotland Labour gained most seats but not a majority as a
consequence of additional member proportional representation and had to
share power in a coalition with the Liberal Democrats, while in Wales,
despite Labour's dominance in the Principality, the party formed a minority
administration. New Labour influence over the devolved Welsh Assembly
quickly ran into difficulties as the Government's preferred candidate for the

post of First Minister, Ron Davies, was forced to resign over his reaction to a minor scandal. Alun Michael, Blair's favoured replacement, secured approval by the Welsh Labour Party only with the help of behind the scenes wire-pulling by the Labour national leadership with the trade unions. His leadership of a minority government proved unpopular with his party's backbenchers, and in October 2000 he felt obliged to resign and was replaced by the rival candidate of the Left, Rhodri Morgan, whom Blair had striven to avoid.

Re-creating London

The promised resurgence of a strategic authority for London was initiated in parallel with the devolution policies for Scotland and Wales. Much groundwork as to the structure of the new London authority had been completed prior to the 1997 election. In the previous year Blair had been persuaded that an elected mayor for London would provide stronger and more visible leadership.[28] The idea was mooted in April in a consultation paper[29] and soon afterwards formed part of the 1997 *Manifesto*.[30] Behind the scenes, the idea was opposed by more traditional Labour leaders, including the shadow Environment spokesman Frank Dobson, a former leader of Camden Borough Council.[31] Under Blair's direction the Government, once elected, poured the reformist enthusiasms of New Labour into the task of creating a strategic authority for London. A Green Paper[32] was published in 1997 to be followed by a 1998 White Paper which proposed the creation of a Greater London Authority (GLA), to cover the same area as the former GLC, with strategic powers for transport, economic development and town planning.[33] The new authority could also co-ordinate plans for health care. An all too rare reversal of power from the centre to the locality gave control of the Metropolitan Police to sub-national government rather than the Home Office and, in addition, the fire services also returned to the control of the strategic authority for London. The GLA more clearly and logically divided the strategic planning and area-wide public protection services from more routine governance of localities in the capital than had been achieved during the preceding 200 years of reorganisation of metropolitan government.

The blueprint for the new GLA demonstrated New Labour's enthusiasm for changing the policy-making structure of local governance by proposing that executive power be separated from the legislative role through a directly elected mayor responsible for devising and implementing policy. The power of the mayor would be mediated by a relatively small twenty-five-person council which, in the spirit of throwing out the old, was to be called an Assembly. Its principal function would be to scrutinise the actions of the mayor and publicly report its views of the incumbent's stewardship. The Assembly could also reject the budget for the GLA as devised by the mayor, but only with a two-thirds majority. The arrangement was based on a US strong mayor system and gave only marginal influence to its councillors. For the majority of its functions the GLA would have an enabling role and preside over several agencies, such as the Metropolitan Police, a London Fire and Emergency Planning Authority and a London Development Agency that would have functions similar to those of other proposed regional planning agencies for England. The mayor, supported by a cabinet of their own choosing, set the overall policies for the agencies, leaving detailed implementation to their chief executives. As in Scotland and Wales, further innovatory spirit was put into the electoral procedures for the mayor and the Assembly. The mayor was chosen by a two-stage supplementary vote while the Assembly was selected through a German-style hybrid system in which the 14 members were elected on a constituency basis and a further 11 by proportional representation of the London-wide vote.

The White Paper's proposals were approved by a 72 per cent vote in their favour in a referendum held in May 1998, at the same time as elections for the London boroughs, but on a thin turnout of only 34 per cent.[34] The complex legislation that brought the GLA into being was completed by November 1999. Even during its preparation, New Labour enthusiasts began to realise, as the Major Cabinet had foreseen in relation to Heseltine's proposals, that elected mayors could give rise to local leaders who may be difficult to control politically through the machinery of party discipline. The role of mayor of London was tailor-made for Ken Livingstone.

Following the demise of the GLC, Livingstone had been elected to Parliament, but, in contrast to David Blunkett, had not been warmly received into the inner circle of New Labour, and so he resumed the role of waspish critic of right-wing Labour policies. Despite, or perhaps because of, hostility from the party leadership, he continued to remain in the public eye and became the overwhelmingly popular choice among Labour voters for the first directly elected mayor of London. New Labour leaders refused to countenance a potential left-wing critic in the office and arranged a complex selection procedure that obliged Frank Dobson to step down from his Cabinet post to become the official Labour candidate for a role he had opposed behind closed doors. The aggrieved Livingstone decided to face inevitable expulsion from the Labour Party by standing as an independent candidate. In May 2000 Dobson secured only the third-highest number of first-preference votes, and after a count of second-preference votes Livingstone was elected Mayor by a majority of over 200,000 over the rival Conservative candidate on a low turnout of 35 per cent.[35] The failure of the Blair Government to secure its preferred candidate, added to their difficulties in Wales, gave some cabinet members serious doubts about the wisdom of pursuing devolved government and elected mayors for the rest of England. By this stage, however, the policy was firmly established as the way forward for other local authorities.

English regions

The commitment to develop English regions that had been trailed within
the Redcliffe-Maud report and included in the 1997 *Manifesto* was slow
to develop due to indifference or hostility among many Labour leaders.
The policy was favoured largely by MPs, like John Prescott, from a northern trade union background who wanted economic regeneration policy to
be made outside Whitehall and placed in the hands of elected regional
agencies.[36] However, some cabinet members close to Blair saw elected
regional authorities as organisations that would be unpopular additions
to local authority structures, adding a further and unnecessary tier of
bureaucracy to the arthritic systems of local government. In 1995 there
had been attempts to develop policy that would bring together regional
and local government reforms into a unified framework,[37] but these ran
into the sand when Jack Straw moved his opposition portfolio to the
Home Office, taking with him responsibility for political organisation of
the regions and leaving his successor in the shadow environment portfolio, John Prescott, to deal with the regions solely in the context of
economic development.[38] Straw was not eager to develop the electoral
element of regionalism.

These divisions led to the compromise of the 1998 Regional
Development Act that established nine unelected RDAs to promote
economic development for their areas,[39] using the boundaries established
in 1994 by John Major for the Regional Government Offices. The GLA
became effectively the metropolitan RDA. The new creations were
QUANGOs rather than local government agencies. The boards of the
RDAs comprised but four local government nominees, who were outnum-
bered by members representing predominantly business interests. They
appointed an executive director to manage the organisation. The boards
were paralleled by regional chambers, representing a wider constituency
of business, public sector and voluntary agencies, which would scrutinise
the work of the boards.[40]

The possibility was left open for the new regional organisations to
develop into fully fledged elected regional governments. It was recognised
that such a development could become established asymmetrically, so that
areas where there was popular support for regional tiers of government
could become institutionalised more rapidly. Three RDAs, for the the
north east, the north west and Yorkshire–Humberside, emerged as possible contenders to evolve into elected regional authorities. Following
renewed support in the 2001 Labour *Manifesto* for regional development,
a White Paper, published in 2002, proposed that the three more advanced
regions could, subject to a referendum, establish elected regional assem-

blies.[41] The proposals in the White Paper did not greatly increase the powers of the potential elected regions beyond those held by the RDAs, which were to be governed, following the policy of separating executive from assembly, by a leader and a 6-member cabinet elected by and accountable to a relatively small assembly of no more than 35 representatives. Legislation[42] that brought the proposals into being also required voters in a referendum to decide not only whether to accept the idea of an elected region but whether they wanted to remove county councils or district authorities in areas within the region that had two-tier status. This development arguably presses forward the pre-New Labour enthusiasms within the party to complete the process begun with the Redcliffe-Maud report to pave Britain with a single tier of unitary authorities. The first referendum, conducted by a postal ballot for the north-east where there was considered to be the strongest popular support for the idea, produced in November 2004 a decisive vote against an elected regional government and the probability that the idea has been laid to rest for several decades to come. In a nation now divided by large and, consequently, remote local, or rather sub-regional, units of multi-purpose governance, it may be suggested that the English public had little appetite for a further even more distant and yet possibly costly extension of this pattern.

Modern local government

New Labour's ideas on local government reform were set out in February 1998 in the White Paper *Modern Local Government: In Touch With the People*,[43] which was the blueprint for change in English local government during the party's first term in office. It was accompanied by a booklet, with Blair named as the author, further explaining the need for change. It was argued that local government faced three challenges: firstly 'a lack of a clear sense of direction' by which Blair meant the absence of leadership at the local level, secondly a lack of cohesion between the many agencies delivering public services and thirdly that services were provided unevenly in terms of quality.[44] 'The answer to today's problems cannot be to go back to the local government model of a bygone age.'[45] Local governments had failed to communicate the reasons behind their budget decisions, to engage participation by local citizens, to work in partnerships and to put the needs of service users ahead of those of service providers.[46]

The White Paper proposed separating the executive and representative roles within councils by the imposition of cabinet government and reform in the methods of voting. Service quality would be monitored and improved under a scheme for 'best value' that removed the crude system of CCT but would replace it with an obligation on local authorities to establish quality targets for the majority of their services unless, as in education, these were imposed already by central government. The White Paper made it clear that 'retaining work in-house', without subjecting it to real competitive pressure, 'can rarely be justified'.[47] It was expected that the modern local authority would provide services working in partnership with the private and voluntary sectors, thus retaining its enabling role. However, in contrast to the ideas of the preceding Conservative administrations, the enabling role was not to be simply a residual activity distributing contracts to private sector services but would involve strategic leadership for the locality, and to that end local governments were given in the Local Government Act, 2000, the duty to promote the economic, social and environmental well-being of their communities.

The view was entrenched in the new Government that there was a malaise in the relationship between local government and the citizen, as shown in the decreasing turnout at elections, and that this issue was certainly more deep seated than the difficulties of casting a vote. Attempts following the 1998 White Paper to overhaul balloting arrangements through electronic voting and more frequent – usually annual – elections, within each local authority were not particularly successful. In selected areas elections in 2002 and 2003 were conducted in some wards by postal ballot, by telephone or through the internet. Not all electronic systems worked perfectly and voting turnout increased substantially only when postal balloting was used, as in the case of the North-East Regional Referendum. The Blair Government realised from the outset that more drastic change was needed, but it is questionable whether it has diagnosed effectively the cause of public indifference.

The 1988 blueprint for local government reform did not suggest that the structure of the system, especially in terms of the remoteness of its units, created a problem. Perhaps wisely, on account of the changes flowing from the Banham review, restructuring of tiers and boundaries did not enter the policy process of the Blair administration until its final years. Internal debate on the structure of the system prior to the 2006 White Paper *Strong and Prosperous Communities*[48] suggest considerable divisions on strategy. Much discussion revolved around creating even larger city region structures, effectively re-inventing the 1969 Senior proposals but from a different, though not necessarily opposed, position there has been interest among some ministers in more community-based structures and local partnership schemes. The White Paper has suggested more support for the latter strategy and also proposes to more easily facilitate the creation of unitary authorities but gives only faint support for fully fledged city regions.

Best value

Legislation to establish BV formed the centrepiece of the 1999 Local Government Act.[49] Local authorities generally supported the idea and a number of authorities freely agreed to adopt the arrangements to allow a full evaluation to be made of the ideas before the Act came into effect.[50]

In contrast to CCT, BV had the merit of allowing local authorities some initiative in determining standards, and did not necessarily throw them open to the mercies of the marketplace unencumbered by concern for the quality of a service. Acceptance of the proposals also reflected the shift in opinion within local government itself and a readiness to seek external contractors for many services rather than to rely on in-house provision. However, the regime also placed local authority services under even further restraints. The standards by which each service was to be measured, although proposed by the local authority itself, were sanctioned by the Audit Commission, if there was no other established structure for inspection such as OFSTED, and were based on a comparison of performance between authorities of similar population size and demographic base. Each local authority service was therefore subject to inspection at least every five years with the findings made public. BV schemes normally require local authorities to conduct surveys to evaluate public support for their services or to record and publicise the number of complaints they receive. While not obliged to contract-out services, local authorities had to justify why they continued to conduct services on an in-house basis. The system also included incentives to induce them to secure excellent service delivery by awarding the accolade of beacon status to specific local authority service delivery units which appeared to be exemplars of good practice. Authorities given this status would be expected to help and guide other councils to meet their standards. The White Paper suggested that 'beacon' authorities and services could be given some measure of competence to develop their policies, but thus far the means to secure this power has yet to emerge.

Following the 2001 election Stephen Byers, Secretary of State for the Department of Environment, Trade and Regions (DETR), published a White Paper that refined the BV system by integrating evaluations into Local Authority Comprehensive Performance Assessments that graded the service activities of each authority on a scale ranging from excellent to poor.[51] The system replicated a strategy, already established for schools and hospitals, but was in the case of local government applied to democratically elected organisations. Local authorities are, therefore, evaluated as if they are agencies rather than separately elected governments subject to the values and priorities of their electorates. A local authority that chooses to spend less on a particular service, knowing this will mean a lower standard of services, has its decision subjected to a critical rating by central government. Although the 2001 White Paper expressed the intention to free local government from excessive restraints there is, as indicated in the Preface of this book, a cavernous gulf between the nineteenth-century practice, where even operating a library was an option for local authorities, to unelected government agencies criticising minute details on the operation of a such a service.

The 2000 Local Government Act also provided, as trailed in the 1998

White Paper, a further guarantee of quality by creating new systems to deal with unethical conduct of councillors. These took shape nationally as the Standards Agency, charged with establishing a code of ethical conduct for elected members that had to be adopted by each local authority. Individual councils could change the code to suit its particular needs. If a councillor transgressed the code the Standards Agency would review the case and would be able to disqualify the individual from holding office. The arrangement was intended to remove the previous cumbersome machinery of surcharge, bankruptcy and disqualification, and to that end seemed a more liberal process; in practice, however, the machinery has yet to be tested in circumstances such as the 1985 rates rebellion, in which it would probably have led to more rapid and widespread disqualification of the disaffected local representatives.

Elected mayors, cabinets and scrutiny

The proposals to restructure policy-making were put into practice through the 2000 Local Government Act.[52] They have been, at best, only moderately successful and much of the enthusiasm for elected executive mayors has trickled into the sand. The White Paper had proposed three forms of local executive that would be chosen by councils or by the electorate through local referenda. These comprised an executive cabinet chaired by the leader of council, an elected mayor choosing his own cabinet from among elected councillors or, most radically, the system, used in some US cities, of an elected mayor who appoints a city manager to run the authority on a day-to-day basis.[53] The creation of a streamlined executive would leave the remaining councillors with greater time to liaise with their electorate and also serve on scrutiny committees to critically review the activities of the executive cabinet and mayor. The majority of the local authorities that were required to remodel their decision-making structures quickly adopted the least disruptive arrangement of the leader–cabinet model. In those authorities dominated by cohesive majority parties, the restructuring has probably made little difference to the central task of major decision-making. Policy can still be hammered out in the ruling party group's deliberations behind closed doors, which, for the most part, involves decision-making by the senior executive members and their leader who occupy seats in the cabinet. The more significant change in fortunes under the leader–cabinet system concerns the role of backbench councillors, especially within the majority parties, who may find themselves isolated from their local authority role. A particular casualty is the councillor who once gained his or her *raison d'être* from chairing a minor committee and championing modest yet worthy policy arenas such as the chair of a market's or a school buildings' sub-sub-committee. It can be seriously questioned whether scrutiny presents a more valuable or attractive task for the backbencher. Travers[54] observes that in the first council to adopt a scrutiny system, the Greater London Authority, 'after the first three years of the Assembly's existence, it still had not found an effective role'. A study of the early years of its implementation in Wales suggests that while cabinet members will attend scrutiny meetings the composition of the committees is structured on party lines, which may limit the extent of criticism.[55] Only 24 per cent of the councillors surveyed felt they had powers over the budget for the services they were monitoring, and overall 73 per cent of the respondents who chose to add their own comments on the activity did so from a negative perspective. In terms of publicity, the local press is from time to time reporting findings of scrutiny committees, although not extensively.[56] There is to date little research evidence to show whether a further aim of the restructuring into a separate executive and council has promoted greater enthusiasm among councillors to work within their communities rather than be mired in endless committee meetings in the town hall, but as Snape points out there is little evidence that backbench councillors have yet found their feet within the new organisational structures.[57]

While the jury may still be out concerning the effectiveness of scrutiny, enthusiasts for the elected mayor and the city manager systems can find little solace in the outcome of this provision in the 2000 Act. The idea had received a measure of support among the general public in surveys conducted prior to the development of the idea,[58] but this favourable attitude did not translate into widespread adoption of the system. The 2000 Act and later Statutory Instruments refining the process of establishing elected mayors gave councils the power to call referenda to approve the adoption of one of the structural options requiring an elected mayor. If councils refused to call this a referendum could be triggered by a petition requiring the signatures of 20 per cent of the local electorate. Few local authorities were enthusiastic supporters of the idea and only 24 decided to hold a referendum to adopt a mayoral system, while in only 5 cases to date was there sufficient enthusiasm and organisation among the public at large to successfully petition a reluctant authority to organise a referendum. Only 11 of the 29 referenda held up to 2003 amassed the simple majority of votes sufficient to be successful. More disappointingly for the Government, turnout in these contests was in almost each case even lower than for normal council elections.[59] As Rao suggests, the majority of local electors who support an elected mayor are also members of the public, with no interest in, or an aversion to, local politics.[60]

The elections that have taken place have often thrown up candidates who would not be, as in the London mayoral contest, the choice of Westminster politicians. Of the 11 contests 5 were won by independent candidates and results suggested a preference among many voters to support a candidate who could be seen as an antidote to established party leaders. The most embarrassing contest for both local and national politicians took place in Hartlepool where public favour alighted on Independent Stuart Drummond whose popularity stemmed largely from his alter-ego as the local football team's mascot H'Angus the Monkey.[61] Middlesbrough elected a tough-on-crime police superintendent who was under suspension by his force. Not all independent candidates were colourful opportunists. In Stoke on Trent, which was the only authority to hold a referendum for the mayor and city manager structure, the successful candidate was a popular local advice worker campaigning against corruption in the local authority. Enthusiasm for elected mayors within central government quickly waned. In 2001 Minister for Local Government Nick Raynsford suggested that all local authorities should be required to hold mayoral referenda by 2005 and one authority, Southwark, was forced by the Government to hold a referendum that led to a resounding defeat for the mayoral principle. Following the May 2002 local elections, when several mayoral elections took place, Charles Clarke, then chairman of the Labour Party, argued in a radio interview that the mayoral system was an experiment whose results would have to carefully evaluated.[62] In local elections in May 2005, the first in which elected mayors stood for re-election, large numbers of voters in the Stoke on Trent election wrote on their ballot papers that they wanted the office of elected mayor to be terminated, but in Hartlepool H'Angus the Monkey was again successful.

Despite the limited enthusiasm for elected mayors among local authorities and, judging from the results of referenda, the public, the Labour Government pressed on with its strategy of enforcing more visibly unitary rather than collective leadership on local authorities. The 2006 White Paper *Strong and Prosperous Communities* proposed that all local authorities should vest their executive powers in a leader who would be elected either directly or indirectly by their council for four years. Three structures were proposed: a directly elected mayor; a directly elected cabinet whose members would be on a slate agreed by their leader; or one would be elected for a four-year term by the councillors who could, presumably on a change of party control in the authority, remove that leader by a vote of no confidence. To enable authorities to develop directly elected leaderships, the referendum would be replaced with a requirement only to widely consult the electorate on such a change. The momentum is being rolled onward by a central prime-ministerial government towards what for national leaders is a familiar pattern of dictatorial democracy rather than the collective democracy established by municipalities after 1834.

Finance

Although Gordon Brown kept in place the Conservative spending plans for the first two years of the Blair Government, there was a significant improvement in financial harmony due to a greater willingness of the Government to consult with local authorities on their financial needs and hence respond more effectively to problems identified at local level. Following a *Manifesto* pledge to abolish 'crude and universal council tax capping',[63] John Prescott announced that capping restriction would be eased for 1997–98 and they were to be removed all together for 1998–99 although several authorities were formally warned after the announcement that continued increases in expenditure would not be tolerated.[64] The Government, nevertheless, had no intention of removing its control entirely over levels of council tax. The 1999 Local Government Act modified the capping system to allow the Government to take account of a local authority's spending patterns over a number of years before forwarding any capping order[65] and subsequently, despite warnings to some local authorities, no capping orders were introduced during the first Blair Government.

Changes to the business rate were also made to allow local authorities the chance to retain some of the tax for their direct use rather than for redistribution by the Treasury. Increased funding was made available for specific schemes to alleviate social problems which were often tied to partnership working based on service agreements between a government department and the Treasury to secure that funding based on a promise to achieve pre-determined targets of achievement. These arrangements could then be translated into similarly structured service agreements with a local authority or a local strategic partnership. The Government also relaxed controls on capital spending. In 2003 the ODPM established a single allowance for capital spending to cover all services other than education and police services[66] and later moved to a regime in which a local authority's capital expenditure would be limited by a general requirement to keep within limits set by the Government their overall debt, their year-by-year increases in borrowing and their capacity to repay their interest.[67] The capacity of local authorities to raise capital was, however, being limited by the Treasury's enthusiasm for the Public Finance Initiative which requires public sector organisations to develop their major projects in partnership with the private sector by persuading private contractors to construct public buildings at their own risk with an agreement that they would then lease the buildings to the public authority at a rate that would allow the contractor a probable substantial profit. The arrangement was imposed on London Transport for modernisation of the underground and occasioned the most serious quarrel between the Government and Ken Livingstone. Several reports have argued that the arrangement is in the long term more expensive for local authorities.[68]

The changes in the financing of local government, while relatively minor, suggested to local authorities that they would be able to gain rather more freedom to arrange their finances from the Blair Government than its predecessors. Local government after 2000 began to receive more generous grants, especially for favoured services such as education, but for many services such as housing and transport, despite Chancellor Gordon Brown's pre-2001 election war chest, there was comparatively little increase in funding. The Government also ensured that the extra expenditure for education was channelled direct to this service. Reassessment of the needs element in grant allocation accompanied by the not so generous increases in grant revenue led many rural authorities to demand increases in the council tax considerably in advance of the rate of inflation. The stresses in the system prompted Raynsford to apply his capping powers in 2004 to fourteen local authorities and to develop a rather low-key review of local government funding initiated in 2002 into a much wider investigation which once again brought into play the possibility of a local income tax.[69] However, the idea did not form part of Labour's 2005 electoral manifesto but following the election discussion continued within the Government, against the background of 'can't pay, won't pay' protests from elderly pensioners. In July 2005 the Government appointed former Chief Executive of Birmingham Sir Michael Lyons to review the system of local government funding and was two months later asked to extend this investigation to a wider study of the strategic role of local government with regard to its functions and relations with central government.

Functions

The less hostile relationship between central and local government of the Blair administrations compared with the preceding New Right administration developed steadily during the early years of the Labour Government. In general local government was seen as an important strategic agency and through the 2000 Act gained broad powers of competence over the economic, social and environmental well-being of their areas, although if such powers are taken in directions not acceptable to the Government the Secretary of State could disallow such action. More specifically local government was seen as having a role in shaping local economies and also in developing, as suggested in the Rio Environmental Summit, a much more determined role in securing sustainable policies.[70] The Blair governments have been happy to allow local authorities to innovate so long as they can step in and control or curtail ideas that are contrary to central interests.

Several services which the Major Government seemed to be prising away from local government were once again reaffirmed as a local responsibility. LEAs were reassigned a clear strategic role in the local provision of schools. David Blunkett wound up the Funding Agency for Schools and the capacity of schools to opt out of local government control and returned to LEAs the strategically important function of determining school catchment areas.[71] However, the role of LEAs was to remain predominantly at the strategic level of co-ordination rather than hands-on control within schools, and proposals to further embed the LEAs in this role were consolidated in the 2006 Education and Inspections Act.[72] The 2000 Green Paper on housing[73] established a parallel framework for local government housing. Local authorities were reaffirmed as having an important strategic role in ensuring that community housing needs were adequately met but were not encouraged to directly manage their housing stock. Financial incentives were provided for local authorities to transfer their estates to housing associations by writing off accumulated debts on their housing accounts. New Labour continued the policies of Conservative governments, although more through incentives than threats. Between 1988 and 2000 more than 400,000 houses had been transferred to housing associations[74] and the direct management of housing by local authorities was increasingly being wound down. The pattern of local authorities shedding their direct responsibility for running services has extended to most other aspects of their activities. In the area of leisure provision most local authorities have been encouraged to set up trusts in order to manage parks, museums and galleries.

In the longer term the Blair governments may have embraced local authorities only to gently but insidiously strangle their importance. Labour has slowed but not ended local authorities' decline as a hands-on provider of services, even if it has continued to be a strategic enabler for service provision. Despite the closer relationship between central government and the local authorities, many of the powers lost during the Conservative years of the 1980s and 1990s have never been returned to local stewardship. Although LEAs have a strategic role, local self-management of schools, the National Curriculum and league tables have remained firmly in place. Local regeneration might still be steered by local government but only in partnership with the private and voluntary sectors. New Labour has continued to encourage the sale of council houses in addition to their transfer to housing associations. Local authorities were not encouraged to operate homes for the elderly. Bus services remained privatised, water and drainage continued to be in private hands and under BV refuse collection was still in the main contracted out to the private sector.

Joining-up and dividing

Alongside the implementation of the 1999 and 2000 Local Government Acts, the Labour Party was more insidiously changing the structure and role of the local government system through the pursuit of principles and programmes that were not designed solely with local government in mind and, in some cases, without any thought to their implications for local governance. Soon after New Labour attained power, supportive think-tanks such as Demos, under the leadership of Perri 6,[75] began to press on the Government such modernisation mantras as the need for 'joined-up government' and community solutions for resolving problems of social deprivation. Urban deprivation was not a function just of poor housing, unemployment, crime or bad education but was the product of the interaction of those issues. The idea also reflected an element of management ideology where numerous studies abandoned with the value of decentralisation, albeit within a 'loose–tight'[76] framework that in the final analysis places innovation under central stewardship. These values, nurtured by separate standard-bearers from different branches of government, have created a complex and often unconnected range of initiatives that further disperses the powers of traditionally large-scale local governments. These ideas were grist to the mill of the modernisers who considered local government to be out of touch with people. An enthusiasm emerged for devolving powers to communities not represented by the established local government system. This trend is indicative of the limited confidence in local government among many senior New Labour ministers. The 1998 White Paper was strangely indifferent to the possibility of decentralisation within local government, acknowledging that local authorities could establish area committees, but also stating: 'Decentralisation is a valuable way – but not the only way of achieving this', that is bringing decisions closer to the people.[77] Effectively the Government showed little sympathy with the growing realisation in many local authorities that they were too large to be 'in touch with the people' and were in many cases capable of devising methods to remedy this problem.

The 1998 White Paper urged local authorities to

> encourage and facilitate more joined up working between Government departments and agencies, and also with the rest of the public sector, like local government. The goal? High quality, modern, accessible and responsive local services.[78]

Local authorities were consequently expected in the 2000 Local Government Act to develop community plans to ensure that, rather than being a monolithic institution imposing policy on their communities, they would draw together community groups to develop policy and the relevant agencies to implement their solutions. The point was valid if not particularly original. Governments have been constantly reforming the scope of ministries and agencies to join-up policy-makers to deal with problems that they deemed to be a priority. The formation of the LGB in 1872 was driven by a desire to 'join-up' government surveillance of local health and social care responsibilities. The development of new towns was a response to the need for a joined-up solution to urban overcrowding, as was the corporate management movement of the 1970s in the context of policy-making.

From these concerns has emerged a multitude of initiatives to deal with problems of community deprivation and poor service delivery through collective action focused on the deprived communities. Sullivan and Skelcher have identified around 60 types of partnership body operating in the local sector and over 5,000 individual partnership bodies.[79] These have included, for example, Action Zones for education,[80] health and sport, and partnership initiatives dealing with the application of Agenda 21, crime prevention, children in deprived areas or regeneration.[81] Local authorities have been encouraged to establish multi-agency organisations – the LSPs – to co-ordinate the development of the many agencies. Many of the partnership schemes, such as Education Action Zones, require local authorities to take the initiative in working with other private, voluntary or public agencies in order to bid for government funds to revive run-down facilities and in some cases the implementation of policy remains predominantly in local authority hands. However, some schemes require the local authority to step back from the management of the partnerships they have promoted. The National Strategy for Neighbourhood Renewal, co-ordinated nationally through the Cabinet Office, was established to deal with the problem of multi-faceted urban deprivation in the most run-down and neglected communities of England and Wales. The scheme provides funding to partnership groups forged by local authorities for deprived communities to enable local people to sponsor the regeneration of their areas in relation to specific community problems. The areas covered are generally the size of a small parish, or French commune, although located in areas governed by monolithic unitary authorities. Once established, it is the partners rather than the local authority that manage the initiative, and in many cases they have a majority of representatives elected from the neighbourhood in which they are based with a minority presence of local councillors. An executive director is normally appointed as the full-time manager of the project.[82] The election turn-out for these neighbourhood groups, according to Shaw and Davidson, has to date been generally much higher than for the local authority elections for the same area.[83] The initiative has, in effect, created a further strand of ad hoc, semi-elected, limited-purpose, as opposed to single-purpose, local governance in addition to the existing local government structures.

In the late nineteenth century politicians and civil servants grasped the value of joining-up the chaotic patchwork of the many separate ad hoc agencies engaged in limited projects for delivering community services. Their policies, as I have discussed in earlier chapters, have led to the creation of multi-purpose local authorities throughout Britain which, outside the major cities, were divided into a strategic county tier and smaller authorities that in many cases embraced locally recognised communities. The value of community government had been strongly recognised also by many, although not all the creators of the late nine-teenth-century system. However, throughout the twentieth century the proponents of community declined in the courts of Westminster to create large-scale, sub-regional, multi-purpose local governments. The joined-up and community initiatives of the Blair governments are now a response to the long-term, gradual but insidious undermining of any semblance of community government. Their response appears to be a return to the nine-teenth-century Chadwickian expediency of ad hoc solutions creating fragmentation, forgetting the late nineteenth-century concern to ensure that disparate policy-making could be resolved by multi-purpose, joined-up, local councils. Perhaps it will dawn on future governments that the conflicting goals of ensuring co-ordinated policy and service delivery, on the one hand, and community involvement, on the other, could be secured by establishing a tier of community-based, multi-purpose, elected local authorities as characterises most other local government systems in Western liberal democracies.

The 2006 White Paper,[84] while further reinforcing the trend to partnership working, has at least recognised the potential role of multi-purpose geographical communities rather than single-purpose communities in helping citizens participate in the governance of their neighbourhoods. It proposes that local areas within urban authorities can petition for parish status with the assumption that such requests are viewed with some favour and that parishes would also have a strategic duty to provide for the well-being of their communities. Such proposals are far from rediscovering the ideals behind some proponents of the 1894 'Parishes' Act or the values underlying the French communal system, but they may mark the beginnings of a sea change in attitudes to community and participation.

Local government in Scotland and Wales

Devolution has established a possibility that the arrangements for local governance in different provinces of Britain could become increasingly diverse and evolve in different directions just as British local government has departed over the last 100 years from Irish practice and over several centuries from French or US practice. Evidence to suggest that this will happen is as yet far from clear. Any radical deviation would require not only differences in sovereignty but also social and economic differences in the regimes that underlie their policy development. Partly to alleviate fears of domination of local government in Scotland by the new Scottish Assembly and Executive, before the Scotland Act was passed, Donald Dewar established a Commission under the chairmanship of former Chief Executive for Strathclyde Neil McIntosh to report on the relationship between the devolved system of government and the local authorities. Presented in 1999, the report argued that the principle of subsidiarity should apply to central–local relations and that the Scottish Assembly would have to show good reason why it should take powers from any lower tier of government. The report proposed the creation both of a covenant between central government and the local authorities to set out their respective spheres of interest and of a joint consultative council between local representatives and members of the Scottish Parliament and also a similar forum between ministers and local leaders. McIntosh further recommended legislation to allow Scottish local authorities a power of general competence. The immediate response from the Scottish

Executive was to create a leadership forum of Scottish ministers and local authority leaders and to consult, but not act, on the issue of general competence.[85]

As Scottish devolution unfolds it appears that its local government may not become an exact clone of the English system. Some aspects of post-2000 English legislation have been adapted by the Scottish Executive to apply to the Province's local authorities. Scotland's local authorities are financed through a framework of grants from the Executive, a business rate set and distributed from Edinburgh and a locally determined council tax, accruing, as in England, only some 20 per cent of local government revenue. The BV idea has been accepted and approval, and monitoring of standards is under the guidance of a section of the Scottish Audit Commission which can, however, develop standards different from those applied in England. The Assembly has also followed the English trend of developing local authorities as strategic authorities, especially in relation to housing, although the Housing (Scotland) Act 2001 does not push local authorities down the track of divesting their property to housing associations as firmly as does the Blair Government. In its restructuring of decision-making, the Scottish Executive has not pursued English practice. The McIntosh report was noncommittal about establishing executive cabinet-style government, recommending that authorities reviewed their structures. Very few adopted a cabinet structure. The largest authority to do so was Edinburgh, but the city's lead was not followed by Glasgow or Aberdeen. Scottish authorities have nevertheless developed a variety of innovative decision-making structures. Several authorities that, like Aberdeenshire, cover sparsely populated territory have created area committees. Stirling has subsumed most business into three major decision-making committees. Scotland has also been more adventurous on reform of voting and established single transferable voting for local elections.[86]

The Welsh Assembly, with less freedom to develop its own policies, has generally followed English practice in relation to local government. A Council for joint policy-making between Welsh local authorities and the Assembly was formed by the 1988 Government of Wales Act which, under the chair of the Welsh Local Government Minister, meets quarterly with local authority and local public agency representatives and establishes joint working parties on policy issues. The Welsh Executive establishes policy agreements with its twenty-two principal local authorities to set what are, in effect, BV performance targets under which efficiency can be measured, and these are evaluated under a Programme for Improvement by the Wales Audit Office. A policy statement of the Welsh Assembly in 2002 set out an overall framework in which local government in the Principality should operate.[87] This included a requirement to operate within the framework of the 2000 Local Government Act and hence requires the adoption of one of the four possible forms of cabinet-style government. Only one referendum has taken place for the adoption of an elected executive mayor in 2004, and the proposal for Ceredigion was heavily defeated.[88] Thus, in the early years of Welsh devolution, while there is closer consultation between the Assembly and Welsh local governments than in England or Scotland, there is little sign of any interest in breaking away from English procedures. Such practice may reflect not only the limited freedom of the Welsh Assembly to amend English law but the predominance of Labour control in the relatively small Principality that can therefore sustain close informal ties and understandings between national and community leaders.

New Labour and the future

Since 1997 a restless New Labour leadership has been trying to resolve its ideas on the role and purpose of local governance. Despite the enthusiasm of *Local Government Closer to the People* the strategy for elected mayors has thus far been taken up by few authorities and has occasioned no significant increase in electoral turnout. Any semblance of powers of general competence, as suggested in the opening sections of the 2000 Local Government Act, have yet to be seriously realised and most experiments on voting methods seem to have been abandoned. On finance Lyons in an interim report has rehearsed the grounds covered by the many surveys on rating and the balancing of local and nationally raised expenditure that have been chronicled in this book without any sign of the Government resolutely abandoning a system dominated increasingly by central controls.[89]

The party is now caught in a serious dilemma. There is a growing awareness among Labour leaders, perhaps long-established among many Liberal Democrats and also emerging within the Cameron 'social responsibility' wing of the Conservatives, that the partial failures of the initial New Labour strategy to revive public enthusiasm for and participation in local government reflects widespread alienation from large and relatively powerless units of local government that are too distant from the continuing interest of many citizens in their local neighbourhoods. The 2005 *Manifesto* stated, alongside a suggestion that parish councils be created in London that 'People need a sense of control over their own neighbourhood. Not a new tier of neighbourhood government but new powers for the problems that confront them.'[90] Such a mixed message does not suggest certainty as to the way ahead, but into 2006 David Miliband in the newly established post of Minister for the Communities has been associated with calls for local neighbourhood government. However, along with the talk of neighbourhood authorities is the continuing hostility to multi-tier structures of local government, with suggestions emerging in the press, presumably from informed leaks, that county councils are to be abolished. The underlying tensions in New Labour will undoubtedly derive from differing views among senior ministers as to the future and value of local government, as was illustrated by the failure of the initiatives on the English regions but it reflects also a deeper concern. BV may be now well entrenched in local government operations, but it is a policy that is essentially motivated by the legacy which New Labour, as with many of its predecessors, inherited from Lloyd George and Addison. New Labour has staked its reputation in part on improving local services, and once governments make such a promise and are required by the media to maintain it, they cannot afford to allow local governments to be local in the sense that their policies derive from community opinion which may differ sharply on matters of taxation, service priority and social equity from those of central government.

Notes

1 S. H. Beer, 'New Labour: Old Liberalism', in S. White (ed.), *New Labour: The Progressive Future* (Basingstoke: Palgrave, 2001).

2 P. Seyd, *The Rise and Fall of the Labour Left* (Basingstoke: Macmillan, 1987), p. 145.

3 Labour Party, *Manifesto: New Hope for Britain* (London: Labour Party, 1983), p. 49.

4 *Ibid.*, pp. 30–1.

5 *Ibid.*, p. 31.

6 Labour Party, *Local Government Reform in England and Wales* (London: Labour Party, 1987).

7 Labour Party, *Manifesto: Britain Will Win With Labour* (London: Labour Party, 1987), pp. 9–12.

8 *Ibid.*

9 Labour Party, *Manifesto: It's Time to Get Britain Working Again* (London: Labour Party, 1992).

10 Labour Party, *Local Government Reform in England and Wales*, p. 7.

11 T. Blair, *New Britain: My Vision of a Young Country* (London: Fourth Estate, 1996), pp. 70, 220, 313–14.

12 *Ibid.*, pp. 313–14.

13 T. Blair, *The Third Way: New Politics for the New Century* (London: Fabian Society, 1998), p. 4.

14 P. Stephens, *Tony Blair: The Price of Leadership* (London: Politico's, 2004), pp. 29–30.

15 Macmurray emphasises, however, the family as the quintessence of community as it is comprised of selfless relationships based on affection for others, unlike a society that is a group united solely by common aims. Thus government and also local government for Macmurray, and probably for Blair, is not the ideal of community: J. Macmurray, *Persons in Relation* (London: Faber & Faber, 1961), pp. 156–7.

16 Blair, *The Third Way*, p. 16.

17 G. Stoker, *Transforming Local Governance: From Thatcherism to New*

Labour (Basingstoke: Palgrave, 2003), p. 83.

18 UNISON formed from the merger of NALGO, NUPE and the health union COHSE in 1993.

19 Commission for Local Democracy, *Taking Charge: The Rebirth of Local Democracy* (London: Municipal Journal, 1995).

20 *Financial Times*, 4 June 1997, p. 9.

21 D. Walker, 'Councils to seek value in service', *Independent*, 3 June 1997, p. 2.

22 *Ibid.*, p. 16.

23 D. Walker, 'Councils told to embrace a new era', *Independent*, 24 July 1997, p. 6.

24 Scottish Office, *Scotland's Parliament*, Cm 3658 (London: HMSO, 1997); Welsh Office, *The Government's Proposals for a Welsh Assembly*, Cm 3718 (London: HMSO, 1997).

25 The Scotland Act, 1998: Eliz. II, c. 46.

26 The Government of Wales Act, 1998: Eliz. II, c. 38.

27 V. Bogdanor, *Devolution in the United Kingdom* (Oxford: Oxford University Press, 2nd edn, 1999), p. 260.

28 T. Travers, *The Politics of London* (Basingstoke: Palgrave, 2004), p. 46; Blair was persuaded by journalist Simon Jenkin who had established the Commission for Local Democracy.

29 Labour Party, *A Voice for London* (London: Labour Party, 1996).

30 Labour Party, *New Labour: Because Britain Deserves Better* (London: Labour Party, 1997), p. 34.

31 Travers, *Politics of London*, p. 47.

32 DETR, *New Leadership for London: The Government's Proposals for a Greater London Authority*, Cm 3924 (London: HMSO, 1997).

33 DETR, *A Mayor and Assembly for London*, Cm 3897 (London: HMSO, 1998).

34 Travers, *Politics of London*, p. 62.

35 *Ibid.*, pp. 75–7.

36 Interview with Richard Caborn, MP.

37 Alan Whitehead, leader of Southampton City Council and, from 1997 MP for Southampton West and Under Secretary of State for Local Government 2001–3, with Professor John Stewart were advising on this design: interview with Alan Whitehead.

38 *Ibid.*

39 The Regional Development Agencies Act, 1998: Eliz. II, c. 45.

40 Chandler, *Local Government*, pp. 31–2.

41 Department of Transport, Local Government and the Regions, *Your Region, Your Choice*, Cm 5511 (London: HMSO, 2002).

42 Eliz. II, 1999, c. 45.

43 DETR, *Modern Local Government: In Touch With the People*, Cm 4014 (London: HMSO, 1998).

44 T. Blair, *Leading the Way: New Vision for Local Government* (London: IPPR, 1998).

45 *Ibid.*, p. 11.

46 *Ibid.*, pp. 11–12.

47 DETR, *Modern Local Government*, para. 7.28.

48 Department for Communities and Local Government, *Strong and Prosperous Communities*, Cm 6939 (London, HMSO, 2006).
49 The Local Government Act, 1999: Eliz. II, c. 27.
50 D. Wilson and C. Game, *Local Government in the United Kingdom* (Basingstoke: Palgrave, 3rd edn, 2002), p. 338.
51 DETR, *Strong Local Leadership – Quality Public Services*, Cm 5372 (London: HMSO, 2001).
52 The Local Government Act, 2000: Eliz. II, c. 22.
53 It was also possible for a local authority to propose some other form of cabinet government for approval by the ODPM, although no authority has so far taken up the offer.
54 Travers, *Politics of London*, p. 117.
55 R. Ashworth, 'Toothless tigers? Councillor perceptions of new scrutiny arrangements in Welsh local government', *Local Government Studies*, 29:2 (2003), pp. 1–18.
56 A web search of newspapers using LEXIS/NEXIS for the term 'scrutiny committee' for the week 24 June–1 July 2005 revealed 40 articles reporting local authority scrutiny committees' findings and for the week 22–9 Nov. 2006, 31 separate articles.
57 S. Snape, 'A role for non-executive councillors?', in G. Stoker and D. Wilson (eds), *British Local Government into the 21st Century* (Basingstoke: Palgrave, 2004).
58 N. Rao, 'Options for change: cabinets or the status quo?', *Local Government Studies*, 29:1 (2003), pp. 1–16.
59 C. Rallings, M. Trasher and D. Cowling, 'Mayoral referendums and elections', *Local Government Studies*, 28:4 (2002), pp. 70–4.
60 Rao, 'Options for change', pp. 1–16.
61 A remembrance of an event in the Napoleonic Wars where credulous locals hanged a monkey which ill-fate had washed up on their shores under the belief that this was, if not Napoleon himself, at least one of his soldiers.
62 Rallings, Trasher and Cowling, 'Mayoral referendums and elections', p. 88.
63 Labour Party, *New Labour: Because Britain Deserves Better*, p. 34.
64 H. Atkinson and S. Wilks-Heeg, *Local Government from Thatcher to Blair* (Cambridge: Polity Press, 2000), p. 256.
65 J. D. Stewart, *Modernising British Local Government: An Assessment of Labour's Reform Programme* (Basingstoke: Palgrave, 2003), p. 230.
66 The Local Government Act, 2003: Eliz. II, c. 26.
67 A. Travers, 'Local government finance: busy going nowhere?', in G. Stoker and D. Wilson (eds), *British Local Government into the 21st Century* (Basingstoke: Palgrave, 2004), p. 157.
68 See for example 'Public–private partnerships', *Financial Times*, 22 Nov. 2002.
69 *Guardian*, 'Society' section, 26 May 2004, p. 6.
70 D. J. Pell, 'Political commitment by the UK's environment cities to the expectations of Agenda 21', Ph.D thesis, Sheffield Hallam University, 1998, pp. 56–78; S. C. Young, 'Participation strategies and environmental politics: local Agenda 21', in G. Stoker (ed.), *The New Politics of British Local Governance* (Basingstoke: Macmillan, 2000).
71 The Schools Standards Framework Act 1998: Eliz. II, c. 31.

72 This followed the White Paper from the Department of Educations and Skills, *Higher Standards: Better Schools for All*, Cm 6677 (London: HMSO, 2005).
73 DETR, *Quality and Choice: A Decent Home for All* (London: HMSO, 2000).
74 *Ibid.*, para. 7.10.
75 Perri 6 (ed.), *Towards Holistic Governance* (Basingstoke: Palgrave, 2002),
76 The ambiguous term was coined in Peters and Waterman, *In Search of Excellence.*
77 DETR, *Modern Local Government*, para. 3.52; only paras 3.48–52 discuss decentralisation strategies.
78 *Ibid.*
79 H. Sullivan and C. Skelcher, *Working Across Boundaries: Collaboration in Public Services* (Basingstoke: Palgrave, 2002), pp. 228–37.
80 They are now being transformed into Education in Cities Action Zones.
81 Wilson and Game, *Local Government in the United Kingdom*, pp. 142–3, provides an accessible list of such schemes.
82 K. Shaw and G. Davidson, 'Community elections for regeneration partnerships: a new deal for local democracy?', *Local Government Studies*, 28:2 (2002), pp. 1–15.
83 *Ibid.*
84 Department for Communities and Local Government, *Strong and Prosperous Communities*, Cm 6939 (London: HMSO, 2006).
85 J. McFadden and M. Lazarowicz, *The Scottish Parliament: An Introduction* (Edinburgh: T. & T. Clark, 2nd edn, 2000), pp. 108–10.
86 The Local Governance (Scotland) Act, 2004: Eliz. II, asp 9.
87 Welsh Assembly Government, *Freedom and Responsibility in Local Government: A Policy Statement* (Cardiff: Welsh Assembly Government, 2002).
88 See 'News releases', 20 May 2004, online at www.ceredigion.gov.uk.
89 Lyons Inquiry into Local Government, *Consultation Paper and Interim Report* (London: HMSO, 2005).
90 Labour Party, *Britain Forward, Not Back: Manifesto for 2005* (London: Labour Party, 2005), chapter 6.

13

Accounting for the evolution of local government in Britain

There is no single factor that accounts for the distancing of the British system of local government from that of France or the USA. The evolution of the British system can be explained as an accretion of changes that have accumulated over the last 200 years and most significantly between 1900 and 1920. In 1832 the structure of sub-national government in Britain, although by no means a replica of the system in France or the USA was, nevertheless, far more comparable than is the case 175 years later. Each country had developed large sub-national territorial units. In Britain these were the counties, in America the states which, in turn, were sub-divided into counties, and in France a variety of institutions such as the *généralités* and *intendances*,[1] which were, after the 1789 revolution, transformed into the departments. Most towns and cities had their own governments and could trace their varied powers and decision-making structures to statutes and charters which gave them some independence from county or federal control. Rural areas were divided into community governments, the parish in Britain, the commune in France and the township or city in the USA, that allowed a measure of self-government for small villages, hamlets and scattered farms under the tutelage of the department, county or State government. In all of these systems inter-governmental relations could at one level be described as a dual polity in the sense that Bulpitt characterises early twentieth-century local government in Britain as a system in which 'national and local *politics* were largely divorced from one another'.[2]

Despite the similarities, there were some significant differences between Britain, France and the USA. The interplay between monarchy, bourgeoisie and peasantry that, as Barrington Moore suggests, explains the differing patterns of democracy which emerged in the three countries had important implications for inter-governmental relationships.[3] In the USA pressures for democracy was bound up with nationalism and nation-building, and led to the War of Independence against British aristocratic colonial rule and the foundation of a new federal nation based on ideals of freedom and the sanctity of property rights. Concern among landed and capitalist entrepreneurs to rid themselves of subservience to a specific powerful overlord, in this case the British, generated a Constitution that was designed, as theorised by Madison in the 'Federalist Papers', to prevent the emergence of rule by any single dominant group.[4] The ideology of a separation of powers involved securing locally as much freedom as possible through the application of what was, in effect, a high level of subsidiarity, with power passing down to the individual or the smallest community unit capable of providing collective services. In their purest form such values created the democratic township governments much praised by De Tocqueville that were modelled on the British structure of open vestries but were not subject to control by the unelected county magistrate.[5]

In France the interests of the landowners, closely co-ordinated by the dominant, central, monarchic government, suppressed pressures for reforms that might empower the bourgeoisie. The animosity between these estates, with the additional complexity of a divided and substantial peasantry, created the revolutionary century after 1789 in which the regime oscillated between centralising autocracy and more open democratic governance. Within this structure industrialisation could not keep pace with developments in the politically more stable Britain or the USA, and there remained a strong peasant community with a measure of political power in any democratic phase of government. The system eventually stabilised as a liberal democracy from the 1870s to establish a system of local government that was in formal terms highly centralised, mirroring the controls over localities built initially by Louis XIV and perfected by Napoleon I. The departments acted as agencies led by the prefect, a state-appointed civil servant, whose role was legally to ensure tutelage of the smallest organic element of the system of local governance. In practice, however, in its democratic phases the French prefectoral system could not be used as a means by which the centre rigidly controlled urban and rural areas. The dominance of monarchy in the *ancien régime* ensured that the French revolutions were not specifically national struggles between bourgeoisie and aristocracy but rather a patchwork of local rebellions, involving business interests and peasant farmers, against the centre. The democratic settlement therefore had to acknowledge the power of local notables in France who were accommodated within strongly established patron–client networks.[6] The local patron gained support from local electors to represent their interests in Paris. The local notable ensured in national political bargaining that in practice the prefect was not wholly a creature of the centre and would follow local custom and interest as much as he would the legal requirements of the State, and reconcile their differences in the National Assembly and Senate.

In Britain the 'dual state' was more apparent than real. Parliament was predominantly the forum in which landowners settled their differences and established the rules of the game, allowing them considerable freedom to govern the communities in which they had an interest. Lords and MPs respected each others' commercial interests and for most of the country they could shut other classes out of local politics by establishing the rules for the local system or the concession of special privileges. Nevertheless, the ruling class feared a centralising autocratic government, as had been attempted by the Stuarts, that could, as in France, seriously tax their estates and commercial interests. The dominant landowning interest consequently developed strongly entrenched myths of the free-born Englishman whose home was his castle. Both Whig and Tory supporters in the eighteenth and into the nineteenth century were deeply antagonistic to reforms that suggested any measure of centralisation. Industrialisation was to challenge this *status quo*. Manufacturers needed a Parliament to encourage free trade rather than the protection of land, and as long as the ownership of estates was the key to the House of Commons, the distribution of the majority of seats to decayed chartered towns was a major barrier to their political progress.

In Britain democracy emerged through compromise and concession. During the early nineteenth century democratic pressures created plutocracy, as the mercantile and manufacturing classes, based largely in the cities, pressed major landowners for a share in power through a uniform franchise based on the ownership of capital rather than land and ancient custom. The 1832 Electoral Reform Act transferred seats in the House of Commons from small, decayed boroughs dominated by landed interests to the larger industrialising towns. The landowners did not abandon power but were obliged to live with new money from commerce and industry and to concede power to them in the geographic areas, largely the industrialising northern towns, where they had the greatest economic interest. The liberal breakthrough of 1832 immediately accelerated a reform of the system of local government in the towns. Throughout the eighteenth century, manufacturing and commercial interests were securing control over local infrastructures by establishing improvement commissions through private acts. The Municipal Reform Act of 1835 consolidated this trend, allowing the larger industrialising towns to establish councils elected by a rate-payer franchise and, therefore, brought to power local industrial and commercial interests who were concerned to develop the infrastructure of their area in order to secure a competitive advantage over entrepreneurs in other towns. In many smaller established boroughs the legislation allowed outmoded cartels of craftsmen to be replaced by manufacturing interests. Not all rate-payers in eligible towns leapt at the opportunities open to them, given that they were fuelled by relatively high taxation, but, by the end of the nineteenth century the initiative created the great city governments of Birmingham, Manchester and Leeds. The major cities in Britain, as in the USA, developed and owned water and sewage industries, generated gas and electricity and organised effective local transport using the wealth of the city. After the 1832 Reform Act, liberal capitalists could more easily use their wealth and influence to extend the powers of their municipalities through private acts which became large enough to establish a pattern of control that ensured the borough implemented most of its services rather than relying on private contractors.

The liberal breakthrough did not have such a marked effect on rural society even though the creation of the reformed Poor Law is seen as the quintessentially major legacy of the immediate post-1832 Whig governments. The most immediate impact was that legislation relating to local matters began to be established on a uniform country-wide basis rather than being the accretion of many separate acts tailored to the needs of a specific community at a specific time. This still enabled magistrates to exert a dominant influence over the countryside. The creation of a reformed Poor Law under a centrally supervised government agency was far from a resounding success in terms of securing central control over non-industrial rural society. The consolidated Poor Law boards could find support both among liberals and Tories as a means of reducing the heaviest economic burden on the parish, but it did little to seriously diminish the power of the local landowner over the structures of rural governance, as they could in practice still exert considerable influence over local boards of guardians. The dual polity thus survived the 1832 liberal entry into the political system. Palmerston informed the Commons in 1854 that 'he thought it quite impossible to overrate the national importance of employing the persons connected with the different districts of the country in administering the affairs of those districts'.[7]

Histories of the development of local government in the nineteenth century focus much attention on the growth of a centralising zeal within government and the emerging Civil Service.[8] Chadwick's importance as a reformer in the development of local government can, however, be overplayed. The development of Whitehall consensus in relation to central control had to wait until the early twentieth century. The growth of *laissez faire* and utilitarian liberalism created a current of highly contradictory thought among the liberal intelligentsia who considered themselves to be at the cutting edge of policy innovation. On the one hand utilitarianism suggested that in an emerging democracy Parliament should be dominant over local interests. If supplying clean water promoted the general happiness, then government, as the executive of Parliament, should guide this policy. However, Adam Smith and Ricardo had counselled *laissez faire* as regards the relationship between the central State and the economy, and there developed an equally important strand of opposition to centralism from agrarian radicals such as Cobden, in the first half of the century, and later from the Anti-Centralization Union of Toulmin Smith advocating a De Tocqueville style of direct democracy and subsidiarity.

In the nineteenth century many of the problems of modernisation could have been administratively resolved by transferring issues such as responsibility for highways and the poor to the larger counties but radicals were opposed to moving functions from the more democratic parish to the unelected landowner dominated county while Tory, Whig and many *laissez faire* liberals objected to a centralised solution as advocated by supporters of Bentham. Allowing commercial, privatised interest to secure change was also not a suitable answer. Even where this may have seemed initially practicable, as in the provision of turnpike roads, lack of capital ensured that the services were too deficient in quality to be acceptable and also were costly to local users.[9] The solution to these conflicting pressures was the creation of the numerous ad hoc local government agencies for special purposes, elected largely through a rate-payer franchise that characterised what was seen as the muddled structure of mid-Victorian local governance, although during the twentieth century the quest for uniformity has perhaps overplayed the problems caused by ad hoc governance.

Creeping centralisation

Although in Britain concessions by landowners to capitalists did not promote strong moves towards centralisation there were forces at work that were slowly undermining the dual polity. Landowners were never wholly territorial but through inter-marriage and purchase could have estates in various parts of the country and hence many owed little loyalty to a specific locality. In addition, the eighteenth-century State could accommodate professionals, such as Lord Sidmouth, who through ability and deference could reach high office by national service irrespective of local loyalties and who subsequently had little interest in the concepts of subsidiarity and community.[10] The absence of a centralising monarchy in Britain ensured that, in contrast to France, there was far less concern among industrialists to establish a peripheral power base to offset the dominance of national government. Capitalists in the 1832 compromise gained a share of power in Parliament and government. They could, therefore, buy into the arrangement, previously benefiting largely the substantial landowner, that local authorities have a high level of discretion on the grounds that the elite should be left to take care of their localised interests and, if necessary, reconcile their differences through the mediation of their peers in Parliament. Capital was moreover soon courted by the Conservative Party, as built by Peel and perfected by Disraeli, and was therefore increasingly not represented solely by radicals and the Liberal Party.

The comparative decline in agricultural wealth in relation to industrial growth was to generate demands from landowners that they shared an unfair burden of local taxation. By the late nineteenth century the campaign to decrease the rate for agricultural land was politically a powerful interest within the Conservative Party but could, in the long run, be conceded only by opening the door to further subsidies for rural services from the Exchequer which gave central government greater resources to supervise and manipulate service development. With the merging of the economic interests of landowners and capitalists as British agriculture became increasingly commercialised,[11] the old Tory squirearchy was increasingly prone to allowing, in relation to local controls, the application of greater central supervision of local service provision. These values combined to make centralising solutions to national problems an increasingly acceptable strategy, despite the established rhetoric condemning such theory. Modernising centralist liberals, such as Chadwick or Simon, were far from popular but could offer answers to problems of public health that worked, and hence began insidiously to build into the central bureaucracy values that supported a 'one size fits all' solution to policy problems.

These pressures led to the cautious introduction of central inspection that, in addition to the contested Poor Law inspectors, included the establishment of Her Majesty's Inspectors of Education in 1839, Police inspectorates in 1856 and the beginnings of local government auditing by central government in 1868. However, these changes in the late nineteenth century did not demonstrate that the nation had for those reasons begun the irrevocable march toward a local government system composed of a few large authorities with relatively little discretion. Britain was no different from France or the USA in having to adapt local government practice and capacity to changing technology. A similar trend modified the role of central and local governments in France and in the USA and required governments to establish a measure of social development through grants that built the need for central auditing. Auditing does not, however, necessitate excessive centralisation, and in Britain during the nineteenth century it proceeded with a light touch geared only to exposing the worst abuses of central largesse.[12] As in the USA, until the development of Johnson's 'Great Society', British local governments in 1900 were rarely obliged to take grants proffered by the centre and the majority of their tasks were permissive rather than mandatory.

The politics of redistribution

The most far reaching changes in intergovernmental relations in Britain emerged in the first decades of the twentieth century as a belated consequence of a mass franchise and greater working-class demand for redistributive welfare policies. Ideologically, these demands popularised New Liberal values and the belief that the State had a duty to secure equality of opportunity. Perceptive capitalists also realised the value of the State in ensuring the reproduction of labour. As a relatively wealthy polity, the British Government could also afford to adopt redistributive policies that could buy-off working-class dissent and yet still ensure government by the wealthy educated elite. The Liberal landslide of 1906 demonstrated the strength of popular support for New Liberal values. Both New Liberals and social democrats believed that expensive systems for social security could be achieved only through uniform provision funded and shaped by national rather than local government. These views applied not only to pensions and health insurance but to more localised schemes such as the provision of public housing. Addison, for example, considered local authorities to be inefficient and accepted only with reluctance that they were sufficiently adequate bodies to undertake Lloyd George's promise to build 'homes fit for heroes'.[13] Churchill and Beveridge saw little value in local authorities as a means of resolving unemployment. New Liberals had no time for the bureaucratic LGB which upheld the nineteenth-century values of the dual polity, stigmatised poverty and showed marked reluctance to promote nationally schemes for social welfare. Interventionist values were further promoted by the emergence of the Labour Party which took much of the erstwhile New Liberal electoral support from a divided Liberal Party. The Labour Party had, as Miliband and Howell[14] show, a veneer of cautious Fabian socialism but in practice became the embodiment of New Liberalism and gathered to its ranks advanced liberals such as Addison who found common ground with socialists wishing to see a Labour government impose equality of opportunity uniformly within the State. The power brokers between Left and Right in the party were, however, the trade unions whose leaders, like Bevin and Citrine, for the most part had little experience of or interest in local government. Their work in establishing country-wide unions led them to envisage national solutions through national rather than local pay bargaining as the route to raising the income and conditions of the working classes. Similarly the framework for equal opportunities required national rather than local solutions.

The rise of the Labour Party, with its rhetoric of socialism, further advanced centralisation by forcing Conservatives into establishing greater controls over local government as many believed that socialist councillors could use the local government system in urban areas to initiate egalitarian policies by adapting liberal zeal for municipalisation into a programme for the collective ownership of the means of production. Redistributive policies on workers' pay and Poor Law payments as pursued in Poplar had to be eradicated.[15] The rebellion that had been sparked off by the Labour councillors of Poplar may have been a local success, but its longer term effect was to ensure that Conservatives were far less amenable to an ethos in which local authorities should be left to pursue their own agendas. Within the Labour Party, Poplarism did nothing to alleviate suspicions of its more moderate New Liberal members.[16] The immediate consequence was a reluctance among the Conservative majority in Parliament to pass private acts creating further municipalised services or extended municipal boundaries, as had been the case prior to 1914.[17]

A further consequence of the success of the Labour Party in gaining seats and, by the 1920s, political control of many large city governments at the expense of local Conservative and Liberal politicians was to force out of town halls the businessmen and professionals who a generation earlier had built those magnificent palaces as gentlemen's clubs. In addition to the loss of seats, businessmen by the 1920s were becoming much less interested in serving within the local authority.[18] This may have also been the result of the growth of joint stock companies. As businesses merged into national concerns their infra-structure needs required resolution at a national level in several localities rather than within specific towns. An additional factor that set the British polity along a centralising trend was the emergence of increasingly centralised mass parties in Britain. Nomination to a safe parliamentary seat became dependent, not so much on patronage from diverse landowning factions, as in the early nineteenth century, but on the approval of party machines controlled by leaders who required far greater obedience in Parliament to sustain their party in power or to have a hope of forming a government following a general election. Party loyalty was far more important than loyalty to the locality.

In the USA tendencies towards the kind of substantial redistributive policies as characterised Poplarism were curbed by the internal political processes within cities and states without recourse to much intervention by federal government. The Democrats and occasionally the Republicans formed patron–client-based mass parties in the late nineteenth century that allowed local leaders to mobilise the working-class vote in exchange for a share in the spoils of municipal office. The more corrupt of these systems, for example Plunkett's Tammany Hall, New York,[19] or the 1920s machine politics of Chicago, could yield high levels of tax from business and industry, and secure positions in the city hall staff for loyal supporters as a form of crude social security. Later, some cities developed effective local systems for health care, secondary and higher education or social aid and welfare on a scale that was never permissible in Britain. Reaction against the high rates of the urban proletarian political machines mitigated fears that such a mode of government would lead to substantive nationwide socialist redistributive policies. From the late nineteenth century business leaders, alongside academics like Woodrow Wilson, initiated a reform movement to clean up urban government from what they saw as corrupt populist practices through reforms such as banning party political electoral contests, voting for councillors at large rather than on a ward basis and establishing structures dominated by a powerful mayor or a small group of commissioners. These strategies were aimed at removing party politics from local government and effectively gave power in many cities to the wealthy business interests with the funding and organisational skills to fight personal, apparently non-partisan, campaigns.[20] Their success ensured that the threat of serious redistributive policies which businesses felt would be ruinous to their commercial interests had ceased to be a major issue in most cities by the 1930s. In some eastern cities where there were strong radical movements the pattern of city-led munic-ipalisation continues to reflect the pattern of nineteenth-century Britain, epitomised by Joseph Chamberlain's Birmingham. The municipalisation of services, as much as they were established in US cities, was not seen to be the trojan horse of socialism and created little pressure on federal or state governments to exert greater controls over the cities.

In France the redistributive challenge led to the creation of nationally powerful communist and socialist parties and, as in Britain, more exten-sive social welfare redistributive policies than in the US, but, given the influence local interests could exert on the centre, the development of social welfare programmes required the consent and co-operation of local authorities. As Timothy Smith shows, French cities, such as Lyon with its socialist reformist Mayor Edouard Herriot, worked in co-operation with central government to provide the necessary funding to improve health and social welfare provision:

> Several years before the Conseil national de la resistance proclaimed the need for a truly national system of social security, the general council of the Rhone, the municipal councils of Lyon and Paris, and several others took steps to do their part. They called on the state to do its part too.[21]

These initiatives led to a piecemeal development of social policy between the two world wars that continued to involve State funding but nevertheless needed the co-operation of local interests to be effective.[22] It may be argued that in the early 1920s mayors of London boroughs were similarly demanding reforms from the State, but they encountered argu-ments from Lloyd George that the State was already doing as much as politically possible and, following him, Conservative administrations that, unlike a French coalition composed largely of local notables, were inclined to undermine what they saw as potentially hostile hotbeds of socialism.

Restructuring the system

By the early 1920s British local governance had reached a stage where it was evolving into a new organisational species from the systems of France and the US. From this point, the structures, functions and discretion of the systems could evolve in wholly different directions. The development of a centrally established welfare state in Britain created a gradual but insidi-ous circle of centralisation. Within a competitive pluralist democracy votes were to be won by securing better welfare services and, as these were being piloted by the centre the competing parties, tentatively at first but by the latter half of the twentieth century as a central plank in electoral contests, began vying with one another as to their capacity to deliver to citizens better redistributive services than their rivals. This trend was also enhanced by the media in Britain, which operated far more on a national than a local basis than in most liberal democracies, so that for the citizen issues affecting the locality became less and less communicated as opposed to the policies generated among party leaders and civil servants in London. The consequence of this development was the embedding of an assumption in Whitehall and Westminster that delivery of effective public service is a responsibility of central government and that it is electorally unthinkable to allow a local authority the power to determine for its own community standards of service provision different from those of a neighbouring area. Electoral necessity has also within the Labour Party and for many Liberal Democrats an ethical dimension in that both parties regard New Liberal ideals of equality of opportunity as a central foundation of their political values, and in 2006 under Cameron's leadership the Conservative Party's future seems to be framed by those values.

From the 1930s, as circumstances ensured that central government was increasingly obliged to involve itself in delivering policy at the local level, local authorities began to shed powers or, when they received new tasks from the centre such as planning responsibility, undertake these only under central supervision. Thus, in 1934 responsibility for Poor Law functions for the relief of poverty became a national function. The NHS in 1948 was not included within local government but was managed by unelected agencies steered, as Chadwick had always wanted, from Whitehall. Modernisation of productive gas, electricity or water services initiated and developed by local government, as in the USA, could not be even considered feasible through contractual arrangements between small local authorities and private or public suppliers. They had to be steered by national public monopolies whose efficiency was, in the final analysis, to be laid at the door of central government.

The attitude that the activities of local government required central supervision created the ground for the restructuring of the system in the 1950s and 1960s. Conservative fears in the 1930s that large urban authorities would harbour socialism had frozen the evolution of structures, despite, or perhaps because of, growing academic demands for larger, more professional, authorities that would generate economies of scale capable of resisting central controls. By the 1950s the widespread belief that a more mobile, commuting population had lost any sense of community, alongside the realisation in the Conservative Party that the possibility of socialism from the Labour Party could be safely discounted, created conditions in which, if a minister was minded to reform structures, change was possible. The reformist ministers emerged as Henry Brooke, who pushed through the restructuring of London, and Crossman and Walker, who managed the creation, in comparison to the European states or the USA, of the super-sized authorities of Britain. The eventual intention of many in Whitehall was to create, when possible, single-tier authorities, although remnants of rural loyalties within the Conservative Party countered the consummation of this trend.

Finance similarly followed the path to ever greater central control. Although throughout the twentieth century both politicians and official reports have extolled the sense of allowing localities to generate a greater proportion of their own finance, reality has obliged the reverse. A number of government departments, for example those responsible for education, pressed their preference for special grants to secure more control over their services. Even more serious were the pressures created by the growing public expectation that central government rather than localities was ultimately responsible not only for service quality but also service costs. To assuage the danger of leaking votes, central government by the 1960s increasingly was subsidising rates through general or direct grants.

The spiral to ever greater central controls was also, in part, developed and then heightened by the growing professionalisation and uniformity among members and officers of local councils. In general, local government officers in 1900 expected to progress to senior positions by promotion within their authorities. As senior officers were increasingly recruited from graduates, these posts were filled through a process of headhunting the best candidates nationally. Chief officers were no more bound to the loyalties of place than are the managers of major football teams. While councillors were required to be resident within their authorities many of the more able and ambitious saw service with their local authorities more as a stepping-stone to national political careers.

In the late 1970s R. A. W. Rhodes argued that the pattern of central–local relations that had emerged was not based on the subordination of localities to the role merely of agents of the centre or, from a contrasting perspective, partners of central government. They maintained considerable discretion, using their legal and financial resources and their legitimacy within the system to bargain with central government. It is not suggested here that local government has come to be solely an agent of the centre or a partner, although it is argued that those positions are not necessarily incompatible and that the state of central–local relations can be seen as encapsulating both characteristics of agency and partnership. For many councillors and local government officers, the centre was not always a constraining force, and many local authorities saw their role as working with central government to supply effective services. However, in as much as a partnership had developed, local government was much the junior partner, and if the centre was intent on pursuing a policy local authorities found it difficult, if not impossible, to resist as they could never match the resources of a central government that could, where necessary, change the rules of the game. The relationship may more be typified as stewardship, akin to the relationship between the eighteenth-century landowner and the stewards who managed their estates. The steward had considerable influence and on occasion was given complete authority over the management of an estate, but was always subject to interference if and when the landowning aristocrat left the high life he was leading in the gambling salons of London or Bath and decided to interest himself in some aspect of governance previously left to the steward.[23]

The generally accepted balance of interest between central and local government and many of the commonly held assumptions between councillors and local government officers, ministers and civil servants were, however, much eroded by the arrival of New Right values under the administrations of Thatcher and John Major. New Right values opposed the assumption that redistributive services should be provided largely by the public sector and that local authorities should be monolithic organisations supplying all aspects of their tasks on an 'in-house' basis. Exposure to private sector competition would create efficiency, would lower costs and, although never a stated aim, would turn many a non-profit-making service into a scheme through which capital could generate private profit. The tensions re-awakened the latent but growing militancy of left-wing grassroots activists that led to the confrontations which culminated in the rate-capping crisis of 1985. The capacity of the Thatcher administration to defeat this movement is indicative of the extent to which a focused central government can destroy local authority intransigence. Local socialism, while it left a legacy of re-awakening local authorities to their capacity to influence local economic development or to facilitate tolerance of diversity, was never likely to succeed in achieving the rather diverse aims of its proponents. Indeed, over time the effectiveness of the New Right views on the private provision of services within a strategy that was established by central and local authorities became, by the late 1980s, sufficiently absorbed into the partnership–stewardship framework of most local officers and politicians that by 1997 most local authorities had accepted the Government's perspective and established NPM practices, according to which they did not necessarily have to implement all their services.

In the context of local government, New Labour has more in common with turn-of-the-century Lloyd George's New Liberals than the Thatcher Conservatives have with the Conservative and Unionist Party of Lord Salisbury. Local government is for Blair, as it was for J. S. Mill, necessary as the means by which to implement principles determined by the centre to suit local circumstance. New Labour accepted the values of NPM and the enabling authority, but with less confidence in the New Right's view that the competitive market would ensure efficiency, and also harboured a distaste for the Conservative acceptance of inequity that flowed from such practice. By embracing the New Liberal goals of equality of opportunity within a competitive capitalist society, the Blair Government has with little difficulty re-forged a sound working partnership with local government. The ideals of equality of opportunity alongside the desperate need to ensure that the Government could deliver more efficient public service recast CCT into BV. The NPM values absorbed by Blair also motivated the Labour leadership to seek private sector management techniques

to resolve what were seen as local inefficiencies and so to adopt streamlined managing director and board, as the mayor and cabinet systems of
governing, to revive flagging local interests in the over-large local authorities. At the same time the Blair Government realised that many of the
worst pockets of deprivation were not authority-wide but were sunk in
much smaller communities that needed not only the injection of targeted
funds but a multi-dimensional resolution to problems, not all of which
spanned the domain of local authority powers. The consequence, in the
absence of any semblance of neighbourhood representative organisations
in urban areas or parishes with effective powers, is the re-emergence of ad
hoc neighbourhood solutions to highly localised problems which are in an
uneasy partnership or sometimes outright rivalry with the local government systems. If pursued further such strategies would lead to the
Balkanisation of most local authorities. After some seven years of pursuing those goals the pay-off in terms of public enthusiasm for the local
government system has not emerged, and at the time of writing some
segments of the Labour Party are at last turning to the possibility that
public indifference to the present structure may reflect that, in its present
format, it is far from being 'in touch with the people'.

Behind the arguments are crucial ethical issues which cannot be
resolved in this study. Britain and its party leaders are faced with resolving serious ethical dilemmas over the role that local government should
play in society. On the one hand, few in today's society would wish to
deny the principles of equality of opportunity for all citizens, and there is
much to be said against harbouring a situation in which the capacity of an
individual to gain a good education, health care and the chance of
employment is determined by the policies of his or her local authority,
however democratic that authority might be. Nevertheless, it is also unacceptable, and indeed arguably unrealistic, to expect central government to
determine in detail the implementation of services to a particular community or to govern in a form that does not take counsel from local opinions
that may differ in different parts of the nation. There is, moreover, a
strong ethical argument favouring freedom for the individual or for
groups of individuals who wish to undertake activities of advantage to
themselves that have little consequence to others.[24] New Labour governments face the problem of reconciling these issues, which might perhaps
be better achieved if we can govern ourselves through neighbourhood
authorities on matters affecting small communities, as in France or the
USA, and through one or two tiers of larger authorities where a community of greater population is significantly affected.

Notes

1 V. A. Schmidt, *Democratizing France: The Political and Administrative History of Decentralisation* (Cambridge: Cambridge University Press, 1990), p. 14.

2 J. Bulpitt, *Territory and Power in the United Kingdom* (Manchester: Manchester University Press, 1983), p. 235; the italics are Bulpitt's.

3 Barrington Moore Jr, *The Social Origins of Dictatorship and Democracy* (Harmondsworth: Penguin Books, 1969).

4 A. Syed, *The Political Theory of American Local Government* (New York: Random House, 1966).

5 A. de Tocqueville, *Democracy in America*, ed. J. P. Mayer (London: Fontana Press, 1994), pp. 61–80.

6 Schmidt, *Democratizing France*, pp. 389–40.

7 Hansard, vol. 138, col. 1266, June 1854.

8 Smellie, *History of Local Government*.

9 Webb and Webb, *The Story of the King's Highway*, pp. 199ff.

10 F. M. L. Thompson, *English Landed Society in the Nineteenth Century* (London: Routledge & Kegan Paul, 1963), p. 180, notes that Lord Sidmouth rarely visited his estates in Devon, which were inherited by his son in a very run-down condition.

11 Commercialisation of agriculture is used here, as it is by Barrington Moore, to refer to the consolidation of estates into large farms manufacturing produce for sale on a national or international market.

12 Redlich and Hirst, *Local Government in England*, vol. 2, p. 102.

13 Addison Papers, C150, fo. 141.

14 R. Miliband, *Parliamentary Socialism* (London: George Allen & Unwin, 1961); D. Howell, *British Social Democracy* (London: Croom Helm, 1976).

15 Branson, *Poplarism 1919–1925*.

16 *Ibid.*

17 Keith-Lucas and Richards, *History of Local Government in the Twentieth Century*, p. 39.

18 J. D. Dearlove, *The Reorganisation of British Local Government* (Cambridge: Cambridge University Press, 1979), pp. 79–105; G. Montague-Harris, *Municipal Self-Government in Britain* (London: P. S. King, 1939), pp. 36–8; E. L. Hasluck, *Local Government in England* (Cambridge: Cambridge University Press, 2nd edn, 1949), pp. 45–58.

19 W. L. Riordon, *Plunkitt of Tammany Hall* (New York: E. P. Dutton, 1963).

20 D. R. Judd, *The Politics of American Cities: Private Power and Public Policy* (Boston, MA: Little, Brown & Co., 1979), pp. 87–117.

21 T. B. Smith, *Creating the Welfare State in France, 1880 –1940* (Montreal: McGill–Queens University Press, 2003), p. 189.

22 *Ibid.*

23 Chandler, *Local Government Today*, pp. 95–8.

24 As implied but never developed by J. S. Mill in *On Liberty*, in *John Stuart Mill: Three Essays*, ed. R. Wollheim (Oxford, Oxford University Press, 1975), p. 125.

Appendices

Appendix 1

Table A1 *Changes in borough and county borough functions 1875–2000*

Function	1875	1925	2000
Police and fire services	X	X	
Education		X	X
Housing		X	X
Planning		X	X
Social services			X
Hospitals		X	
Gas	X	X	X
Electricity		X	
Transport		X	
Highways	X	X	X
Water		X	X
Markets	X	X	X
Libraries	X	X	X

Appendix 2

Table A2 *Expenditure (£10 millions) of local authorities in Britain 1913–2002*

Years	Expenditure
1913–14	120
1924–25	284
1933–34	368
1946–47	711
1956–57	1,503
1966–67	3,664
1976–77	4,095
1986–87	5,899
1996–97	7,072
2001–2	7,859

Sources: Data to 1966–67 from G. Rhodes, 'Local government finance 1918–1966', in *Report of the Royal Commission on Local Government Finance* (London, HMSO, 1976) after 1966–67 from ODP (2004) Local Government Financial Statistics (London: HMSO).

Appendix 3

Table A3 *Average populations of lower tiers of local government systems and voting turnout*

	Average population[a] of lower tier	% Turnout Local[b]	% Turnout National[c]
Britain Metropolitan, non-metro-politan districts and unitary authorities	139,300	30	59[d]
Belgium Municipalities	17,000	80	91
Denmark Municipalities	19,000	80	87
Ireland Cities and boroughs	93,000	62	66
France Communes	1,500	68	72[e]
Germany Gemeinden	9,000	72	82
Italy Communes	7,120	85	87
Netherlands Municipalities	49,000	88	90
Portugal Municipalities	32,349	60	61
Spain Municipalities	4,877	64	69
Sweden (1985) Municipalities[f]	29,200	88	90

Notes

[a] National populations from International Institute for Democracy and Electoral Assistance (IDEA), online at www.idea.int; number of authorities from www.carlbro/library/subnat/RLGinEU.

[b] Rallings, Thrasher and Downe (1966), 'Enhancing local electoral turnout', cited in DETR, *Modern Local Government: In Touch With the People*, para. 1.12.

[c] IDEA.

[d] General election 2001.

[e] Parliamentary election.

[f] Number of authorities and local turnout for 1985 from A. Gustafsson, *Local Government in Sweden* (Stockholm, Swedish Institute, 1988).

Bibliography

Archived papers

Addison, Christopher, Bodleian Library, Oxford.
Asquith, Herbert, Bodleian Library, Oxford.
Attlee, Clement, Bodleian Library, Oxford.
Bright, John, British Library, London.
Brougham (Lord), British Library, London.
Burns, John, British Library, London.
Chadwick, Edwin, University College Library, London.
Chamberlain, Joseph, University of Birmingham Library, Birmingham.
Chamberlain, Neville, University of Birmingham Library, Birmingham.
Cobden, Richard, British Library, London.
Conservative Party Archives, Bodleian Library, Oxford.
Dodson, J. G. (Lord Monk-Bretton), Bodleian Library, Oxford.
Disraeli, Benjamin, Bodleian Library, Oxford.
Gladstone, William, British Library, London.
Labour Party Archives, People's History Museum, University of
    Manchester.
Lloyd George, David, House of Lords, London.
Parkes, Joseph, University College Library, London.
Passfield Papers (Sydney and Beatrice Webb), London School of
    Economics, London.
Peel, Robert, British Library, London.
Place, Francis, British Library, London.
Liverpool, Lord, British Library, London.
Newman Diaries, National Archive.

Interviews

Richard Caborn MP
Alan Whitehead MP
Patrick Jenkin MP

Official papers

Audit Commission (1984) *The Impact on Local Authorities' Economy: Efficiency and Effectiveness of the Block Grant Distribution System*, London, Audit Commission.

Audit Commission (1990) *We Can't Go On Meeting Like This: The Changing Role of Local Authority Members*, Management Papers No. 8, London, Audit Commission.

AMC Minutes (1907) Meeting of a Special Committee of the Council and Representatives of Distress Committees, 12th December 1907 (Birmingham University Library).

Balfour, A. J. (chair) (1901) *Royal Commission on Local Taxation: Final Report*, Cd 638, London, HMSO.

Beveridge, W. H. (chair) (1942) *Social Insurance and Allied Services*, Cmd 6404, London, HMSO.

Board of Education (1926) *The Education of the Adolescent* (Hadow report), London, HMSO.

Board of Education (1938) *Report on Secondary Education* (Spens report), London, HMSO.

Board of Trade (1940) *Report of the Royal Commission on the Distribution of Industrial Population* (Barlow report), Cmd 6153, London, HMSO.

County Councils' Association (1943) *Local Government Reform: Final Report*, 18 Feb.

Department of Education and Science (1977) *A New Partnership for our Schools*, London, HMSO.

Department of Education and Skills (2005) *Higher Education: Better Schools for All*, Cm 6677, London, HMSO.

DoE (1971*) Local Government in England: Government Proposals for Reorganisation*, Cmnd 4584, London, HMSO.

DoE (1971) *Fair Deal for Housing*, Cmnd 4728, London, HMSO.

DoE (1971) *The Future Shape of Local Government Finance*, Cmnd 4741, London, HMSO.

DoE (1975) *Local Government Finance (England and Wales)*, Cmnd 209, London: HMSO.

DoE (1977) *Report of the Committee on the Remuneration of Councillors* (Robinson report), Cmnd 7010, London, HMSO.

DoE (1979) *Organic Change in Local Government*, Cmnd 7457, London, HMSO.

DoE (1981) *Alternatives to the Domestic Rates*, Cmnd 8449, London, HMSO.

DoE (1983) *Streamlining the Cities*, Cmnd 9063, London, HMSO.

DoE (1986) *Paying for Local Government*, Cmnd 9714 London, HMSO.

DoE (1986) *The Conduct of Local Authority Business* (Widdecombe report), Cmnd 9797, 4 vols, London, HMSO.

DoE (1987) *Housing: The Government's Proposals*, Cm 214, London, HMSO.

DoE (1993) *Community Leadership and Representation: Unlocking the Potential, Report of the Working Party on the Internal Management of Local Authorities in England*, London, HMSO.

DoE (1997) *Leadership for London: The Government's Proposals for a Greater London Authority*, Cm 3924, London, HMSO.

DoE (1998) *A Mayor and Assembly for London*, Cm 3897, London, HMSO.

DoE and LAAs (1972) *The New Local Authorities: Management and Structure* (Bains report), London, HMSO.

DoE and Welsh Office (1971) *Local Government Finance*, Cmnd 4813, London, HMSO.

DETR (1997) *New Leadership for London: The Government's Proposals for a Greater London Authority*, Cm 3924, London, HMSO.

DETR (1998) *A Mayor and Assembly for London*, Cm 3897, London, HMSO.

DETR (1998) *Modern Local Government: In Touch with the People*, Cm 4014, London, HMSO.

DETR (2000) *Quality and Choice: A Decent Home for All*, London, HMSO.

DETR (2001) *Strong Local Leadership – Quality Public Services*, Cm 5372, London, HMSO.

DETR (2002) *Your Region Your Choice*, Cm 5511, London, HMSO.

Department of Health (1988) *Caring for People: Community Care in the Next Decade and Beyond*, Cm 849, London, HMSO.

Department of Health and Social Security (1968) *The Organisation and Structures of the Medical and Related Services in England and Wales*, London, HMSO.

Department for Health and Social Security (1988) *Community Care: Agenda for Action in 1988* (Griffiths report), London, HMSO.

Department of Local Government and Regional Planning (1970) *Reform of Local Government in England*, Cmnd 4276, London, HMSO.

Department of Transport, Local Government and the Regions (2002) *Your Region, Your Choice*, Cm 5511, London, HMSO.

HM Government (1835) *Inquiry into the Municipal Corporations of England and Wales*, in *British Parliamentary Papers*, vol. 23: *Government: Municipal Corporations*, Shannon, Irish University Press, 1956.

HM Government (1909) *Report of the Royal Commission on the Poor Laws and the Relief of Distress*, Cd 4499, London, HMSO.

Herbert, E. (chair) (1960) *Report on the Royal Commission on Local Government in Greater London 1957–60*, Cmnd 1164, London, HMSO.

Home Office (1968) *Committee on Local Authority and Allied Personal*

Social Services 1967–1968 (Seebohm report), Cmnd 3703, London, HMSO.

Kilbrandon, Lord (chair) (1973) *Royal Commission on the Constitution 1969–1973*, Cmnd 5460, London, HMSO.

Layfield, F. (chair) (1976) *Local Government Finance: Report of the Committee of Inquiry*, Cmnd 6453, London, HMSO.

LGB (1914) *Local Taxation*, Cd 7315, London, HMSO.

LGB (1917) Transfer of Function of Poor Law Authorities: England and Wales, Cd 8917, London, HMSO.

Lord President of the Council (1975) *Our Changing Democracy: Devolution to Scotland and Wales 1975–76*, Cmnd 6348, London, HMSO.

Ministry of Health (1934) *Qualifications, Recruitment, Training and Promotion of Local Government Officers* (Hadow report), London, HMSO.

Ministry of Health (1934) *Report of the Departmental Committee on Qualifications, Recruitment, Training and Promotion of Local Government Officers*, London, HMSO.

Ministry of Health (1943) *A National Health Service*, Cmd 6502, London, HMSO.

Ministry of Health (1945) *Local Government in England and Wales during the Period of Reconstruction*, Cmd 6579, London, HMSO.

Ministry of Health and Ministry of Town and Country Planning (1946) *New Towns Committee: Interim Report*, Cmd 6759, London, HMSO.

Ministry of Health and Scottish Office (1947) *Report of the Interdepartmental Committee on Expenses of Members of Local Authorities* (chair: A. D. Lindsay), Cmd 7126, London, HMSO.

MHLG (1956) *Local Government: Areas and Status of Local Authorities in England and Wales*, Cmd 9831, London, HMSO.

MHLG (1965) *Report of the Committee of Inquiry into the Impact of Rates on Households* (Allen report), Cmnd 2582, London, HMSO.

MHLG (1966) *Local Government Finance in England and Wales*, Cmnd 2923, London, HMSO.

MHLG (1966) *The Staffing of Local Government* (Mallaby report), London, HMSO.

MHLG (1967) *The Management of Local Government* (Maud report), London, HMSO.

MHLG (1967) *Local Government in Wales*, Cmnd 3340, London, HMSO.

Ministry of Town and Country Planning (1945) *National Parks in England and Wales* (Dower report), Cmd 6628, London, HMSO.

Ministry of Town and Country Planning (1947) *National Parks (England and Wales)* (Hobhouse report) Cmd 7121, London, HMSO.

Ministry of Transport (1936) *Electricity Distribution*, London: HMSO.

Ministry of Works and Building (1942) *Report of the Expert Committee on Compensation and Betterment* (Uthwatt report) Cmd 6386, London, HMSO.

Ministry of Works and Building, *Report of the Committee on Land Utilisation in Rural Areas* (Scott report), Cmd 6378, London, HMSO.

ODPM (2003) *Your Region, Your Choice; What the Government's Policy Means for Yorkshire and the Humber*, London, ODPM.

Onslow, Lord (chair) (1925) *First Report of the Royal Commission on Local Government*, Cmd 2506, London, HMSO.

Onslow, Lord (chair) (1928) *Second Report of the Royal Commission on Local Government*, Cmd 3213, London, HMSO.

Onslow, Lord (chair) (1929) *Final Report of the Royal Commission on Local Government*, Cmd 3436, London, HMSO.

Redcliffe-Maud, Lord (chair) (1969) *Royal Commission on Local Government in England, 1966–1969*, Cmnd 4040, London, HMSO.

Redcliffe-Maud, Lord (chair) (1969) vol. 2: *Memorandum of Dissent by Mr D. Senior*, London, HMSO.

Report of the Inquiry into the Municipal Corporations of England and Wales (1835), in *British Parliamentary Papers*, vol. 23: *Government: Municipal Corporations*, Shannon, Irish University Press, 1956.

Robbins, Lord (chair) (1963) *Report of the Committee on Higher Education*, Cmnd 2165, London, HMSO.

Robinson Committee (1977) *Report on the Remuneration of Councillors*, Cmnd 7010, London, HMSO.

Royal Sanitary Commission (1970) Minutes of Evidence, 26 April 1869, in *British Parliamentary Papers*, vol. 9: *Health General*, Dublin, Irish University Press, 1970.

Royal Sanitary Commission (1871) *Report*, C 4281, London, HMSO.

Salmon, Lord (chair) (1976) *Report of the Royal Commission on Standards of Conduct in Public Life*, Cmnd 6524, London, HMSO.

Scott Committee (1942) *Report on Land Utilisation in Rural Areas*, London, HMSO.

Scottish Office (1966) *Social Work and the Community: Proposals for Reorganising Local Authority Services in Scotland*, Cmnd 3605, London, HMSO.

Scottish Office (1971) *Reform of Local Government in Scotland*, Cmnd 4583, London, HMSO.

Scottish Office (1975) *Local Government Finance in Scotland*, Cmnd 208, London, HMSO.

Scottish Office (1993) *The Structure of Local Government – Shaping the Future: The New Councils*, Cm 2267, London, HMSO.

Scottish Office (1997) *Scotland's Parliament*, Cm 3658, London, HMSO.

Statistical Office (2004) *Annual Abstract of Statistics*, London, HMSO.

Treasury (1991) *Competing for Quality: Buying Better Public Services*, Cm 1730, London, HMSO.

Welsh Office (1993) *Local Government in Wales*, Cm 2155, London, HMSO.

Welsh Office (1997) *The Government's Proposals for a Welsh Assembly*, Cm 3718, London, HMSO.

Welsh Assembly Government (2002) *Freedom and Responsibility in Local Government: A Policy Statement*, Cardiff, Welsh Assembly Government.

Wheatley, Lord (chair) (1970) *Reform of Local Government in Scotland: Report of the Royal Commission for Local Government in Scotland*, Cmnd 4150, London, HMSO.

Willink, H. (chair) (1962) *Royal Commission on the Police*, Cmnd 1728, London, HMSO.

Workington Borough Council (1893), Minutes of Workington Borough Council 1893–94, December.

Websites

Ceredigion County Council: www.ceredigion.gov.uk.

Local Government Chronicle Elections Centre, University of Plymouth: www.plymouth.ac.uk/research.

Theses and dissertations

Isaac-Henry, K. (1980) 'The Association of Municipal Authorities and the County Councils' Association: a study of the influences and pressures on the reorganisation of local government 1945–1972', Ph.D thesis, University of London.

Mathers, H. (1979) 'Sheffield municipal politics 1893–1926: parties, personalities and the rise of Labour', Ph.D thesis, University of Sheffield.

Pell, D. J. (1998) 'Political commitment by the UK's Environment Cities to the expectations of Agenda 21', Ph.D thesis, Sheffield Hallam University.

Smitham, K. (1991) 'The new urban Right: a study of Bradford City Council 1988–1990', B.A. dissertation, Sheffield Hallam University.

Books and articles

Addison, C. (1924) *Politics from Within: 1911–1918*, London, Herbert Jenkins.

Addison, P. (1994) *The Road to 1945: British Politics and the Second World War*, London, Pimlico.

Alexander, A. (1985) *Borough Government and Politics: Reading 1835–1985*, London, George Allen & Unwin.

Anon. (1836) 'Municipal reform, as required for the metropolis', *Westminster Review*, 25 January–July.

Anti-Centralization Union (1857) *Government and its Measures in 1857*, London, Edward Stanford.

Ashford, D. E. (1981) *British Dogmatism and French Pragmatism*, London, George Allen & Unwin.

Ashworth, R. (2003) 'Toothless tigers? Councillor perceptions of new scrutiny arrangements in Welsh local government', *Local Government Studies*, 29:2.

Atkinson, H. and Wilks-Heeg, S. (2000) *Local Government from Thatcher to Blair*, Cambridge, Polity Press.

Attlee, C. (1937) *The Labour Party in Perspective*, London, Left Book Club–Gollancz.

Axon, W. (1917) *Cobden as a Citizen: A Chapter in Manchester's History*, London, T. Fisher & Unwin.

Baker, K. (1993) *The Turbulent Years: My Life in Politics*, London, Faber & Faber.

Ball, A. (1987) *British Political Parties*, Basingstoke, Macmillan.

Banham, J. (1994) *The Anatomy of Change: Blueprint for a New Era*, London, Weidenfeld & Nicolson.

Barber, B. (1993) 'Sheffield Borough Council 1843–1993', in Binfield, C. et al. (eds) *The History of the City of Sheffield*, Sheffield, Sheffield Academic Press, vol. 1.

Barnard, H. C. (1961) *A History of English Education*, 2nd edn, London, London University Press.

Barnett, N. and Harrison, S. (1996) 'The Citizen's Charter in local government', in Chandler, J. A. (ed.) *The Citizen's Charter*, Aldershot, Dartmouth.

Barron, J., Crawley, G., and Wood, T. (1991) *Councillors in Crisis*, Basingstoke, Macmillan.

Bealey, F., Blondel, J., and McCann, W. J. (1965) *Constituency Politics: A Study of Newcastle under Lyme*, London, Faber & Faber.

Beer, S. H. (2001) 'New Labour: Old Liberalism', in White, S. (ed.) *New Labour: The Progressive Future*, Basingstoke, Palgrave.

Bellamy, C. (1988) *Administering Central–Local Relations 1871–1919*, Manchester, Manchester University Press.

Beresford, P. (1987), *Good Council Guide: Wandsworth 1978–1987*, London, Centre for Policy Studies.

Binfield, C., Childs, R., Harper, R., Hey, D., Martin, D. and Tweedale, G. (1993) *History of the City of Sheffield 1843–1993*, vol. 1: *Politics*; vol. 2: *Society*; vol. 3: *Images*, Sheffield, Sheffield Academic Press.

Birch, A. H. (1959) *Small Town Politics: A Study of Political Life in Glossop*, Oxford, Oxford University Press.

Birley, A. (1981) *Life in Roman Britain*, 2nd edn, London, Batsford.

Blair, J. (1994) *Anglo Saxon Oxfordshire*, Oxford, Sutton Publishing.

Blair, T. (1996) *New Britain: My Vision of a Young Country*, London, Fourth Estate.

Blair, T. (1998) *The Third Way: New Politics for the New Century*, London, Fabian Society.

Blair, T. (1998) *Leading the Way: New Vision for Local Government*, London, IPPR.

Blaxland, G. (1964) *J. H. Thomas: A Life for Unity*, London, Fredrick Muller.

Blunkett, D. and Jackson, J. (1987) *Democracy in Crisis*, London, Hogarth Press.

Boddy, M. and Fudge, C. (eds) (1984) *Local Socialism?*, Basingstoke, Macmillan.

Bogdanor, V. (1999) *Devolution in the United Kingdom*, 2nd edn, Oxford, Oxford University Press.

Bosanquet, B. (1965) *The Philosophical Theory of the State*, 4th edn, London, Macmillan

Bowman, M. and Hampton, W. (1983) *Local Democracies: A Study in Comparative Government*, Melbourne, Longman Cheshire.

Bradbury, B. J. (1995) *History of Cockermouth*, Workington, Richard Byers.

Branson, N. (1979) *Poplarism 1919–1925*, London, Lawrence & Wishart.

Briggs, A. (1952) *History of Birmingham*, Oxford, Oxford University Press, vol. 2.

Briggs, A. (1963) *Victorian Cities*, London, Odhams.

Brooke, J. (1964) *The House of Commons 1754–1790*, Oxford, Oxford University Press.

Brown, J. (1977), *John Burns*, London, Royal Historical Society.

Bruce, M. (1968) *The Coming of the Welfare State*, London, Batsford.

Bulpitt, J. G. (1967) *Party Politics in English Local Government*, London, Longmans.

Bulpitt, J. G. (1983) *Territory and Power in the United Kingdom*, Manchester, Manchester University Press.

Bunce, J. T. (1885) *History of the Birmingham Corporation*, Birmingham, Cornish Brothers, vol. 2.

Burns, D., Hambleton, R. and Hoggett, P. (1994) *The Politics of Decentralisation*, Basingstoke, Macmillan.

Burns, N. (1994) *The Formation of American Local Governments*, Oxford, Oxford University Press.

Burton, J. H. (1934) *The Finance of Local Government Authorities*, London, Charles Griffen.

Butler, D. (1953) 'Local Government in Parliament', *Public Administration*, 31:1.

Butler, D. and Stokes, D. (1969) *Political Change in Britain*, London, Macmillan.

Butler, D., Adonis, A. and Travers, T. (1994) *Failure in British Government: The Politics of the Poll Tax*, Oxford, Oxford University Press.

Byrne, T. (1981) *Local Government in Britain*, Harmondsworth, Penguin.

Cannadine, D. (ed.) (1982) *Patricians, Power and Politics in Nineteenth Century Towns*, Leicester, Leicester University Press.

Cannnan, E. (1912) *The History of Local Rates in England*, 2nd edn, London, P. S. King.

Carr, H. and Knox, W. (1984) 'Patrick Dollan', in Knox, W. (ed.) *Scottish Labour Leaders 1918–1939*, Edinburgh, Mainstream Publishing.

Cartwright, T. J. (1975) *Royal Commissions and Departmental Committees in Britain*, London, Hodder & Stoughton.

Castells, M. (1977) *The Urban Question*, London, Edward Arnold.

Castle, B. (1980) *The Castle Diaries 1974–1976*, London, Book Club Associates edn, Weidenfeld & Nicolson.

Chamberlain, N. (2000) *The Neville Chamberlain Diary Letters 1921–27*, vol. 2, ed. Self, R., Aldershot, Ashgate.

Chandler, J. A. and Lawless, P. (1985) *Local Authorities and the Creation of Employment*, Farnborough, Gower.

Chandler, J. A. (1988) *Public Policy Making for Local Government*, London, Croom Helm.

Chandler, J. A. (1989) 'The Liberal justification for local government: values and administrative expediency', *Political Studies*, 37:4.

Chandler, J. A. (1998) 'Regenerating South Yorkshire: how the public sector dominates business partnerships in Britain', in Walzer, N. and Jacobs, B. (eds) *Public–Private Partnerships for Local Economic Development*, Westport, CT, Praeger.

Chandler, J. A. (2001) *Local Government Today*, 3rd edn, Manchester, Manchester University Press.

Chandler, J. A. and Kingdom, J. E. (1999) 'MPs and local government: the case of Sheffield', paper presented to the Political Studies Association Annual Conference, University of Nottingham.

Chapman, B. (1955) *The Prefects and Provincial France*, London, Allen & Unwin.

Checkland, S. G. and Checkland, E. O. A. (eds) (1974) *The Poor Law Report of 1834*, Harmondsworth, Penguin.

Clarke, A. (1987) *The Rise and Fall of the Socialist Republic: A History of the South Yorkshire County Council*, Sheffield, Sheaf Publishing.

Clarke, J. J. (1955) *A History of Local Government of the United Kingdom*, London, Herbert Jenkin.

Clements, R. V. (1969) *Local Notables and the City Council*, London, Macmillan.

Clifford, F. (1885) *A History of Private Bill Legislation*, vol.1, London, Butterworths.

Clifton, G. (1989) 'Members and officers of the LCC, 1889–1965', in Saint, A. (ed.) *Politics and the People of London*, London, Hambledon Press.

Cobbett, W. (1834) *Cobbett's Legacy to the Labourers*, Cobbett, London.

Cobden, R. (1835) 'Incorporate your borough', in Axon, W. (1917) *Cobden as a Citizen: A Chapter in Manchester's History*, London, T. Fisher & Unwin.

Cockburn, C. (1977) *The Local State*, London, Pluto Press.

Cole, G. D. H. (1921) *The Future of Local Government*, London, Waverley Book Co.

Cole, G. D. H. (1947) *Local and Regional Government*, London, Cassell.

Cole, I. and Furbey, R. (1994) *The Eclipse of Council Housing*, London, Routledge.

Collings, J. and Green, J. (1920) *Life of the Right Honourable Jesse Collings*, London, Longmans.

Commission for Local Democracy (1995) *Taking Charge: The Rebirth of Local Democracy*, London, Municipal Journal.

Conservative Party (1970) *A Better Tomorrow*, London, Conservative Party.

Cowans & Gray Ltd (1902) *The Lords Provosts of Glasgow 1833–1902*, Glasgow, Cowans & Gray.

Craig, F. W. S. (ed.) (1975) *British Election Manifestos 1900–1974*, London, Macmillan.

Crick, M. (1986) *The March of Militant*, London, Faber & Faber.

Crick, M. (1997) *Michael Heseltine: A Biography*, London, Hamish Hamilton.

Crossman, R. H. S. (1975) *The Diaries of a Cabinet Minister*, vol. 1, London, Hamish Hamilton & Jonathan Cape.

Crowther, M. A. (1981) *The Workhouse System 1834–1929*, London, Methuen.

Cullingworth, J. B. (1976) *Town and Country Planning in Britain*, 6th edn, London, George Allen & Unwin.

Curtis, S. J. and Boultwood, M. E. A. (1966) *An Introductory History of English Education since 1800*, 4th edn, Cambridge, University Tutorial Press.

Curwen, P., Hunt, M., Chandler, J. A., and Turner, R. (1995) *Charging for Services: Approaches to Price Setting in Local Authorities*, London, Local Government Management Board.

Dalton, H. (1935) *Practical Socialism in Britain*, London, Routledge.

Dalton, H. (1986) *The Political Diary of Hugh Dalton, 1918–40, 1945–60*, ed. B. Pimlott, London, Jonathan Cape.

Darwin, L. (1903) *Municipal Trade*, London, John Murray

Daunton, M. J. (1995) *Progress and Poverty: An Economic and Social History of Britain 1700–1850*, Oxford, Oxford University Press.

Davis, J. (1988) *Reforming London: The London Government Problem 1855–1900*, Oxford, Oxford University Press.

Dearlove, J. D. (1973) *The Politics and Policy of Local Government*, Cambridge, Cambridge University Press.

Dearlove, J. D. (1979) *The Reorganisation of British Local Government*,

Cambridge, Cambridge University Press.

De Toqueville, A. (1994) *Democracy in America*, ed. J. P. Mayer, London, Fontana Press.

DoD (various years) *Parliamentary Companion*, London, DoD.

Donoughue, B. and Jones, G. W. (1973) *Herbert Morrison: Portrait of a Politician*, London, Weidenfeld and Nicolson.

Dorey, P. (1999) 'The 3Rs – reform, reproach and rancour: education policies under John Major', in Dorey, P. (ed.) *The Major Premiership*, Basingstoke, Macmillan.

Dunleavy, P. (1980) *Urban Political Analysis*, London, Macmillan.

Dundas, W. C. (1942) *Development of Local Government in Counties in Scotland, London*, William Hodge.

Duverger, M. (1964) *Political Parties*, London, Methuen.

Eastwood, D. (1994) *Governing Rural England: Tradition and Transformation in Local Government 1780–1840*, Oxford, Clarendon Press.

Edsall, N. C. (1971) *The Anti-Poor Law Movement*, Manchester, Manchester University Press.

Elcock, H. (1986) *Local Government: Politicians, Professionals and the Public in Local Authorities*, 2nd edn, London, Methuen.

Electoral Commission and Hansard Society (2005) *An Audit of Political Engagement 2*, London, Electoral Commission–Hansard Society.

Elliott, A. (1982) 'Municipal government in Bradford in the mid-nineteenth century', in Fraser, D. (ed.) *Municipal Reform and the Industrial City*, Leicester, Leicester University Press.

England, J. (1986) 'The characteristics and attitudes of councillors', in Widdecombe, D. (chair) *The Conduct of Local Authority Business*, Cmnd 9797, London, HMSO, vol. 2.

English, J., Madigan, R. and Norman, P. (1976) *Slum Clearance*, London, Croom Helm.

Evans, E. J. (1994) *The Great Reform Act of 1832*, 2nd edn, London, Routledge.

Eyler, J. M. (1997) *Sir Arthur Newsholme and State Medicine 1885–1935*, Cambridge, Cambridge University Press.

Field, J. (1981) 'Police, power and community in a provincial English town: Portsmouth 1815–1875', in Bailey, V. (ed.) *Policing and Punishment in Nineteenth Century Britain*, London, Croom Helm.

Finer, H. (1941) *Municipal Trading*, London, George Allen & Unwin.

Finer, S. E. (1952) *The Life and Times of Sir Edwin Chadwick*, London, Methuen.

Finlayson, B. A. M. (1969) *England in the Eighteen Thirties*, London, Edward Arnold.

Firth, J. F. B. (1888) *Reform of London Government*, London, Swan Sonnenschein.

Flick, C. (1978) *The Birmingham Political Union*, Folkstone, Archon & Dawson.

Foot, M. (1962) *Aneurin Bevan 1897–1945*, London, Macgibbon Kee.

Foot, M. (1973) *Aneurin Bevan 1945–1960*, London, Davis-Poyner.

Foster, C. D., Jackman, R. A. and Perlman, M. (1980) *Local Government Finance in a Unitary State*, London, George Allen & Unwin.

Fowler, E. H. (1912) *The Life of Lord Wolverhampton*, London, Hutchinson.

Frangopulo, N. J. (1962) *Rich Inheritance: A Guide to the History of Manchester*, Manchester, Manchester Education Commmittee.

Frankenberg, R. (1957) *Village on the Border*, London, Cohen & West.

Fraser, D. (1976) *Urban Politics in Victorian England*, London, Macmillan.

Fraser, D. (ed.) (1982) *Municipal Reform and the Industrial City*, Leicester, Leicester University Press.

Fraser, D. (1984) *The Evolution of the British Welfare State*, 2nd edn, Basingstoke, Macmillan.

Frears, J. (1995) 'The role of the depute in France', in Bogdanor, V. (ed.) *Representatives of the People?*, London, George Allen & Unwin.

Fudge, C. (1984) 'Decentralisation: socialism goes local?', in Boddy, M. and Fudge, C., *Local Socialism?*, Basingstoke, Macmillan.

Gamble, A. (1988) *The Free Economy and the Strong State: The Politics of Thatcherism*, Basingstoke, Macmillan.

Garrard, J. (1983) *Leadership and Power in Victorian Industrial Towns*, Manchester, Manchester University Press

Gash, N. (1961) *Mr Secretary Peel*, London, Longmans.

Gladwin, I. (1974) *The Sheriff: The Man and His Office*, London, Gollancz.

Gneist, R. von (1891) *History of the English Constitution*, trans. P. A. Ashworth, London, William Clowes.

Gordon, I. and Whitely, P. (1979) 'Social class and political attitudes: the case of Labour councillors', *Political Studies*, 27:1.

Goschen, G. J. (1871) *Local Taxation*, London, Macmillan.

Gosling, H. (1927) *Up and Down Stream*, London, Methuen.

Goss, S. (1988) *Local Labour and Local Government*, Edinburgh, Edinburgh University Press.

Grant, W. (1977) *Independent Local Politics in England and Wales*, Farnborough, Saxon House.

Green, D. G. (1981) *Power and Party in an English City*, London, George Allen & Unwin.

Greenleaf, W. H. (1975) 'Toulmin Smith and the British political tradition', *Public Administration*, 53:1.

Greenwood, R. and Stewart, J. (1974) *Corporate Planning in Local Government*, London, Charles Knight.

Gyford, J. (1985) *The Politics of Local Socialism*, London, George Allen & Unwin.

Gyford, J. (1985) 'The politicisation of local government', in Loughlin,

M., Gefland, D. and Young, K. (eds) *Half a Century of Municipal Decline*, London, George Allen & Unwin.

Gyford, J. and James, M. (1983) *National Parties and Local Politics*, London, George Allen & Unwin.

Hamer, D. A. (1968) *John Morley*, Oxford, Oxford University Press.

Hamlin, C. (1998) *Public Health and Social Justice in the Age of Chadwick: Britain 1800–1854*, Cambridge, Cambridge University Press.

Hampton, W. (1970) *Democracy and Community: A Study of Politics in Sheffield*, Oxford, Oxford University Press.

Hanham, H. J. (1959) *Elections and Party Management*, London, Longmans.

Hanham, H. J. (1969) 'The development of the Scottish Office', in Wolfe, J. N. (ed.) *Government and Nationalism in Scotland*, Edinburgh, Edinburgh University Press.

Hanham, H. J. (1969) *The Nineteenth Century Constitution: Documents and Commentary*, Cambridge, Cambridge University Press.

Hannah, L. (1979) *Electricity Before Nationalisation: A Study of the Electricty Supply Industry in Britain to 1948*, London, Macmillan.

Harding, C., Hines, B., Ireland, R. and Rawlings, P. (1985) *Imprisonment in England and Wales*, London, Croom Helm.

Harris, J. (1977) *William Beveridge: A Biography*, Oxford, Oxford University Press.

Hasluck, E. L. (1936) *Local Government in England*, Cambridge, Cambridge University Press.

Hay, J. R. (1983) *The Origins of the Liberal Welfare Reforms 1906–1914*, London, Macmillan.

Hayek, F. A. (1944) *The Road to Serfdom*, London, Routledge.

Hennessy, P. (1992) *Never Again: Britain 1945–51*, London, Jonathan Cape.

Hennock, E. P. (1973) *Fit and Proper Persons*, London, Edward Arnold.

Henney, A. (1984) *Inside Local Government*, London, Sinclair Brown.

Heseltine, M. (1987) *Where There's a Will*, London, Hutchinson.

Hill, C. (1967) *Reformation to Industrial Revolution*, Harmondsworth, Pelican.

Hindess, B. (1971) *The Decline of Working Class Politics*, London, Mcgibbon Key.

Hodgkinson, R. G. (1967) *The Origins of the National Health Service*, London, Welcome Trust.

Hogg, S. and Hill, J. (1995) *Too Close to Call: Power and Politics – John Major in No. 10*, London, Warner.

Hollis, P. (1987) *Ladies Elect: Women in English Local Government 1865–1914*, Oxford, Oxford University Press.

Honigsbaum, F. (1970) *The Struggle for the Ministry of Health*, London, Social Administration Research Trust,

Hood, C. (1991) 'A public management for all seasons', *Public Administration*, 69.

Howell, D. (1976) *British Social Democracy*, London, Croom Helm.

Hunt, T. (2004) *Building Jerusalem: The Rise and Fall of the Victorian City*, London, Weidenfeld & Nicolson.

Hyndman, H. M. (n.d.) *A Commune for London*, London, Justice Printery.

Jay, R. (1981) *Joseph Chamberlain: A Political Study*, Oxford, Oxford University Press.

Jefferys, K. (1999) *Anthony Crosland*, London, Richard Cohen Books.

Jones, G. W. (1969) *Borough Politics*, London, Macmillan.

Jones, G. W. and Stewart, J. D. (1983) *The Case for Local Government*, London, George Allen & Unwin.

Jones, K. (2003) *Education in Britain, 1944 to the Present*, Cambridge, Polity Press.

Judd, D. R. (1979) *The Politics of American Cities: Private Power and Public Policy*, Boston, MA, Little, Brown.

Kahn, U. (1989) 'Neighbourhood forums: the Islington experience', *Local Government Policy Making*, 16:2.

Keble Hawson, H. (1968) *Sheffield: The Growth of a City, 1893–1926*, Sheffield, J. W. Northend.

Keith-Lucas, B. (1952) *The English Local Government Franchise*, Oxford, Blackwell.

Keith-Lucas, B. (1980) *The Unreformed Local Government System*, London, Croom Helm.

Keith-Lucas, B. and Richards, P. G. (1978) *A History of Local Government in the Twentieth Century*, London, George Allen & Unwin.

Kellas, J. (1968) *Modern Scotland*, London, Pall Mall Press.

Kelly, J. (2003) 'The Audit Commission: guiding, steering and regulating local government', *Public Administration*, 81:3.

Kilfoyle, P. (2000) *Left Behind: Lessons from Labour's Heartland*, London, Politico's.

Kingdom, J. E. (1999) 'Centralisation and fragmentation: John Major and the reform of local government', in Dorey, P. (ed.) *The Major Premiership*, Basingstoke, Macmillan.

Kingdom, J. E. (2003) *Government and Politics in Britain*, 3rd edn, Cambridge, Polity Press.

Kynaston, D. (1994) *The City of London: A World of its Own 1815–1890*, London, Pimlico.

Labour Party (1930) *Annual Report*, London, Labour Party.

Labour Party (1964) *Let's Go with Labour for the New Britain: The Labour Party's Manifesto for the 1964 General Election*, London, Labour Party.

Labour Party (1974) *Bringing Power Back to the People*, London, Labour Party.

Labour Party (1975) *Devolution and Regional Government in England*, London, Labour Party.

Labour Party (1977) *Regional Authorities and Local Government Reform*, London, Labour Party.

Labour Party (1977) *Building Britain's Future: Labour's Policy on Construction*, London, Labour Party.

Labour Party (1983) *Manifesto: New Hope for Britain*, London, Labour Party.

Labour Party (1987) *Local Government Reform in England and Wales*, London, Labour Party.

Labour Party (1987) *Manifesto: Britain Will Win With Labour*, London, Labour Party.

Labour Party (1992) *Manifesto: It's Time to Get Britain Working Again*, London, Labour Party.

Labour Party (1996) *A Voice for London*, London, Labour Party

Labour Party (1997) *1997 Manifesto: New Labour: Because Britain Deserves Better*, London, Labour Party.

Labour Party (1997) *Local Government Reform in England and Wales*, London, Labour Party.

Laffin, M. (1989) *Managing Under Pressure: Industrial Relations in Local Government*, Basingstoke, Macmillan.

Lambert, R. (1963) *Sir John Simon 1816–1904*, London, MacGibbon & Kee.

Lamont, N. (1999) *In Office*, London, Little Brown.

Langford, D. A. (1982) *Direct Labour Organisations in the Construction Industry*, Aldershot, Gower.

Lawson, N. (1992) *The View from No. 11*, London, Bantam Press.

Layburn, K. (1988) *The Rise of Labour*, London, Edward Arnold.

Leach, S., Game, C., Gyford, J. and Midwinter, A. (1986) 'The political organisation of local authorities', in Widdecombe, D. (chair) *The Conduct of Local Authority Business*, Cmnd 9797, London, HMSO, vol. 2.

Leach, S. and Stewart, J. (1992) *The Politics of Hung Authorities*, Basingstoke, Macmillan.

Leach, S. (1995) 'The strange case of the Local Government Review', in Stewart, J. and Stoker, G. (eds) *Local Government in the 1990s*, Basingstoke, Macmillan.

Lee, J. M. (1988) *Social Leaders and Public Persons: A Study of County Government in Cheshire Since 1888*, Oxford, Oxford University Press.

Lipman, V. D. (1947) *Local Government Areas*, Oxford, Blackwell.

Littlejohn, J. (1963) *Westrigg*, London, Routledge.

Livingstone, K. (1987) *If Voting Changed Anything, They'd Abolish It*, London, Fontana.

Lloyd, J. (1910) *London Municipal Government: History of a Great Reform 1880–1888*, London, P. S. King.

Local Government Manual and Directory (1942) London, Charles Knight–Shaw & Co.

Lowell, L. (1910) *The Government of England*, vol. 1, London, Macmillan.

Lubnow, W. C. (1971) *The Politics of Government Growth*, Newton Abbott, David & Charles.

Lynch, P. (2001) *Scottish Government and Politics*, Edinburgh, Edinburgh University Press.

McBriar, A. M. (1966) *Fabian Socialism and English Politics 1884–1918*, Cambridge, Cambridge University Press.

McFadden, J. and Lazarowicz, M. (2000) *The Scottish Parliament: An Introduction*, 2nd edn, Edinburgh, T. & T. Clark.

Machin, H. (1977) *The Prefect in French Public Administration*, London, Croom Helm.

McIntyre, I. (1994) *The Expense of Glory: A Life of John Reith*, London, Harper Collins.

Mackenzie, N. and Mackenzie, J. (1977) *The First Fabians*, London, Weidenfeld & Nicolson.

McKenzie, R. T. (1963) *British Political Parties*, 2nd edn, London, Mercury.

Mackenzie, W. J. M. (1951) 'Local government in Parliament', *Public Administration*, 29.

Mackenzie, W. J. M. (1954), 'Local government in Parliament', *Public Administration*, 32.

McKibben, R. (1974) *The Evolution of the Labour Party 1910–1914*, Oxford, Oxford University Press.

Mackintosh, J. (1970) *The Government and Politics of Britain*, London, Hutchinson.

Macmillan, H. (1969) *Tides of Fortune 1945–55*, London, Macmillan.

Macmurray, J. (1961) *Persons in Relation*, London: Faber & Faber.

Major, J. (1999) *John Major: The Autobiography*, London, Harper Collins.

Malpass, P. (2000) *Housing Associations and Housing Policy: An Historical Perspective*, Basingstoke, Macmillan.

Marris, N. M. (1900) *Joseph Chamberlain*, London, Hutchinson.

Marsh, A. (1991) *Directory of Trade Unions*, 5th edn, Aldershot, Gower.

Marsh, D. and Rhodes, R. A. W. (eds) (1992) *Policy Networks in British Government*, Oxford, Oxford University Press.

Marsh, P. T. (1994) *Joseph Chamberlain: Entrepreneur in Politics*, New Haven, CT, Yale University Press.

Marshall, J. D. (1969) *The English Poor in the Eighteenth Century*, London, Routledge & Kegan Paul.

Marshall, T. H. (1975) *Social Policy*, 4th edn, London, Hutchinson.

Mathew, H. G. C. (1997) *Gladstone 1808–1889*, Oxford, Oxford University Press.

Maver, I. (2000) *Glasgow*, Edinburgh, Edinburgh University Press.

Mellors, C. (1974) 'Local government in Parliament – 20 years later', *Public Administration*, 52:2.

Midwinter, A. (1983) *The Politics of Local Spending*, Edinburgh, Mainstream Publishing.

Midwinter, A. and Monaghan, C. (1993) *From Rates to the Poll Tax*, Edinburgh, Edinburgh University Press.

Miles, D. (1988) *Francis Place 1771–1854*, Brighton, Harverster Press.

Mill. J. S. (1840) 'Democracy in America', reprinted in Williams, G. L. (ed.) (1976) *John Stuart Mill on Politics and Society*, London, Fontana.

Mill, J. S. (1975) *Considerations on Representative Government*, in *John Stuart Mill: Three Essays*, ed. R. Wollheim, Oxford, Oxford University Press.

Mill, J. S. (1924) *Autobiography*, ed. H. J. Laski, Oxford, Oxford University Press.

Miller, W. (1986) 'Local electoral behaviour', in Widdecombe, D. (chair) *The Conduct of Local Authority Business*, Cmnd 9797, London, HMSO, vol. 3.

Milliband, R. (1961) *Parliamentary Socialism*, London, George Allen & Unwin.

Minns, R. and Thornley, J. (1978) *State Shareholding: The Role of Local and Regional Authorities*, London, Macmillan.

Montague-Harris, G. (1939) *Municipal Self-Government in Britain*, London, P. S. King.

Morley, J. (1879) *Burke*, London, Macmillan.

Morrell, J. B. and Watson, A. G. (eds), 1928, *How York Governs Itself*, London, George Allen & Unwin.

Morgan, K. O. (1970) *Wales in British Politics 1868–1902*, Cardiff, University of Wales Press.

Morgan, K. O. (1975) *Keir Hardie: Radical and Socialist*, London, Weidenfeld & Nicolson.

Morgan, K. O. (1984) *Labour in Power 1945–51*, Oxford, Clarendon Press.

Morgan, K. O. and Morgan, J. (1980) *Portrait of a Progressive: The Political Career of Christopher, Viscount Addison*, Oxford, Clarendon Press.

Moore, Barrington, Jr (1969) *The Social Origins of Dictatorship and Democracy*, Harmondsworth, Penguin Books.

Murrell Martin, N. (1900) *Joseph Chamberlain: The Man and the Statesman*, London, Hutchinson.

Namier, L. (1957) *The Structure of Politics at the Accession of George III*, 2nd edn, London, Macmillan.

Newton, K. (1976) *Second City Politics*, Oxford, Oxford University Press.

Nicholson, P. P. (1990) *The Political Philosophy of the British Idealists*, Cambridge, Cambridge University Press.

Niskanen, W. A. (1971) *Bureaucracy and Representative Government*, Chicago, IL, Aldine Atherton.

Oakes, C. (1928) *Wright and Hobhouse on Local Government and Local Taxation in England and Wales*, 6th edn, London, Sweet & Maxwell.

Odgers, W. B. and Naldrett, E. W. (1909) *Local Government*, 2nd edn, London, Macmillan.

Olney, R. J. (1979) *Rural Society and County Government in Nineteenth Century Lincolnshire: History of Lincolnshire*, vol. 10, Lincoln, History of Lincolnshire Committee.

O'Neill, B. J. (2000) 'The development of the electricity supply industry in north west Kent 1882–1914', *Local Historian*, 30:2.

Orbach, L. F. (1977) *Homes for Heroes: A Study of the Evolution of British Public Housing 1915–1921*, London, Seeley Service.

Ostrom, V., Bish, R. and Ostrom, E. (1988) *Local Government in the United States*, San Francisco, CA, Institute of Contemporary Studies Press.

Ottewill, R. M. (2004) 'Redrawing the boundaries: politics and outcomes of the county review process in Surrey 1929–1933', *Southern History*, 26.

Ottewill, R. M. (2004) 'The changing character of municipal election 1835–1974', *Local Historian*, 34:3.

Ottewill, R. M. (2005) 'County elections in Surrey: the first sixty years, 1889 to 1949', draft of unpublished paper.

Owen, D. (1982), *The Government of Victorian London 1855–1889*, Cambridge, MA, Harvard University Press.

Paine, T. (1969) *The Rights of Man*, ed. H. Collins, Harmondsworth, Penguin.

Parekh, B. (ed.) (1973) *Bentham's Political Thought*, London, Croom Helm.

Parkinson, M. (1985) *Liverpool on the Brink*, Hermitage, Berkshire, Policy Journals.

Peacock, A. (1981), 'George Leeman and York politics', in Feinstein, C. H. (ed.) *York 1831–1981*, York, William Sessions.

Peardon, T. P. (1974) 'Bentham's ideal republic', in Parekh, B. (ed.) *Jeremy Bentham: Ten Critical Essays*, London, Frank Cass.

Pelling, H. (1965) *The Origins of the Labour Party 1880–1900*, Oxford, Clarendon Press.

Pennybacker, S. (1995) *A Vision for London 1889–1915*, London, Routledge.

Perri 6 (2002) *Towards Holistic Governance*, Basingstoke, Palgrave.

Peters, P. and Waterman, R. (1982) *In Search of Excellence*, New York, Harper Collins.

Philo, G. (1995) 'Television, politics and the rise of the New Right', in Philo, G. (ed.) *Glasgow Media Group Reader*, vol. 2, London, Routledge.

Pimlott, B. (1985) *Hugh Dalton*, London, Jonathan Cape.

Poole, K. P. (1978) *The Local Government Service in England and Wales*, London, George Allen & Unwin.

Poole, K. P. and Keith-Lucas, B. (1994) *Parish Government 1894–1994*, London, National Association of Parish Councils.

Porter, R. (1990), *English Society in the Eighteenth Century*, Harmondsworth, Penguin.

Prest, J. (1990) *Liberty and Locality: Parliament, Permissive Legislation and Ratepayers' Democracies in the Nineteenth Century*, Oxford, Clarendon Press.

Rallings, C., Trasher, M. and Cowling, D. (2002) 'Mayoral referendums and elections', *Local Government Studies*, 28:4.

Rao, N. (1996) *Towards Welfare Pluralism*, Aldershot, Dartmouth.

Rao, N. (2003) 'Options for change: cabinets or the status quo?', *Local Government Studies*, 29:1.

Rathbone, W., Pell, A. and Montague, F. C. (1885) *Local Administration*, London, Swan Sonnenschein.

Rawlings, P. (2002) *Policing: A Short History*, Cullompton, Willan Publishing.

Reddlich, J. and Hirst, F. W. (1903) *Local Government in England*, 2 vols, London, Macmillan.

Rhodes, G. (1970) *The Government of London*, London, Weidenfeld & Nicolson.

Rhodes, G. (1976) 'Local government finance 1918–1966', Layfield, F. (chair) *Report of the Royal Commission on Local Government Finance*, Cmnd 6453, London, HMSO, Appendix 6.

Rhodes, R. A. W. (1981) *Control and Power in Central–Local Government*, Farnborough, Gower.

Rhodes, R. A. W. (1986) *The National World of Local Government*, London, Allen & Unwin.

Rhodes, R. A. W. (1988) *Beyond Westminster and Whitehall*, London, Allen & Unwin.

Rhodes, R. A. W. (2000) *Control and Power in Central–Local Government Relations*, 2nd edn, Aldershot, Ashgate.

Rhodes, R. A. W. and Marsh, D. (1992) 'Policy networks in British politics: a critique of existing approaches', in Marsh, D. and Rhodes, R. A. W. (eds) *Policy Networks in British Government*, Oxford, Oxford University Press.

Richards, P. G. (1956) *Delegation in Local Government*, London, George Allen & Unwin.

Ridley, F. and Blondel, J. (1964) *Public Administration in France*, London, Routledge & Kegan Paul.

Ridley, N. (1988) *The Local Right: Enabling, Not Providing*, London, Centre for Policy Studies.

Ridley, N. (1992) *My Style of Government*, London, Harper Collins.

Rivet, A. L. F. (1958) *Town and Country in Roman Britain*, London, Hutchinson.

Riordon, W. L. (1963) *Plunkitt of Tammany Hall*, New York, Dutton.

Roberts, A. (1999) *Salisbury: A Victorian Titan*, London, Weidenfeld & Nicolson.

Roberts, D. (1974) 'Jeremy Bentham and the Victorian administrative State', in Parekh, B. (ed.) *Jeremy Bentham: Ten Critical Essays*, London, Frank Cass.

Robson, W. A. (1931) *The Development of Local Government*, London, George Allen & Unwin.

Robson, W. A. (1939) *The Government and Misgovernment of London*, London, George Allen & Unwin.

Robson, W. A. (1954) *The Development of Local Government*, 3rd edn, George Allen & Unwin.

Roots, I. (1968) 'The central government and the local community', in Ives, E. W. (ed.) *The English Revolution 1600–1660*, London, Edward Arnold.

Rose, M. E. (1971) *The English Poor Law 1780–1930*, Newton Abbott, David & Charles.

Rose, R. (1982) *The Territorial Dimension in Government*, Chatham, NJ, Chatham House.

Ryde, W. C. (1894) *The Local Government Act 1894*, London, Reeves & Turner.

Salzman L. F. (1926) *English Life in the Middle Ages*, Oxford, Oxford University Press.

Saunders, P. (1979) *Urban Politics: A Sociological Interpretation*, London, Hutchinson.

Saunders, P. (1981) *Social Theory and the Urban Question*, London, Hutchinson.

Schmidt, V. A. (1990) *Democratizing France: The Political and Administrative History of Decentralisation*, Cambridge, Cambridge University Press.

Searle, G. R. (1993) *Entrepreneurial Politics in Mid-Nineteenth Century Britain*, Oxford, Oxford University Press.

Seyd, P. (1987) *The Rise and Fall of the Labour Left*, Basingstoke, Macmillan.

Sharp, E. (1962) 'The future of local government', *Public Administration*, 40.

Sharp, E. (1969) *The Ministry of Housing and Local Government*, London, George Allen & Unwin.

Shaw, G. B. S. (1908) *The Common Sense of Municipal Trading*, London, A. C. Fifield.

Shaw, K. and Davidson, G. (2002) 'Community elections for regeneration partnerships: a new deal for local democracy?', *Local Government Studies*, 28:2.

Sheffield Telegraph Year Books and *Sheffield Red Guide* Year Books.

Sheldrake, J. (1992) *Modern Local Government*, Aldershot, Dartmouth.

Sheppard, F. (1971), *The Infernal Wen: London 1808–1870*, London, Secker & Warburg.

Simon, E. D. (1926) *A City Council from Within*, London, Longmans.

Skinner, D. and Langdon, J. (1974) *The Story of Clay Cross*, Nottingham, Spokesmen Books.

Slack, P. (1988) *Poverty and Policy in Tudor and Stuart England*, London, Longman.

Smallwood, F. (1965) *Greater London: The Politics of Metropolitan Reform*, Indianapolis, IN, Bobbs-Merrill.

Smellie, K. B. (1946) *A History of Local Government*, London, George Allen & Unwin.

Smith, A. (1964) *The Wealth of Nations*, vol. 1, ed. E. Seligman, London, Dent.

Smith, F. B. (1979) *The People's Health*, London, Croom Helm.

Smith, J. T. (1851) *Local Self-Government and Centralization*, London, John Chapman.

Smith, J. T. (1852) *The Metropolis and its Municipal Administration*, London, Trelawny Saunders.

Smith, J. T. (1854) *The Parish*, London, J. Sweet.

Smith, T. B. (2003) *Creating the Welfare State in France, 1880–1940*, Montreal, McGill–Queens University Press.

Snape, S. (2004) 'A role for non-executive councillors?', in Stoker, G.and Wilson, D. (eds) *British Local Government into the 21st Century*, Basingstoke, Palgrave.

Spoor, A. (1967) *White Collar Union: 60 Years of NALGO*, London, Heinemann.

Stacey, F. (1975) *British Government 1966–1975*, Oxford, Oxford University Press.

Stanyer, J. (1970) 'The Local Government Commissions', in Wiseman, V. H. (ed.) *Local Government in England 1958–1969*, London, Routledge & Kegan Paul.

Stanyer, J. (1976) *Understanding Local Government*, London, Fontana.

Stanyer, J. (1989) *A History of Devon County Council 1889–1989*, Exeter, Devon Books.

Steedman, C. (1984) *Policing the Victorian Community*, London, Routledge & Kegan Paul.

Steel, D. (1980) *A House Divided*, London, Weidenfeld & Nicolson.

Stephens, P. (2004) *Tony Blair: The Price of Leadership*, London, Politico's.

Stewart, J. (2000) *The Nature of British Local Government*, Basingstoke, Macmillan.

Stewart, J. (2003) *Modernising British Local Government: An Assessment of Labour's Reform Programme*, Basingstoke, Palgrave.

Stewart, J. and Stoker, G. (1995) *Local Government in the 1990s*, Basingstoke, Macmillan.

Stoker, G. (1996) *The Reform of the Institutions of Local Representative Democracy: Is There a Role for the Mayor–Council Model?*, London, Commission for Local Democracy.

Stoker, G. (2000) 'Introduction', in Stoker, G. (ed.) *The New Politics of British Local Governance*, Basingstoke, Macmillan.

Stoker, G. (2003) *Transforming Local Governance: From Thatcherism to New Labour*, Basingstoke, Palgrave.

Stoker, G. and Mossberger, K. (1995) 'The post-Fordist local state: the dynamics of its development', in J. D. Stewart and G. Stoker, *Local Government in the 1990s*, Basingstoke, Macmillan.

Stoker, G. and Wilson, D. (eds) (2004) *British Local Government in the 21st Century*, Basingstoke, Palgrave.

Stoker, G. and Wilson D. (2004) 'Conclusions: New Ways of Being Local' in Stoker, G. and Wilson, D. (eds) *British Local Government in the 21st Century*, Basingstoke, Palgrave.

Street, J. (1930) *A Treatise on the Doctrine of Ultra Vires*, London, Sweet & Maxwell.

Stuart Maclure, J. (ed.) (1965) *Educational Documents*, 5th edn, London, Methuen.

Sullivan, H. and Skelcher, C. (2002) *Working Across Boundaries: Collaboration in Public Services*, Basingstoke, Palgrave.

Swanson, H. (1999) *Medieval British Towns*, Basingstoke, Macmillan.

Syed, A. (1966) *The Political Theory of American Local Government*, New York, Random House.

Taafe, P. and Mulhearn, T. (1988) *Liverpool: A City that Dared to Fight*, London, Fortress Press.

Tate, W. E. (1960) *The Parish Chest: A Study of the records of Parochial Administration in England*, Cambridge, Cambridge University Press.

Thackery, W. M. (1985) *Vanity Fair*, Harmondsworth, Penguin Books.

Thane, P. (1996) *Foundations of the Welfare State*, 2nd edn, London, Longman.

Thatcher, M. (1995) *The Path to Power*, London, Harper Collins.

Thomas, W. (1979) *The Philosophic Radicals: Nine Studies in Theory and Practice, 1817–1841*, Oxford, Clarendon Press.

Thompson, E. P. (1968) *The Making of the English Working Class*, Harmondsworth, Penguin.

Thompson, F. M. L. (1963) *English Landed Society in the Nineteenth Century*, London, Routledge & Kegan Paul.

Thorpe, A. (1993) 'The consolidation of a Labour stronghold', in Binfield, C. *et al.* (eds) *The History of the City of Sheffield 1843–1993*, vol. 1: *Politics*, Sheffield, Sheffield Academic Press.

Tiebout, C. M. (1956) 'A pure theory of local expenditures', *Journal of Political Economy*, 64 October.

Towler, W. G. (1908) *Socialism in Local Government*, London, George Allen & Sons.

Travers, A. (2004) 'Local government finance: busy going nowhere?', in Stoker, G. and Wilson, D. (eds) *British Local Government into the 21st Century*, Basingstoke, Palgrave.

Travers, T. (1986) *The Politics of Local Government Finance*, London, George Allen & Unwin.

Travers, T. (2004) *The Politics of London*, Basingstoke, Palgrave.

Travis, A. (1990) 'Poll tax fears leave Prime Minister Cold', *Guardian*, 2 April.

Tressell, R. (1965) *The Ragged Trousered Philanthropists*, London, Granada.

Tristam-Hunt, G. (2004) *Building Jerusalem: The Rise and Fall of the Victorian City*, London, Weidenfeld & Nicolson.

Walker, D. (1983) *Municipal Empire: The Town Halls and their Beneficiaries*, London, Temple-Smith.

Walker, D. (1997) 'Councils to seek value in service' *Independent*, 3 June, p. 2.

Walker, D. (1997) 'Councils told to embrace a new era', *Independent*, 24 July, p. 6.

Waller, P. J. (1983) *Town, City and Nation*, Oxford, Oxford University Press.

Walsh, K. (1995) *Public Services and Market Mechanisms*, Basingstoke, Macmillan.

Walsh, K. (1995) 'Competition and service in local government', in Stewart, J. and Stoker, G. (eds) *The Future of Local Government*, Basingstoke, Macmillan.

Webb, S. (1890) *Socialism in England*, London, Swan Sonnenschein.

Webb, S. and Webb, B. (1906) *English Local Government from the Revolution to the Municipal Corporations Act*, vol. 1: *The Parish and the County*, London, Longmans, Green.

Webb, S. and Webb, B. (1906) *English Local Government: The Parish and the County*, London, Longmans, Green.

Webb, S. and Webb, B. (1913) *English Local Authorities*, vol. 5: *The Story of the King's Highway*, London, Longmans, Green.

Webb, S. and Webb, B. (1927) *English Local Government*, vol. 7 *English Poor Law History*, Part 1: *The Old Poor Law*, London, Longmans, Green.

Webb, S. and Webb, B. (1929) *English Local Government*, vol. 8: *English Poor Law History*, Part 2: *The Last Hundred Years*, 2 vols, London, Longmans, Green.

Webb, S. and Webb, B. (1963) *English Local Government*, vol. 3: *The Manor and the Borough*, London, Frank Cass.

Webb, S. and Webb, B. (1963) *English Local Government*, vol. 6: *English Prisons Under Local Government*, London, Frank Cass.

Webb, S. and Webb, B. (1963) *History of Liquor Licensing in England*, London, Frank Cass.

Webb, S. and Webb B. (1975) *A Constitution for the Socialist Commonwealth of Great Britain*, 3rd edn, Cambridge, Cambridge University Press.

Western, J. R. (1965) *The English Militia in the Eighteenth Century*, London, Routledge & Kegan Paul.

Whetstone, A. (1981) *Scottish County Government in the Eighteenth and Nineteenth Centuries*, Edinburgh, John Donald.

White, B. D. (1951) *A History of the Corporation of Liverpool 1835–1914*, Liverpool, Liverpool University Press.

Whitely, P. (1983) *The Labour Party in Crisis*, London, Methuen.

Whyte, W. E. (1925) *Local Government in Scotland*, Edinburgh, William Hodge.

Whyte, W. E. (1936) *Local Government in Scotland*, 2nd edn, London, William Hodge.

Williams, A. (1999) *Kingship and Government in Pre-Conquest England*, Basingstoke, Macmillan.

Williams, O. P. (1971) *Metropolitan Political Analysis*, New York, Free Press.

Williams, T. I. (1981) *A History of the British Gas Industry*, Oxford, Oxford University Press.

Williams, W. M. (1956) *The Sociology of an English Village: Gosforth*, London, Routledge.

Wilson, D. and Game, C. (2002) *Local Government in the United Kingdom*, 3rd edn, Basingstoke, Palgrave.

Wiseman, V. H. (ed.) (1970) *Local Government in England 1958–1969*, London, Routledge & Kegan Paul.

Wood, B. (1976) *The Process of Local Government Reform*, London, George Allen & Unwin.

Woodward, L. (1962) *The Age of Reform 1815–1870*, Oxford, Clarendon Press.

Wright, W. (1905) *The Life of George Dawson*, Birmingham, Percival Jones, 1905.

Wright, R. S. and Hobhouse, H. (1884) *An Outline of Local Government and Local Taxation*, London, W. Maxwell & Son.

Young, K. (1975) *Local Politics and the Rise of Party*, Leicester, Leicester University Press.

Young, K. (1986) 'Party politics in local government: an historical perspective', in Widdecombe, D. (chair) *The Conduct of Local Authority Business*, Cmnd 9797, London, HMSO, vol. 4.

Young, K. and Rao, N. (1997) *Local Government Since 1945*, Oxford, Blackwell.

Young, S. C. (2000) 'Participation strategies and environmental politics: local Agenda 21', in Stoker, G. (ed.) *The New Politics of British Local Governance*, Basingstoke, Macmillan.

Zeigler, P. (1976) *Melbourne*, London, Collins.

Index

Dale, Robert 78–9, 90, 115
Dalton, Hugh 165–6
Dawson, George 90, 115
decentralisation 101, 206, 297, 318
Department for Communities and
    Local Government 282
Department of the Environment
    194, 222, 260, 282
democracy 226, 308, 309, 314
devolution 206–10, 279, 280,
    283–5
Devon County Council 226, 229,
    232
Dilke, Charles 99, 144
direct labour organisations 150–1,
    246–7
Disraeli, Benjamin 52, 61, 82, 89,
    97, 310
Dobson, Frank 281, 285, 286
doctors 40, 84, 85, 121, 162–3,
    168, 200
Dodson, J. G. 99, 109
Doncaster 71, 142
dual polity 4, 6, 110, 306–8

economic development 32, 198,
    220, 249, 259, 269–70, 285,
    287, 317
Ede, Chuter 166, 170, 173, 177
education 58–9, 107–9, 163–4, 258,
    268, 295–6
education boards 58–9, 103, 107,
    108
elections 224–5, 233, 237, 254, 286,
    292
electricity supply 79, 168
employment creation 249
enabling authority 256–9, 267–70
enclosures 3, 5,
English regions 206, 287–8
Enterprise Zones 247
European Charter of Local Self-
    Government 283
European Union 283
Eve, Trustram 174–5

excise duty 23

Fabians 121, 131–4, 312
farm colonies 122
finance 22–4, 60–3, 98, 102–3, 135,
    147–50, 173, 185–7, 194–6,
    208–10, 293–5, 301, 316
  business rate 260–1, 262, 283,
    294, 300
  capital spending 21, 75, 154, 171,
    185, 195, 211, 245, 259, 294
  council tax 263–4, 293–4, 300
  cuts 208, 209, 244
  equalisation 135, 173
  grants 58, 60–1, 149, 173, 244–6
  rate support grant 208, 250
Firth, J. F. B. 82–3, 104, 131
Foot, Michael 249, 278–9
Fowler, Henry 101,106
France 3, 49, 89, 133, 235, 298,
    306–7, 314
franchise 6–7, 31, 37–9, 87, 100
freemen 6, 13, 153
Funding Agency for Schools 268

garden cities 127
gas supply 78, 93, 168
General Board of Health 54, 63, 81
general competence 204, 283, 295
Germany 122
Gilbert Acts 4, 18, 52
Gladstone, William 30, 61, 62, 88,
    99, 107, 109
Glamorgan 203
Glasgow 76, 78, 88, 212, 227, 246,
    300
Glossop 88, 221, 26
Goschen, George 61, 64, 98, 103,
    105
Greater London Authority 285–6,
    287
Greater London Council 81, 190–2,
    249, 251, 253–6, 257, 285
Greater London Enterprise Board
    249, 259

Lightning Source UK Ltd.
Milton Keynes UK
UKOW04f0205101217
314159UK00009B/346/P